George W. Field

A Treatise on the County and Township Officers of Iowa

being a complete official guide for clerks, sheriffs, boards of supervisors, auditors, treasurers, recorders, coroners, surveyors, notaries public, and township trustees, clerks, constables

George W. Field

A Treatise on the County and Township Officers of Iowa
being a complete official guide for clerks, sheriffs, boards of supervisors, auditors, treasurers, recorders, coroners, surveyors, notaries public, and township trustees, clerks, constables

ISBN/EAN: 9783337367923

Printed in Europe, USA, Canada, Australia, Japan

Cover: Foto ©Andreas Hilbeck / pixelio.de

More available books at **www.hansebooks.com**

A TREATISE

ON THE

COUNTY AND TOWNSHIP

OFFICERS OF IOWA,

BEING A COMPLETE

OFFICIAL GUIDE

FOR

CLERKS, SHERIFFS, BOARDS OF SUPERVISORS, AUDITORS, TREASURERS, RECORDERS, CORONERS, SURVEYORS, NOTARIES PUBLIC, AND TOWNSHIP TRUSTEES, CLERKS, CONSTABLES, ASSESSORS, AND COLLECTORS.

SHOWING THEIR

POWERS, DUTIES AND LIABILITIES,

WITH ALL THE

FORMS REQUIRED IN THEIR OFFICIAL BUSINESS, AND AN APPENDIX OF FORMS FOR GENERAL USE, ADAPTED TO THE CODE OF 1873, AND AS AMENDED BY THE LAWS OF THE LAST GENERAL ASSEMBLY.

BY GEORGE W. FIELD,
COUNSELOR AT LAW.

DES MOINES:
MILLS & COMPANY, LAW PUBLISHERS.
1875.

STEREOTYPED AND PRINTED
BY MILLS & COMPANY,
DES MOINES, IOWA.

PREFACE.

A large number of county and township officers are annually installed into office, and new duties and obligations are imposed upon them, with which they usually have little acquaintance.

The directions relating to those duties, and the obligations imposed upon them, scattered through various sections and chapters of the Code, are many times indefinite and obscure; but these, with casual consultations with attorneys, in particular cases, are generally the only guides and sources of light practically accessible to them.

Impressed with these facts, and the great utility of some more complete guide for them, this volume has been prepared.

It will be conceded by those competent to judge, that anything like an exhaustive treatise in relation to the duties, obligations and liabilities of any one of several of the officers herein treated of, would form a volume as large as this, and that such a treatment of all of those officers would swell the volume to a size that would be too expensive and inconvenient for general use by them.

In view of these facts, it has been the aim of the author to select and condense in this volume, the most useful and important matters relating to those duties, obligations and liabilities.

The author entertains a hope that the treatise may also be convenient and useful to attorneys. Under the pressure of professional business, they will, perhaps, accept the results of investigations herein contained, and especially the carefully prepared forms, as a great convenience.

The laws relating to the duties of County Superintendents of common schools, with instructions and forms, are generally furnished them by the Superintendent of Public Instruction; the laws relating to highways, and the duties of road supervisors, with directions and forms required by them, are furnished them under the provisions of the statute; while the excellent and exhaustive treatise of CONKLIN and BISSELL on the Powers and Duties of Justices of the Peace, furnishes that important township officer with a complete guide. For these reasons any consideration of them, has been omitted in this treatise.

The author acknowledges his obligations to T. W. SHAPLEY, cashier of the First National Bank of Anamosa, Iowa, for the forms furnished herein for treasurer's accounts, and to T. R. ERCANBRACK, ESQ., of the Anamosa Bar, for valuable assistance in the final preparation of this volume for the press.

G. W. FIELD.

ANAMOSA, IOWA, JAN., 1875.

CONTENTS.

PART FIRST.

COUNTY OFFICERS.

CHAPTER I.

CLERK.

CHAPTER II.

CHAPTER III.

CHAPTER IV.

CHAPTER V.

CHAPTER VI.

CHAPTER VII.

SHERIFF.

CHAPTER VIII.

CHAPTER IX.

Of His Duties.

CHAPTER X.

CHAPTER XI.

CHAPTER XII.

Of the Process of Execution,

CHAPTER XIII.

On Replevin.

CHAPTER XIV.

Of Property taken for Internal Improvements.

CHAPTER XV.

Of the Foreclosure of Chattel Mortgages.

CHAPTER XVI.

Of Injunction Cases.

CHAPTER XVII.

Subpœnas.

CHAPTER XVIII.

Certiorari.

CHAPTER XIX.

Writ of Habeas Corpus.

CHAPTER XX.

Writ of Mandamus.

CHAPTER XXI.

Commitment for Insanity.

CHAPTER XXII.

Other Process.

CHAPTER XXIII.

Crimes.

CHAPTER XXIV.

Bench Warrants.

CHAPTER XXV.

Jails, Prisoners, etc.

CHAPTER XXVI.

Courts.

CHAPTER XXVII.

Liability.

CHAPTER XXVIII.

Fees and Compensation.

COUNTY SUPERVISORS.

CHAPTER XXIX.

CHAPTER XXX.

Records.

CHAPTER XXXI.

Powers.

AUDITOR.

CHAPTER XXXII.

TREASURER.

CHAPTER XXXIII.

RECORDER.

CHAPTER XXXIV.

SURVEYOR.

CHAPTER XXXV.

CORONER.

CHAPTER XXXVI.

NOTARIES PUBLIC.

CHAPTER XXXVII.

PART SECOND.

TOWNSHIP OFFICERS.

CHAPTER I.

TOWNSHIP TRUSTEES.

CHAPTER II.

TOWNSHIP CLERK.

CHAPTER III.

CONSTABLES.

CHAPTER IV.

TOWNSHIP ASSESSOR.

CHAPTER V.

TOWNSHIP COLLECTOR.

CHAPTER VI.

CHAPTER VII.

APPENDIX.

PART FIRST.

OF COUNTY OFFICERS.

CHAPTER I.

COUNTY OFFICERS.

I. STATUTES: GENERAL PROVISIONS.

Many of the provisions of the Code have a general application to all or several county and township officers; and in treating of these officers frequent reference must necessarily be made to them. For the purposes of convenience, and of avoiding the necessity of frequent repetition, it is considered advisable to insert these provisions together in this chapter. Of this character are those relating to *the election of county and township officers*.

II. OF THE ELECTION OF OFFICERS AND THEIR TERMS.

The Code provides in reference thereto:

General Elections.—SECTION 573. The general election for State, County, District and Township Officers, shall be held throughout the State on the second Tuesday of October, in each year, except the years of the Presidential Election, when it shall be held on the Tuesday next after the first Monday of November.

Special Elections.—SEC. 574. Special elections authorized by any law, or held to supply vacancies in any office, to be filled by the vote of the qualified voters of the entire State, or of any district or county, or township, may be held at the time designated by such law, or by the officer authorized to order such election.

Vacancies.—SEC. 575. All vacancies in office created by the expiration of a full term, shall be supplied at the general election next preceding the time of expiration.

Term of office.—SEC. 576. The term of office of all officers chosen at a general election for a full term, shall commence on the first Monday of January next thereafter, except when otherwise provided by the constitution. The term of an officer chosen to fill a vacancy, shall commence as soon as he is qualified therefor.

County officers.—SEC. 589. Each county shall elect at the general election in each even-numbered year, a clerk of the district and circuit courts, and a recorder of deeds; and in each odd-numbered year, an auditor, a treasurer, a sheriff, a coroner a county superintendent, and a surveyor; and each of said officers shall hold his office for the term of two years.

Justices and constables.—SEC. 590. Two justices of the peace and two constables shall be chosen by the qualified voters of each township at the general election of each even-numbered year, and shall hold their offices for the term of two years.

Township officers.—SEC. 591. Three township trustees, a township clerk, one assessor, and one highway supervisor for each highway district in each civil township in this State, shall be chosen by the qualified voters of each township at the general election annually, and shall hold their offices for the term of one year.

Additional justices and constables.—SEC. 592. One or two additional justices of the peace, and one or two additional constables may be elected in each township if the trustees so direct, by posting up notices of the same in three of the most public places in the township, at least ten days before election.

Justices and constables county officers.—SEC. 593. Justices of the peace and constables shall be considered as county officers under the provisions of this title, but they shall be voted for by the voters of their respective townships.

III. OF QUALIFICATION FOR OFFICE.

Constitutional Provision.—Section Five, of Article Eleven, of the Constitution of the State, provides as follows:

"Every person elected or appointed to any office shall before entering upon the duties thereof, take an oath or affirmation to support the Constitution of the United States, and of this State, and also an oath of office."

Statutory provisions.—The Code further provides in relation thereto as follows:

Must qualify.—SECTION 670. No civil officer shall enter on the duties of his office until he has qualified himself as required in this chapter.

Who to give bond: form of.—SEC. 674. County supervisors and township trustees are not required to give bond. All other civil officers elected by the people with those specified hereafter in this chapter, are required to give bond with a condition in substance as follows:

That as . . . . (naming the office) in . . . . . township, ... county, (or State of Iowa), he will render a true account of his office and of his doings therein to the proper authority when required thereby or by law; that he will promptly pay over to the person or officer entitled thereto all money which may come into his hands by virtue of his office; that he will promptly account for all balances of money remaining in his hands at the termination of his office; that he will, exercise all reasonable diligence and care in the preservation and lawful disposal of all money, books, papers, securities, or other property appertaining to his said office, and deliver them to his successor, or to any other person authorized to receive the same; and that he will faithfully and impartially, without fear, favor, fraud, or oppression, discharge all duties now or hereafter required of his office by law.

Oath.—SEC. 675. Every civil officer who is required to give bond, shall take and subscribe on the back of his bond, or on a paper attached thereto, to be certified by the officer administering it, an oath that he will support the constitution of the United States and that of the State of Iowa, and that to the best of his knowledge and ability he will perform all the duties of the office of (naming it) as provided by the condition of his bond within written.

SEC. 676. The oath of office provided by article eleven of the constitution for all civil officers not otherwise expressly provided for, may be substantially in the following form: I, ... do solemnly swear that I will support the constitution of the United States and the constitution of the State of Iowa, and that I will faithfully and impartially, to the best of my ability, discharge all the duties of the office of . . . . (naming it) in . . . . (naming the township, county, district, or state, as the case may be), as now or hereafter required by law.

Bond.—SEC. 677. The bonds of state and district officers shall be given to the state, those of county and township officers to the county.

SEC. 678. The bonds of county treasurers, clerks of the district and circuit courts, county recorders, coroners, county surveyors, township assessors, auditors, county superintendents, sheriffs, and of justices of the peace and constables, shall each be in a penal sum to be fixed by the board of supervisors; but those of the treasurer, clerks of the district and circuit courts, auditors, and sheriffs, shall not be in a less sum than five thousand dollars each, and those of justices and constables, not less than five hundred dollars each.

Number of sureties.—SEC. 679. Every official bond shall be given with at least two sureties, and all sureties shall be freeholders within the state; the bonds of the state printer and binder shall be given with at least three sureties, and those of the treasurer of state and each county treasurer with at least four sureties.

Approval of bonds.—SEC. 680. The bonds of state officers must be approved by the governor before being filed; those of district attorneys, by the district judges of their respective districts; those of county officers and township clerk, by the board of supervisors, and of township officers, by the township clerk. The approval shall in all cases be indorsed upon the bond and signed by the officer approving, or the president of the board. But in case the board of supervisors should decide that a bond which is to be approved by them is insufficient, or such bond is not approved the first day of the session, then a reasonable time, not to exceed five days, is to be allowed the officer elect, to supply a sufficient bond, or to approve the same.

SEC. 681. If the board of supervisors refuse or neglect to approve the bond of any county officer elect, he may present the same for approval to the judge of the circuit court, who shall fix a day for the hearing. Notice of such hearing shall be served upon the board of supervisors, as provided by law for the service of original notice; and due proof of such service being made to the judge at the time fixed, he shall, unless good cause for postponement be shown, proceed to hear and determine the sufficiency of the bond, and if satisfied that the same is sufficient, he shall approve the same, and such approval shall have the same force and effect as an approval by the board of supervisors, at the time the same was presented to them for approval would have had.

State officer's filed and recorded.—SEC. 682. The bonds and oaths of state officers shall be filed in the office of the secretary of state, except those of the secretary, which shall be filed and recorded in the office of the auditor; those of county and township officers in the county auditor's office, except those of the county auditor, which shall be kept in the county treasurer's office, and those of justices of the peace, which shall be filed by the auditor in the office of the clerk of the district court, after the same have been approved and recorded.

Penalty.—SEC. 684. Any county officer who shall enter upon the discharge of the duties of his office, without first having caused his official bond to be recorded shall forfeit to the county of which he is an officer, the sum of five dollars for each official act by him performed prior to the recording of said bond, and the chairman of the board of supervisors of each county is hereby required to bring suit for, or collect such penalty in the name of his county; and it shall be considered a misdemeanor for any officer who is required to give bond to act in such official capacity without giving such bond as is provided by law, and he shall be liable to a fine for an amount not exceeding the amount of the bond required of him.

When Governor and Lieutenant Governor shall qualify.—SEC. 685. The governor and lieutenant-governor shall qualify within ten days after the result of the election shall be declared by the General Assembly; judges of the supreme, district, and circuit courts, by the first day of January following their election; and all other officers by the first Monday of January following their election.

Refusal to serve.—SEC. 686. A failure to qualify within the time prescribed shall be deemed a refusal to serve.

Election contested.—SEC. 687. When any election is contested, the person elected shall have twenty days in which to qualify after the day of the decision.

Effect of bonds.—SEC. 688. The bonds of officers shall be construed to cover duties required by law subsequent to giving them.

None void.—SEC. 689. No official bond shall be void for want of compliance with the statute, but it shall be valid in law for the matter contained therein.

Bond not approved until all public property has been accounted for.—SEC. 690. When the incumbent of an office is re-elected, he shall qualify as above directed; but when the re-elected officer has had public funds or property in his control, under color of his office, his bond shall not be approved until he has produced and fully accounted for such funds and property to the proper person to whom he should account therefor; and the officer or board approving the bond shall indorse upon the bond before its approval the fact that the said officer has fully accounted for and produced all funds and property before that time under his control as such officer; and when it is ascertained that the incumbent holds over another term by reason of the non-election of a successor, or for the neglect or refusal of the successor to qualify, he shall qualify anew within a time to be fixed by the officer who approves of the bonds of such officers.

Temporary officer.—SEC. 691. Any person temporarily appointed to fill an office during the incapacity or suspension of the regular incumbent, shall qualify in the manner required by this chapter for the office so to be filled.

IV. REMOVAL—SUSPENSION—DEPUTIES—SURETIES AND VACANCIES.

The Code provides in reference to removal and suspension from Office as follows:

Causes.—SECTION 746. All county and township officers may be charged, tried, and removed from office for the causes following:

1. For habitual or willful neglect of duty;
2. For gross impartiality;
3. For oppression;
4. For extortion;
5. For corruption;
6. For willful mal-administration in office;
7. Upon conviction of a felony;
8. For a failure to produce and fully account for all public funds and property in his hands at any inspection or settlement.

By whom made.—SEC. 747. Any person may make such a charge, and the district court shall have exclusive original jurisdiction thereof by the service of original notice.

Proceedings.—SEC. 748. The proceedings shall be as nearly like those in other actions at law as the nature of the case admits, excepting where otherwise provided in this chapter.

Petition.—SEC. 749. The petition shall be by an accuser against the accused, and shall contain the charges with the necessary specifications under them and be verified by any elector.

Notice.—SEC. 750. It will be sufficient that the notice require the accused to appear and answer the petition of A B (naming the accuser) for "official misdemeanors;" but a copy of the petition must be served with the notice.

When clerk is the accused.—SEC. 751. If the person who holds the office of clerk of the district and circuit court is accused in either of those capacities, his removal or suspension shall operate in both courts and the petition may be filed with the county auditor, and both he and the clerk may issue subpœnas for witnesses, and the county auditor shall deliver the papers to the judge of the district court, on its sitting.

Suspension.—SEC. 752. If a continuance of the action take place beyond the return term, the court may suspend the accused from the functions of his office until the determination of the matter, if sufficient cause appear from testimony, or affidavits then presented; and if such suspension take place, the board of supervisors shall temporarily fill the office by appointment.

Appointments.—SEC. 753. When the accused is an officer of the court and is suspended, the court may supply his place by appointment for the term.

Trial: judgment.—SEC. 754. The question of fact shall be tried as in other actions, and if the accused is found guilty, judgment shall be entered removing the officer from his office, and declaring the latter vacant; and a copy thereof shall be certified to the county auditor, who shall cause it to be entered in the election book.

Costs.—SEC. 755. The accuser and the accused are liable to costs as in other actions.

Judge may suspend clerk and sheriff.—SEC. 756. The judges of the district and circuit courts in their respective districts, shall have authority on their own motion, to suspend from office any clerk of those courts, or sheriff of a county, for any of the causes mentioned in this chapter coming to their own knowledge, or manifestly appearing from the papers or testimony in any proceeding in court.

Direct a petition to be filed.—SEC. 757. Upon such suspension the court may direct the district attorney to file a petition in the name of the county; but it need not be verified.

Suspension certified.—SEC. 758. Such order of suspension shall be certified to the county auditor, and be by him entered in the election book.

OF DEPUTIES.

What officers may appoint.—SEC. 766. The secretary, auditor, and treasurer of state, the superintendent of public instruction, the register of the state land office, each clerk of the district and circuit courts, county auditor, treasurer, sheriff, surveyor, and recorder, may appoint a deputy for whose acts he shall be responsible, and from whom he shall require bonds; which appointment must be in writing and be approved by the officer who has the approval of the principal's bond, and shall be revocable by writing under the principal's hand, and both the appointment and the revocation shall be filed and kept in the office of the secretary of state and county auditor respectively.

Powers of deputy.—SEC. 767. In the absence or disability of the principal, the deputy shall perform the duties of his principal pertaining to his own office; but when any officer is required to act in conjunction with, or in place of another officer, his deputy cannot supply his place.

Who may be appointed.—SEC. 768. The secretary, treasurer, and auditor of state can neither of them appoint either of the others his deputy; nor can either the clerk of the district court, auditor, recorder, treasurer, or sheriff of a county appoint either of the others.

Sheriff.—SEC. 769. The sheriff may appoint such number of deputies as he sees fit.

Oath.—SEC. 770. Each deputy shall take the same oath as principal, which shall be indorsed upon and filed with the certificate of his appointment.

Compensation.—SEC. 771. When a county officer receiving a salary is compelled by the pressure of the business of his office to employ a deputy, the board of supervisors may make a reasonable allowance to such deputy.

OF ADDITIONAL SECURITY, AND THE DISCHARGE OF SURETIES.

Bonds of State officers increased.—SEC. 772. Whenever the governor shall deem it advisable that the bonds of any state officer should be increased and the security enlarged, or a new bond given, he shall notify said officer of the fact, the amount of new or additional security to be given, and the time when the same shall be executed, which said new security shall be approved and filed as provided by law.

Additional security required.—SEC. 773. Any officer or board who has the approval of another officer's bond, when of opinion that the public security requires it, upon giving ten days' notice to show cause to the contrary, may require him to give such additional security by a new bond, as may be deemed requisite, within a reasonable time to be prescribed.

Security in force: vacancy.—SEC. 774. If a requisition made under either of the foregoing sections be complied with, both the old and the new security shall be in force; and if not complied with, the office shall become and be declared vacant, and the proceeding be certified to the proper officer, to be recorded in the election book, or township record.

When a surety deems himself insecure.—SEC. 775. When any surety on the bond of a civil officer conceives himself in danger by remaining surety, and desires to be relieved of his obligation, he may petition the approving officer or board above referred to for relief, stating the ground of his apprehension.

Notice of petition.—SEC. 776. The surety shall give the principal at least twen-four hours' notice of the presenting and filing of the petition, with a copy thereof. At the expiration of this notice the approving officer may hear the matter, or may postpone the hearing as the case permits or requires.

Hearing: order: effect.—SEC. 777. If, upon the hearing, there appears substantial ground for apprehension, the approving officer or board may order the principal to give a new bond and to supply the place of the petitioning surety within a reasonable time to be prescribed; and upon such new bond being given, the petitioning surety upon the former bond shall be declared discharged from liability on the same for future acts; which order of discharge shall be entered in the proper election book, but the bond will continue binding upon those who do not petition for relief.

Failure to comply.—SEC. 778. If the new bond is not given as required, the office shall be declared vacant, and the order to that effect entered in the proper election book.

Justice of the peace.—SEC. 779. If the proceedings relate to a justice of the peace, and he is removed from office, the county auditor shall notify the proper township trustees, or clerk, of the removal.

Subpœnas.—SEC. 780. The approving officer may issue subpœnas in his official name for witnesses, compel their attendance, and swear them.

OF VACANCIES AND SPECIAL ELECTIONS.

Civil office when vacant.—SEC. 781. Every civil office shall be vacant upon the happening of either of the following events, at any time before the expiration of the term of such office, as follows:

1. The resignation of the incumbent;
2. His death;
3. His removal from office;
4. The decision of a competent tribunal declaring his office vacant;
5. His ceasing to be a resident of the state, district, county or township in which the duties of his office are to be exercised, or for which he may have been elected;
6. A failure to elect at the proper election, there being no incumbent to continue in office until his successor is elected and qualified, nor other provision relating thereto;
7. A forfeiture of office as provided by any law of the state;
8. Conviction of an infamous crime, or of any public offense involving the violation of his oath of office;
9. The acceptance of a commission to any military office, either in the militia of this state, or in the service of the United States, which requires the incumbent in the civil office to exercise his military duties out of the state for a period not less than sixty days;

Resignations: how made. SEC. 782. Resignation of civil officers may be made as follows:

1. By the governor to the general assembly, if in session, if not, to the secretary of state;
2. By senators and representatives in congress, and by all officers elected by the qualified voters of the state, and by judges of courts of record, and district attornies, to the governor;
3. By senators and representatives in the general assembly, to the presiding officer of their respective bodies, if in session, who shall immediately transmit information of the same to the governor; if such bodies are not in session to the governor;
4. By all county officers to the board of supervisors, and by members of the board of supervisors, to the county auditor;
5. By all township officers, to the township clerk; and by the township clerk to the township trustees, or any one of them;
6. By all officers holding by appointment, to the officer or body by whom they were appointed.

Vacancies: how filled.—SEC. 783. Vacancies shall be filled as follows:

In the offices of the clerk and reporter of the supreme court, by the supreme court;

In all other state offices, and in the membership of any board or commission created by the state, where no other method is specially provided, by the governor;

In county offices by the board of supervisors; and in the membership of such board by the county clerk, auditor and recorder;

In township officers by the trustees, but where the offices of the three trustees are all vacant the clerk shall appoint, and if there be no clerk, the county auditor shall appoint.

Term continued until successor qualifies. SEC. 784. Every officer elected or appointed for a fixed term, shall hold office until his successor is elected and qualified unless the statute under which he is elected or appointed expressly declares the contrary; *provided*, that this section shall not be construed in any way to prevent the removal or suspension of such officer during or after his term, in cases provided by law.

Appointments.—SEC. 785. Appointments under the provisions of this chapter shall be in writing and continue until the next election at which the vacancy can be filled and until a successor is elected and qualified, and be filed with the secretary or proper township clerk, or in the proper county office, respectively.

Qualification.—SEC. 786. Persons appointed to office as herein provided, shall qualify in the same manner as those elected, within a time to be prescribed in their appointments, and the provisions of the chapter relating to qualification for office are extended to them.

Removed.—SEC. 787. A person appointed as herein contemplated, may be removed by the officer appointing, and no person can be appointed who has been removed from office within one year.

Who may take possession of office.—SEC. 788. When a vacancy occurs in a public office, possession shall be taken of the office room, and of the books, papers, and all things pertaining to the office, to be held until the election or appointment and qualification of a successor, as follows:

Of the office of the county auditor, by the clerk of the district court;

Of that of the clerk or treasurer, by the county auditor;

Of any of the state officers, by the governor; or in his absence or inability at the time of the occurrence, as follows:

Of the secretary, by the treasurer;

Of the auditor, register of the land office, or superintendent of public instruction, by the secretary;

Of the treasurer, by the secretary and auditor, who shall make an inventory of the money and warrants therein, sign the same, and transmit it to the governor if he be in the state; and the secretary shall take the keys of the safes and desks after depositing the books, papers, money, and warrants therein, and the auditor shall take the key of the office room.

Election to fill vacancies.—SEC. 789. Vacancies occurring in the township officers, ten days; in county offices, fifteen days; and in all other public elective offices, thirty days prior to a general election, shall be filled thereat. When a vacancy occurs in the office of representative in congress, or senator or representative in the general assembly, and the body in which such vacancy exists will convene prior to such election, the governor shall order a special election to fill such vacancy, at the earliest practicable time, and ten days' notice of such election shall be given.

Members of the general assembly; vacancy.—SEC. 790. Whenever a vacancy shall occur in the office of a senator or representative in the general assembly, the auditor of the county in which such vacancy occurs shall notify the governor of such fact, and the cause of the vacancy; and if more than one county is represented in the district in which such vacancy may occur, then such notice shall be given by the auditor of the county in which the late member resided.

V. FEES AND OTHER MATTERS.

Statutory provisions.—The Code further provides, in relation to public officers, as follows:

Where no other fees are fixed.—SECTION 3819. Any officer legally called on to perform any of the following services, in cases where no fees have been fixed therefor, shall be entitled to receive:

For drawing and certifying an affidavit, or giving a certificate not attached to any other writing, twenty-five cents;

For affixing his official seal to any paper, whether the certificate be under seal or not, thirty-five cents;

For making out a transcript of any public papers or records under his control, for the use of a private person or corporation, or recording articles of incorporation, for every one hundred words, ten cents.

For publication of legal notices.—SEC. 3832. In all cases where publication of legal notices of any kind are required or allowed by law, the person or officer desiring such publication shall not be required to pay more than one dollar per square of ten lines of brevier type, or its equivalent, for the first insertion, and fifty cents per square for each subsequent insertion; and any person desiring such publication, who shall have tendered such notice to the editor, proprietor, or person conducting some newspaper, published weekly or oftener in such county, having the largest circulation, and has offered to pay for the publication of the same at the rate herein named, and in case the publication of such notice is refused at the price above fixed, then the officer or person desiring such publication shall procure the insertion of such notice in the newspaper nearest the county seat of such county having a general circulation that will publish such notice at the rate herein provided; which publication shall in all respects have the same effect in law and equity as if such notice had been published in the county where such action was commenced or sale to take place. And in all cases of publication of notices in connection with commencement of actions in court, or sales upon execution, the plaintiff may designate the newspaper published within the county in which such notice shall be published.

For printing delinquent tax list.—SEC. 3833. The compensation for printing the delinquent tax list, shall be at a rate not exceeding twenty cents for each tract of real property advertised for sale; and in case there is no newspaper published in the county where such lands lie, then the treasurer shall cause the publication to be made in the nearest newspaper having a circulation in such county, provided that no newspaper shall be considered as one of general circulation unless it has two hundred regular weekly subscribers.

Arbitrators.—SEC. 3834. The compensation of arbitrators shall be, for each day actually and necessarily spent in the discharge of their duty, two dollars, or such other sum as may be agreed upon by the parties in interest. The fees of referees acting under a submission made by or agreed to by the parties in a case pending in a court of record, shall be fixed by the court or judge and taxed as a part of the costs in the case.

Depositions.—SEC. 3835. Any officer or person taking depositions is authorized to charge therefor at the rate of ten cents per hundred words, exclusive of the certificate,

Receipt for fees paid.—SEC. 3836. Every person charging fees shall, if required by the person paying them, give him a receipt therefor, setting forth the items and the date of each.

Bill of particulars.—SEC. 3837. When no other provision is made on the subject, the party requiring any service shall pay the fees therefor upon the same being rendered, and a bill of particulars being presented if required.

Putting up advertisements.—SEC. 3838. In all cases where an officer in the discharge of his duty is required to set up an advertisement, he shall, when not otherwise provided, be allowed twenty-five cents, and if an advertisement is required to be published in a newspaper, the money therefor shall be paid by the party, and may be taxed in the bill of costs.

Officers to keep list of fees posted up.—SEC. 3839. Every officer entitled to fees shall keep posted up in his office a fair table thereof on pain of forfeiture of two dollars per day, for the benefit of the county, for each day he fails to keep such tables of fees thus posted up.

Penalty for taking more than allowed.—SEC. 3840. Any officer who wilfully takes higher or other fees than are allowed by law, is guilty of a misdemeanor, and may be fined therefor a sum not less than than ten nor more than fifty dollars.

When paid by a county.—Where costs are paid by a county other than the one where the offense was committed, the amount of such costs shall be deemed a charge in favor of such county and against the one in which the offense was committed, and may be recovered by action in any court having jurisdiction.

When fees must be paid in advance.—SEC. 3842. No officer or other person mentioned in this title is entitled to any of the fees in advance, where the same grows out of any criminal prosecution. But in all other cases, except where the fees or compensation is payable by the state or county, or when the orders, judgments, or decrees of courts, or justices of the peace are to be entered or performed, or their writs executed, the officer performing any of the services named in this chapter is entitled to his fees in advance if he demand them. After the expiration of sixty days from the rendition of a final judgment not appealed, removed or reversed, the clerk of the court or a justice of the peace in whose office the judgment is entered, may, and on demand of any party entitled to any part thereof, shall issue a fee bill for all costs of such judgment, which shall have the same force and effect as an execution issued by such officer, and shall be served and executed in the same manner.

When fees are payable by state or county.—SEC. 3843. In all cases where fees or compensation, as distinguished from a certain and fixed salary, are by the provisions of this title to be paid any officer or other person, out of the county or state treasury, no part of the same shall be audited or paid, until a particular account has been filed in the auditor's office of the county or state, verified by affidavit, and showing clearly for what services such fees or compensation are claimed, and when the same was rendered.

Supervisors to furnish officers with fuel and stationery.—SEC. 3844. The board of supervisors shall furnish the clerk of the district and circuit court, sheriff, recorder, treasurer, auditor, and county superintendent, with offices at the county seat, together with fuel, lights, blanks, books and stationery necessary and proper to enable them to discharge the duties of their respective offices; but in no case shall any of such officers be permitted to occupy an office also occupied by a practicing attorney.

County officers control advertisements.—SEC. 306. The clerk of the district court, sheriff, auditor, treasurer and recorder shall designate the newspapers in which the notices pertaining to their several offices shall be published, and the board of supervisors shall designate the papers in which all other county notices shall be published; and in counties having a population exceeding eighteen thousand inhabitants, the board shall designate as one of such papers, a paper published in a foreign language, if there be such in its county.

VI. OF THE ADMINISTRATION OF OATHS.

Who authorized.—SECTION 277. The following officers are authorized to administer oaths, and take and certify the acknowledgment of instruments in writing:

Each judge of the supreme court;

Each judge of the district court;

Each judge of the circuit court;

The clerk of the supreme court;

Each clerk of the district court as such, or as clerk of the circuit court;

Each deputy clerk of the district and circuit courts;

Each county auditor;

Each deputy county auditor;

Each sheriff and his deputies, in cases where they are authorized by law to select commissioners or appraisers, or to empanel jurors for the view or appraisement of property, or are directed as an official duty to have property appraised, or to take the answers of garnishees;

Each justice of the peace within his county;

Each notary public within his county.

Affirmation.—SEC. 278. Persons conscientiously opposed to swearing may affirm, and shall be subject to the penalties of perjury, as in case of swearing.

VII. OF SECURITIES AND INVESTMENTS.

SECTION 246. Whenever security is required to be given, by law or by order on judgment of a court, and no particular mode is prescribed, it shall be by bond.

SEC. 247. Such security, when not otherwise directed, may, if for the benefit of individuals, be given to the party intended to be thereby secured. If in relation to the public matters concerning the inhabitants of one county or part of a county, it may be made payable to the county; if concerning the inhabitants of more than one county, it may be made payable to the state. But a mere mistake in these respects will not vitiate the security.

SEC. 248. No defective bond or other security, or affidavit in any case, shall prejudice the party giving or making it, provided it be so rectified within a reasonable time after the defect is discovered as not to cause essential injury to the other party.

SEC. 249. The surety in every bond provided for by this code, must be a resident of this state, and worth double the sum to be secured, beyond the amount of his debts, and have property liable to execution in this state equal to the sum to be secured. Where there are two or more sureties in the same bond, they must, in the aggregate, have the qualification prescribed in this section.

SEC. 250. The officer whose duty it is to take a surety in any bond provided for by this code, shall require the person offered as surety to make affidavit of his qualification, which affidavit may be made before such officer, or other officer qualified to administer oaths. The taking of such an affidavit shall not exempt the officer from any liability to which he might otherwise be subject, for taking insufficient security.

SEC. 251. Where investments of money are directed to be made, and no mode of investment is pointed out by statute, they must be made in the stock or bonds of this State or of those of the United States, or upon bond or mortgage of real property of clear unincumbered value of at least twice the investment.

SEC. 252. When such investment is made by order of any court, the security taken shall in no case be discharged, impaired, or transferred without an order of the court to that effect entered on the minutes thereof.

SEC. 253. The clerk or other person appointed in such cases to make the investment, must receive all moneys as they become due thereon, and apply or re-invest the same under the direction of the court, unless the court appoint some other person to do such acts.

Account, when rendered.—SEC. 254. Once in each year, and oftener if required by the court, the person so appointed must, on oath, render to the court an account in writing of all moneys so received by him, and of the application thereof.

Delivery of property or deposit of money.—SEC. 255. When it is admitted by the pleading or examination of a party that he has in his possession, or under his control, any money or property capable of delivery, which is in any degree the subject of litigation, and which is held by him as trustee for another party, the court, or judge thereof, may order the same to be deposited in the office of the clerk, or delivered to such party, with or without such security, subject to the farther direction of the court; or may order such money to be deposited in a bank with the consent of the parties in interest, to the credit of the court in which the action is pending, and the same shall be paid out by such bank, only upon the check of the clerk annexed to the certified order of the court directing such payment.

SEC. 256. Whenever a court or judge, in the exercise of its or his authority, has ordered the deposit or delivery of money or other property, and the order is disobeyed, the court, besides punishing the disobedience, may make an order requiring the sheriff to take the money or property, and deposit or deliver it in conformity with the directions of the court or judge.

SEC. 257. The sheriff has the same power in such cases, as when acting under an order for the delivery of personal property.

VIII.—CRIMES AND THEIR PUNISHMENT.

The Code defines crimes and misdemeanors of officers, and provides for their punishment as follows:

Sheriff and other officers receiving bribes.—SECTION 3948. If any sheriff, deputy sheriff, constable, or coroner, receive from a defendant, or any other person, any money or other valuable thing as a consideration or inducement for omitting or delaying to arrest any defendant, or to carry him before a magistrate or to prison; or for postponing, delaying, or neglecting the sale of property on execution; or for omitting or delaying to perform any other duty pertaining to his office, he shall be punished by fine not exceeding five hundred dollars, or be imprisoned in the county jail not exceeding six months, or by both fine and imprisonment at the discretion of the court.

Refusing to execute process in criminal cases.—SEC. 3949. If any officer authorized to serve process, wilfully refuse to execute any lawful process to him directed, requiring him to apprehend or confine any person charged with, or convicted of, any public offense; or wilfully delay or omit to execute such process, whereby such person escape, he shall be punished by imprisonment in the county jail not more than one year, or by fine not exceeding one thousand dollars, or by both fine and imprisonment at the discretion of the court.

Extortion.—SEC. 3950. If any person corruptly and wilfully demand and receive of another, for performing any service or official duty for which the fee or compensation is established by law, any greater fee or compensation than is allowed or provided for the same; or if any witness falsely and corruptly certify that as such he has traveled more miles, or attended more days than he has actually traveled or attended, he shall be punished by fine not exceeding one hundred dollars for each offense, or imprisoned in the county jail not exceeding six months.

Compounding felonies.—SEC. 3951. If any person having knowledge of the commission of any offense punishable with imprisonment in the penitentiary for life, take any money, or valuable consideration, or gratuity, or any promise therefor, upon an agreement or understanding, expressed or implied, to compound or conceal such offense, or not to prosecute the same, or not to give evidence thereof, he shall be punished by imprisonment in the penitentiary not more than six years, or by fine not exceeding one thousand dollars.

SEC. 3952. If any person having knowledge of the commission of any offense punishable by imprisonment in the penitentiary for a limited term of years is guilty of the offense described in the preceding section, he shall be punished by imprisonment in the county jail not more than one year, and by fine not exceeding four hundred dollars.

Suffering prisoner to escape.—SEC. 3953. If any jailor or other officer voluntarily suffer any prisoner in his custody upon a charge or conviction of a felony punishable by imprisonment for life to escape, he shall be punished by imprisonment in the penitentiary not more than ten years, nor less one year.

SEC. 3954. If any jailor or other officer voluntarily suffer any prisoner in his custody upon charge or conviction of any other felony to escape, he shall be punished by imprisonment in the penitentiary not more than eight years, or by fine not more than one thousand dollars.

SEC. 3955. If any jailor or other officer suffer any prisoner in his custody upon charge or conviction of any public offense to escape, he shall be punished by fine not exceeding one thousand dollars, and by imprisonment in the penitentiary not exceeding five years.

Falsely assuming to be an officer.—SEC. 3962. If any person falsely assume to be a judge, justice of the peace, magistrate, sheriff, deputy sheriff, coroner, or constable, and take upon himself to act as such, or require any one to aid or assist him in any matter pertaining to the duty of any such officer, he shall be punished by imprisonment in the county jail not more than one year or by fine not exceeding three hundred dollars.

Exercising office without authority.—SEC. 3963. If any person take upon himself to exercise or officiate in any office or place of authority in this state, without being legally authorized; or if any person by color of his office, wilfully and corruptly oppress any person under pretense of acting in his official capacity, he shall be punished by fine not exceeding one thousand dollars, or imprisonment in the county jail not more than one year; or by both fine and imprisonment.

Stirring up quarrels.—SEC. 3964. If any judge, justice of the peace, clerk of any court, sheriff, coroner, constable, attorney or counsellor at law, encourage, excite or stir up any suit, quarrel, or controversy between two or more persons, with intent to injure such person or persons, he shall be punished by fine not exceeding five hundred dollars, and shall be answerable to the party injured in treble damages.

Neglect of duty.—SEC. 3965. When any duty is or shall be enjoined by law upon any public officer, or upon any person holding any public trust or employment, every willful neglect to perform such duty, where no special provision has been made for the punishment of such delinquency, is a misdemeanor.

Misdemeanors.—SEC. 3966. When the performance of any act is prohibited by any statute, and no penalty for the violation of such statute is imposed, the doing of such act is a misdemeanor.

Punishment of when none other prescribed.—SEC. 3967. Every person who is convicted of a misdemeanor, the punishment of which is not otherwise prescribed by any statute of this state, shall be punished by imprisonment in the county jail not more than one year, or by fine not exceeding five hundred dollars, or by both such fine and imprisonment.

Making false entries and returns.—SEC. 3968. If any public officer fraudulently make or give false entries, or false returns, or false certificates of receipts in cases where entries, returns, certificates, or receipts are authorized by law, he shall be fined not exceeding five hundred dollars, or be imprisoned in the county jail not exceeding one year, or both, at the discretion of the court.

Oppression by officers.—SEC. 3969. If any judge or other officer by color of his office, willfully and maliciously oppress any person under pretense of acting in his official capacity, he shall be punished by fine not exceeding three hundred dollars and imprisonment in the county jail not less than five nor more than thirty days, and be liable to the injured party for any damage sustained by him in consequence thereof.

Failing to pay over fees.—SEC. 3970. If any justice of the peace, clerk of the district or other court, county recorder, or any other officer who by law is authorized to receive and required to pay over fees of office, or who is or may be authorized to impose or collect fines, shall fail, neglect, or refuse to pay over as prescribed or as may hereafter be prescribed by law, all such fees and fines, he shall be deemed guilty of a misdemeanor, besides being liable in a civil action for the amount of such fines and fees as he may have thus illegally withheld or appropriated.

Making false entries in relation to fees.—SEC. 3971. If any justice of the peace, clerk of the district or other court which is now or may hereafter be established, county recorder, or other officer, who by law is authorized or required to keep a record docket, or who is or may be required to keep an account of fees or fines, and to pay over, or in any way account for the same, shall in any manner falsify such docket or account, or shall fail, neglect, or retuse to make an entry upon such docket, or account of such fees and fines as are required to be paid over according to law, such justice of the peace, clerk of the district court, or clerk of any other court, county recorder and other officer shall be guilty of a misdemeanor, and shall be subject and liable to be prosecuted therefor in any court having jurisdiction of the offense.

Officers appropriating fees to their own use.—SEC. 3972. Any justice of the peace, clerk of the district or of any other court which is or may be established, county recorder, or other officer who may be found guilty of the offense of appropriating to his own use fees of office or fines collected for violation of law, or of neglecting to pay over the same as prescribed by law, shall be removed from office by the court before or by whom the offense may be tried and judgment or conviction had, and each and every person so found guilty shall be punished by a fine not exceeding three hundred dollars nor less than ten dollars, or imprisonment in the county jail for a period not exceeding one year, or by both such fine and imprisonment, in the discretion of the court.

Officers to report fees to supervisors.—SEC. 3973. All officers required by the provisions of this code to collect and pay over fines and fees, shall, on the first Monday in January in each year, make report thereof under oath to the board of supervisors of the proper county, showing the amount of fines assessed and the amount of fines and fees collected, together with the vouchers for the payment of all sums by him collected, to the proper officer required to keep the same.

Clerks and justices to report fines, fees, etc: penalty for failure.—SEC. 3974. The clerks of the several courts of this state, except of the supreme court, and all mayors of incorporated towns and cities, and justices of the peace, shall on the first Monday of January of each year, make a report in writing to the board of supervisors of their respective counties, of all forfeited recognizances in their several offices; of all fines, penalties, and forfeitures imposed in their respective courts, and which by law go into the county treasury for the benefit of the school fund; in what cause or proceedings, when, for what purpose, against whom, and for what amount rendered; whether said fines, penalties, forfeitures and recognizances have been paid, remitted, cancelled, or otherwise satisfied; if so, when, how, and in what manner; if not paid, remitted, canceled, or otherwise satisfied, what steps have been taken to enforce the collection thereof, and the prospect of such collection. Such report must be verified under oath, to the effect that the same is full, true, and complete of the matters therein contained, and of all things required by this section to be reported; and any officer failing so to do shall be deemed guilty of a misdemeanor, and upon conviction thereof, may be fined in any sum not less than one hundred dollars.

Notary public exercising improperly duties of office.—SEC. 3975. If any notary public exercise the duties of his office after the expiration of his commission, or when otherwise disqualified, or appends his official signature to documents when the parties have not appeared before him, he shall be deemed guilty of a misdemeanor, and be punished by a fine of not less than fifty dollars, and shall also be removed from office by the governor.

Failure to take oath before entering on duties of office.—SEC. 3976. If any officer or person willfully fails to take the oath required by law before entering on the discharge of the duties of any office, trust, or station, or makes any contract which contemplates an expenditure in excess of the law under which he was elected or appointed, or fails to report to the proper officer showing the expenditure of all public moneys with proper vouchers therefor by the time required by law, he shall be punished by a fine not exceeding five thousand dollars, or by imprisonment in the penitentiary not exceeding five years, or by both at the discretion of the court.

IX.—EVIDENCE.

General provisions of the Code, in reference to records, and certified copies thereof:

Copies of record and entries.—SECTION. 3702. Duly certified copies of all records and entries, or papers belonging to any public office, or by authority of law filed to be kept therein, shall be evidence in all cases of equal credibility with the original record or papers so filed.

Officer to give copies.—SEC. 3706. Every officer having the custody of a public record or writing is bound to give any person, on demand, a certified copy thereof on payment of the legal fees therefor.

X.—RESISTANCE TO PROCESS AND SUPPRESSION OF RIOTS.

Calling out power of county.—SECTION. 4145. When the sheriff or other officer authorized to execute process, finds or has reason to apprehend, that resistance will be made to the execution thereof, he may command as many male inhabitants of the county as he may think proper, and any military companies of his county, armed and equipped, to assist him in overcoming the resistance, and if necessary, in seizing, arresting, and confining the resisters, and their aiders and abettors to be punished by law.

Certify to court names of resisters.—SEC. 4146. The officer shall certify to the court from which the process issued, the names of the resisters and their aiders and abettors, to the end that they may be punished for a contempt.

Refuses to assist.—SEC. 4147. Every person commanded by a public officer to assist him in the execution of process, as provided in section four thousand one hundred and forty-five of this chapter, who, without lawful cause, refuses or neglects to obey such command, is guilty of a misdemeanor.

When power of county not sufficient.—SEC. 4148. If it appear to the governor that the power of any county is not sufficient to enable the sheriff to execute process delivered to him, he may, on the application of the sheriff, order such posse or military force from any other county or counties as is necessary.

Unlawful assemblages.—SEC. 4149. When persons to the number of twelve or more, armed with dangerous weapons, or persons to the number of thirty or more, whether armed or not, are unlawfully or riotously assembled in any city or town, the judges, sheriff, and his deputies if they be present, the mayor, aldermen, marshal, constables, and justices of the peace of such city or town, must go among the persons assembled, or as near them as may be safe, and command them in the name of the state, immediately to disperse.

Arrest.—SEC. 4150. If the persons assembled do not immediately disperse, the magistrates and officers must arrest them, that they may be punished according to law, and for that purpose may command the aid of all persons present or within the county.

Refusing to aid.—SEC. 4151. If any person commanded to aid the magistrate or officer, without good cause neglect to do so, he is guilty of a misdemeanor.

Failure of duty.—SEC. 4152. If a magistrate or officer having notice of an unlawful or riotous assembly as above provided in this chapter, neglect to proceed to the place of assembly, or as near thereto as he can with safety, and to exercise the authority with which he is invested for suppressing the same and arresting the persons, he is guilty of a misdemeanor.

Assembly will not disperse.—SEC. 4153. If the persons so assembled and commanded to disperse, do not immediately disperse, any two of the magistrates or officers before mentioned, may command the aid of a sufficient number of persons, and may proceed in such manner as, in their judgment, is necessary to disperse the assembly and arrest the offenders.

When armed force is called out.—SEC. 4154. When an armed force is called out for the purpose of suppressing an unlawful or riotous assembly, or arresting the offenders, it must obey such orders in relation thereto as have been made by the governor, or by a judge of the supreme, district, or circuit court, a sheriff or magistrate, as the case may be.

CHAPTER II.

THE CLERK.

I. HIS ELECTION, QUALIFICATION, ETC.

Election.—Each county is required to elect at the general election in each even-numbered year, a clerk of the District and Circuit Courts. Code Sec. 589. His term of office, in case of election for a full term, commences on the first Monday of January after his election, provided he qualifies according to law, and continues for two years, and until his successor is elected and qualified, unless he should resign, or be removed, as provided by law.

Qualification.—He cannot enter upon the duties of his office until he gives a bond and subscribes to an oath required by the constitution of the State, and the provisions of the Code, which may be found in Chapter One.

Official Bond.—The bond should be in a penal sum to be fixed by the board of supervisors of the county, but cannot be in a less sum than five thousand dollars. Code, Sec. 678. And his bond should be given with at least two sureties, freeholders of the State, and be approved by the board of supervisors. The approval should be indorsed on the bond, and signed by the president of the board. Code, Secs. 679, 680. He should qualify as aforesaid, by the first Monday of January, following his election, and a failure to qualify shall be deemed a refusal to serve. Code, Secs. 685, 686.

Refusal to approve the bond.—If the board refuse or neglect to approve the bond, the clerk may proceed as directed by Section 681, of the Code, found in Chapter One.

Construction of official bonds.—The bond is construed to cover any duty required by law, subsequent to giving it; and it is not void for want of compliance with the statute, but is valid in law for the matter contained therein. Code, Secs. 688, 689.

In case of re-election.—If any officer is re-elected, he is required to qualify in the same way, but when re-elected, and he has public funds, or property in his control, under color of his office, his bond shall not be approved until he has produced, and fully accounted for such funds and property to the person to whom he should account therefor; and the officer or board approving the bond shall indorse upon it before its approval, the fact that said officer has fully accounted for, and produced all funds and property before that time under his control, as such officer.

In case he holds over.—When it is ascertained that the incumbent holds over another term, by reason of the non-election of a successor, or by reason of the neglect or refusal of the person elected to qualify, the incumbent should qualify anew, within the time to be fixed by the officer who approves the bonds of such officers. Code, Sec. 690.

FORM OF OFFICIAL BOND.

No. 1.

Know all men by these Presents: That we, A B as principal, and C D and E F, as sureties, of the county of ...., and State of Iowa, are held and firmly bound unto the county of ...., in said State, in the penal sum of .... dollars, for the payment of which we bind ourselves firmly by these presents.

The above bond is to be void upon condition that the said A B, as clerk of the District and Circuit Courts of said county, (or as sheriff or treasurer, or auditor or other officer, according to the fact,) will render a true account of his said office and his doings therein, to any person or board, or officer whenever he may be lawfully required so to do; that he will promptly pay over and deliver to the person or officer entitled thereto, all money and property that may come into his hands by virtue of said office; that he will promptly account for all balances of money, and all property remaining in his hands at the termination of his office; that he will hereafter exercise all reasonable diligence, and care in the preservation and lawful disposal of all money, books, papers, securities, or other property appertaining to his said office, and deliver them to his successor, or to any any other person authorized to receive the same; and that he will faithfully and impartially, without fear, favor, fraud or oppression discharge all the other duties now, or hereafter required of his said office by law.

Witness our hands this .... day of ...., 18..

A.... B....
C.... D....
E ... F....

FORM OF OFFICIAL OATH.

No. 2.

STATE OF IOWA, }
.... County, } ss.

I, A B, do solemnly swear that I will support the constitution of the United States, and the constitution of the State of Iowa, and that to the best of my knowledge and ability, I will perform all the duties of the office of clerk of the District and Circuit Courts of .... county, State of Iowa, now, or hereafter required by law. A.... B....

Subscribed and sworn to before me, this .... day .... A. D., 18.... C.... D....

FORM OF APPROVAL OF BOND.

No. 3.

STATE OF IOWA, }
.... County. } ss.

I, J C, chairman of the board of supervisors of said county, hereby certify that the foregoing, (or within) bond of A B, as clerk, etc., and the sureties thereto, were this day approved by the said board.

Dated this .... day of ...., 18....

J.... C ...., *Chairman.*

Extent of liability of sureties.—The official bond of a public officer is construed as a security to the body politic or civil corporation of which he is an officer, and also to all the members thereof severally, who are intended to be thereby secured. And a judgment in favor of a party for one delinquency does not preclude the same or another party from maintaining an action on the same for another delinquency, except that sureties can be made liable in the aggregate only to the extent of their undertaking. Code, Secs. 3368, 3369.

II. VACANCIES, AND REMOVAL AND SUSPENSION FROM OFFICE.

Vacancies.—Vacancies occurring fifteen days prior to a general election, should be filled at said election. Code, Sec. 789. The provisions of the Code relating to vacancies, and removal and suspension from office may be found in Chapter One.

Right to resign.—The right to resign and vacate an office is clearly recognized in this State. The tendering of a resignation of a public office in writing to the officer authorized by law to receive it, and the filing of the same without objection by such officer, operate to vacate the office resigned, according to the tenor of the resignation ; and the officer to whom the resignation is by law to be made, cannot forbid it or refuse to receive it. 12 Iowa, 405.

III. DEPUTIES.

The clerk may appoint.—The general provisions of the Code in reference to deputies may be found in Chapter One.

The clerk may in writing appoint a deputy, for whose acts he is responsible, and from whom he is required to take a bond for the faithful discharge of his duties. The bond should be satisfactory to the principal, but need not be otherwise approved ; but the appointment should be approved by the officer who has the approval of the principal's bond ; and the appointment may be revoked at any time by a writing under the principal's hand, and both the appointment and the revocation should be filed and kept in the office of the auditor of the county when it relates to a county office. Code, Sec. 766.

FORM FOR THE APPOINTMENT OF DEPUTY.

No. 4.

STATE OF IOWA, }
........, County, } ss.

To the Board of Supervisors of said county :

I, J C, clerk of the District and Circuit Courts of said, county, (or sheriff, treasurer, or other officer), do hereby certify, that I hereby appoint E F, my deputy clerk in and for said county, and that he has given a satisfactory bond, duly approved by me as required by law. Said appointment is subject to your approval.

Witness my hand this .... day of ...., 18...

J.... C...., *Clerk.*

The approval.—The approval of the appointment should be by the board of supervisors of the county, and in analogy to the requirements in relation to the approval of bonds, the better practice would be to have the approval indorsed on the appointment, and certified by the chairman of the board.

FORM OF APPROVAL OF APPOINTMENT.

STATE OF IOWA, }
.... County, } ss.

I, H S, chairman of the board of supervisors of said county, hereby certify that the appointment by J C, clerk, etc., of E F, as his deputy, etc., as shown by the above (or within) certificate of his appointment, was this day duly approved by said board.

Witness my hand this ..... day of ......, 18...

J.... C ..., *Chairman.*

Official oath.—The usual official oath taken and subscribed by the deputy should be indorsed on the appointment and filed with the auditor.

Revocation and removal.—The appointment is at any time revocable by the principal in writing, and should also, like the appointment, be filed in the office of the county auditor. This is necessary and important, that the public may know who is lawfully authorized to act as deputy.

FORM OF REVOCATION.

To the Auditor of.. ... County, Iowa, and all others whom it may concern:

I, J C, clerk of the District and Circuit Courts of said county, (or sheriff or treasurer or other officer as the case may be), hereby revoke the appointment of E F as my deputy in said county. Said revocation to take effect at this, (or some future) date.

Dated this....day of....18.. J.... C...., *Clerk.*

The power of removal important.—The power of removal of deputies by the principal is absolute and unqualified, and is demanded by considerations of private security and public policy.

Deputy to give bond to the principal.—The deputy is required, as we have seen, to give a bond to the principal; but it need not be filed in the office of the auditor or approved by the board of supervisors. It is intended for the protection of the principal and his sureties, who are alone liable for the acts of the deputy. 12 Iowa, 346.

Powers of the deputy.—The deputy is vested with the general powers of the principal, and may do any act in the name of the principal which the principal could do, except when he is required to act in conjunction with, or in the place of another officer. Code, Sec. 767. The acts of the deputy are the acts of the principal, and unless he is removed, his authority continues as long as the authority of the principal. This is in accordance with the statute, and the principles of the common law. 7 Com. Dig., 543; Chit. Black. 260, and notes.

Applicable to the deputies of all officers.—The provisions of the Code with the general principles of law and the directions furnished herein in reference to deputies, apply to all other officers authorized under the statute, to appoint deputies.

When a new bond is required.—In certain cases provided for by the Code, a new official bond may be required of officers. The duty of the officer in such case is sufficiently pointed out by the statutes, which may be found in the first chapter of this volume. If a new bond is required, it should be approved, indorsed and filed, as required in case of original bonds; but no new oath of office would be required.

CHAPTER III.

THE CLERK'S DUTIES.

I. STATUTES RELATING THERETO.

The general provisions of the Code, in reference to the duties of the clerk, are as follows:

Of circuit court.—SECTION 193. The clerk of the district court is, by virtue of his office, clerk of the circuit court.

Official duty.—SEC. 194. He shall keep his office at the county seat; shall attend the sessions of the district and circuit courts himself, or by deputy; keep the records, papers, and seals of both courts, and record their proceedings as hereinafter directed under the direction of the judges of each court respectively.

How designated.—SEC. 195. The clerk of the district court shall, while acting as clerk of the circuit court, be known and designated as "clerk of the circuit court;" and in all certificates and records relating to said court, signed by him, he shall so designate himself. The deputy of the clerk of the district court may perform any of the duties required by the clerk of the district court, to be performed in and for said circuit court: and may sign all certificates and records thereof, in the same manner and with the same force and effect as the clerk of the district court.

Records consist of.—SEC. 196. The records of each court consist of the original papers constituting the causes adjudicated or pending in that court, and the books prescribed in the next section.

Books kept.—SEC. 197. The clerk is required to keep the following books for the business of the district and circuit courts severally:

1. A book containing the entries of the proceedings of the court, which may be known as the "record book," and which is to have an index referring to each proceeding in each cause under the name of the parties, both plaintiff and defendant, and under the name of each person named in either party;

2. A book containing an abstract of the judgments, having in separate and appropriate columns the names of the parties, the date of the judgment the damages recovered, costs, the date of the issuance and return of executions, with the entry of satisfaction and other memoranda; which book may be known as the "judgment docket," and is to have an index like that required for the record book;

3. A book in which to enter in detail the costs and fees in each action or proceeding under the title of the same, with an index like that required above, and which may be known as the "fee book;"

4. A book in which to enter the following matters in relation to any judgment

under which real property is sold, entering them after the execution is returned—the title of the action, the date of the judgment, the amount of damages recovered, the total amount of costs, and the officer's return in full—which book may be known as the "sale book," and is to have an index like those required above;

5. A book in which to make a complete record when required by law;

6. A book to be called the "incumbrance book," in which the sheriff shall enter a statement of the levy of every attachment on real estate, as required by Part III. of this code;

7. A book to be known as the "appearance docket," with an index to the same, in which all actions, entered in said docket shall be indexed directly in the name of each plaintiff; and reversely in the name of each defendant therein:

8. A book in which an index of all liens in district or circuit courts shall be kept.

Appearance docket.—SEC. 198. The clerk shall enter in said appearance docket, each suit that shall be brought in the court, numbering them consecutively in the order in which they shall have been commenced, which number shall not be changed during the further progress of the suit. In entering the suits, the clerk shall set out the full name of all the parties, plaintiffs and defendants, as contained in the petition, or as subsequently made parties by any pleading, proceeding, or order, and shall give the date of the filing of the petition.

SEC. 199. When the original notice shall be returned to the office of the clerk, he shall enter in said docket so much of the return thereon as to show who of the parties have been served therewith, and the manner and time of service.

SEC. 200. The clerk shall, immediately upon the filing thereof, make in the appearance docket a memorandum of the date of the filing of all petitions, demurrers, answers, motions, or paper of any other description in the cause: and no pleading of any description shall be considered as filed in the cause, or be taken from the clerk's office, until the said memorandum is made.

SEC. 201. Immediately upon the sustaining or overruling of any demurrer or motion; the striking out or amendment of any pleading; trial of the cause; rendition of the verdict; entry of judgment; issuing of execution, or any other act or thing done in the progress of the cause, the like memorandum thereof shall be made in said docket, giving the date thereof, and the number of the book and page of the record where the entry thereof shall have been made, it being intended that the appearance docket shall be an index from the commencement to the end of a suit.

Records of both courts kept.—SEC. 202. The district and circuit judges of any county, may, by a joint order under their hands, direct that the records and minutes of both courts be kept in one set of books. But all matters touching decedents' estates, wills, administrations, guardians and heirs, and all business relating thereto transacted in the circuit court, and also the record of marriage licenses, shall be kept separate, in proper books prepared for that purpose, as heretofore.

Report criminal returns.—SEC. 203. The clerk of the district court is required to report to the secretary of state, on or before the first Monday in November of each year, the number of convictions for all crimes and misdemeanors in that court in his county for the year preceding; and such report shall show the character of the offense and the sentence of punishment, the occupation of the convict, whether he can read and write, his general habits, and also the expenses of the county for criminal prosecutions during the year, including, but distinguishing, the compensation of the district attorney.

Not act as attorney.—SEC. 204. The clerk, or deputy clerk of the district court is prohibited from holding the office of justice of the peace, or practicing, directly or indirectly, as an attorney or solicitor in the district or circuit court.

II. THE RECORDS.

Among the duties prescribed by the statute, we find he is required to keep the records, papers, and seals of the District and Circuit Courts. The records consist of the original papers in causes adjudicated or pending, and the books prescribed by the statute.

Record book.—The most important of these books is the "Record Book," in which he is required to record the proceedings of the court. This should contain in full all the proceedings.

Opening of the court.—At the beginning of each term, the clerk should therein record the presence of the judge and other officers of the court in attendance on the same, the time of opening the court, and the proceedings of the court in its order, such as the impaneling of the grand and trial juries, the rulings of the court and proceedings therein, and the orders and decisions of the court on motions and demurrers; and the judgments of the court on verdicts of the trial jury, and on trials to the court.

Judge's minutes.—A brief minute of the orders and judgments of the court is usually made by the judge in each cause, on a calendar of the causes furnished him by the clerk; from this calendar the clerk usually transcribes these entries on one kept by himself for his own convenience; and from these transcribed minutes he writes up the record relating thereto.

Orders and decisions.—The ingenuity and resources of the clerk are frequently taxed to the greatest extent to place these orders and decisions in proper form on the record, so as to embrace all that is intended and required, and avoid superfluous and useless matter.

Uniformity of records.—The records in similar cases are usually in a certain uniform and stereotyped language, which is very common in legal papers and records, and is adopted for its convenience and accuracy.

Forms of entry in important cases.—In unusual, important and complicated cases, forms for entry of orders, judgments, and decrees on the records, are usually furnished the clerk by the attorney of the prevailing party; and this is the proper practice, as it would in such cases be usually unsafe to trust to the clerk, who may have little acquaintance with legal forms and the requirements in such cases. And in all cases these forms of entry should be submitted to the opposing counsel for his approval.

To record the names of jurors.—At the opening of the court at which grand and trial jurors are required to appear, the clerk should call the jurors summoned, and the names of those who appear should be entered on the record as hereinafter set forth.

III. FORMS OF RECORD ENTRIES.

ORGANIZATION OF THE COURT.

No. 5.

STATE OF IOWA,........COUNTY DISTRICT COURT,
........Term, 187.., First day....187..

STATE OF IOWA, } ss.
........County, }

Be it Remembered, that on this....Monday of...., A. D. 187.., it being the....day of...., 187.., at the court house in said county was begun and holden a District Court of said State, within and for said county, in the .... judicial district of said State, at which are present:

The Honorable J H R, sole Presiding Judge;
W G G, District Attorney for said district;
A J B, Sheriff of said county;
J C D, Clerk of said court.

The following officers are also in attendance on said court, as bailiffs, to-wit:

S D P, in attendance upon the grand jury;
S P S, in attendance upon the trial jury;
D W X, in attendance upon the court.

And the court being duly organized, is thereupon duly opened by proclamation of the sheriff, and the following proceedings had:

SHERIFF'S RETURN OF SUMMONS OF GRAND JURORS—

The sheriff, by virtue of a precept to him duly directed and delivered, makes return thereof in open court, from which it appears that the following named persons were duly summoned as grand jurors for this term of court, and appear on the call of their names, and take their seats in the jury box, to-wit: [Here: insert the names of the fifteen jurors summoned, and who appear;

if less than fifteen appear, the court should order the sheriff to summon a sufficient number of persons to complete the panel, which facts should appear in the record.] Code, Sec. 4256.

MOTION TO SET ASIDE THE PRECEPT, ETC.—

And thereupon the district attorney, W G T, files a motion to set aside the precept under which the grand jurors were summoned, and for an order that a new precept issue to the sheriff to summon forthwith a sufficient number to make a panel for this term of court, for the reason that said jurors were not duly selected and drawn.

PRECEPT SET ASIDE, AND A NEW PRECEPT ISSUED—

Whereupon the court having examined the evidence in relation thereto, and duly considered the premises, sustains said motion, and it is ordered by the court that said precept be set aside, and that the clerk issue a new precept to the sheriff, commanding him to summon forthwith from the body of the county, fifteen persons, duly qualified to serve as jurors during this term. And thereupon said precept is issued, and said jurors are summoned and appear in open court and answer to their names, and take seats in the jury box, to-wit: [Here insert the names of the jurors.]

OPPORTUNITY GIVEN PARTIES TO OBJECT—

And thereupon opportunity is given by the court to parties held to appear at this court on criminal charges, to interpose objections to said jurors. Whereupon E K, Esq., attorney for C D, a defendant held to appear at this term of court on a criminal charge, having examined said jurors under oath, doth interpose and challenge one of the jurors aforesaid, to-wit: E F, on the ground that he is the prosecutor in the charge against said C D, (or has formed or expressed such an opinion as to the guilt of the defendant as would prevent him from rendering a true verdict upon the evidence submitted on a trial; or, that he is a minor, insane, or otherwise not competent in law to serve as such juror.) And the court having heard the evidence relating to said challenge, sustains the same, and orders and directs that said juror shall not be present nor take any part in the consideration of the charge against the said defendant C D; and thereupon, by order of the court, another juror was duly summoned by the sheriff to fill the panel on the examination of the charge against said defendant before said jury, (or in case the objection relates to his want of qualification in general, the court should discharge said juror) to-wit: E F, duly qualified to serve as grand juror as aforesaid, on the examination of the charge against the said defendant, before the grand jury in the place of A B, challenged as aforesaid, (or, in case said A B is discharged for general incompetency, the record should show that the said E F was duly selected and sworn as a grand juror in the place of the said A B).

JURY ORGANIZED, SWORN AND CHARGED—

And thereupon no further challenge being made to the panel, or to the individual jurors, fifteen good and lawful men, electors of the State, selected, drawn and summoned as aforesaid, and duly qualified as jurors, the court appoints C L as foreman of said grand jury, and said foreman is duly sworn, and said grand jurors are duly sworn. And said grand jurors being thus duly selected, drawn, summoned, impaneled and sworn as aforesaid, are charged by the court, and retire to the grand jury room with a sworn bailiff, to inquire of and concerning matters and things that may lawfully come before them.

PRECEPT FOR TRIAL JURORS RETURNED—

And thereupon the sheriff, aforesaid, returns into open court the precept duly issued and delivered to him to summon .... persons to act as trial jurors at this term of the court, from which it appears that said .... persons have been duly summoned, and said persons being duly called, appear and take their seats in the jury box, to-wit: [Here insert the names of the persons appearing. If the full number summoned as directed do not appear, the clerk should draw from the box of ballots containing the names of persons selected for that purpose, the requisite number of persons to supply the deficiency, and they should be summoned by the sheriff, on a precept issued for that purpose, as in the first instance]. Code, Sec. 232.

PANEL OF TRIAL JURORS DULY ORGANIZED—

And thereupon said panel of trial jurors being duly summoned and completed, the following proceedings were had:

RECORD ENTRY IN A CRIMINAL CAUSE ON A PLEA OF GUILTY.

No. 6.

THE STATE OF IOWA
v.
M.... W....

Now, to-wit: this ...... day of ....., 187., this cause comes on to be heard, G W T, Esq., district attorney, appearing for the State, and the defendant appearing in person, and also by M & M, his attorneys. Whereupon the defendant is arraigned, says he is indicted by his true name, and pleads guilty to the charge of keeping a nuisance, as set forth in the indictment herein.

And afterwards, to-wit: ...., 187., this cause comes up for the judgment of the court herein.

Whereupon the defendant is informed of the nature of the indictment and of his plea, and is asked whether he has any legal cause to show why judgment should not be pronounced against him.

And it appearing that no legal cause exists why judgment should not be pronounced:

It is therefore ordered and adjudged by the court, that said defendant pay a fine of .... dollars and the costs of this prosecution, taxed at $...., and that in default of the payment of said fine, he be committed to the jail of this county for....days, unless said fine be sooner paid.

RECORD IN A CRIMINAL CAUSE TRIED BY A JURY.

No. 7.

THE STATE OF IOWA,
v.
J.... M....

Now, to-wit: this....day of....187.., this cause comes on to be heard, W G T, district attorney, appearing for the State, and T R E, Esq., appearing for the defendant.

Issue being joined, a jury is called to try the same, to-wit: [Here insert the names of the twelve jurors.] Twelve good men and lawful jurors, duly impaneled and sworn to well and truly try said issue.

The evidence on the part of the plaintiff and defendant being adduced, the cause is argued by the respective counsel, and fully submitted.

The court duly instructs the jury in the premises, and they retire to their room, under the charge of a sworn bailiff to consider on their verdict.

And afterwards, to-wit: on the same day the jury return with their verdict into open court, and in the presence of the counsel aforesaid (if the indictment is for a felony the defendant should be present, and the record should so state), and say, that they find the defendant guilty.

Whereupon the defendant, by his counsel, T R E, files a motion for a new trial herein.

And afterwards, on the ...day of....187.., this cause comes up for a hearing on the motion for a new trial, and the court having heard the arguments of the counsel thereon, the motion is overruled by the court, to which decision the counsel for the defendant duly excepts.

And afterwards, to-wit: this....day of...., 187.., this cause comes up before the court for judgment therein, and the defendant being present is informed by the court of the nature of the indictment, his plea, and the verdict of the jury thereon, and the defendant is asked whether he has any legal cause to show why judgment should not be pronounced against him thereon. And no legal cause being shown against the same, it is therefore ordered and adjudged by the court, that the defendant pay a fine of ...dollars, and the costs of this prosecution taxed at $.... ; and that in default in the payment of said fine, he be committed to the jail of....county, State of Iowa, for the term of.... days, unless said fine be sooner paid.

RECORD ENTRY IN A CIVIL CAUSE TRIED BY THE COURT.

No. 8.

M..... W..... }
v.
W..... M..... }

Now, to-wit: this .... day of ....., 1874, this cause comes up to be heard on the demurrer to plaintiff's petition, J. L. S., Esq., appearing as attorney for plaintiff, and S. T. P., Esq., as attorney for the defendant. And the court having heard the arguments of the respective attorneys, overrules the demurrer; and thereupon the defendant files his answer. Issue being joined and a jury being waived, this cause by consent of the parties is tried to the court; and thereupon the testimony for the plaintiff and the defendant is adduced to the court and the court having heard the arguments of counsel for the respective parties finds for the plaintiff for the amount due on one promissory note, to-wit: the sum of .... dollars.

It is therefore adjudged by the court that the plaintiff have and recover of the defendant .... dollars, and costs herein taxed at $...

ENTRY JUDGMENT ON NOTE AND DECREE OF FORECLOSURE, AFTER DEFAULT.

No. 9.

R.... R.... }
v.
J.... D.... }

Now, to-wit: this .... day of ....., 187., this cause comes on to be heard, J L S, Esq., appearing for the plaintiff, and no one for the defendant. And it appearing to the court that the defendant is in default herein, the evidence for the plaintiff is heard by the court. And it appearing to the court that the plaintiff's cause of action is founded upon a promissory note; that the same is due and unpaid, and amounting to .... dollars, and that the same is secured by a mortgage upon property hereinafter described.

It is therefore ordered and adjudged by the court, that the plaintiff, R R, have and recover of the defendant, J D, said sum of .... dollars, together with interest to accrue thereon at the rate of ten per centum per annum, and the costs herein taxed at $...

And it is further adjudged and decreed, that the mortgage aforesaid be foreclosed, and that a special execution issue against the mortgaged premises, to-wit: [Here describe the premises], in .... county, Iowa, and that the same, or so much thereof as may be necessary, be sold to satisfy this judgment, interest and costs; and that if said property shall not sell for sufficient to satisfy the same, that a general execution issue against the property of said defendant for the remainder.

And thereupon the court adjourns until to-morrow morning, ..., at .. o'clock, . M.

...... DAY, ...TERM, 18.., ..., ...

The court convened pursuant to adjournment, and was opened by proclamation of the sheriff.

ANOTHER ENTRY OF DEFAULT, JUDGMENT AND DECREE.

No. 10.

T.... T....
v.
G.... G....

Now, to-wit: this .... day of ...., 187., this cause comes on for hearing, M R, attorney, appearing for the plaintiff, and no one appearing for the defendant.

And thereupon, the court having inspected the original notices and return of service of the same, finds that the defendant has been duly served with the same, and the said defendant though solemnly called comes not, but makes default; he is therefore adjudged to be in default.

And the court having inspected the pleadings, and heard the evidence and proofs of the plaintiff, and being fully advised in the premises finds that the allegations of the petition are true; that the notes and mortgage described in the petition are genuine; that the notes are due and unpaid, and that the plaintiff is entitled to a judgment on said notes for .... dollars, and to a foreclosure of said mortgage given to secure the same as prayed for in the petition, against said defendant; that plaintiff is entitled under the stipulations of the mortgage to .... dollars, as a remuneration for counsel in this foreclosure, and to .... dollars for taxes paid on the premises, since the giving of said mortgage, and to .... dollars paid for necessary abstracts of title, and other documentary evidence, to be taxed as costs.

It is therefore, adjudged by the court that the plaintiff have, and recover of the defendant .... dollars, and interest thereon to accrue at 10 per cent., besides costs herein including the amounts found as above, amounting to .... dollars, which the clerk is ordered to enter with the other costs in the case, amounting in all to the sum of $....

It is further adjudged and decreed by the court that the right of redemption of the said defendant, in and to said mortgaged premises, to-wit: [Here describe the premises,] be, and the same is, hereby barred and foreclosed, and that said judgment for .... dollars, with interest and costs as aforesaid, be declared a lien on said premises from the date of said mortgage, to-wit: ... .., 187., till the same is fully paid.

And it is further ordered, adjudged and decreed that said premises, or so much thereof as shall be necessary, be sold to satisfy this judgment, with interest and costs; that a special execution issue accordingly, and that a general execution issue for any balance remaining unsatisfied after exhausting said mortgaged property.

ANOTHER FORM IN CASE OF DEFAULT.

No. 11.

A B, *Plaintiff*,
v.
C D, *Defendant.*

This day comes the said plaintiff by S T P, Esq., his attorney, and the said defendant, although duly served with an original notice herein, as required by law, and being three times solemnly called in open court, comes not, but herein makes default.

It is therefore considered by the court that plaintiff do have and recover of and from the defendant, C D, damages by plaintiff herein sustained. And it appearing to the court that this suit is brought upon a money demand, and the damages being unknown to the court, it is ordered by the court that the clerk assess the same; thereupon the clerk assessed and reported the damages in the sum of .... dollars and .... cents, which report is accepted by the court.

It is therefore ordered by the court that plaintiff have and recover of the said defendant, the sum of .... dollars and .... cents, damages assessed as aforesaid, together with interest at the rate of .. per cent. per annum, and .... dollars and .... cents, costs, and that execution issue therefor.

RECORD ENTRY ON RE-TAXATION OF COSTS.

No. 12.

J.... J....
v.
S.... S....

Now, to-wit: This ...... day of ...., 187., this cause comes on to be heard before the court on defendant's motion to re-tax costs herein.

And the court being fully advised in the premises, it is ordered that the costs herein be re-taxed, and that the defendant be taxed with the cost only of those witnesses of the plaintiff who were sworn and used on the trial of said cause, and who claimed their fees to the clerk before the final adjournment of this court at the last term thereof; and that the clerk re-tax them accordingly.

ENTRY ON AN ORDER FOR SECURITY FOR COSTS.

No. 13.

T.... H.... }
v.
M.... P.... }

Now, to-wit: this .... day of ...., 187., this cause comes on to be heard on the motion of defendant to require the plaintiff to give security for costs herein.

And the court being fully advised in the premises, it is ordered by the court, that the plaintiff give a bond as security for costs herein in the penal sum of .... dollars, to be approved by the clerk within .... days.

ENTRY ON AN ORDER FOR AN ATTACHMENT.

No. 14.

THE STATE OF IOWA, }
v.
J.... S.... }

Now, to-wit: this ...., 187., this cause comes up on the motion of W S T, the prosecuting attorney, for an attachment against the defendant. And it appearing to the court, that the defendant is guilty of contempt of court, in refusing as a witness to day, before the grand jury, to answer proper questions put to him by the foreman thereof:

It is therefore ordered, that an attachment be issued by the clerk against him, and that he be brought forthwith before the court to show cause, if any he has, why he should not be punished for said contempt.

RECORD ENTRY ON DEFAULT, ON A NOTE BY TWO MAKERS, AND DECREE OF FORECLOSURE AGAINST ONE OF THEM, AND SEVERAL OTHERS.

No. 15.

A.... B ... }
v.
C.... D....
E.... F.... } *In Equity.*
G.... H ...
I .... J ....
K.... L.... }

Now, to-wit: ...., 187., this cause comes up for a hearing J G, Esq., appearing as attorney for the plaintiff, and no one appearing for the defendants or either of them; and the court inspects the original notice herein, and the return of service thereon by the sheriff, and finds that each of said defendants has been duly served with said notice; and thereupon each of said defendants was solemnly called but came not, and makes default.

It is therefore adjudged by the court that they, and each of them, are in default.

And thereupon the court having inspected the petition, and seen and heard the proofs of the plaintiff herein, and being fully advised in the premises, finds that the allegations of the petition are true; that the note sued on is genuine, and due and unpaid; that said note executed by C D and G H, and the mortgage given to secure the same, executed by the said defendants C D and E F, to J S have been duly assigned by the said J S the mortgagee, to the plaintiff; that the interest in or lien on said premises, described in said mortgage held by the defendants I J, and K L, or either of them, are junior and inferior to the lien of plaintiffs said mortgage, and that the plaintiff is entitled to a foreclosure of said mortgage against all of said defendants, and to a judgment on said note against the said defendants C D and G H, for the sum due thereon, and a decree as prayed against all of said defendants; and said note is referred to the clerk to compute the amount due thereon, which is computed by him at the sum of $——

It is therefore adjudged by the court, that the plaintiff have and recover of the defendants C D and G H, the sum of $...., and costs herein taxed at $....

It is further adjudged and decreed by the court that the right of defendants, I J and K L to, or their interest in, the premises described in said mortgage is junior and inferior to the lein of said mortgage, and that the right and equity of redemption of the said mortgaged premises, to-wit: [Here describe the lands] be, and the same is hereby barred and foreclosed, and the said judgment is declared a lien on the same, from the date of said mortgage, to-wit: ...., 187., until the same is fully paid and satisfied.

It is further ordered, adjudged, and decreed that said premises, or so much thereof as shall be necessary, be sold to satisfy said judgment, with interest and costs; that a special execution issue therefor, and that the plaintiff have a general execution against the said C D and G H, for any balance of said judgment that may remain after exhausting said mortgaged property.

RECORD ENTRY ON LICENSE OF AN ATTORNEY.

No. 16.

In the matter of the application of J J for license to practice as Attorney and Counsellor-at-Law, in the courts of this State. }

Now, to-wit: ...., 187., J J applies to the

court for a license to practice as attorney and counselor-at-law in the courts of the State of Iowa. And it appearing to the court that said applicant is over twenty one years of age, and an inhabitant of this State; that he is of good moral character, and possesses the requisite learning and ability; the said J J is sworn to support the constitution of the United States, and of the State of Iowa, and to faithfully discharge the duty of an attorney and counselor of the courts of this State, according to the best of his ability.

Wherefore it is ordered by the court that the said J J be licensed and admitted to practice as attorney and counselor-at-law in all the courts of the State of Iowa.

ENTRY OF A DECREE AGAINST PLAINTIFF, AND IN FAVOR OF DEFENDANTS, ON A COUNTER-CLAIM.

No. 17.

W.... L ... B.... }
v. } *In Equity—Decree.*
P.... T.... }

Now, to-wit: ...., 187., this cause comes on to be tried to the court on the pleadings and proofs, S & M appearing as attorneys for the plaintiff, and M & M as attorneys for defendants.

And the court having heard the evidence and the arguments of counsel, and being fully advised in the premises, finds that the equity of the case is with the defendants, and that the material averments of the defendant's counter-claim are true.

It is therefore adjudged and decreed that the plaintiff's petition herein be dismissed.

It is further adjudged and decreed that the deed executed by G W F and his wife, to said plaintiff, dated ...., 187., and filed for record in the office of the recorder of ...... county, Iowa, ..., 187., was made to the said plaintiff at the request of J B, who paid the consideration therefor, and also at the request of the plaintiff, and was so procured to be made by them, with intent to hinder and delay, and to cheat and defraud, the defendants as the creditors of the said J B; and that the sales of said lands described in said deed, to-wit: [The south-west quarter of the south-west quarter of section ten, township 86, north range three west of the 5th P. M.], by the sheriff of said county, made on the .... day of ...., 187.., and on the ... day of ...., 18.., without appraisement, under and by virtue of executions issued on judgments in favor of said defendants, and against the said J B, were valid sales, and the deeds executed by said sheriff on said sales to the defendants as purchasers thereof, and of the dates of said sales, were valid deeds, and conveyed the title thereto to the defendants.

It is further adjudged and decreed by the court, that the sale of said lands by the sheriff of said county to the defendants, by virtue of an execution issued on a judgment in favor of said G W F, and against said plaintiff, on which said land was appraised, and on which a deed was made to the defendants as the purchasers at the date of said sale, to-wit: ...., 187., and which deed was filed for record, in the office of the recorder of said county, on the .. day of ...., 187., and recorded in book ... of deeds, page .., in said, recorder's office, was a valid sale, and said deed was legal and valid, and conveyed all the title and interest of said plaintiff in and to said land to the defendants.

It is further adjudged and decreed, that the title in fee, in and to said real estate, be and the same is, established in the defendants, and that said plaintiffs pay the costs herein taxed at $.....

RECORD ENTRY ON THE PARTITION OF LANDS.

No. 18.

A...... B......,
v.
C.... D.... and E.... F.....

Now, to-wit: ...., 18.., this cause comes on to be heard on report of the referees herein appointed, to make partition of the premises described in the petition herein, to-wit: [The north half of the south-west quarter, and the north-west quarter of section one, and the east half of the north east quarter of section two, in township 84, north, range 4, west of the 5 P. M., situate in ..... county, Iowa,] by special allotment to said parties:

And it appearing that said referees after being duly sworn, to faithfully and impartially perform said duty, have made such partition and reported thereon to this court in writing, in the words and figures following, to-wit:

In the District Court .... County, Iowa, ... Term, 18...

A.... B...., *Plaintiff*,
v. — *Report of Referees.*
C... D... and E... F..., *Defendants.*

To the District Court aforesaid:

We, the undersigned, referees appointed by the court at said term, to make partition of the lands belonging to the parties in this cause, respectfully report:

That after being duly qualified and subscribing an oath hereto attached, we proceeded to make partition of the lands and premises described in the petition herein, upon a personal and actual examination of the said premises, and that we have partitioned said premises by special allotment, as follows:

First. We have set off and allotted to the plaintiff A B, as his share, the following described premises, to-wit:

The east half of the north-east quarter of section two, and the west half of the west half the north-west quarter of section one, all in township 84, north, range 4, west of the 5th P. M.

Second. We have set off and allotted to the defendant, C D, as his share of said premises, the following described premises, to-wit:

The east half, and the east half of the west half of the north-west quarter of section one, in township 84, north of range 4, west of the 5th P. M.

Third. We have set off and allotted to the defendant, E F, as his share of said premises, the following described premises, to-wit:

The north half of the south-west quarter of section one, township 84, north range 4, west of the 5th P. M.]

We further report, that the subjoined plat is a true plat of said premises partitioned; that we placed stakes at the corners as shown by said plat; that the share set off and allotted to the said plaintiff, A B, is marked on said plat "No. 1;" that the share set off and allotted to the said defendant, C D, is marked on said plat "No. 2;" and that the share set off and allotted to the defendant, E F, is marked on said plat, "No. 3."

All of which is respectfully submitted.

Dated this....day of....187...

R.... O.... P....
H.... S.... K....
W.... H.... Q....

PLAT.

TOWNSHIP 84, RANGE 4.

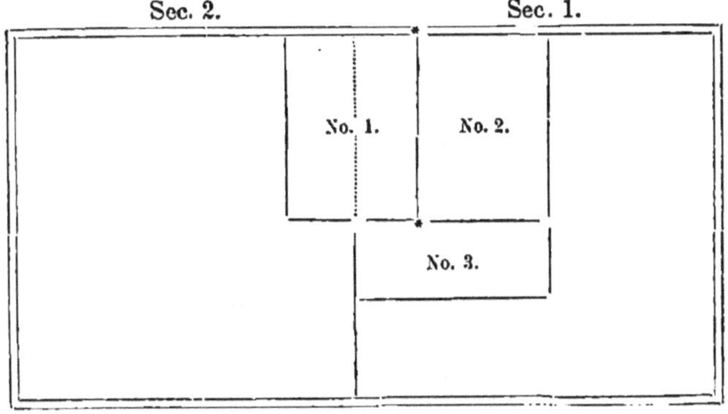

* Stake.

It is therefore ordered, adjudged and decreed by the court, that the said report be and the same is approved.

It is further adjudged and decreed, that the said parties respectively have and hold in fee simple and exclusively, the lands and premises so set off and allotted to them respectively, as described and contained in said report and plat.

It is further ordered and adjudged that D M C, attorney for the plaintiff, be allowed the sum of....dollars, as fees for services herein as attorney, to be taxed as costs in this case and to be a lien on said lands until the same is paid.

It is further ordered and adjudged, that the costs herein be paid by the parties hereto in equal shares; that each of said parties pay one-third of said costs, and that each one's share of costs, be a lien upon the lands set off, attached and adjudged to him, and that the costs herein be taxed at $....

PROBATE RECORD.

CIRCUIT COURT OF THE STATE OF IOWA, IN AND FOR.... COUNTY.

....*Term*, 187.., ...*Day*, ...187..

RECORD ENTRY ON PROBATE OF A WILL.

No. 10.

In the matter of the Estate of A.... B...., *deceased.* } *Probate of Will.*

Now, to-wit: ....187.., it being the day set for a hearing of this cause, it comes on for a hearing before the court.

And it appearing that due notice has been given of the time of final hearing on this application for admission of the will to probate, to all parties interested, by publication thereof as required by law, and no one appearing to resist the probate of said will; and the instrument purporting to be the last will of said deceased being produced, and the testimony of the subscribing witnesses thereto being heard, the court finds: that the said instrument was duly signed and executed by the deceased, A B, at the time it purports to have been, as and for his last will; that at that time said deceased was of sound mind; that he then declared the said instrument to be his last will, in the presence of C D, and E F, the subscribing witnesses thereto, who then, and in the presence of said deceased, and in the presence of each other, and at the special request of the said A B, deceased, signed their names as witnesses thereto.

It is therefore ordered and adjudged by the court, that said will be admitted to probate as and for the last will of the said A B, deceased, and that said will be recorded in the proper record of wills in....county, Iowa.

It is further ordered that G H, the person named in said will as the executor thereof, be appointed and confirmed as such executor, upon his filing a bond as such executor, with the clerk of this court, and to be approved by him in the penal sum of $ ...

FORM OF JUDGMENT BY CONFESSION IN VACATION.

No. 20.

A.... B...., *Plaintiff*,
v.
C.... D...., *Defendant.*

Be it remembered: That on this day, to-wit: ...., 187., comes A B, the plaintiff herein and files in the office of the clerk of this court a written statement and confession of judgment, made and signed by the defendant, C D, and duly verified by his oath thereto attached, whereby said C D confesses himself justly indebted to the said plaintiff in the sum of .... dollars and ...... cents, and authorizes the clerk of this court to enter judgment thereon for said sum with costs.

Now, therefore, it is considered and adjudged, that the plaintiff have and recover of said defendant said sum of ... . dollars and ...... cents, with costs herein taxed at $......

The recorded judgments to be entered on the judgment docket.—The judgments entered in the "Record Book," should also be entered by the clerk in the "Judgment Docket," with the names of each of the parties, plaintiffs and defendants, and the names of each party should also be properly entered on the index of said "Judgment Docket."

Unless the index refers to each of the parties defendant, it would not operate as notice to third parties, who were included in the judgment as defendants.

The entry of the judgment in the "Index Book," as A B, *et al.*, defendants, may be good notice of plaintiff's rights, as to the defendant named, but not as to the others. The name of each should be entered therein.

CHAPTER IV.

OATHS IN COURT.

I. BY WHOM ADMINISTERED.

Although there is no express provision of the statute making it the duty of the clerk to administer oaths required in open court, still he usually performs that act, and he may administer oaths at any time; and those parties who object to being sworn, may affirm. Code, Sec. 277.

II. FORMS OF OATHS.

OATH ON APPLICATION TO BE EXCUSED, BY JUROR.

No. 21.

You do solemnly swear, (or affirm), that you will true answers make to such questions as shall be put to you, touching your application to be excused from attendance as a grand juror at this term of court. So help you God. [In case of affirmation in all cases omit the last sentence.]

OATH TO JUROR FOR REMISSION OF FINE.

No. 22.

You do solemnly swear, (or affirm), that you will true answers make to such questions as shall be put to you, touching your application for the remission of your fine on a default in attending as a juror at this term of this court. So help you God.

OATH AS TO QUALIFICATIONS OF GRAND JURORS.

No. 23.

You, and each of you, do solemnly swear, (or affirm), that you will true answers make to such questions as shall be put to you touching your qualifications as a grand juror for .... county. So help you God.

OATH TO THE FOREMAN OF THE GRAND JURY.

No. 24.

You, as foreman of the grand jury, shall diligently inquire and true presentment make of all public offenses against the people of this state committed or triable within this county of which you have or can obtain legal evidence; you shall present no person through malice, hatred, or ill will, nor leave any unpresented through fear, favor, or affection, or for any reward or the promise or hope thereof; but in all of your presentments you shall present the truth, the whole truth, and nothing but the truth, according to the best of your skill and understanding. So help you God.

OATH TO THE OTHER GRAND JURORS.

No. 25.

The same oath which your foreman has now taken before you on his part, you, and each of you, shall well and truly observe on your part. So help you God.

OATH ON CHALLENGE TO THE PANEL, IN CRIMINAL CASES.

No. 26.

You do solemnly swear, (or affirm), that you will true answers make to such questions as shall be put to you touching the challenge to the panel of trial jurors selected, drawn, and summoned for this term of the court. So help you God.

OATH TO TRIAL JURORS, TOUCHING THEIR QUALIFICATION.

No. 27.

You, and each of you, do solemnly swear, (or affirm), that you will true answers make to such questions as shall be put to you touching your qualifications to sit as a juror in this cause. So help you God.

OATH TO TRIAL JURORS.

No. 28.

You, and each of you, do solemnly swear, (or affirm), that you will well and truly try the issues joined in this cause between A B, plaintiff, and C D, defendant, and a true verdict give according to the evidence, and the instructions given you by the court. So help you God.

OATH TO WITNESSES ON THE TRIAL.

No. 29.

You do solemnly swear, (or affirm), that the evidence you shall give in the cause now pending before this court shall be the truth, the whole truth, and nothing but the truth. So help you God.

ANOTHER FORM—OATH TO SEVERAL WITNESSES.

No. 30.

You, and each of you, do solemnly swear, (or affirm), that the testimony you shall give in this cause wherein A B is plaintiff, and C D is defendant, shall be the truth, the whole truth, and nothing but the truth. So help you God.

OATH TO INTERPRETER.

No. 31.

You do solemnly swear, (or affirm), that you will well and truly interpret between the court, the jury, the counsel and the witness A B, in the cause now pending wherein C D is plaintiff, and E F is defendant. So help you God.

OATH TO BAILIFF IN CHARGE OF A TRIAL JURY IN CRIMINAL CASE DURING ADJOURNMENT OF COURT.

No. 32.

You do solemnly swear, (or affirm), that you will keep all the members of this jury together in some safe and convenient place during the adjournment of this court, and suffer no person to speak to or cummunicate with them on any subject connected with this trial, nor do so yourself, and return them into the court at the opening of the same after the adjournment. So help you God.

OATH TO BAILIFF IN CHARGE OF TRIAL JURY.

No. 33.

You do solemnly swear, (or affirm), that you will keep this jury together in some private and convenient place, without meat or drink, water excepted; that you will not suffer any person to speak to or communicate with them, nor speak to or communicate with them yourself, unless it be to ask them whether they have agreed upon their verdict; that you will not communicate to any one the state of their deliberations, or the verdict agreed upon, until after the same shall have been declared in open court, and received by the court; and that you will return them into court when they shall have so agreed upon their verdict, unless by permission or order of the court, or they be sooner discharged. So help you God. Code, Sec. 4442.

OATH TO BAILIFF ON RETIRING WITH A GRAND JURY.

No. 34.

You do solemnly swear, (or affirm), that you will faithfully attend upon this grand jury, obey all their lawful behests, and keep secret all their doings that may come to your knowledge. So help you God.

OATH TO ATTORNEYS AND COUNSELORS.

No. 35.

You do solemnly swear, (or affirm), that you will support the constitution of the United States and of the State of Iowa, and faithfully discharge the duties of an attorney and counsellor of the courts of said State. So help you God.

CHAPTER V.

OTHER BOOKS, RECORDS AND DUTIES.

I. BOOKS AND RECORDS.

Fee book.—He is required to keep a Fee Book, Sale Book, Complete Record Book, Incumbrance Book, Appearance Docket, and Index Book. These books are usually prepared with printed headings and forms, in compliance with the law, and these with the directions of the statute, will be a sufficient guide to the clerk in making the proper records therein.

Calendar of causes.—The clerk is further required to keep a calendar of causes in court, distinguishing first, criminal, and next the civil causes, and arranging each in the order of their commencement; and under the direction of the judge to apportion the same to as many days as is believed necessary, and at the request of any party or his attorney, to issue subpœnas accordingly. And he is required to furnish the court and the bar with a sufficient number of printed copies of the calendar. Code, Sec. 2747.

II. OTHER DUTIES.

Drawing jurors.—When a jury is required, the clerk should select twelve jurors by lot from the regular panel, and if they are excluded on challenges made for any cause, their places should be filled by jurors drawn in the same manner from the regular panel, until the panel is exhausted, when the requisite number can be supplied by talesmen, selected by the sheriff from the body of the county. Code, Sec. 2761, 2765.

Entering judgment and satisfaction.—He is required to

enter all orders and judgments on the record of the court, and specify clearly the relief granted, or order made, in the action, for which we have already furnished the requisite forms in many cases; and when the judgment is set aside, or satisfied by execution, or otherwise, the clerk should at once enter a memorandum thereof, on the column left for that purpose, in the judgment docket.

Complete record: when to make.—In cases where the title to land is involved, and expressly settled or determined, the clerk should make a complete record of the whole cause, and enter it in the proper book; but in no case need a complete record be made, except at the request of a party who will pay the expense of such record. Code, Secs. 2864, 2865, 2866.

To compute amounts due in certain cases.—When the action is for a money demand, and the amount of the proper judgment is a mere matter of computation, the clerk should ascertain the amount, but no fee shall be charged therefor. Code, Sec. 2872.

To tax costs.—The clerk is required to tax costs in favor of the party recovering costs, the allowance of his witnesses, the fees of officers, the compensation of referees, the necessary expenses of taking depositions by commission, or otherwise, and any further sum for any other matter which the court may have awarded as costs in the progress of the cause, or may deem just to be taxed; and any person aggrieved by the taxation of a bill of costs may upon application have the same re-taxed by the court or by a referee, appointed by the court, in which the application or proceeding was had; and in such re-taxation all errors shall be corrected; and if the party aggrieved shall have paid any unlawful charge, by reason of the first taxation, the clerk shall pay the costs of re-taxation, and also to the party aggrieved the amount which he may have paid by reason of the allowing of such unlawful charges. Code, Secs. 2942, 2944.

CHAPTER VI.

DUTY RELATING TO PROCESS.

I. OF EXECUTION.

To make a record of what.—The clerk is required to issue an execution on the demand of any party entitled thereto; and upon its issuance, he is required to enter on the judgment docket the date of its issuance, to what county and officer issued; and shall also enter on said docket the return of the officer, with the date of the return, the dates and amount of all moneys received into or paid out of the office thereon; and these entries shall be made at the time of the thing done. Code, Sec. 3029.

Liability for failure of duty.—Any clerk willfully neglecting to perform any one of these duties, is liable to a penalty of five hundred dollars, and to damages to the party aggrieved, and is guilty of a misdemeanor in office; and on conviction thereof shall be removed from office. Code, Sec. 3030.

Execution to another county.—If execution is issued to any county, other than that in which judgment is rendered, a transcript of such judgment must be filed in the office of the clerk of the District Court of such county, who shall make an entry thereof in the judgment docket of such court, and the officer having such execution shall return a copy thereof, with his return and doings indorsed thereon, to such clerk, who shall make entries thereof in the same manner, and to the same extent, as if such judgment had been entered in, and execution issued from, such court. Code, Sec. 3033.

What the execution must contain.—The execution must intelligibly refer to the judgment, stating the time and place at which it was rendered, the names of the parties to the action, as well as the judgment, its amount, and the amount still to be collected thereon, if for money; and if not for money, it must state what specific act is required to be performed.

If for money and against property.—If it be against the property of the judgment debtor, it shall require the sheriff to satisfy the judgment, interest and costs, out of the property of the judgment debtor subject to execution. Code, Sec. 3033.

If it be against real or personal property in the hands of personal representatives, heirs, devisees, legatees, tenants of real property, or trustees, it shall require the sheriff to satisfy the judgment out of said property. Code, Sec. 3034.

If for the delivery of real or personal property.—If for the delivery of real or personal property, it shall require the sheriff to deliver the possession of the same, particularly describing it, to the party entitled thereto; and it may at the same time require the sheriff to satisfy any costs, damages, rents, and profits, with interest, recovered by the same judgment, out of the property of the party against whom it was rendered, subject to execution, and the value of any property for which judgment was recovered, to be specified therein; and if a delivery thereof cannot be had, it shall in that case, and in that respect, be deemed an execution against property. Code, Sec. 3035.

If for the performance of any other act.—When it requires the performance of any other act, a certified copy of the judgment may be served on the person against whom it is given, or upon the person or officer who is required thereby, or by law, to obey the same and his disobedience enforced. Code, Sec. 3036.

If the judgment is against a principal.—If the judgment is against a principal and his sureties, and the judgment shows that fact, the clerk issuing execution on the judgment, shall state the order of liability.

When execution may issue: one at a time.—Executions may issue into any county, at any time within ten years, when they are barred by the statute of limitations; but only one execution can issue and be in existence at the same time. If one has been issued, no other can properly issue, until some return of the first has been made, and then only to satisfy any balance of the judgment that may remain unsatisfied. Code, Secs. 3025, 3086.

Stay of execution: how taken, and effect.—Surety for the stay of execution may be taken and approved by the clerk, and the bond given therefor should be recorded in a book to be kept by the clerk for that purpose, and it has the force and effect of a judgment confessed from the date thereof, against the property of the sureties; and the clerk should enter and index the same in the proper judgment docket, as in case of other judgments. Code, Sec. 3061.

When stayed after execution has issued.—When the stay is entered after execution is issued, the clerk should immediately notify the sheriff of the stay, and he should forthwith return the execution with his doings thereon. Code, Sec. 3065.

When a surety may have execution issued.—When any surety for the stay of execution files with the clerk an affidavit stating that he verily believes he will be liable for the judgment, interest and costs thereon, unless execution issues immediately, the clerk should issue execution thereon, forthwith, unless other sufficient surety be entered before the clerk as in other cases.

STAY BOND.

No. 36.

...., *Plaintiff,*	*In the ....Court of the State of Iowa,*
v.	*in and for....county.*
...., *Defendant.*	*Amount of judgment, $....Costs $...*

....do hereby acknowledge....suret....for the defendant.. herein, for the payment of the judgment and costs, and interest thereon, rendered by the....Court of the State of Iowa, in and for....county, in the above entitled action, on the....day of.... A. D. 187.., against said defendant.., for the purpose of a stay of execution thereon for....months; and to that end....hereby undertake and promise to pay the said judgment, interest and costs, that may accrue at or before the expiration of the said term of the stay of execution, and upon the expiration of said term....

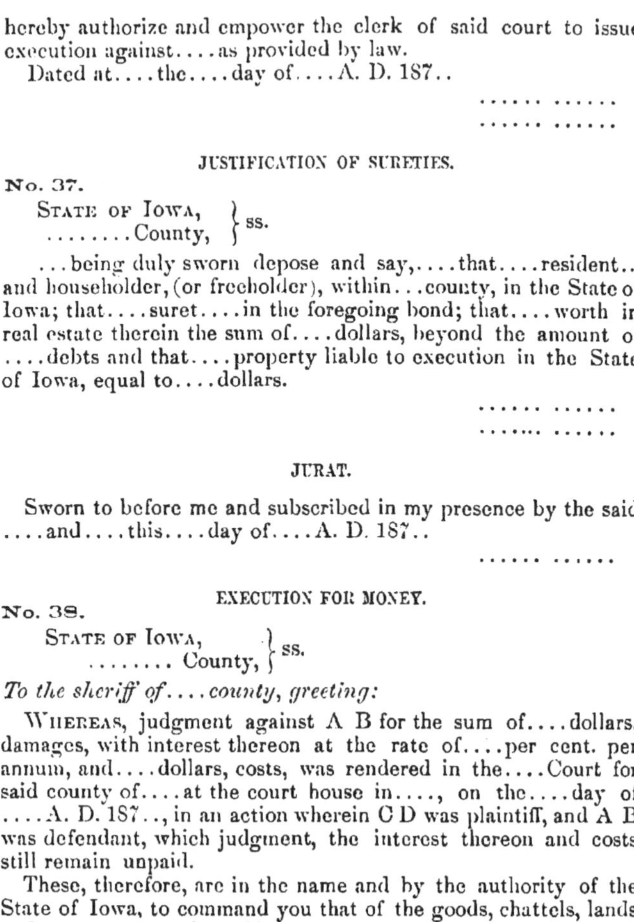

hereby authorize and empower the clerk of said court to issue execution against....as provided by law.

Dated at....the....day of....A. D. 187..

....
....

JUSTIFICATION OF SURETIES.

No. 37.

STATE OF IOWA, }
........County, } ss.

...being duly sworn depose and say,....that....resident... and householder, (or freeholder), within...county, in the State of Iowa; that....suret....in the foregoing bond; that....worth in real estate therein the sum of....dollars, beyond the amount of ....debts and that....property liable to execution in the State of Iowa, equal to....dollars.

....
....

JURAT.

Sworn to before me and subscribed in my presence by the said ....and....this....day of....A. D. 187..

....

EXECUTION FOR MONEY.

No. 38.

STATE OF IOWA, }
.... County, } ss.

To the sheriff of....county, greeting:

WHEREAS, judgment against A B for the sum of....dollars, damages, with interest thereon at the rate of....per cent. per annum, and....dollars, costs, was rendered in the....Court for said county of....at the court house in...., on the....day of ....A. D. 187.., in an action wherein C D was plaintiff, and A B was defendant, which judgment, the interest thereon and costs still remain unpaid.

These, therefore, are in the name and by the authority of the State of Iowa, to command you that of the goods, chattels, lands and tenements of the said......if sufficient be found in your county which are subject to execution, you cause to be made the said sum, with interest thereon and costs, and accruing costs, by levy and sale thereof according to law, and have you said sums of money before us within seventy days from the date hereof, to render unto those who may be legally entitled thereto, and have you then and there this writ, with a return of your doings in the premises hereon indorsed or annexed.

Witness,......clerk of said court, with the seal thereof hereunto affixed at......, in said county, this......day of......, A. D. 187..

...... *Clerk.*

SPECIAL EXECUTION.

No. 39.

STATE OF IOWA, }
......County, } ss.

To the sheriff of said county, greeting:

WHEREAS, on a day of the term of the....Court of....county, State aforesaid, holden at....therein, on the....day of....in the year of our Lord one thousand eight hundred and seventy ..., a judgment was rendered in favor of A B, plaintiff, against C D, defendant, for....dollars, damages, and....dollars, costs; and the court adjudged and decreed, that the following described tract or parcel of land, situate in said county, to-wit: [Here describe the land,] or so much thereof as shall be sufficient to satisfy the amount of said judgment, interest and costs, be sold to satisfy the same; and whereas, the said defendant..ha..failed to pay the said judgment, interest and costs, or either or any part thereof:

Therefore, we command you, that of the lands hereinbefore described in your county, you cause to be made the sum of.... dollars and....cents, principal and interest....; also....dollars and...cents, costs of suit, which, in our said...court of...county, at the time aforesaid, the said plaintiff..recovered against the said defendant.. ....together with interest thereon at the rate of....per cent. per annum, from the ....day of....A. D, 187.., the time of the rendition of the judgment and decree aforesaid, as being the amounts now due said plaintiff.., as appears to us of record, and have you the money before us within seventy days to render to those who may be legally entitled thereto, with a return of your doings hereon indorsed or annexed; and hereof fail not at your peril.

Witness,....clerk of the said court, and the seal thereof hereto affixed at my office in...., this....day of....A. D. 187..

......*Clerk.*
......*Deputy.*

II. OF CERTIORARI.

May grant writs of.—The clerk may grant writs of certiorari; and when directed so to do by the judge or court, may approve the bond required in certain cases.

WRIT OF CERTIORARI.

No. 40.

STATE OF IOWA, }
.... County. } ss.

The State of Iowa to A B, C D and E F, members of the Board of Supervisors of said county:

WHEREAS, On the petition of G H, it has been made to appear to the (naming the court,) that you have exceeded your jurisdiction as the board of supervisors of said county, by ordering the erection of a court-house in said county, and letting contracts therefor, at a cost of over five thousand dollars, (or where the probable cost will exceed five thousand dollars), without a submission of a proposition therefor to the legal voters of said county at any election, and are proceeding illegally in the matter of erecting a court-house for said county, (or state any other illegal act.)

You are therefore, hereby commanded to certify and return fully to our said court, on the .... day of ..., 18.., a transcript of the records and proceedings, as well as the facts in the case in reference to said order, and any evidence you may have of the cost of said court-house, (or of the probable cost of the same, and in reference to any vote that may have been taken on the proposition to build said court-house, if any), as fully as the same are now before you, and have you then and there this writ.

Witness .... clerk of said court, with the seal thereof, hereto affixed this .... day of .... 18..

...., *Clerk.*

III. OF ATTACHMENTS.

Provisions of the Code.—The following are the provisions of the Code, in reference to the clerk's duty in attachment cases:

Plaintiff must give bond.—SECTION 2959. In all cases before it (the attachment) can be issued, the plaintiff must file with the clerk a bond for the use of the defendant with sureties to be approved by such clerk, in a penalty at least double the value of the property sought to be attached, and in no case less than two hundred and fifty dollars in a court of record, nor less than fifty dollars if in a justice's court, conditioned that the plaintiff will pay all damages which the defendant may sustain by reason of the wrongful suing out of the attachment.

Additional security.—SEC. 2960. The defendant may, at any time before judgment, move the court or judge for additional security on the part of the plaintiff, and if, on such motion, the court or judge is satisfied that the surety in the plaintiff's bond has removed from this state, or is not sufficient, the attachment may be vacated and restitution directed of any property taken under it, unless, in a reasonable time to be fixed by the court or judge, security is given by the plaintiff.

Action on or by way of counter-claim.—SEC. 2961. In an action on such bond, the plaintiff therein may recover if he shows that the attachment was wrongfully sued out, and that there was no reasonable cause to believe the ground upon which the same was issued to be true, the actual damages sustained and reasonable attorney's fees to be filed by the court; and if it be shown such attachment was sued out maliciously, he may recover exemplary damages, nor need he wait until the principal suit is determined before suing on the bond.

To whom directed.—SEC. 2962. The clerk shall issue an attachment, directing the sheriff of the county therein named to attach the property of the defendant to the requisite amount therein stated.

More than one attachment.—SEC. 2963. Attachments may be issued from courts of record to different counties, and several may, at the option of the plaintiff, be issued at the same time, or in succession and subsequently, until sufficient property has been attached; but only those executed shall be taxed in the costs, unless otherwise ordered by the court; and if more property is attached in the aggregate than the plaintiff is entitled to have held, the surplus must be abandoned and the plaintiff pay all costs incurred in relation to such surplus.

ATTACHMENT BOND.

No. 41.

Know all men by these presents, That we, A B, principal, and C D and E F, sureties, are held and firmly bound unto G H in the penal sum of ...... dollars, for the true payment of which we bind ourselves firmly by these presents.

The condition of the above obligation is such that, whereas A B has this day sued out of the office of the clerk of the ... Court of .... county, Iowa, an attachment against the property of said G H.

Now if the said A B shall pay the said defendant all the damages that .... may sustain by the wrongful suing out of said writ of attachment, then this bond to be void, otherwise in full force.

Dated at .... this .... day of .... A. D. 18...

A.... B....
C.... D....
E.... F....

[*For Form of Affidavit of Sureties, see No.* 37.]

FORM OF WRIT OF ATTACHMENT.

No. 42.

STATE OF IOWA, *To the sheriff of .... county, greeting:*

WHEREAS, A B has filed his petition in the clerk's office of the .... Court of the State of Iowa, in and for .... county, duly sworn to according to law, claiming of C D the sum of .... dollars as money due on (note, account, or other matter), and alleges [here state the grounds of the attachment], and asking a writ of attachment against the lands and tenements, goods, chattels, rights and credits of the said C D.

Now therefore you are hereby commanded to attach the lands tenements, goods and chattels, rights and credits of the said C D, (except such as is exempt from execution) wherever the same may be found in your county, or so much thereof, as may be necessary to satisfy said amount of .... dollars, with interest and costs, and safely preserve the same, to be dealt with as required by law. And of this writ you will make due and legal service, and return to our said court on or before the first day of the next term thereof.

In witness whereof, I ...., clerk of said court have hereunto set my hand and affixed the seal thereof the .... day of ...., 18...

...., *Clerk.*

IV. OF REPLEVIN.

Bond: sureties.—In actions for the recovery of specific personal property, the clerk is required to take a bond, with sureties, to be approved by him, where the plaintiff desires the immediate possession thereof, for the use of any person injured by the proceedings. Whereupon the clerk should issue an order under his hand, and the seal of the court, directed to the sheriff and requiring him to take the property therein described, and deliver the same to the sheriff.

And where the petition shows that the property has been wrongfully removed into another county, from the one in which the action is commenced, the order may issue from the county whence the property is so wrongfully taken, and may be served in any county where the property can be found, in the same manner and with the same effect; and if the property is moved after suit is brought, counterparts of the order may be issued to such other county.

REPLEVIN BOND.

No. 43.

Know all men by these Presents: That we, A B principal, and C D and E F, sureties, are held and firmly bound unto G H, in the sum of .... dollars, lawful money of the United States, well and truly to be paid to the said G H, his heirs, executors and assigns.

The condition of this obligation is such, that whereas, the said A B, did on the ... day of ...., 18.., file his petition in the clerk's office, of the .... Court of the State of Iowa, in and for .... county, claiming of the said G H, the present possession of [here particularly describe the property,] and asking the issuance of a writ of replevin therefor. Now if the said A B, shall appear at the next term of said court, and prosecute his said suit to judgment, and return the property if a return be awarded, and also pay all costs and damages that may be adjudged against him in said action, then this obligation to be void, otherwise to remain in full force and virtue.

Dated, ... 18...

A.... B...., *Principal.*

C.... D...., } *Sureties.*
E.... F..... }

WRIT OF REPLEVIN.

No. 44.

STATE OF IOWA, }
.... County, } ss.

IN THE DISTRICT COURT, ... TERM, A. D., 18..

The State of Iowa, to the sheriff of said county, greeting:

For as much as A B, as plaintiff has given approved security for prosecuting his suit with effect against C D, as defendant for the wrongful detention of the following, viz: [here describe particularly and fully the property claimed.] as it is said and alleged in said plaintiff's petition, now filed in my office, and also for making return of said property with costs and damages, if the same shall be adjudged against him. Therefore you are hereby commanded in the name of the State of Iowa, that without delay you replevy and deliver to the said plaintiff, the property above described, and that you make return of your doings hereon to our next .... Court, to be holden at .... in said county, on the first day of the next regular term thereof.

Witness, ... clerk of said .... Court, and seal of said court, hereto affixed at office in ...., this the .... day of .... A. D. 18... ...., *Clerk of* .... *Court.*

V. OF INJUNCTION.

Allowance of writ and bond.—An order for the allowance of an injunction can only issue after the filing of a bond, in the office of the clerk of the proper court, in a penalty to be fixed by the court or judge, with sureties to be approved by the clerk, and conditioned to pay all damages which may be adjudged against the petitioner by reason of said injunction; and where proceedings in a civil action or on a judgment are sought to be enjoined, the bond must be further conditioned to pay such judgment or comply with such final orders, if the injunction is not made perpetual, or to pay any judgment that may ultimately be recovered against the party obtaining the injunction, on the cause of action enjoined. Code Sec. 3396.

The bond may be in the following form:

INJUNCTION BOND.

No. 45.

Know all men by these presents, That we, A B, principal, and C D and E F, sureties, are held and firmly bound unto G H in the penal sum of .... dollars, lawful money of the United

States, well and truly to be paid to the said ...., and to .... heirs, executors and assigns.

The condition of the obligation is such, that whereas, the said A B, on this .... day ...., filed in the office of the clerk of the .... Court of the State of Iowa, in and for .... county, a petition praying the issuance of an injunction to restrain the said defendant from [here state the act or thing to be enjoined.]

And whereas on the .... day of ...., 18.., the Honorable .... judge of said court, made an order indorsed on said petition, allowing said writ upon filing a bond in the penal sum of .... dollars, to be approved by the clerk of said court.

Now therefore if the said A B shall and will pay all the damages which may be adjudged against him by reason of such injunction, then this obligation to be void, otherwise to remain in full force and virtue.

Dated this .... day of ...., A. D. 18...

...., *Principal.*

...., } *Sureties.*
.... }

[*Annex affidavit of sureties and approval of the bond by the clerk.*]

WRIT OF INJUNCTION.

No. 46.

THE STATE OF IOWA *to C D, defendant:*

WHEREAS, A B, as plaintiff, has this day filed in the office of the .... Court of the State of Iowa, in and for .... county, a petition duly sworn to, making C D defendant therein, and praying for the allowance of a writ of injunction against said defendant: And whereas, the Honorable ...., judge of the .... Court of said county, has made an order allowing said writ of injunction to issue, upon the filing of a bond with sureties, pursuant to said order. And whereas, said order has been complied with, and such bond filed and approved: Now, therefore you, the said C D, defendant, as aforesaid, in the name and by the authority of the State of Iowa, are hereby strictly enjoined and restrained from [here insert the matter or thing the defendant is restrained doing] until the further order of our said court in the premises.

To the sheriff of .... county:

You are hereby commanded to make due service of this writ upon said defendant, and hereof fail not, and make return of this writ unto our said .... Court, with your doings hereon, on the first day of the next term of our said .... Court.

Witness, ..., clerk of the court, and the seal thereof hereto affixed, this .... day of ...., A. D. 18...

...., *Clerk.*

VI. OF THE SELECTION AND SUMMONING OF JURORS.

Duties of the clerk.—In reference to the number of grand and trial jurors and the mode of selecting and summoning them, and the clerk's duty connected therewith, the Code provides as follows:

Number.—SECTION 231. The number of grand jurors shall be fifteen, and in counties containing less than fifteen thousand inhabitants as shown by the last preceding census, the trial jurors shall consist of the same number, unless the judge otherwise orders. But in counties containing a greater number of inhabitants, the number of trial jurors shall be twenty-four.

Failure of trial jurors to attend.—SEC. 232. Should there not be the number of trial jurors in attendance, as provided in the preceding section, by reason of the failure of the persons summoned to attend, or because excused as provided in section two hundred and thirty of this chapter, the requisite number of persons to supply the deficiency shall be drawn in the same manner as provided in sections two hundred and forty and two hundred and forty-one of this chapter. The persons so drawn shall be forthwith summoned to appear, and serve as trial jurors during the term.

Discharge of.—SEC. 233. If, in the judgment of the court, the business of the term does not require the attendance of all, or a portion of the trial jurors, they, or such portion as the court deems proper, may be discharged. Should it afterward appear that a jury is required, the court may direct them to be resummoned, or empanel a jury from the bystanders.

Lists.—SEC. 234. Two jury lists, one consisting of seventy-five persons to serve as grand jurors, and one consisting of one hundred and fifty persons, or, in counties containing more than twenty thousand inhabitants, of two hundred and fifty persons to serve as trial jurors, and composed of persons competent and liable to serve as jurors, shall annually be made in each county from which to select jurors for the year commencing on the first day of January.

SEC. 235. Should there be less than the required number of such persons in any county, the list shall compose all those who answer the above description in the same proportion.

How selected.—SEC. 236. On or before the first Monday in September in each year, the county auditor shall apportion the number to be selected from each election precinct, as nearly as practicable in proportion to the number of votes polled therein at the last general election, and shall deliver a statement thereof to the sheriff.

Sheriff to serve notice.—SEC. 237. The sheriff shall cause a written notice to be delivered to one of the judges of election in each precinct of the county, on or before the day of the general election in each year, informing them of the number of jurors apportioned for the ensuing year to their respective precincts.

Duty of judge of election.—SEC. 238 The judges shall thereupon make the requisite selection, and return lists of names as selected to the auditor with the returns of the election, and in case the judges of election shall fail to make and return said lists as herein required, the county canvassers shall, at the meeting to canvass the votes polled in the county, make such lists for the delinquent precincts, and the auditor shall file said lists in his office and cause a copy thereof to be recorded in the election book.

Term of service.—SEC. 239. Grand jurors shall be selected for the first term in the year at which jurors are required, commencing next after the first day of January in each year, and shall serve for one year. Trial jurors shall be selected for each term wherein they are required; but no person shall be required to attend as a trial juror more than two terms in the same year, and in counties containing a population, of more than five thousand inhabitants, it shall be a cause of challenge that the person has served on a jury in a court of record within one year, unless he be a member of the regular panel.

Auditor write names.—SEC. 240. At least twenty days prior to the first day of any term at which a jury is to be selected, the auditor, or his deputy, must write out the names on the lists aforesaid which have not been previously drawn as jurors during the year, on separate ballots, and the clerk of the district court, or his deputy, and sheriff having compared said ballots with the lists, and corrected the same if necessary, shall place the ballots in a box provided for that purpose.

Clerk to draw: issue precept.—SEC. 241. After thoroughly mixing the same the clerk, or his deputy, shall draw therefrom the requisite number of jurors to serve as aforesaid, and shall, within three days thereafter, issue a precept to the sheriff, commanding him to summon the said jurors to appear before the court as provided in section two hundred and thirty of this chapter.

Sheriff to serve.—SEC. 242. The sheriff shall immediately obey such precept, and, on or before the day for the appearance of said jurors, must make return thereof, and on failure to do so, without sufficient cause, is liable to be fined for a contempt in any amount not exceeding fifty dollars.

Grand jurors to attend.—SEC. 243. Except when required at a special term which has been called in vacation, the grand jury need not be summoned after the first term, but must appear at the next term without summons, under the same penalty as though they had been regularly summoned.

When precept is set aside.—SEC. 244. Where, from any cause, the persons summoned to serve as grand or trial jurors fail to appear, or when from any cause the court shall decide that the grand or trial jurors have been illegally elected or drawn, the court may set aside the precept under which the jurors were summoned, and cause a precept to be issued to the sheriff commanding him to summon a sufficient number of persons from the body of the county, to serve as jurors at the term of court then being holden, which precept may be made returnable forthwith, or at some subsequent day of the term, in the discretion of the court.

VII. OF COMMISSION TO TAKE DEPOSITIONS.

The Code provides as follows in reference to the clerk's duty on applications for commissions to take depositions.

Notice: action before a justice.—SECTION 3727. Reasonable notice must be given the adverse party of a time when a commission will be sued out of the office of the clerk of the court in which the action is pending; if such action is in an inferior court, then from the office of the clerk of the circuit court for taking the deposition of the witness, naming him, which notice must be accompanied with a copy of the interrogatories to be asked such witness.

Cross interrogatories.—SEC. 3728. At or before the time thus fixed, the opposite party may file cross-interrogatories. If cross-interrogatories are not filed, the clerk shall file the following:

1. Are you directly or indirectly interested in this action? and if interested, explain the interest you have;

2. Are all your statements in the foregoing answers made from your personal knowledge? and if not, do your answers show what are made from your personal knowledge, and what are from information, and the source of that information? if not, now show what is from information, and give its source;

3. State everything you know concerning the subject of this action, favorable to either party.

Rules.—SEC. 3729. Subject to the regulations herein contained, the court may establish farther rules for taking depositions and all other acts connected therewith.

Reasonable notice: what deemed.—SEC. 3730. The notice hereinbefore mentioned, is at least, when served on the attorney, ten days, and when served on the party within the county, five days; if served on the party anywhere else, the notice shall be that required under other similar circumstances in the service of an original notice; and when depositions are to be taken in pursuance of the first of the above methods, one day in addition must be allowed for every thirty miles travel from the place where the notice is served, to that where the depositions are to be taken. No party shall be required to take depositions when the court is in actual session.

How served.—SEC. 3731. The notice, or notice and copy of interrogatories, may be served by the same persons on the same persons in the same manner, and may be returned, and the return shall be authenticated in the same way, as should be an original notice in the same cause when served other than by publication.

On attorney.—SEC. 3732. It may also be served personally on any attorney of the adverse party of record in the cause.

By filing in clerk's office.—SEC. 3733. Whenever the adverse party has been notified by publication only, and has not appeared, he shall be deemed served with the notice, or the notice and interrogatories, by the filing of the same with the clerk in the cause.

Commission: form of.—SEC. 3734. The commission issues in the name of the court and under its seal. It must be signed by the clerk, and need contain nothing but the authority conferred upon the commissioner, instructions to guide him, and a statement of the cause and court in which the testimony is to be used, and a copy of the interrogatories on each side appended.

No. 47.

COMMISSION TO TAKE DEPOSITION.

STATE OF IOWA, }
......County, } ss.

To........ ... Know ye that we, the....Court of the county of...., State of Iowa, reposing full confidence in your integrity and fidelity, do by these presents, constitute, empower, and commission you to summon and cause to come before you at such time and place as you shall appoint, according to the notice hereto attached, the witnesses hereinafter named; to-wit: ....material witnesses, as it is said, on the part and behalf of the....in a suit wherein....plaintiff, and....defendant, now pending in our said court, and....to examine on corporal oath or affirmation, first to....administered, true answers to make to the several interrogations accompanying this commission, and the same, when taken, to certify, seal up, and forward to the clerk of said court, with all convenient dispatch, according to the instructions hereto attached.

Witness,....clerk of said court, and the seal thereof affixed, at office in....in said county, this the....day of....A. D. 18..

......*Clerk.* .

Instructions for taking depositions.—Section 3738, Code 1873, requires that, "Where a deposition is taken upon interrogatories, neither party, nor his agent or attorney, shall be present at the examination of a witness, unless both parties are present or represented by an agent or attorney, and the certificate shall state such fact, if party or agent is present."

The officer taking the depositions will observe the following forms and mode of proceeding, commencing thus:

Deposition of witnesses produced, sworn and examined at.... in the county of...., and State of...., before me [name of officer and style of office], in a certain case, now pending in the.... Court of....county, State of Iowa, between...., plaintiff, and ...., defendant, on the part of the....A B, of lawful age, being produced, sworn, and examined on the part of the...., deposeth and saith; [Here insert each interrogatory as it occurs, and the answer thereto, immediately following.]

Every deposition must be reduced to writing by some person who is neither of the parties, attorneys of either, nor in anywise interested in the event of the suit, in presence of the officer before whom it is taken, and signed by the witness.

If any paper or exhibit is produced and proved, or referred to by a witness, it should be described in his deposition, and referred to by the deponent in such a manner that it may be identified when the deposition is read, and all such papers and exhibits must be attached to and returned with the deposition.

The officer will annex at the foot of the deposition of each witness, the following certificate:

I, [insert the name of officer and style of office], do hereby certify that A B, the deponent, whose place of residence is.... was by me sworn, (or affirmed), to testify the whole truth of his (or her) knowledge, touching the matter in controversy in the cause aforesaid, that deponent was examined, and his (or her) examination reduced to writing by...., who is neither of the parties, nor attorney of either, nor in any wise interested in the suit, and after being carefully by me read over to the said deponent, the same was sworn to and subscribed by the said deponent in my presence, on the....day of...., A. D. 187.., between the hours of....A. M., and....P. M., of said day. At [here name the place, county, and State]. Given and certified [here give the date], under my hand and seal official, this....day of...., A. D. 18.. [If the officer has a seal it must be affixed.]

....

Then proceed with other depositions (if any), in the same form, annexing a certificate to each.

When all the witnesses who appear have been sworn and examined, and their depositions reduced to writing, subscribed and certified as above, the officer will attach to the deposition all papers and exhibits proved or referred to in the examination, the commission and notice [herewith inclosed,] with the following certificate indorsed thereon or attached thereto:

THE STATE OF...... } ss.
........County, }

I, [name of officer and style of office], within and for [name the place], or duly commissioned for that purpose, do certify that, in pursuance of the within [or annexed] commission and notice, came before me at [name the place where the testimony was taken], A, B, C, D, etc., [insert the names of all witnesses] who were there by me then sworn and examined, and such examination reduced to writing by [the name of the person], who is neither of the parties, their attorney, nor in anywise interested in the event of the suit, and after being by me read over to each of said deponents, the same was sworn to and subscribed to by said witnesses respectively in my presence, and their depositions are now herewith returned. [State if either or both parties were present at the examination personally, or by agent or attorney.] Given under my hand and seal official hereto affixed, at [name of place, county, and State], this [give date].

....

The return must be accompanied by a certificate of the official character of the officer when the depositions are taken by any judge, notary public, or justice of the peace, attested by the seal of the State of, or by the seal of any court of record of the county or city wherein such depositions shall be taken, which may be in the following form:

IT IS HEREBY CERTIFIED, that...., on [here insert the date at which the depositions were taken and certified],....was (and now is)....[state the style of office], ..., State of...., duly commissioned and acting as such, and that full faith and credit are due to his acts as such.

In testimony whereof, I, A B, [here state the style of office], have hereunto subscribed my name and affixed [L. S.] the seal of said court at office, this....day of...., eighteen hundred and....

....

The officer taking the depositions is required to enclose in a strong envelope, securely sealed, the depositions, papers and exhibits, commission notice and certificates, and direct the same to the clerk of the....Court of....county, Iowa, noting on some convenient part of the envelope the style of the cause and contents; thus:

.... }
v. } *Depositions on the part of....*
.... }

The depositions must be begun on the day mentioned in the notice. If they cannot be completed on that day, the taking of them may be adjourned to the succeeding day, at the same place and between the same hours. The person taking them should, in such case, make the following entry closing the business for that day, viz:

Not being able to complete the taking of said depositions, by reason that [here insert the reason], I adjourn the further taking of the same until tomorrow, then to be continued at the same place, and between the same hours, mentioned in the annexed notice.

....

On the succeeding day, let the person taking the depositions commence as follows:

Pursuant to the adjournment as above stated, on the....day of ...., in the year eighteen hundred and...., between the hours of....in the forenoon, and....in the afternoon, I continued the taking of said depositions, as follows:

A B, in continuance of his depositions, commenced yesterday on his oath, further says, etc.

The foregoing directions must be strictly observed, or the deposition will be unavailing.

If the officer taking the deposition has a seal of office, it must be affixed to every certificate.

The officer taking the deposition must write out each interrogatory in full, and insert the answer just below the proper question.

The depositions must be returned by mail, unless some mode is agreed upon between the parties.

CROSS-INTERROGATORIES.

No. 48.

.... }
v.
.... }

WHEREAS, the....has failed to appear and file cross-interrogatories in the above entitled case as by law he was privileged to; Now, therefore, I,....clerk of said court, agreeable to Sec. 3728 of the Code of 1873, do file the following, to-wit:

1st. Are you directly or indirectly interested in this action? and if interested, explain the interest you have.

2d. Are all your statements in the foregoing answers made from your personal knowledge; and if not, do your answers show what are made from your personal knowledge, and what from information, and the source of the information? if not, show what is from information and give the source.

3d. State everything you know concerning the subject of this action, favorable to either party.

Witness,....clerk of said court, this....day of....A. D. 18...

....

CHAPTER VI.

OTHER DUTIES, AND COMPENSATION.

I. OF ENTERING MINUTES ON THE MARGIN OF MORTGAGES.

Whenever a judgment of foreclosure shall be entered in any court, the clerk thereof should make upon the margin of the record of the mortgage foreclosed, in the recorder's office, a minute showing that said mortgage was foreclosed; in what court foreclosed, and giving the date of the decree; and when such decree shall be fully paid and satisfied upon the judgment docket of such court, the clerk should enter satisfaction in full upon the margin of such mortgage, and he is allowed for such services twenty-five cents, to be taxed as a part of the costs in the case. Code, Sec. 3328.

MINUTE OF FORECLOSURE.

No. 49.

STATE OF IOWA }
...... County. } ss.

I, A B, clerk of the .... Court of said county, hereby certify that a judgment and decree of foreclosure of this mortgage was entered in said court on the .... day of 18..

Dated this .... day of ...., 18....

A.... B ...., *Clerk.*

ENTRY OF SATISFACTION BY THE CLERK.

No. 50.

STATE OF IOWA, }
......County, } ss.

I, A B, clerk of the .... Court of said county, hereby certify, that the judgment and decree of foreclosure of this mortgage is fully paid, and satisfied upon the judgment docket of said court where entered, and this mortgage is thereby satisfied in full.

Dated this .... day .... 18...

A.... B...., *Clerk.*

II. TO CERTIFY RECORDS.

Every officer having the custody of a public record or writing, is bound to give any person on demand a certified copy thereof on payment of the legal fees therefor; and the certificate of a public officer that he has made diligent and ineffectual search for a paper in his office, is of the same efficacy in all cases as if such officer had personally appeared and sworn to such facts, and the signature of the officer is presumed to be genuine until the contrary is shown. Code, Sec. 3706, 3708.

How proved.—A judicial record of this State, or of any of the federal courts of the United States, may be proved by the production of the original or by a copy thereof, certified by the clerk or person having the legal custody thereof, and authenticated by his seal of office if he have one. Code, Sec. 3712.

CAPTION AND CERTIFICATE.

No. 51.

STATE OF IOWA, } ss.
.... County, }

Be it remembered, That heretofore, to-wit: At a term of the .... Court of the State of Iowa, begun and held at ...., in and for said county, on the .... Monday, the .... day of ...., A. D. 18 .., present the Hon. ...., Judge of the .... Judicial .... of the State of Iowa, ..., Sheriff of said county, and ...., clerk of said court, and the following entitled causes coming on to be heard, on the ... day of ...., A. D. 18.., and still during said term of said court, the following among other proceedings were had therein, to-wit:

...... *Plaintiff*, }
v. }
...... *Defendant.* }

[Here set forth the whole or any part of the record that may be required.]

STATE OF IOWA, } ss.
.... County. }

I, ... clerk of the .... Court of the State of Iowa, in and for said county, do hereby certify that the above and foregoing is a true and perfect transcript of the record entry of .... in the above entitled causes as fully as the same remains on record in my office.

In testimony whereof, I have hereunto set my hand and affixed the seal of said court, at the court house in ...., in said county, this .... day of .... A. D. 18...

...., *Clerk of said Court,*
By ...., *Deputy.*

III. DUTY ON APPEALS TO THE SUPREME COURT.

When perfected: and transcript.—An appeal to the Supreme Court is not perfected until the notice thereof has been served upon both the adverse party and the clerk, and the clerk paid, or secured his fees, for a transcript; whereupon the clerk should forthwith transmit by mail, express, or messenger not a party nor the attorney of a party to the action, a transcript of the record, or so much thereof as the appellant in writing may direct; to which the clerk should append copies of the notice of appeal, and the supersedeas bond if any. Code, Sec. 3179.

Form of certificate thereto: and evidence.—With a little change the certificate No. 51, may be used by the clerk in certifying transcripts on appeal. If the evidence is required to be certified, it should be certified in its original form, and as all the evidence used on the trial of the cause. Code, Sec. 3184.

To approve the supersedeas bond.—The clerk has also the approval of the bond given for a stay of execution in appealed causes. It should be in a penalty at least twice the sum of the judgment and costs; and if the judgment is not for the payment of money, the penalty to be fixed by the clerk, should be sufficient to save the appellee harmless from the consequences of taking the appeal, and if execution has issued before the bond is filed, the clerk should countermand the same. Code, Sections 3186, 3187, 3190, 3191, 3192.

SUPERSEDEAS BOND.

No. 52.

Know all men by these presents: That we, A B, principal, and C D and E F, sureties, are held and firmly bound unto G H, in the sum of .... dollars, lawful money of the United States, well and truly to be paid to the said G H, his heirs, executors, and assigns.

The condition of this obligation is such, that whereas, the said A B has appealed from the judgment of the .... Court of the State of Iowa, in and for .... county, rendered on the .... day of ...., A. D. 18.., in an action, then pending in said court, wherein the said ...., plaintiff, and the said ...., defendant, ...

Now, if the said appellant, A B, shall pay to the said appellee all costs and damages that shall be adjudged against said appellant on said appeal, and shall also satisfy and perform the said judgment appealed from, in case it shall be affirmed, and any judgment or order which the Supreme Court may render or order to be rendered by the said .... Court, then this obligation to be void, otherwise to remain in full force and virtue.

Dated this .... day of...., A. D. 18...

A.... B...., *Principal.*
C.... D...., } *Sureties.*
E ... F..... }

[*Add qualification of sureties and approval*].

IV. SUMMARY OF OTHER DUTIES, ETC.

The clerk is required to attest and date all process issued by him on the day on which it is issued; Code, Sec. 188; issue orders for the seizure of the property of absconding father, etc.; Code, Sec. 1343; issue marriage licenses; Code, Sec. 2187; to keep a register of marriages; Code, Sec. 2187; to bind out paupers by indenture; Code, Sec. 2283; to watch over the interests of apprentices; Code, Sec. 2287; to consent to the adoption of orphan children; Code, Sec. 2308; to approve bonds in probate cases; Code, Sec. 2321; to open and read wills of testators; Code, Sec. 2338; to fix a day for proving wills and keep the probate records; Code, sections 2341, 2490; to make a complete record in case of a sale of real estate by an executor or administrator; Code, Sec. 2492; to record the bonds of guardians; Code, Sec. 2493; to issue a fee-bill on the demand of any person entitled to fees in any cause, after sixty days from the rendition of a judgment, which shall have the force and effect of an execution; Code, Sec. 3842; to file transcript of justice docket delivered to him for that purpose, and enter a memorandum thereof in his judgment docket, noting the time of such filing; Code, Sec. 3568; to enter judgments on confessions; Code, Sec. 2897; to approve the bonds of receivers; Code, Sec. 2904; to make out a bill of costs on appeals to the Supreme Court; Code, Sec. 2945; to pay costs to witnesses entitled thereto when received; Code, Sec. 2947; to render a verified statement of fees received to the board of supervisors at each regular session of the board; Code, Sec. 3785; to pay all witness fees unclaimed for six months into the county treasury, giving the treasurer a written statement of the title of the cause, and style of the court in which the same was pending, with the name of the witnesses, and the amount each one is entitled to receive; Code, Sec. 3786; to report to the Secretary of State, on or before the first Monday of November in each year, the number of convictions of all crimes and misdemeanors in the District Court of his county for the year preceding, which report shall show the character of the offense, the sentence of punishment, the occupation of the convict, whether he can read and write, his general habits, and also the expenses of the county for criminal prosecutions during the year, including, but distinguishing the compensation of the district attorney; Code, Sec. 203; to give attested copies of the records of notaries, deposited in his office; Code, Sec. 266; to issue subpœnas in trials of contested elections; to make an entry of proceedings in habeas corpus cases; Code, Sec. 3490; to issue bench warrants on the order of the judge therefor, and into different counties; Code, Sec. 4320; to issue warrants on the order of the court for contempt; Code, Sec. 3498; to issue letters of administration; Code, Sec. 2365; and in vacation of the Probate Court to appoint executors, administrators and guardians, and to issue citations and other notices; Code, Sec. 2315 and Chap. 43, Ses. L., 1874.

FEE-BILL EXECUTION.

No. 53.

THE STATE OF IOWA, *To the sheriff of .... county, greeting:*

WHEREAS, on the .... day of ...., A. D. 18.., by the judgment of the .... Court of the State of Iowa, in and for .... county, ... recovered against ...., as principal, and .... as surety, the sum of .... dollars debt, and the further sum of .... dollars costs, in a certain action then pending in said court, wherein the said .... was plaintiff, and the said .... w.. defendant., which said sum of .... dollars costs is still due.

AND WHEREAS, more than sixty days have now expired from the rendition of said judgment, and said judgment has not been appealed, removed or reversed.

AND WHEREAS, the following schedule contains a full, true and complete statement of all the costs in said cause as the same appears of record in Fee-Book No. .., page .., of the records of the clerk's office of said county, to-wit:

	$ Cts.	$ Cts,

AND WHEREAS, the said .... is entitled to a part of said costs, and has demanded that a fee-bill for all costs of said judgment shall be issued, and served as by statute in such cases made and provided.

You are therefore hereby commanded to cause to be made of the goods and chattels, lands and tenements of the said .... in your county, subject to execution, the said sum of ... dollars costs, together with all legal costs that may accrue by virtue of this writ. And have said moneys in our said court in seventy days to render the same or his portion thereof unto the said .... ; and have you then and there this writ with your doings hereon.

Witness ...., clerk of said court, with the seal thereof hereto affixed, at ...., this .... day of ...., A. D. 18...

...., *Clerk.*

BENCH WARRANT.

No. 54.

STATE OF IOWA, }
.... County. } SS.

To any peace officer in the State:

An indictment having been found in the District Court of said county, on the .... day of ...., A. D. 18.., charging .... with the crime of [state the charge as in the indictment].

You are, therefore, hereby commanded to arrest the said ...., and bring him before said court to answer said indictment, if the said court be then in session in said county, or, if the said court be not then in session in said county, that you deliver him into the custody of the sheriff of said county.

Given under my hand and the seal of said court, at my office in ...., in the county aforesaid, this .... day of ...., A. D. 18...

By order of the judge of the court.

...., *Clerk.*

WRIT OF ATTACHMENT FOR CONTEMPT.

No. 55.

STATE OF IOWA, ⎫
.... County. ⎭ ss.

To the sheriff of said county, greeting:

WHEREAS, in the presence of the District Court of said county now in session, it has been proven that A B has been regularly summoned as a grand juror at the term of the District Court of said county, to be begun and held at the court house in . .., on the .... day of ...., 18.., and he having failed to obey said summons, this is therefore to command you to arrest the said A B, and bring him before the District Court now in session forthwith to answer for contempt, and fail not at your peril.

Given under my hand and the seal of the District Court affixed this .... day of ...., A. D. 18...

...., *Clerk.*

VENIRE.

No. 56.

STATE OF IOWA, ⎫
........County, ⎭ ss.

.... *Court*, ... *Term*, 18..

To the sheriff of .... county, greeting:

You are hereby commanded to summon ...., to be and appear before the .... Court of .... county, Iowa, at the court house in said county, at ... o'clock, A. M., on the .... day of ...., A. D. 18.., to serve as .... jurors, and then and there to continue until duly discharged, and have you then and there this writ.

In testimony whereof, I have hereunto set my hand, and affixed the seal of said court, at ...., this the .... day of ...., A. D. 18..

...., *Clerk.*

V. CRIMES AND MISDEMEANORS.

For the statute, prohibiting certain acts, and defining and punishing crimes and misdemeanors in office the reader is referred to Chapter One.

Session Laws 1874.—Additional powers and duties of the clerk, are provided for by the Session Laws of 1874, which are as follows:

He is required at the close of each term of court to make out a certificate for each juror, of the amount to which he is entitled for his services. Ses. Laws 1874, Chap. 16. To keep the true and correct time actually occupied by the jury in each case, and tax the *per diem* fees therefor, as costs in the case, and when collected to pay the same to the county treasurer, and report the same to the board of supervisors, at each regular session thereof. Ses. Laws 1874, Chap. 32.

He has power to appoint guardians. Ses. Laws 1874, Chap. 42; and is required to give notice of the hearing, on a petition for the vacation of a plat of town lots, in some newspaper published in the county. Ses. Laws 1874, Chap. 61.

VII. FEES AND COMPENSATION OF THE CLERK.

The Code provides as follows, in reference to fees and compensation of the clerk:

Fees.—SECTION 3781. The clerk of the district and circuit court shall be entitled to charge and receive the following fees:

For filing any petition, appeal, or writ of error, and docketing the same, one dollar and fifty cents;

For every attachment, fifty cents;

For every cause tried by jury, one dollar and fifty cents;

For every cause tried by the court, seventy-five cents;

For every equity cause, one dollar and fifty cents;

For each injunction, or other extraordinary process or order, one dollar;

For all causes continued on application of a party by affidavit, fifty cents;

For all other continuances, fifteen cents;

For entering any final judgment or decree, seventy-five cents;

For taxing costs, fifty cents;

For issuing execution or other process after judgment or decree, fifty cents;

For filing and properly entering and indorsing each mechanic's lien, the same to be taxed as other costs in case a suit is brought thereon, one dollar;

For certificate and seal, fifty cents;

For filing and docketing transcript of judgment from another county or a justice of the peace, fifty cents;

For entering any rule or order, twenty-five cents;

For issuing writ or order, not including subpœnas, fifty cents;

For issuing commission to take depositions, fifty cents;

For entering sheriff's sale of real estate, fifty cents;

For entering judgment by confession, one dollar;

For entering satisfaction of any judgment, twenty-five cents;

For all copies of record or papers filed in his office, transcripts, and making complete record, ten cents for each hundred words;

For taking and approving a bond and sureties thereon, fifty cents;

For declaration of intentions by an alien to become a citizen, twenty-five cents;

For all services on naturalization of aliens, including oaths and certificates, fifty cents;

In criminal cases.—In criminal cases, and in all causes in which the state or county is a party plaintiff, the same fees for same services as in suits between private parties. When judgment is rendered against the defendant, the fees shall be collected from such defendant. Where the state fails, the clerk's fees shall be paid by the county;

For making out transcripts in criminal cases appealed to the supreme court, when the defendant is unable to pay, for each one hundred words, ten cents, to be paid by the county.

Pensions and bounties.—SEC. 3782. The clerk of the district court shall certify under the seal of such court, to all applications and other papers requiring the certificate and seal of a court of record to procure pensions, bounties, and back pay for soldiers or other persons entitled thereto, whenever requested by the applicant, his agent, or attorney, and such clerk shall be entitled to the sum of ten cents only for such services.

In probate matters.—SEC. 3783. There shall be such compensation paid such clerk for his services in probate matters out of the fees collected by him for probate business, as the board of supervisors may allow.

Compensation limited.—SEC. 3784. The total amount of compensation of such clerk for all official services, shall not exceed the sum of two thousand dollars in any one year, except that in each county having two county seats, such compensation, including the amount paid to deputies, shall not exceed three thousand dollars in any one year, and if the fees received by said clerk shall amount in the aggregate to more than the sum above stated for any one year, the excess shall be paid into the county treasury. In case the amount of fees so received by such clerk is deemed an inadequate compensation, the board of supervisors may allow such additional compensation as they deem best and proper.

Report to supervisors: fees collected.—SEC. 3785. The clerk of the district court as such, and as clerk of the circuit court, shall report to the board of supervisors of his county at each regular session, a full and complete statement of the amount of fees received by him, which shall be verified by the affidavit of such clerk.

Money received that is uncalled for.—SEC. 3786. The clerk of the district and circuit courts shall pay into the county treasury all money received for witness fees remaining unclaimed in his hands for six months after the receipt of the same, and at the time of so doing shall deliver to the treasurer a written statement, giving the title of the cause and style of the court in which the same was pending, with the name of the witnesses and the amount each one is entitled to receive and the treasurer shall keep an account of the money thus received separate from other funds, and shall pay the same to the persons entitled thereto as shown by such statement, taking proper receipts therefor.

For marriage licenses and fees in probate matters.—SEC. 3787. There shall be paid the clerk of the circuit court the following fees;

For issuing marriage licenses, one dollar;

For all services performed in the settlement of the estate of any decedent, except where actions are brought by the administrator or against him, or as may be otherwise provided herein, where the value of the estate does not exceed three thousand dollars, three dollars;

Where such value is between three and five thousand dollars, five dollars;

Where such value is between five and seven thousand dollars, eight dollars;

Where the value exceeds eight thousand dollars, ten dollars;

And in addition to the foregoing, for making a complete record in cases where the same is required by law or directed by an order of the court, for every one hundred words, ten cents;

All of which fees shall be paid into the county treasury.

Cannot charge fees except expressly allowed.—Neither the clerk nor any other public officer, is authorized to charge or exact fees for any service or duty performed by him unless the fee therefor is expressly provided for, and authorized by the statute. If there are no fees expressly allowed for the performance of certain duties required of them, it is to be presumed that the legislature did not intend to allow them fees therefor, but that the fees or compensation provided for them was intended as a complete consideration for all duties devolving upon them; and no recovery can be had by them for services upon a *quantum meruit*. These principles were authoritatively settled by the Supreme Court in a recent case. *Sprout v. Kelly*, June Term, 1873. (Not reported).

CHAPTER VIII.

THE SHERIFF.

I. THE ANTIQUITY AND IMPORTANCE OF THE OFFICE.

Antiquity and early duties.—The office of sheriff is one of great antiquity, and under the ancient laws of England, it was an exalted and highly honorable one. He was keeper of the king's peace, did the king's business, and was superior in rank to any nobleman in the county.

The sheriff not only possessed great executive authority, but also extensive judicial functions, both civil and criminal.

Its dignity and importance.—The dignity and importance of the office was frequently maintained by great displays and extravagance, as is disclosed by an ancient English statute which provided, that no sheriff should keep any table at the time and place of holding the courts, except for his own family, or have more than forty men in livery; but it was further provided, that for the purpose of maintaining the proper security, respect, and dignity of the office, or in the language of the statute, "for the sake of safety and decency," he should not have less than twenty men in England and twelve in Wales.

The common law in construction of statutes.—It being an ancient office, the duties and liabilities of it were regulated by the common law, which became a part of our inheritance from the mother country, so far as the same was applicable to the changed condition and circumstances; and although the duties of the office are here largely regulated by statute, it is necessary for us to go to the common law for guidance and instruction in solving the problems of the meaning and the proper construction of the statutes relating to those duties.

The office continues an important one.—As under the early laws of England, so the sheriff in this country continues to be the executive officer of the county, and the office is one of honor and great responsibility, although shorn of much of its former dignity and power.

II. HIS ELECTION.

By reference to the statutes contained in the first chapter of this treatise, it will be seen that the sheriff is elected in each odd-numbered year, at the general election, for the term of two years; that the term of office commences on the first Monday of January next after the election, Code, Sec. 573, except when elected to fill a vacancy, and that the term of office of an officer elected to fill a vacancy shall commence so soon as he has qualified therefor. Code, Sec. 576.

III. QUALIFICATION—DEPUTIES—VACANCIES—REMOVAL—SUSPENSION.

General statutes.—The general provisions of the Code in reference to qualification, deputies, vacancies and removal or suspension from office, may be found in Chapter One.

Forms given for clerk, etc. The directions and forms to guide the clerk, in such cases, given in treating of that officer, will serve the sheriff also in those cases.

CHAPTER IX.

SHERIFF'S DUTIES.

Provisions of the statutes.—The Code contains the following general provisions, in reference to his duties:

Duties.—SECTION 337. The sheriff shall, by himself or his deputies, execute according to law, and return all writs and other legal process issued by lawful authority and to him directed or committed, and shall perform such other duties as may be required of him by law.

Disobedience.—SEC. 338. His disobedience of the command of any such process is a contempt of the court from which it issued, and may be punished by the same accordingly, and he is further liable to the action of any person injured thereby.

Jail: charge of.—SEC. 339. He has the charge and custody of the jail or other prison of his county, and of the prisoners in the same, and is required to receive those lawfully committed, and to keep them himself, or by his deputy or jailor, until discharged by law.

Conservators of the peace.—SEC. 340. The sheriff and his deputies are conservators of the peace, and to keep the same, or to prevent crime, or to arrest any person liable thereto, or to execute process of law, may call any person to their aid, and when necessary, the sheriff may summon the power of the county.

Attend courts.—SEC. 341. The sheriff shall attend upon the district and circuit courts of his county, and while either remains in session he shall be allowed the assistance of such number of bailiffs as either may direct. They shall be appointed by the sheriff, and shall be regarded as deputy sheriffs, for whose acts the sheriff shall be responsible.

Not appear as attorney or counsel.—SEC. 342. No sheriff, deputy sheriff, coroner, or constable, shall appear in any court as attorney or counsel for any party, nor make any writing or process to commence, or to be in any manner used in the same, and such writing or process made by any of them shall be rejected.

Purchase void.—SEC. 343. No sheriff, deputy sheriff, coroner or constable, shall become the purchaser, either directly or indirectly, of any property by him exposed to sale under any process of law, and every such purchase is absolutely void.

Execute process when out of office.—SEC. 344. Sheriffs and their deputies may execute any process which may be in their hands at the expiration of their office, and in case of a vacancy occurring in the office of sheriff from any cause, his deputies shall be under the same obligation to execute legal process then in his or their hands, and to return the same, as if the sheriff had continued in office, and he and they will remain liable therefor under the provisions of law as in other cases.

Deliver to successor.—SEC. 345. Where a sheriff goes out of office, he shall deliver to his successor all books and papers pertaining to the office, and property attached and levied upon, except as provided in the preceding section, and all prisoners in the jail, and take his receipt specifying the same, and such receipt shall be sufficient indemnity to the person taking it.

Successor may serve.—SEC. 346. If the sheriff die or go out of office before the return of any process then in his hands, his successor, or other officer authorized to discharge the duties of the office, may proceed to execute and return the same in the same manner as the out-going sheriff should have done, but nothing in this section shall be construed to exempt the out-going sheriff and his deputies from the duty imposed on them by section three hundred and thirty-seven of this chapter, to execute and return all process in their hands at the time the vacancy in the office of sheriff occurs.

SEC. 347. On the election or appointment of a new sheriff all new process shall be directed to him.

SEC. 348. If the sheriff, who has made a sale of real estate on execution, die, or go out of office before the period of redemption expires, his successor shall make the necessary deed to carry out such sale.

CHAPTER X.

ORIGINAL NOTICE.

I. WHAT IT IS.

The most common process.—This is the most common kind of legal process. It is the substitute for the common law summons, and the process provided by law for the commencement of an action.

II. HOW SIGNED AND SERVED.

It may be signed by the party or by his attorney and served by any person not a party to the action.

When delivered to the sheriff for service.—If the notice is delivered to the sheriff for service, he must note thereon the date when received, and proceed to serve the same in his county without delay, and file the same with his return thereon in the office of the clerk of the court in which the suit is instituted, or return the same by mail or otherwise, to the party from whom he received it.

Provisions of the Code relating to service.—The provisions of the Code in reference to service on individuals, and the return thereof, are as follows:

Notice: how served.—SECTION 2603. The notice shall be served as follows:

1. By reading the notice to the defendant, or offering to read it in case he neglects or refuses to hear it read, and, in either case, by delivering him personally a copy of the notice, or if he refuses to receive it, offering to deliver it;

2. If not found within the county of his residence, by leaving a copy of the notice at his usual place of residence with some member of the family over fourteen years of age;

3. By taking an acknowledgment of the service indorsed on the notice, dated and signed by the defendant.

Return when personally served.—Sec. 2604. If served personally, the return must state the time and manner and place of making the service, and that a copy was delivered to defendant, or offered to be delivered. If made by leaving a copy with the family, it must state at whose house the same was left, and that it was the usual place of residence of the defendant, and the township, town, or city in which the house was situated, the name of the person with whom the same was left, or a sufficient reason for omitting to do so, and that such person was over fourteen years of age, and was a member of the family.

Sheriff to note when received.—Sec. 2605. If the notice is placed in the hands of a sheriff, he must thereon note the date when received, and proceed to serve the same without delay in his county, and must file the same with his return thereon in the office of the clerk, or return the same by mail or otherwise to the party from whom he received it.

Penalty for defective return: amendment of.—Sec. 2606. If a notice be not duly filed or returned to the person from whom it was received by the sheriff, or if the return thereon is defective, the officer making the same may be fined by the court, not exceeding ten dollars, and shall also be liable to the action of any person aggrieved thereby. But the court may permit an amendment according to the truth of the case.

Noting the time.—The noting thereon the time when received by him is important, in cases where the statute of limitations may be set up as a defense to a cause of action. That statute provides, that the delivery of a notice to the sheriff of the proper county, with intent that it be immediately served, which intent shall be presumed unless the contrary appears, or the actual service by another person, is a commencement of an action. Code, Sec. 2532.

How served.—It must be served on the defendant and not on an agent, 13 Iowa, 546, by reading the same to the defendant, unless he refuses to hear it read, and by delivering to him a copy of the same, unless he refuses to receive it.

Construction of the statute.—It was held under a former but similar statute, requiring a reading of the notice to the defendant and the giving of him a copy if demanded; that a return of service, "by reading the same in the presence and hearing of the defendant," was defective, and a judgment rendered on such a return of service was reversed by the Supreme Court. But it was also held, that a service by reading in the presence and hearing of the defendant, was made good by a demand of a copy of the notice which was given the defendant. 11 Iowa, 210; 10 Iowa, 553; 4 G. Greene, 345; 6 Iowa, 78.

And in a subsequent case, where the return showed the notice was, "personally served by reading in the hearing of the defendant, and leaving a true copy with him," it was held to be a good service. 27 Iowa, 270.

Where the defendant is not found.—If the defendant cannot be found within the county of his residence, the service should be made by leaving a copy thereof at his usual place of residence with some member of the family over fourteen years of age.

The officer shall use diligence.—Diligence should be used by the officer to make personal service. He should make search and inquiry for him, and merely calling at his residence or place of business and finding him temporarily absent, would hardly justify a return that the defendant could not be found in the county, and a service by copy.

When to serve by copy.—When in the use of reasonable diligence the officer is unable to find the defendant in the county, a service by copy is required.

Where and with whom to leave the copy.—The copy should be left at the usual and not the temporary place of residence of the defendant, not at defendant's shop or store. It should be left with some member of the family over fourteen years of age. If left with the wife of defendant, the return should show that she was over fourteen years of age, and not leave it to be presumed.

If the return states, that it was left at the usual place of residence of the defendant, with his wife, a member of his family over fourteen years of age, it would be sufficient if the name of the wife should not be stated. 7 Iowa 56.

Meaning of the words "the family."—The words, "the family," in the statute mean the family of which the defendant is a member. He is not required to be the head of a family. And a return that the officer, "left a copy with Mrs. Gay, at defendant's boarding house, being the residence of E. E. Gay, the above named Mrs. Gay being over fourteen years of age, and being a member of the family of E. E. Gay," was held, "defective in not showing the house of E. E. Gay, was the usual place of residence of the defendant, and that Mrs. Gay, was a member of defendant's family."

The Court in deciding the case, say: "We do not intend to determine here, that the defendant must be the head of a family, with a member of which a copy is left; but only that they must be of the same family." 2 Iowa, 158.

A service on a widowed mother of the defendant residing with him would be good. 17 Mo., 78.

III. WHAT THE RETURN SHOULD SHOW.

The return of service may be written on the notice, and it should show the mode of service. It is not sufficient to state that it was duly served. 6 Iowa, 78.

RETURN OF PERSONAL SERVICE.

No. 57.

STATE OF IOWA, ... County, } ss.

I, A B, sheriff of said county, do hereby certify and return that I received the within, (or annexed), notice for service on the .... day of ...., 18.., and that I served the same personally on C D, the defendant therein named, on the .... day of ...., 18.., at .... in said county, by reading the same to him, (or by offering to read the same to him, he neglecting and refusing to hear the same read), and by delivering to him personally a copy of said notice, (or by offering to deliver to him personally a copy of said notice, he refusing to receive the same).

Dated this .... day of .... 18...

FEES: A.... B...., *Sheriff.*
Service $....
Mileage ....
Copy ....

Where service is made on several defendants.—If there are several defendants personally served at the same time and place, one return might be made for all, by stating the same was personally served on each of the defendants named in the notice, by reading the same to each of them, and by delivering to each of them personally a copy of the same.

If they are served at different times and places, a return of service in each case would be necessary.

ADMISSION OF SERVICE.

No. 58.

I hereby admit due service of the within notice at .... in .... county, State of.....

Dated this .... day of ...., 18...

C.... D...., *Defendant.*

Where made, and what is admission.—The admission of service should be in writing, and indorsed on the notice. A waiver of service of notice indorsed on the back of it, dated and signed by the defendant, in another State, is equivalent to an acknowledgment, and will confer jurisdiction, and it is not necessary that proof of the signature should be made. 13 Iowa, 300.

Service on a firm.—A notice in which a co-partnership is made defendant, should be served on one of the partners, and the return need not show that it was served on the member engaged in the general management of the business. 8 Iowa, 474, 516; 10 Iowa, 445. A service on one member of the firm, in an action against the firm, on a note signed in the firm name, gives the court jurisdiction over all the members of the firm; and if service is made on one, after a dissolution of the firm, it would warrant a judgment against the firm to be satisfied out of the firm property, or the separate property of the party served with notice. 18 Iowa, 19; 10 Iowa, 70. One defendant cannot have a judgment reversed for insufficiency of service upon a co-defendant, who does not complain. 13 Iowa, 304.

Service where a county is defendant.—If a county is defendant, service should be made on the chairman of the board of supervisors, or on the county auditor. Code, Sec. 2610.

RETURN OF SERVICE ON A FIRM.

No. 59.

STATE OF IOWA, } ss.
......County, }

I, A B, sheriff of said county, hereby certify and return, that I received the within original notice for service on the....day of ....18..., and that I served the same on the defendant, C D & Co., therein named, at ..., in said county, by reading the same to C D, a member of said firm of C D & Co., (or by offering to read the same to him, he neglecting and refusing to hear the same read), and by delivering to him personally, a copy of said notice, (or by offering to deliver to him personally, a copy of said notice, he refusing to receive the same.)

Dated....187.... A.... B.... *Sheriff.*

FEES:
Service, $....
Mileage, ...
Copy, ...

RETURN OF SERVICE BY COPY.

No. 60.

STATE OF IOWA }
...... County. } ss.

I, A B, sheriff of said county, hereby certify and return, that I received the within original notice for service on the....day of .....18..., and that I served the same on the defendant, C D, therein named, by leaving a copy thereof at the dwelling house of the defendant, (or the residence of E F), situated in the city (or township), of...., in said county, that being the usual place of residence of said defendant, with E D, wife of the defendant, (or with Mrs. G F, wife of the said E F), she being over fourteen years of age and a member of the family; the said defendant not being found within said county.

[*Dated and signed as in No.* 59.]

RETURN WHERE A COUNTY IS DEFENDANT.

No. 61.

STATE OF IOWA, }
.... County. } ss.

I, A B, sheriff of said county, do hereby certify and return, that I received the within original notice for service on the.... day of....18..., and that I served the same on the defendant therein named by reading the same to C D, chairman of the board of supervisors of said county, (or E F, auditor of said county), at...., in said county, on the....day ...of.....18.., and by then and there delivering to him personally a copy of said notice. Dated....18....

A.... B...., *Sheriff.*

IV. SERVICE ON CORPORATIONS.

The Code provides for the service of the original notice on private and public corporations, as follows:

How served on railway corporations.—SECTION 2611. If the action is against any corporation, or person owning or operating any railway, telegraph line, canal, stages, coaches, or cars, or any express company, service may be made upon any general agent of such corporation, or person, wherever found, or upon any station, ticket, or other agent of such corporation, or person transacting the business thereof in the county where the suit is brought; if there is no such agent in said county, then service may be had upon an agent thereof transacting said business in any other county.

On municipal.—SEC. 2612. When the action is against a municipal corporation, service may be made on the mayor or clerk, and if against any other corporation, or any trustee or officer thereof, or on any agent employed in general management of its business, or on any of the last known or acting officers of said corporation, and if no person can be found on whom service can be made as provided in this and the preceding section, service may be made by publication as provided in other cases.

Agents: service on.—SEC. 2613. When a corporation, company, or individual, has, for the transaction of any business, an office or agency in any county other than that in which the principal resides, service may be made on any agent or clerk employed in such office or agency, in all actions growing out of or connected with the business of that office or agency.

Service on a R. R. corporation.—In an action against a railroad corporation, service cannot properly be made on a baggage-master or track-master, in the service of such corporation. He would not be such an agent as the law contemplates; and a return of service upon an agent merely, would not be sufficient; but the return of service should show a service on a general agent or the particular agents named in the statute. 8 How. Prac. R., 308. 13 Iowa, 546; 8 Iowa, 260.

RETURN OF SERVICE ON R. R. CORPORATION.

No. 62.

STATE OF IOWA, }
......County, } ss.

I, A B, sheriff of said county, hereby certify and return, that I received the within original notice for service on the....day of ....18..., and that on the....day of ...18..., at...., in said county, I served the same on the defendant therein named, by reading the same to C D, the general agent of said defendant, (or the station or ticket agent of said defendant, or the person transacting the business of the defendant in said county, or the agent of said defendant transacting business in another county and having no agent in said county where suit is brought), and by delivering to him personally a copy of said notice.

Dated....18... A.... B...., *Sheriff.*

RETURN OF SERVICE ON MUNICIPAL CORPORATION.

No. 63.

STATE OF IOWA, }
......County, } ss.

I, A B, sheriff of said county, hereby certify and return, that

I received the within original notice for service on the ...day of ....18..., and served the same on the defendant therein named, at...., in said county, on the....day of....18..., by then and there reading the same to C D, mayor of said city, the defendant therein named, (or on the clerk of said city or town, defendant therein named), and by then and there delivering to him personally, a copy of said notice.

Dated....18... A.... B...., *Sheriff.*

V. SERVICE ON MINORS, PRISONERS AND INSANE PERSONS.

The following provisions of the Code, direct the mode of service on minors, prisoners and insane persons:

Minors: how served.—SECTION 2614. When the defendant is a minor under the age of fourteen years, the service must be made on him, and also on his father, or mother, or guardian, and if there be none of these within the state, then on the person within this state having the care and control of such minor, or with whom he shall reside, or in whose service he shall be employed. When the minor is over fourteen years of age, service on him shall be sufficient.

Insane.—SEC. 2615. When a defendant has been judicially declared to be of unsound mind, or who is confined in any state lunatic asylum, service may be made upon him and upon his guardian, and if he have no guardian, then upon his wife or the person having the care of him, or with whom he lives, or the keeper of the asylum in which he may be confined.

When confined in state lunatic asylum.—SEC. 2616. When it becomes necessary to serve personally with a notice or process of any kind, a person who is confined in any state lunatic asylum, the superintendent thereof shall acknowledge service of the same for such person, whenever, in the opinion of such superintendent, personal service would injuriously affect such person, which fact shall be stated in the acknowledgment of service. A service thus made shall be deemed a personal one on the defendant.

Prisoner in penitentiary.—SEC. 2617. When the defendant is a prisoner in the penitentiary, a copy of the petition must be delivered to the prisoner at the time the notice is served, and a copy of the notice must be delivered to the husband or wife of the defendant, if any such there be within this state.

Infants: decision relating to.—The court has no jurisdiction to make any order prejudicing an infant, not even to appoint a guardian *ad litem*, until there has been a complete legal service of process upon him; and any order therefor made in an action against an infant, who has not been legally served with notice, will be absolutely null and void; and the return must show that neither father nor mother are living within the State, to authorize a service on the person having the care and control of the minor. 14 Iowa, 435.

RETURN OF SERVICE ON A MINOR.

No. 64.

STATE OF IOWA, }
........County, } ss.

I, A B, sheriff of said county, hereby certify and return that I received the within original notice for service on the .... day of ...., 18.., and served the same on C D, defendant therein named on the .... day of ...., 18.., at .... in said county, by reading the same to him, and also by then and there reading the same to E F, the father (or mother or guardian of the defendant), of the said defendant, said defendant being under the age of fourteen years, and by then and there delivering to each of them personally a copy of said notice.

Dated ...., 18... A.... B...., *Sheriff.*

RETURN WHERE DEFENDANT IS OF UNSOUND MIND OR INSANE.

No. 65.

STATE OF IOWA, }
.... County. } ss.

I, A B, sheriff of said county, hereby certify and return, that I received the within original notice for service on the ... day of ...., 18.., and that on the ....day of ...., 18.., I served the same personally on C D, the defendant therein named, at ...., in said county, by then and there reading the same to him, and by delivering to him personally a copy of the same; and that on the .... day of ...., 18.., I served the same personally on E D, the wife of the said C D, (or the keeper of the asylum where the defendant is confined), at ...., in ... county, by then and there reading the same to her and delivering to her personally a copy of the same, said defendant having been judicially declared to be of unsound mind, and having no guardian, (or, being confined in the State lunatic asylum at ...., in said State.)

Dated ...., 18...

A.... B...., *Sheriff.*

Where the superintendent of an asylum acknowledges service.—Where the superintendent of a State lunatic asylum acknowledges service under the provisions of section 2615, it would still be necessary, I apprehend, to serve the same on the guardian, or wife of the defendant, as provided by section 2614.

RETURN, WHERE SERVICE CANNOT BE MADE.

No. 66.

STATE OF IOWA, }
.... County. } ss.

I, A B, sheriff of said county, hereby certify and return, that

I received the within original notice for service on the .. day of ...., 18.., and that the defendant therein named cannot be found in said county, and that he has no dwelling house or usual place of residence in said county.

Dated this .... day of ...., 18..

A.... B...., *Sheriff.*

Service on Sunday.—The general rule of law is, that civil process cannot be served on Sunday, but when the plaintiff, his agent, or attorney, makes oath on the original notice, that personal service will not be possible, unless then made, the officer is required to serve the same on Sunday, as on a secular day. Code, Sec. 2607.

The forms of return of service above given can be varied to meet the case where the name of the party with whom the copy is left is not known, and cannot be ascertained, and also where service is by deputy; in which case the return should be the same, with the signature of the sheriff, but to which should be added, "by C D, his deputy."

V. THE EFFECT OF THE RETURN.

Provisions of the statutes.—The Code provides, that if service is made within the State, the truth is proven by the signature of the sheriff or his deputy, and the court shall take judicial notice thereof.

Return of "not found."—And where the sheriff returns "not found," it raises sufficient presumption that the defendant was not found within his bailiwick, to sustain a service made by leaving a copy, and where the notice was directed to Luther Burt, and served on L. Burt, it was held that the court might infer that it was served on the right person. 12 Iowa, 428; 7 Iowa, 56.

In case of admission.—If the defendant admits service in writing, this is good, even though made in another State, and the signature need not be proved. 13 Iowa, 300.

The return as evidence.—The matters set forth in the return of the sheriff, are presumed to be true; such as, that the defendant cannot be found, or has no dwelling house, or usual place of residence in the county, or that the defendant is a minor, or has been judicially declared of unsound mind, or insane, or in the insane asylum of the State, or penitentiary of the State, or that the person on whom service is made, is a guardian, or wife, or father or mother of the defendant.

The return is competent evidence of these facts, and it is questioned if they can be contradicted by parol evidence. 11 Iowa, 387; 19 Iowa, 248; 3 G. Greene, 387; 4 G. Greene, 468.

CHAPTER XI.

PROCESS OF ATTACHMENT.

I. THE SHERIFF'S DUTY RELATING TO SERVICE.

The duty of the sheriff on receiving an attachment for service is pointed out by the Code, as follows:

Property attached: officer's duty.—SECTION 2964. The sheriff shall in all cases attach the amount of property directed if sufficient, not exempt from execution, found in his county, giving that in which the defendant has a legal and unquestionable title a preference over that in which his title is doubtful or only equitable.

SEC. 2965. Where there are several attachments against the same defendant, they shall be executed in the order in which they were received by the sheriff.

May follow to another county: when.—SEC. 2966. If, after an attachment has been placed in the hands of the sheriff, any property of the defendant is moved from the county, the sheriff may pursue and attach the same in an adjoining county within twenty-four hours after removal.

What may be attached, and how done.—SEC. 2967. Stock or interest owned by the defendant in any company, and also debts due him, or property of his held by third persons, may be attached, and the mode of attachment must be as follows:

1. By giving the defendant in the action, if found within the county, and also the person occupying or in possession of the property, if it be in the hands of a third person, notice of attachment;

2. If the property is capable of manual delivery, the sheriff must take it into custody if it can be found;

3. Stock in a company is attached by notifying the president or other head of the company, or the secretary, cashier, or other managing agent thereof, of the fact that the stock has been so attached,

4. Debts due the defendant, or property of his held by third persons, and which cannot be found, or the title to which is doubtful, or attached by garnishment thereof.

Defendant examined on oath before judge.—SEC. 2968. Whenever it appears by the affidavit of the plaintiff, or by the return of the attachment, that no property is known to the plaintiff or the officer on which the attachment can be executed, or not enough to satisfy the plaintiff's claim, and, it being shown to the judge of any court by affidavit, that the defendant has property within the state not exempt, the defendant may be required by such judge to attend before him, or before the court in which the action is pending, and give information on oath respecting his property.

When property bound.—SEC. 2969. Property attached otherwise than by garnishment, is bound thereby from the time of the service of the attachment only.

Receiver appointed: when and how.—SEC. 2970. The court before whom the action is pending, or the judge thereof in vacation, may, at any time, appoint a receiver to take possession of property attached under the provisions of this chapter, and to collect, manage, and control the same, and pay over the proceeds according to the nature of the property and the exigency of the case.

Money attached to be paid clerk.—SEC. 2971. All money attached by the sheriff, or coming into his hands by virtue of the attachment, shall forthwith be paid over to the clerk to be by him retained till the further action of the court.

Other property.—SEC. 2972. The sheriff shall make such disposition of other attached property as may be directed by the court or judge, and where there is no direction upon the subject he shall safely keep the property subject to the order of the court.

Partnership property.—SEC. 2973. In executing an attachment against a person who owns property jointly or in common with another, or who is a member of a partnership, the officer may take possession of such property so owned jointly, in common, or in partnership, sufficiently to enable him to inventory and appraise the same, and for that purpose shall call to his assistance three disinterested persons; which inventory and appraisement shall be returned by the officer with the attachment, and such return shall state who claims to own such property.

Specific attachments.—The Code provides for specific attachments, to enforce a mortgage of or a lien upon personal property, or for the recovery, sale or partition of such property, where it appears that the plaintiff has a just claim, and that the property is about to be sold, concealed, or removed from the State, and by a vendor of property fraudulently purchased, to secure the same. Code, Secs. 3000, 3001.

The Code further provides in such cases, that the attachment shall have indorsed upon it the direction of the judge as to the disposition to be made of the attached property, and that it shall be directed, executed and returned as other attachments. Code, Secs. 3003, 3004.

Indebtedness due the State.—The Code provides for attachments in case a person is indebted to the State, and the sheriff's duty in such a case, as follows:

No bonds can be required.—SECTION 3007. The attachment so issued shall be levied as in other cases of attachment, and no bond shall be required of the plaintiff in such cases, and the sheriff shall not be authorized to require any indemnifying bond before levying the same.

Property released: how.—SEC. 3008. Any property taken on attachment under the provisions of the two preceding sections, shall be subject to be released upon the execution of a delivery bond, with sufficient security as provided by law in other cases.

Damages paid by sheriff: a debt against the State.—SEC. 3009. In case any sheriff shall be held liable to pay any damages by reason of the wrongful execution of any writ of attachment issued under the three preceding sections, and if a judgment be rendered therefor by any court of competent jurisdiction, the amount of such judgment when paid by such sheriff shall become a claim against the state of Iowa in favor of such sheriff, and a warrant therefor shall be drawn by the auditor upon proper proof.

II. PROVISIONS OF THE CODE ON RETURN.

The following provisions relate to the return, and other proceedings:

Sheriff's return: contents.—SECTION 3010. The sheriff shall return upon every attachment what he has done under it. The return must show the property attached, the time it was attached, and the disposition made of it, by a full and particular inventory; also the appraisement above contemplated, when such has been made. When garnishees are summoned, their names, and the time each was summoned, must be stated. And where real property is attached, the sheriff shall describe it with certainty to identify it, and where he can do so, by reference to the book and page where the deed under which the defendant holds is recorded. He shall return with the writ all bonds taken under it. Such return must be made immediately after he shall have attached sufficient property, or all that he can find; or, at latest, on the first day of the first term on which the defendant is notified to appear.

III. JUDGMENT—APPLICATION OF PROPERTY—INTERVENTION, ETC.

The Code provides:—

Judgment: how satisfied.—SECTION 3011. If judgment is rendered for the plaintiff in any case in which an attachment has been issued, the court shall apply in satisfaction thereof, the money arising from the sales of perishable property, and if the same is not sufficient to satisfy the plaintiff's claim, the court shall order a sale by the sheriff of any other attached property which may be under his control.

Court may control property.—SEC. 3012. The court may, from time to time, make and enforce proper orders respecting the property, sales, and the application of the moneys collected.

Expenses for keeping.—SEC. 3013. The sheriff shall be allowed by the court the necessary expenses of keeping the attached property, to be paid by the plaintiff and taxed in the costs.

Surplus.—SEC. 3014. Any surplus of the attached property and its proceeds shall be returned to the defendant.

Discharge of property.—SEC. 3015. If judgment is rendered in the action for the defendant, the attachment shall be discharged, and the property attached, or its proceeds, shall be returned to him.

Intervention: how made and tried.—SEC. 3016. Any person other than the defendant may, before the sale of any attached property, or before the payment to the plaintiff of the proceeds thereof or any attached debt, present his petition, verified by oath, to the court, disputing the validity of the attachment, or stating a claim to the property or money, or to an interest in, or lien on it under any other attachment or otherwise, and setting forth the facts upon which such claim is founded; and the petitioner's claim shall be in a summary manner investigated. The court may hear the proof or order a reference, or may empanel a jury to inquire into the facts. If it is found that the petitioner has title to, a lien on, or any interest in such property, the court shall make such order as may be necessary to protect his rights. The costs of such proceeding shall be paid by either party at the discretion of the court.

IV. THE WRIT—WHAT IT SHOULD CONTAIN.

The writ should direct the officer to attach the property of the defendant, if sufficient can be found not exempt from execution, to satisfy the claim of plaintiff, the amount of which should be stated in the writ, as a guide to the sheriff, in attaching the requisite amount, which should be fifty per cent. greater than that amount. Code, Sec. 2954. The causes for the issuance of the attachment need not be recited in the writ. 13 Iowa, 576.

V. OF THE SERVICE, ETC.

It is the duty of the officer, on receiving the writ for service, to indorse thereon the time of receiving it, and proceed without unnecessary delay to serve the same.

Writ presumed regular: when.—The writ, if regular on its face, is his sufficient justification for serving the same, and the officer need not stop to inquire whether the proceedings have been authorized or are lawful, or whether there was a sufficient bond or cause of action. 11 Iowa, 387.

He should be diligent.—In seeking property of the defendant not exempt from execution, the officer must be diligent.

He should levy fifty per cent. more.—The statute directs the sheriff to levy fifty per cent. greater in value than the amount claimed by plaintiff; and he is required to attach that amount of property not exempt from execution, if found in his county, giving that in which the defendant has a legal and unquestionable title a preference over that in which his title is doubtful or only equitable. Code, Secs. 2954, 2964.

Not to levy on property exempt.—Under a general writ of attachment the officer should have a care not to attach property exempt from execution. But under a special attachment, as we shall hereafter notice, the officer may attach the property directed to be attached by the order of the judge indorsed thereon.

Bond no protection.—The bond given on suing out the attachment is no protection to the officer who levies on exempt property, or on property which does not belong to the defendant, even though directed so to do by the plaintiff. He acts in these respects at his peril, and is liable to the owner in trespass or replevin. 12 Iowa, 605.

And the attachment, or any part thereof, may be discharged on motion, where it is made to appear that the attachment should not have been levied on all or some of the property held, but the case should be clear and satisfactory. Code, Sec. 3018; 26 Iowa, 297; 9 Iowa, 140.

Intervention by third parties.—Any person other than the defendant may by intervention in the attachment suit, claim the money or property, or an interest in, or lien on the property attached, and on investigation, the court may make such order as may be necessary to protect his rights. Code, Sec. 3016.

What constitutes a valid levy.—To constitute a valid levy on personal property, the officer should be in view, and take actual possession of the property.

Where levy valid, not necessary to remove the property.—But it is not necessary where there has been a valid levy, that he should remove the property from the possession of the defendant. The levy in such a case, would be good as against the defendant, and all those having notice of the levy. 15 Iowa, 104. To constitute a levy, the officer should do that which would render him liable as a trespasser in the absence of the writ. 25 Iowa, 464; 3 Wend., 446; 14 Wend., 123. He should do that which would amount to a change of possession, or something that would amount to a claim of dominion, coupled with a power to exercise it, and make a complete inventory of it. 23 Iowa, 453.

Property must be in view, or in possession.—It is not sufficient to make a levy on a part of the property, and inventory other property not in view, or in possession of, or under the control of the officer. Such a levy is not sufficient on the property not in view of, or in possession of, the officer as against a subsequent attaching creditor, or purchaser in good faith without notice, although the property be entered on the inventory by the assent of the defendant. 19 Wend., 495.

Nor is it sufficient for an officer to seize a few articles outside a store or warehouse, and proclaim a levy on goods locked up in the store or warehouse. He should, if necessary, break open the store or warehouse, and actually seize and possess the goods, and make an inventory thereof. 16 John., 287.

Not necessary to touch or handle the property.—But it is not necessary to a valid levy that the officer should have actually touched and handled the property, or that he should have counted the hogs or cattle levied upon, if he could, and did, otherwise ascertain their number. If he actually saw the property levied upon, and had it in his possession, and under his control, and declared that he levied upon it, and placed it under the control of a person to hold for him, and if by himself or said person he had such possession and control over the property, that it could not well be taken from him, by the defendant in the suit without the knowledge of the sheriff or his agent, or by an officer with another writ, without their knowing it, this would be a sufficient levy. 11 Iowa, 387.

What is not a valid levy.—A valid levy under an execution, or attachment, cannot be made on property the possession of which has been obtained by means of fraud or violence, or an abuse of official authority, and it is error to refuse a motion to set aside an attachment on that ground.

Officer may break open building.—The officer, for the purpose of serving an attachment or execution, may, if necessary, break open buildings, having first demanded entrance.

He would be justifiable in so doing in case admission was refused, or in case there was no proper person at hand from whom to make a demand; provided property on which to levy, is found within; otherwise, and especially in cases where other parties were interested, he would be liable as a trespasser. 16 John., 287.

Not authorized to break open a dwelling house.—No officer, for the purpose of serving an attachment or execution, is authorized to break open or enter, without permission, the dwelling house of another to make a levy; for the law considers the home of a person and his family, too private and sacred to permit the unwelcome intrusion of any one, except to search for property under a search warrant, or to make arrests of parties charged with crimes, which we shall hereafter consider.

The attachment would be no justification to the officer in such a case, and a levy made by such means would be void.

May enter by permission.—The officer may enter a dwelling house of a defendant with his permission, or that of his family in his absence, and when a lawful entrance is once effected he may make a valid levy upon property within; and even break open the doors of rooms within the house, if necessary, to effect this purpose after requesting that they be opened.

Where there are several attachments.—If there are several attachments against the same defendants, in the hands of the officer, they should be executed by him in the order in which they were received by him; and if after an attachment is placed in his hands for service, any property of the defendant is moved from the county, he may pursue and attach the same in an adjoining county within twenty-four hours after the removal. Code, Secs. 2965, 2966.

No appraisement.—No appraisement of the property is necessary, except in certain cases which we shall hereafter notice. 9 Iowa, 376.

Special property in the officer.—By the levy, the officer acquires a especial property in the goods attached, and may maintain trespass or replevin for the same, against any person taking them from him; and if left with a third party as bailee, or receptor, or for safe keeping, such custody is deemed that of the officer, and replevin may be brought therefor; or if the same is stolen, they may be charged in the indictment as the property of the officer. 17 John., 128; 15 Iowa, 47; 10 Wend., 165; 7 Cow., 297; 8 Cow., 137.

Mode of levying on real estate.—The mode of levying upon real estate is to indorse a description of the land upon the writ, and also to enter the same in the "Incumbrance Book" required to be kept by the clerk, with the statement that the same has been attached, and stating the cause in which the same has been attached, and when it was done, which statement should be signed by the sheriff. No attachment of real property is notice to a subsequent vendee or incumbrancer in good faith, until this is done. Code, Sec. 3022.

Money attached.—Money attached by an officer, or coming into his hands by virtue of an attachment, should be forthwith paid over to the clerk, and the officer should make such disposition of other property as may be directed by the court or judge; and where there is no direction on the subject he should safely keep the property subject to the order of the court. Code, Secs. 2971, 2972.

Expenses incurred.—The keeping of attached property will sometimes involve the care and feeding of live stock, and for necessary expenses incurred thereby, or the keeping of attached property, the sheriff is entitled to remuneration, which should be paid in the first instance by the plaintiff, and the amount should be returned by the sheriff and entered up as costs in the case. Code, Sec. 3013.

VI. OF GARNISHMENT, AND PROCEEDINGS UNDER THE CODE THEREIN.

How effected.—SECTION 2975. The attachment by garnishment is effected by informing the supposed debtor or person holding the property, that he is attached as garnishee, and by leaving with him a written notice to the effect that he is required not to pay any debt due by him to the defendant, or thereafter to become due, and that he must retain possession of all property of the said defendant then or thereafter being in his custody, or under his control, in order that the same may be dealt with according to law, and the sheriff shall summon such persons as garnishees as the plaintiff may direct.

SEC. 2976. A sheriff or constable may be garnished for money of the defendant in his hands. So may a judgment-debtor of the defendant, when the judgment has not been previously assigned on the record, or by writing filed in the office of the clerk, and by him minuted as an assignment on the margin of the judgment docket, and also an executor for money due from the decedent to the defendant may be garnished, but a municipal or political corporation shall not be garnished.

SEC. 2977. Where the property to be attached is a fund in court, the execution of the writ of attachment shall be by leaving with the clerk of the court a copy thereof, with notice specifying the fund.

SEC. 2978. If the garnishee die after he has been summoned by garnishment, and pending the litigation, the proceedings may be revived by or against his heirs or legal representatives.

SEC. 2979. Unless exempted, as provided in the next section, the notice must also require the garnishee to appear on the first day of the next term of the court, wherein the main cause is depending, or on the day fixed for trial if in a justice's court, and answer such interrogatories as may be then propounded to him, or that he will be liable to pay the entire judgment which the plaintiff eventually obtains against the defendant.

SEC. 2980. When the plaintiff, in writing, directs the sheriff to take the answer of the garnishee, the sheriff shall put to the garnishee the following questions:

1. Are you in any manner indebted to the defendant in this suit, or do you owe him money or property, which is not yet due? If so, state the particulars.
2. Have you in your possession, or under your control, any property, rights, or credits of the said defendant? If so, what is the value of the same, and state all particulars.
3. Do you know of any debts owing to said defendant, whether due or not due, or any property, rights, or credits belonging to him and now in the possession or under the control of others? If so, state the particulars, and append the examination to his return.

SEC. 2981. If the garnishee refuses to answer fully and unequivocally all the foregoing interrogatories, he shall be notified and required to appear and answer on the first day of the next term of court, or on the day fixed for trial, as above provided, and so he may be required in any event, if the plaintiff so notify him.

SEC. 2982. The questions propounded to the garnishee in court, may be such as are above prescribed, to be asked by the sheriff, and such others as the court may think proper and right.

SEC. 2983. Where the garnishee is required to appear at court, unlesss he has refused to answer, as contemplated above, he is entitled to the pay and mileage of an ordinary witness, and may, in like manner, require payment beforehand, in order to be made liable for non-attendance.

NOTICE OF GARNISHMENT.

No. 67.

In the .... Court of the State of Iowa, in and for .... county.

C.... D...., *Plaintiff*,
v.
E.... F...., *Defendant.*

To G.... H....

You are hereby notified that you are attached as garnishee in the above entitled action; and you are hereby required not to pay any debt due by you to the defendant herein, or hereafter to become due, and that you must retain possession of all property of the said defendant, now or hereafter being in your custody, or under you control, in order that the same may be dealt with according to law.

And you are hereby further required to be and appear at the said court on the first day thereof, which will commence on the .... day of ...., A. D. 18.., and answer such interrogatories as may then be propounded to you, or you will be liable to pay the entire judgment which the plaintiff may eventually obtain against the defendant..

Dated, ..., A. D. 18...

A.... B...., *Sheriff of .... county.*

Answers taken by the sheriff.—The plaintiff may direct the answer of garnishee to be taken by the sheriff, which direction should be in writing.

DIRECTION TO SHERIFF.

No. 68.

In the .... Court of the State of Iowa, in and for.... county.

C.... D...., *Plaintiff*,
v.
E.... F...., *Defendant.*

To the sheriff of said county:

You are hereby directed to garnishee G H, on the attachment issued in the above entitled cause, and take his answers thereon as provided by law.

C.... D...., *Plaintiff*,
By I.... J...., *his attorney.*

QUESTIONS PROVIDED BY STATUTE.

No. 69.

First—Are you in any manner indebted to the defendant in this suit, or do you owe money or property which is not yet due? If so, state the particulars.

Second—Have you in your possession, or under your control any property, rights, or credits of the said defendant? If so, what is the value of the same, and state all the particulars.

Third—Do you know of any debts owing to the said defendant, whether due or not, or any property, rights, or credits belonging to, and now in the possession or under the control of others? If so, state the particulars.

You do solemnly swear that you have made full and true answers to the above questions, touching the matter wherein you have been attached as garnishee, so help .... God.

Subscribed and sworn to before me this .... day of ...., A. D. 18...

...., *Sheriff of .... county.*

Where the plaintiff desires the garnishee to appear.—If the plaintiff in addition to the answers to the officer, desires the garnishee to appear at court on the first day thereof, as provided by the statute, he may add to the notice to the sheriff the following: "And you are required to notify him to appear and answer on the first day of the next term of said court."

Municipal corporations.—The statute provides that municipal corporations shall not be garnished; but they may waive their statutory rights. 5 Iowa, 285; 25 Iowa, 315; 22 Iowa, 261.

Exemptions and limitations.—It will be a matter of interest to officers charged with the service of attachments, as well as of executions, to observe the exemption laws, which provide that the earnings of a debtor for his personal services, or those of his family at any time within ninety days, next preceding the levy, shall be exempt from levy, and also the provision limiting exemptions, where a debtor has started to leave the State. Code, Secs. 3074, 3076.

The provisions of the Code relating to exemptions, may be found in Chapter Six on the process of execution.

Cannot garnish without a writ.—A sheriff without a writ of attachment or execution, (which we shall hereafter consider), is not authorized to notify a party as garnishee, nor take his answers as such, and a judgment rendered against a garnishee under such circumstances and without an appearance on his part, would be erroneous. 8 Iowa, 251.

Answer of garnishee: how made.—The answer of the garnishee need not be made categorically to the questions laid down in the statute, but he may state facts and circumstances, and leave the question of liability to the court. 1 Iowa, 460; 3 Iowa, 325.

Garnishment of a firm: how served.—A garnishment of a firm should be served on a member of the firm the same as an original notice, but the answer of one member of the firm, on a notice directed to him, will not bind the firm. 10 Iowa, 498.

Mortgaged personal property not subject to levy.—Personal property mortgaged, cannot be levied on, but the mortgagee may be garnished and required to reveal the amount of his claim unpaid, the amount and value of the mortgaged property he holds as security for the same, and he should be held responsible from the time of garnishment for the surplus of any property mortgaged, over and above the payment of his own claim. 9 Iowa, 407; 11 Iowa, 435.

VII. RELEASE OF ATTACHED PROPERTY.

The sections of the Code relating to the release of attached property are as follows:

By defendant executing a bond.—SECTION 2994. If the defendant, at any time before judgment, causes a bond to be executed to the plaintiff with sufficient securities to be approved by the officer having the attachment, or, after the return thereof by the clerk, to the effect that he will perform the judgment of the court, the attachment shall be discharged and restitution made of property taken or proceeds thereof. The execution of such bond shall be deemed an appearance of such defendant to the action.

Judgment on bond.—SEC. 2995. Such bond shall be part of the record, and, if judgment go against the defendant, the same shall be entered against him and sureties.

By defendant or person in possession giving bond.—SEC. 2996. The defendant, or any person in whose possession any attached property is found, or any person making affidavit that he has an interest in it, may, at any time before judgment, discharge the property attached, or any part thereof, by giving bond with security, to be approved by the sheriff, in a penalty at least double the value of the property sought to be released, but if that sum would exceed three times the claim, then in such sum as equals three times the claim, conditioned that such property, or its estimated value, shall be delivered to the sheriff to satisfy any judgment which may be obtained against the defendant in that suit within twenty days after the rendition thereof. This bond shall be filed with the clerk of the court.

Appraisement of property.—SEC. 2997. To determine the value of property in cases where a bond is to be given, unless the parties agree otherwise, the sheriff shall summon two disinterested persons having the qualification of jurors, who, after having been sworn by him to make the appraisement faithfully and impartially, shall proceed to the discharge of their duty. If such persons disagree as to the value of the property, the sheriff shall decide between them.

Defense to action on bond.—SEC. 2998. In an action brought upon the bond above contemplated, it shall be a sufficient defense that the property for the delivery of which the bond was given, did not, at the time of the levy, belong to the defendant against whom the attachment was issued, or was exempt from seizure under such attachment.

Delivery Bond: its effect.—An informal delivery bond, though defective as a statutory bond, will hold the parties thereto liable, if it is valid as a common law obligation; and to entitle the plaintiff to recover, it is not necessary for the court to order a sale of the attached property; the execution of the bond takes the property from the custody of the law. 23 Iowa, 21.

Bond takes the place of the attachment lien.—The delivery bond in the form prescribed by law, is a new security and takes the place of the attachment lien, releasing the property from the custody of the law, and leaving it in the possession of the debtor or his personal representatives, free from the attachment. 10 Iowa, 302; 12 Iowa, 22.

To release property in hands of garnishee.—It may be given for the release of property in the hands of garnishees as well as for property actually taken into the possession of the officer.

To be given to the plaintiff.—The bond should be given to the plaintiff; but if made to the sheriff, the plaintiff can sue and recover upon it without an assignment of it to him by the sheriff; and in an action on the bond, it is not necessary to aver and prove an appraisement of the property levied on, or garnished. 9 Iowa, 474; 12 Iowa, 570.

DELIVERY BOND.

No. 70.

Know all men by these presents:

That we, A B, principal, and C D, security, are held and firmly bound unto E F, in the sum of....dollars [here insert a sum equal to double the amount claimed by plaintiff], for the payment of which well and truly to be made, we bind ourselves firmly by these presents. The condition of this obligation is such, that whereas, G H, sheriff of....county, Iowa, by virtue of a writ of attachment to him directed, issued out of the office of the clerk of the....Court of said State, within and for....county, in an action wherein A B is plaintiff, and E F is defendant, did, on the...day of...18..., attach and levy upon the following described property, to-wit: [Here insert a description of the property levied upon.] And whereas, the said E F desires to have said levy discharged, and to obtain a restitution of said property: Now, therefore, if the said E F shall in all things well and truly perform any judgment of said court which may be rendered against him in said action, then this obligation to be void, otherwise to remain in full force and virtue.

Witness our hands and seals, this....day of....18...

A.... B....
C.... D....

The sheriff should indorse an approval of the bond thereon, as follows:

APPROVAL OF BOND.

No. 71.

I hereby approve the within bond and surety therein.
Dated....18... A.... B...., *Sheriff.*

Delivery Bond on claim of property.—The delivery bond required under section 2996, of the Code on a claim of the property, may be as follows:

DELIVERY BOND.

No. 72.

Know all men by these presents:

That we, A B, principal, and C D, surety, are held and firmly bound unto E F, in the sum of....dollars [here insert double the value of the property to be released, unless that sum would exceed three times the amount of the claim, in which case insert three times the amount of the claim], for the payment of which well and truly to be made, we bind ourselves firmly by these presents.

The condition of this obligation is such, that whereas....sheriff of....county, Iowa, by virtue of a writ of attachment to him directed, and issued out of the office of the clerk of the....Court of said State, within and for said county, in an action wherein said E F is plaintiff, and G H is defendant, did, on the....day of ....18.., attach and levy upon the following described property, to-wit: [Here describe the property.] And of the estimated value of $....; and whereas said A B, the person in whose possession said attached property was found (or the person who has made an affidavit that he has an interest in said property), desires to have said property discharged from said attachment and levy:

Now therefore, if the said A B, shall deliver said property or its estimated value as aforesaid to said sheriff, to satisfy any judgment that may be rendered against said defendant in said suit, within twenty days after the rendition thereof, then this obligation to be void, otherwise to remain in full force and virtue.

Witness our hands this .... day of ...., 18..
A.... B...., *Principal.*
C.... D...., *Surety.*

Approval of the bond.—The bond should be approved like the foregoing one, and be returned to, and filed with, the clerk of the court.

Value of the property: how determined.—To determine the value of the property as contemplated in the above bond, unless the parties can otherwise agree, the sheriff should summon two disinterested persons, having the qualification of jurors who being duly sworn by the sheriff to faithfully and impartially appraise the property, shall proceed to appraise the same, and if they cannot agree as to the value, the sheriff shall decide between them.

If a summons is required, it may be served the same as an original notice, and in the following form:

SUMMONS TO APPRAISERS.

No. 73.

STATE OF IOWA, }
......County, } ss.

To B C, and D E.

In the name of theState of Iowa: You, and each of you, are hereby summoned and required to be and appear forthwith, [or at such time as may be required,] at the ...., [naming the house or place], in the city [or town or township] of ...., to examine and appraise the value of certain personal property attached, and now held by me the undersigned sheriff of .... county, by virtue of a writ of attachment issued by the clerk of the .... Court of said county, in a certain action wherein A B, is plaintiff, and C D, is defendant. And hereof fail not at your peril.

Dated .... 18..

A.... B...., *Sheriff of .... county, Iowa.*

OATH TO APPRAISERS.

No. 74.

THE STATE OF...... }
........County, } ss.

We B C and D E, of said county, do each solemnly swear that we will faithfully and impartially appraise the certain personal property attached by A B, sheriff of said county, by virtue of a certain writ of attachment, now in the hands of said officer, and a true report make thereon, according to the best of our knowledge and ability.

B.... C ...,
D.... E.....

The foregoing oath was this....day of....18..., by me administered to, and subscribed by the said B C, and D E, and each of them.

A.... B...., *Sheriff of....county, Iowa.*

REPORT OF APPRAISERS.

No. 75.

STATE OF IOWA, }
.....County, } ss.

We, the undersigned appraisers, summoned and duly sworn as

such by the sheriff of of said county, to appraise the following described property levied upon by such sheriff by virtue of a certain writ of attachment, do find and report, that we have appraised said property, as shown by the following inventory thereof:

INVENTORY.

One two-horse carriage, appraised at	....	$175 00
One span of mules, " "	....	250.00
One gold watch, " "	....	150.00
	Total value,	$575.00

Dated....18...

FEES:—

B C, six hours, $1.50.
D E, " " 1.50.

B.... C.... }
D.... E.... } *Appraisers.*

VIII. PERISHABLE PROPERTY.

Provisions of the statute.—The Code provides for the sale of perishable property taken on attachment as follows:

How and when done.—SECTION 2999. When the sheriff thinks the property attached in danger of serious and immediate waste and decay, or when the keeping of the same will necessarily be attended with such expense as greatly to depreciate the amount of proceeds to be realized therefrom, or when the plaintiff makes affidavit to that effect, the sheriff may summon three persons having the qualification of jurors to examine the same. The sheriff shall give the defendant, if within the county three days' notice of such hearing, and he may appear before such jury and have a personal hearing. If they are of the opinion that the property requires soon to be disposed of, they shall specify in writing a day beyond which they do not deem it prudent that it should be kept in the hands of the sheriff. If such day occurs before the trial day, he shall thereupon give the same notice as for sale of goods in execution, and for the same length of time, unless the condition of the property renders a more immediate sale necessary. The sale shall be made accordingly. If the defendant gives his written consent, such sale may be made without such finding.

Summons and oath to appraisers.—The summons and oath to appraisers under the provision, may be the same with a little modification as in Nos. 73 and 74.

NOTICE TO BE SERVED ON THE DEFENDANT.

No. 76.

To G.... H....:

You are hereby notified that on the....day of....18.., at.... in the town of....., in the county of.....and State of Iowa, a jury of three persons summoned by me, will meet for the purpose of examining and deciding upon the necessity of an immedate sale of certain personal property levied upon by me, by virtue of a certain writ of attachment sued out of the office of the clerk of.... Court of said county, against your property, at the suit of K L, plaintiff, and against you, defendant, and at which time and place you can appear, if you think proper.

Dated...., 18..

A.... B...., *Sheriff of.... County, Iowa.*

REPORT OF JURY FOR A SALE.

No. 77.

STATE OF IOWA, ⎫
.... County. ⎭ ss.

We, the undersigned, jurors duly summoned and sworn by A B, sheriff of said county, to determine the necessity of an immediate sale of certain personal property, to-wit: [here describe the property] levied upon by said sheriff, by virtue of a writ of attachment in favor of L L, and against the property of G H, as is alleged, do find and report, that said property is in danger of serious and immediate waste and decay (or that the keeping of the same will necessarily be attended with such expense as greatly to depreciate the amount of proceeds to be derived therefrom), and we do not deem it prudent that it should be kept in the hands of the said sheriff beyond the.... day of.... 18..

Dated.... day of.... 18..

O.... P.... ⎫
Q.... R.... ⎬ *Jurors.*
S.... T.... ⎭

Finding against a sale.—If the jury should be of opinion that there was no danger of immediate waste or decay of the property, and that the keeping of the same would not necessarily be attended with such expense as greatly to depreciate the amount of proceeds to be realized therefrom, the jury should so find and report, and the above form can be changed to meet that case.

Judge Conklin's remarks.—Judge Conklin, in his valuable "Treatise on the Powers and Duties of Justices of the Peace," makes the following remarks relating to the jury in such cases:

"The jury should be sworn by the officer, though their oath need not be in writing. It will be sufficient if the officer returns that they were sworn.

"If all those summoned do not appear, the officer may complete the number, on the day of the hearing, from any competent persons present, or he may serve the same summons on others in the neighborhood, and require them to appear forthwith. Persons properly served and failing to obey the summons without sufficient excuse, would doubtless be guilty of contempt of the court issuing the writ, and might be cited before such court and dealt with accordingly."

Defendant entitled to a hearing.—From the provision of the Code requiring notice to the defendant, it is evident that the defendant may have a hearing before the jury, on the question presented to them, and every reasonable privilege should be extended to him by the sheriff and the jurors in examining the property, and in presenting evidence, if he so desires, bearing on the question, which might be of such a character as to require the opinion of experts.

Sheriff's duty on the finding.—If the jury find that a sale is necessary, the sheriff should proceed to sell as on execution, except where the time fixed by the jury for a sale would prevent the delay of giving the usual notice, in which case the length of notice might doubtless be made less.

If defendant consents.—In case the defendant consents in writing that the sale may take place without such finding, it may be so made.

DEFENDANT'S CONSENT TO SALE.

No. 78.

I hereby consent that a sale of the property attached by A B, sheriff of .... county, Iowa, on the within (or annexed) writ, may be made immediately, (or specify the time and manner of notice), and without the finding of a jury on the necessity of such sale.

Dated this .... day of ...., 18...

G.... H...., *Defendant.*

IX. SPECIFIC ATTACHMENTS.

The provisions of the Code in reference to specific attachments, have already been referred to. Code, Secs. 3003, 3004.

What the writ must contain.—The writ, in case of specific attachments, must describe the property to be attached, and the directions of the court or judge allowing the attachment, as to the disposition to be made of the attached property, if any, must be indorsed on the writ.

The officer should execute the same on the property, and persue the directions indorsed on the writ, as aforesaid.

If no directions are indorsed, the proceedings should be the same as in case of general attachment.

The officer would be protected in attaching the specific property in all cases, according to the requirements of the writ, even though it would otherwise be exempt from levy.

When levy invalid.—Where the officer receiving a specific attachment, not having upon it the directions of a court or judge, did not take the property into his custody, nor give notice of a levy, nor make such return as the statute requires, the levy was held invalid. 23 Iowa, 453.

XI. THE RETURN OF ATTACHMENTS.

What it should contain.—It is evident from the provisions of the statute, hereinbefore set forth, that the return should contain a complete history of the doings of the officer by virtue of the writ.

It should show how and when the levy was made, and what property was attached, and how disposed of, and an inventory of the same should be attached to the return.

In case a bond or bonds are given for a release or return of the property, these, with the proceedings on the appraisement, if any, should be returned, and where garnishments have been made, the names of the garnishees, the time when each were notified or summoned, and their answers, if any, must be returned.

Where real estate has been attached, the sheriff should describe it, and when he can do so, reference should be made to the book and page where the deed under which the defendant holds the property is recorded. Code, Sec. 3010.

SHERIFF'S RETURN TO ATTACHMENT WRIT.

No. 70.

STATE OF IOWA, } ss.
.... County. }

I, A B, sheriff of said county, hereby certify and return, that I received the within (or annexed) writ, for service on the .... day of ...., 18..; that on the .... day ...., 18.., (or on the same day,) by virtue thereof I attached, and levied upon the following described real estate of the defendant, to-wit: [Here describe the real estate;] that on the .... day of ...., 18.., by virtue of said writ I attached and levied upon the personal property described as follows: [Here describe the property accurately, and give an inventory of each article; or state that an inventory is contained in the Exhibit hereto attached and marked "Exhibit A,"] as the property of said defendant; that on the .... day of ...., 18.., by virtue of said writ, I attached as garnishee F G, by informing him that he was attached as garnishee, and by leaving with him a written notice, a copy of which is hereto attached marked "Exhibit B," and that at the request of the plaintiff made in writing, I took the answers of said garnishee as provided by law, which request and answers, are hereto attached marked "Exhibit C;" that on the .... day of ...., 18.., the defendant with O P, as surety, executed and delivered to me a bond for the release of the personal property attached and levied upon (or the garnishment, or both), as above described, which bond was duly approved by me, and is hereto attached and made a part hereof, marked "Exhibit D." [If there has been a sale of the property after the finding of a jury of the necessity therefor, or by consent of the defendant say:]

I further certify and return, that on the....day of....18.., thinking said personal property in danger of serious and immediate waste and decay, I summoned three competent persons as jurors, to determine that question, at...., on the....day of.... 18.., at...o'clock, ..M., and gave the defendant three days' notice thereof; that said persons met at the time and place last aforesaid, and were duly sworn by me as jurors aforesaid, and did then and there find and report, that said property should be disposed of, and that it would not be prudent to retain the same in my hands beyond the....day of....18..; that said summons to said persons, with their oaths, finding and report, and said notice served on the defendant, are hereto annexed, marked "Exhibit E"; that thereupon after due notice, I proceeded to sell said personal property, on the....day of....18.., and that said property on said sale brought the sum of $...., which was forthwith paid over to the clerk of the court.

I further certify, that on the....day of....18.., I gave the defendant notice of said attachments and levies, and also on the same day I gave V F, who was in possession of said personal (or real) property, notice thereof, at the time of the attachment thereof; and I now return this writ, with my doings in the premises.

Dated this....day of....18..

A ... B...., *Sheriff.*

When the return should be made.—The return should be made as soon as the officer has attached sufficient property, or all that he can find; or at least on the first day of the term at which the defendant is notified to appear.

Presumptions: evidence.—When the return states that the officer served the writ by attaching the property, describing it, it will be presumed that the property attached was the property of the debtor, and the omission to state the ownership of the property, will not affect the levy if legally made, as until the contrary appears, it will be presumed that the officer did his duty. 4 G. Greene, 468.

May amend his return.—If the officer has indorsed upon the writ a return of no property found, yet, if the defendant subsequently, and before the return of the writ, acquires property, or if further search discloses property belonging to him, it is proper for the officer to attach it; and an indorsement by the officer upon a writ, that there is no property of the defendant found within the county, does not preclude his successor, to whom the writ has been delivered, from levying the attachment upon property of the defendant, nor render his acts therein irregular. 6 Iowa, 238.

CHAPTER XII.

OF THE PROCESS OF EXECUTION.

I. ITS PURPOSE AND THE RESPONSIBILITY OF THE SHERIFF.

The execution is a process of the court issued to the proper officer for the purpose of executing the order or judgment of the court, and none of the duties of the sheriff are more responsible and intricate than those which frequently relate to the proper service of this writ.

II. STATUTORY PROVISIONS, AND HIS DUTY THEREUNDER.

The Code provides as follows:

When it may issue.—SECTION 3025. Executions may issue at any time before the judgment is barred by the statute of limitations, and but one execution shall be in existence at the same time.

Judgments: orders enforced by.—SEC. 3026. Judgments or orders requiring the payment of money, or the delivery of the possession of property are to be enforced by execution. Obedience to those requiring the performance of any other act, is to be coerced by attachment for contempt.

From courts of record.—SEC. 3027. Executions from any court of record may issue into any county which the party ordering them may direct.

When issued and served on Sunday.—SEC. 3028. An execution may be issued and executed on Sunday, whenever an affidavit shall be filed by the plaintiff or some person in his behalf, stating that he believes he will lose his judgment unless process issue on that day.

Issued on demand of party: duty of clerk.—SEC. 3029. Upon the rendition of judgment, execution may be at once issued, and shall be by the clerk on the demand of the party entitled thereto; and upon its issuance, the clerk shall enter on the judgment docket the date of its issuance, and to what county and what officer issued, and shall also enter on said docket the return of the officer with the date of the return, the dates and amount of all moneys received into or paid out of the office thereon; and these entries shall be made at the time of the thing done.

Penalty for clerk's failure of duty.—SEC. 3030. The clerk willfully neglecting or refusing to perform any one of the duties in this chapter imposed, shall be liable to a penalty of five hundred dollars, and to damages to the party aggrieved, and shall be guilty of a misdemeanor in office, and on conviction thereof, shall be removed from office.

When issued to another county what done.—SEC. 3031. In case execution is issued to a county other than that in which the judgment is rendered, a transcript of such judgment must be filed in the office of the clerk of the district court of such county, who shall make an entry thereof in the judgment docket of such court; and the officer having such execution shall return a copy thereof, with his return and doings indorsed thereon, to such clerk, who shall make entries thereof in the same manner and extent as if such judgment had been entered in and execution issued from such court.

Return: how made: money: how sent.—SEC. 3032. When sent into any county other than that in which the judgment was rendered, return may be made by mail. But money cannot thus be sent except by the direction of the party entitled thereto, or his attorney.

General form of execution.—SEC. 3033. The execution must intelligibly refer to the judgment, stating the time and place at which it was rendered, the names of the parties to the action as well as to the judgment, its amount, and the amount still to be collected thereon, if for money; and, if not for money, it must state what specific act is required to be performed. If it be against the property of the judgment debtor, it shall require the sheriff to satisfy the judgment and interest out of property of the debtor subject to execution.

When against representatives.—SEC. 3034. If it be against real or personal property in the hands of personal representatives, heirs, devisees, legatees, tenants of real property, or trustees, it shall require the sheriff to satisfy the judgment and interest out of such property.

When for delivery of possession of real property.—SEC. 3035. If it be for the delivery of the possession of real or personal property, it shall require the sheriff to deliver the possession of the same, particularly describing it, to the party entitled thereto, and may, at the same time, require the sheriff to satisfy any costs, damages, or rents and profits, with interest, recovered by the same judgment out of the property of the party against whom it was rendered subject to execution, and the value of the property for which judgment was recovered to be specified therein if a delivery thereof cannot be had, and shall in that respect be deemed an execution against property.

When for performance of any other act.—SEC. 3036. When it requires the performance of any other act, a certified copy of the judgment may be served on the person against whom it is given, or upon the person or officer who is required thereby, or by law, to obey the same, and his obedience thereto enforced.

Officer to receipt for.—SEC. 3037. Every officer to whose hands an execution may legally come shall give a receipt therefor, if required, stating the hour when the same was received, and shall make sufficient return thereof, together with the money collected, on or before the seventieth day from such delivery.

What officer must indorse.—SEC. 3038. The officer to whom an execution is legally issued, shall indorse thereon the day and hour when he received it, and the levy, sale, or other act done by virtue thereof, with the date, and the dates and amounts of any receipts or payment in satisfaction thereof; the indorsements must be made at the time of the receipt or act done.

PRINCIPAL AND SURETY.

Property of principal first liable.—SEC. 3039. When a judgment is against a principal and his surety, the officer having the collection thereof shall exhaust the property of the principal before proceeding to sell that of the surety.

Meaning of term surety.—SEC. 3040. The term "surety" in the foregoing section, shall embrace accommodation indorsers, stayers, and all other persons whose liability on the claim is posterior to that of another; but the surety shall, if requested by the officer, show property of the principal to entitle himself to the benefit of this provision.

Property of surety liable: when.—SEC. 3041. After exhausting the property of the principal, the officer shall subject the property of the other parties in the order of their liability in the execution. But the party subsequently liable, shall, if requested by the officer, show property of the party liable before him, so as to entitle himself to the benefit of this provision.

Judgment recite order of liability.—SEC. 3042. But all the parties will be considered as equally liable in all cases, unless the order of liability is shown to the court and recited in the judgment, and the clerk issuing execution on the judgment containing such recital shall state the order of liability in the execution.

LEVY.

Mode of: duty of officer.—SEC. 3043. When an execution is delivered to an officer, he must proceed to execute the same with diligence; if executed, an exact description of the property at length, with the date of the levy, shall be indorsed upon or appended to the execution, and if the writ was not executed, or only executed in part, the reason in such case must be stated in the return.

SEC. 3044. The officer must execute the writ by levying on the property of the judgment debtor, collecting the things in action by suit in his own name, if necessary, or by selling the same, selling the other property and paying to the plaintiff the proceeds, or so much thereof as will satisfy the execution.

What property he shall take.—SEC. 3045. The officer shall, in all cases, select such property, and in such quantities, as will be likely to bring the exact amount required to be raised, as nearly as practicable, and having made one levy, may, at any time thereafter, make other levies if he deem it necessary. But no writ of execution shall be a lien on personal property before the actual levy thereof.

Judgments, bank bills, things in action.—SEC. 3046. Judgments, bank bills, and other things in action, may be levied upon and sold, or appropriated as hereinafter provided, and assignment thereof by the officer shall have the same effect as if made by the defendant.

Persons indebted to defendant may pay.—SEC. 3047. After the rendition of judgment, any person indebted to the defendant in execution may pay to the sheriff the amount of such indebtedness, or so much thereof as is necessary to satisfy the execution, and the sheriff's receipt shall be a sufficient discharge therefor.

Public property not liable.—SEC. 3048. Public buildings owned by the state, or any county, city, school district, or other municipal corporation, or any other public property which is necessary and proper for carrying out the general purpose for which such corporation is organized, are exempt from execution. The property of a private citizen can in no case be levied on to pay the debt of any such.

Tax levied to pay corporate debt.—Sec. 3049. If no property of a municipal corporation against which execution has issued can be found, or if the judgment creditor elect not to issue execution against such corporation, a tax must be levied as early as practicable to pay off the judgment. When a tax has been so levied and any part thereof shall be collected, the treasurer of such corporation shall pay the same to the judgment creditor, or to the clerk of the court in which the judgment was rendered, in satisfaction thereof.

Stocks or interests levied upon.—Sec. 3050. Stock or interests owned by the defendant in any corporation, and also debts due him, and property of his in the hands of third persons, may be levied upon in the same manner provided for attaching the same.

PROCEEDINGS BY GARNISHMENT.

How done: proceedings.—Sec. 3051. In proceedings by garnishment on execution, the garnishee shall be served as in case of attachment. The plaintiff may, also, if the garnishee is called into court, have a case docketed against him without docket fee, and upon his answer to the officer, issue may be made and notice thereof given him, or issue may be made on his answer in court without any notice theron, if made at the same term; and in all these and every other particular, the proceedings shall be the same as under garnishment on attachment, as near as the nature of the case will allow.

Not affected by expiration of execution.—Sec. 3052. Proceedings by garnishment on execution shall not be in any manner affected by the expiration of the execution or its return; and where parties thereunder have been garnished, the officer shall return to the next term thereafter a copy of the execution with all his doings thereon, so far as the garnishments thereon are concerned.

PARTNERSHIP PROPERTY.

Officer may take possession, inventory, and appraise.—Sec. 3053. When an officer has an execution against a person who owns property jointly, in common, or in partnership with another, such officer may levy on and take possession of the property owned jointly, in common, or in partnership, sufficiently to enable him to appraise and inventory the same, and for that purpose shall call to his assistance three disinterested persons, which inventory and appraisement shall be returned by the officer with the execution, and shall state in his return who claims to own the property.

Lien enforced by equitable proceeding.—Sec. 3054. The plaintiff shall, from the time such property is so levied on, have a lien on the interest of the defendant therein, and may commence an action by equitable proceedings to ascertain the nature and extent of such interest, and to enforce the lien; and, if deemed necessary or proper, the court or judge may appoint a receiver under the circumstances provided in chapter twelve of title seventeen of this code.

INDEMNIFYING BOND.

May be required, when.—Sec. 3055. An officer is bound to levy an execution on any personal property in the possession of, or that he has reason to believe belongs to the defendant, or on which the plaintiff directs him to levy, unless he has received notice in writing from some other person, his agent, or attorney, that such property belongs to him; or, if after levy he receives such notice, such officer may release the property unless a bond is given as provided in the next section; but the officer shall be protected from all liability by reason of such levy until he receives such written notice.

Terms and conditions of.—SEC. 3056. When the officer receives such notice he may forthwith give the plaintiff, his agent, or attorney, notice that an indemnifying bond is required. Bond may thereupon be given by or for the plaintiff, with one or more sufficient sureties, to be approved by the officer, to the effect that the obligators will indemnify him against the damages which he may sustain in consequence of the seizure or sale of the property, and will pay to any claimant thereof the damages he may sustain in consequence of the seizure or sale, and will warrant to any purchaser of the property such estate or interest therein as is sold; and thereupon the officer shall proceed to subject the property to the execution, and shall return the indemnifying bond to the *district* court of the county in which the levy is made.

If not given, levy discharged.—SEC. 3057. If such bond is not given, the officer may refuse to levy, or if he has done so, and the bond is not given in a reasonable time after it is required by the officer, he may restore the property to the person from whose possession it was taken, and the levy shall stand discharged.

Officer protected if bond good when taken.—SEC. 3058. The claimant or purchaser of any property, for the seizure or sale of which an indemnifying bond has been taken and returned by the officer, shall be barred of any action against the officer levying on the property if the surety on the bond was good when it was taken. Any such claimant or purchaser may maintain an action upon the bond, and recover such damages as he may be entitled to.

Application of proceeds of such property.—SEC. 3059. Where property, for the sale of which the officer is indemnified, sells for more than enough to satisfy the execution under which it was taken, the surplus shall be paid into the court to which the indemnifying bond is directed to be returned. The court may order such disposition or payment of the money to be made, temporarily or absolutely, as may be proper in respect to the rights of the parties interested.

Executions issued by justices.—SEC. 3060. The provisions of the preceding sections as bonds, shall apply to proceedings upon executions issued by justices of the peace. Indemnifying bonds shall be returned in such cases with the execution under which they are taken.

General rules relating to levy on attachments, apply to executions.—The general directions heretofore given in the chapter on Attachments in reference to the levy, will apply as well to the levy under an execution, and reference may be had thereto, to show the mode and effect of a levy, and the rights and duties of the officer thereon.

His duty on receiving an execution.—On receiving an execution the officer should proceed at once to execute it; he should give a receipt for it, if required, stating the hour and day when it was received, and make sufficient return thereof with the money collected thereon within seventy days from such receipt; he should indorse on the writ the day and hour when received, and the levy, sale, and every other act done by virtue thereof, with the date and amounts of receipts or payments in satisfaction thereof, and the indorsements must be made at the time of the receipt or act done.

When the execution becomes a lien.—The execution is a lien on personal property only after an actual levy, and is sufficient justification to levy, provided it is regular on its face. 18 Iowa, 380, 474; 16 Iowa, 234.

Only one at a time.—Only one execution can be in existence at the same time. If one has issued, it must be returned before a second one can issue; and under the provisions of the Rev. 1860, it was held that it was necessary to return an execution after property had been levied upon and not sold for any cause, and the execution was not satisfied, before a second execution, commonly called an *alias*, could properly issue; and that a special execution, commonly called a *venditioni exponas*, should issue in such a case to complete the sale. But a sale in such a case under an *alias*, though irregular, would not render it absolutely void. 13 Iowa, 202.

This has been changed by the Code, which provides, in such cases for another execution, and if the property levied upon under the former execution does not satisfy the second one, other property may be taken to satisfy the same. Code, Sec. 3086.

Omission to levy.—If the sheriff omits to levy until the return day is past, the execution is dead, and he will be liable as a trespasser if he levy after that time. 13 John., 255.

Several executions in his hands.—If there are several executions in his hands at the same time, in different cases, they should be executed in the order in which they were received, and ordinarily after a valid levy on property sufficient to satisfy an execution, neither the plaintiff nor the sheriff can withdraw the levy and discharge the property, or treat it as a nullity, and sue out a second writ to be levied on additional property.

Plaintiff may order a return in certain cases.—But under certain circumstances, the plaintiff or his assignees, may order a return after the levy and before sale; as when it is discovered that the proceedings under which it issued were illegal or irregular, or where the sale, if made, would be nugatory, or where a compromise is made with the defendant whereby the debt is liquidated, or the time of its payment extended, or where notice of a claim thereto is made, and an indemnifying bond required and refused. 22 Wend., 569; 10 Iowa, 325; Code, Sec. 3063.

Liability where sufficient property levied on.—If the sheriff levy on sufficient property to satisfy the judgment, the officer becomes liable to the plaintiff for the debt, unless he does his duty according to the requirements of the law, or is released by the plaintiff. 2 G. Greene, 208.

Officer cannot discharge an execution.—The officer cannot discharge an execution without payment, and a note taken by him instead of money, is no satisfaction of the execution, though he return the same satisfied. But the plaintiff might ratify the transaction, and sue the sheriff for the amount. 1 Cow., 46; 4 Cow., 553; 6 Cow., 465. Neither can the sheriff with his own money pay the plaintiff the amount of the judgment, and by arrangement with the defendant, retain the execution as security for the payment. The execution in such a case would not protect the officer, and the defendant could maintain trespass or replevin for goods subsequently taken under it. The sole object of an execution is to raise money to satisfy the judgment, if the judgment is for money; and that object being attained the power conferred by the writ is spent, and the officer is not permitted to use it in enforcing a bargain with the defendant. 15 John., 443.

Property wrongfully or fraudulently obtained.—Property tortiously severed from the freehold, and which would otherwise be exempt, cannot properly be levied upon. 11 Iowa, 533. Nor is property, the possession of which has been obtained fraudulently, subject to levy.

When money is made.—Section 3044 provides, that when money is made under an execution, the sheriff should pay the same to the plaintiff, or so much thereof as will satisfy the execution.

This might appear inconsistent with Section 3037, which provides, among other things, that the officer "shall make sufficient return thereof, together with the money collected, on or before the seventieth day from such delivery."

The proper practice would appear to be, for the officer to pay over to the plaintiff the money he is entitled to receive, and take his receipt therefor, and return the same with his writ; but if the amount due the plaintiff in the execution is not paid over to him, to return the money made with the execution to the clerk.

Any surplus, after satisfying the execution and costs, should be paid to the defendant, unless there are other executions in his hands on which the same should be applied.

III. INDEMNIFYING BOND.

May be required when.—The statute further provides:

SECTION 3055. An officer is bound to levy an execution on any personal property in the possession of, or that he has reason to believe belongs to the defendant, or on which the plaintiff directs him to levy, unless he has received notice in writing from some other person or his agent or attorney, that such property belongs to him; or if after levy he receives such notice, such officer may release the property, unless a bond is given as provided in the next section; but the officer shall be protected from all liability by reason of such levy until he receives such notice.

To give plaintiff notice: terms and conditions.—SEC. 3056. When the officer receives such notice, he may forthwith give the plaintiff, his agent or attorney, notice that an indemnifying bond is required. Bond may thereupon be given by or for the plaintiff, with one or more sufficient sureties, approved by the officer, to the effect, that the obligors will indemnify him against the damages which he may sustain in consequence of the seizure or sale of the property, and will pay to any claimant thereof the damages he may sustain in consequence of the seizure or sale, and will warrant to any purchaser of the property such estate or interest as is sold; and thereupon the officer shall proceed to subject the property to the execution, and shall return the indemnifying bond to the district court of the county in which the levy is made.

If not given, levy discharged.—SEC. 3057. If such bond is not given the officer may refuse to levy, or if he has done so and the bond is not given in a reasonable time after it is required by the officer, he may restore the property to the possession of the person from whose possession the property was taken, and the levy shall stand discharged.

Officer protected if bond good when taken.—SEC. 3058. The claimant or purchaser of any property for the seizure or sale of which an indemnifying bond has been taken and returned by the officer, shall be barred of any action against the officer levying on the property, if the surety on the bond was good when it was taken. Any such claimant or purchaser may maintain an action upon the bond, and recover such damages as he may be entitled to.

Application of proceeds of such property.—SEC. 3059. Where property for the sale of which the officer is indemnified, sells for more than enough to satisfy the execution under which it was taken, the surplus shall be paid into the court to which the indemnifying bond is directed to be returned. The court may order such disposition or payment of the money to be made, temporarily or absolutely, as may be proper in respect to the rights of the parties interested.

These provisions to apply to justices.—SEC. 3060. The provisions of the preceding sections as to bonds, shall apply to proceedings upon executions issued by justices of the peace. Indemnifying bonds shall be returned in such cases, with the execution under which they are taken.

The above provisions obscure.—The above provisions of the Code are in some respects quite obscure, and have materially changed the former law relating to indemnifying bonds.

Probable construction.—The construction given to these provisions, will undoubtedly be that the officer is bound to levy on any property in the possession of the defendant, or on any property not in his possession which he has reason to believe belongs to the defendant, and which in either case is not exempt from execution, and that he is required to levy on any property on which the plaintiff directs him so to do, and which is not exempt from execution, unless he shall receive notice in writing from some other person, his agent or attorney, that said property belongs to him; and that the officer will be protected as to the claims of third parties, until he receives such notice.

INDEMNIFYING BOND.

No. 80.

In the....Court of the State of Iowa, in and for....county.

A.... B ..., *Plaintiff*,
v.
C.... D...., *Defendant*.

Know all men by these presents, that we, A B as principal, and E F as surety, are held and firmly bound unto G H, sheriff of said county, in the sum of....[here insert double the value of the property,] dollars, for the payment of which well and truly to be made we bind ourselves firmly by these presents.

The condition of this obligation is such, that whereas the said G H, sheriff as aforesaid, by virtue of an execution to him duly issued and directed in the above entitled cause, against the goods and chattels, lands and tenements of the said defendant, is about to levy said execution upon (or has levied the same upon) the following described property, to-wit:

[Here describe the property;] and whereas the said G H has received a notice in writing from I J, (or his agent or attorney,) that said property belongs to him, and the said sheriff has given notice thereof to said plaintiff, and that an indemnifying bond is required herein, of said plaintiff.

Now therefore, if said obligors shall and will indemnify the said sheriff against any damage which he may sustain by reason of the seizure and sale of said property, and shall pay to any claimant thereof the damages he may sustain by reason of the seizure and sale of said property, and shall pay to any claimant thereof the damages he may sustain in consequence of the seizure and sale under said execution, and will warrant to any purchaser of the property on said sale, such estate or interest therein as is sold, then this obligation to be void, otherwise in full force and virtue.

Dated this....day of....18... A.... B...., *Principal.*
E.... F...., *Surety.*

APPROVAL OF BOND.

No. 81.

I hereby approve the within bond and the surety therein.

Dated this....day of....18...

G.... H...., *Sheriff.*

These facts should be returned.—These facts should, of course, be set forth in the officer's return, and if a bond is given, it should also be returned to the clerk of the court, and the officer should thereupon proceed to sell the property as in other cases, and the surplus, if any remaining after satisfying the execution, should be paid into the court where the bond is required to be returned.

IV. STAY OF EXECUTION.

Statutory provisions.—The provisions of the Code in reference to a stay of execution, so far as the same relate to the duty of the sheriff, are as follows:

Execution recalled.—SECTION 3065. When the surety is entered after execution issued, the clerk shall immediately notify the sheriff of the stay, and he shall forthwith return the execution with his doings thereon.

Property levied on released.—SEC. 3066. All property levied on before stay of execution, and all written undertakings for the delivery of personal property to the sheriff, shall be relinquished by the officer upon stay of execution being entered.

Execution against: form of.—SEC. 3067. At the expiration of the stay, the clerk shall issue a joint execution against the property of all the judgment debtors and sureties, describing them as debtors or sureties therein.

V. PROPERTY EXEMPT FROM EXECUTION.

Provisions of the statute.—Beside the provisions of the Code exempting a homestead, it contains the following provisions in reference to exemption from execution:

Property enumerated.—SECTION 3072. If the debtor is a resident of this state and is the head of a family, he may hold exempt from execution the following property: All wearing apparel of himself and family kept for actual use and suitable to their condition, and the trunks or other receptacles necessary to contain the same;

one musket or rifle and shot gun; all private libraries, family bibles, portraits, pictures, musical instruments, and paintings, not kept for the purpose of sale; a seat or pew occupied by the debtor or his family in any house of public worship; an interest in a public or private burying ground, not exceeding one acre for any defendant; two cows and calf; one horse, unless a horse is exempt as herein after provided; fifty sheep and the wool [therefrom and the materials manufactured from such wool. Ch. 42, Acts 15 Gen. A., p. 32;] six stands of bees; five hogs, and all pigs under six mon hs; the necessary food for all animals exempt from execution, for six months; all flax raised by the defendant on not exceeding one acre of ground and the manufactures therefrom; one bedstead and the necessary bedding for every two in the family; all cloth manufactured by the defendant, not exceeding one hundred yards in quantity; household and kitchen furniture, not exceeding two hundred dollars in value; all spinning wheels and looms; one sewing machine and other instruments of domestic labor kept for actual use; the necessary provisions and fuel for the use of the family for six months; the proper tools, instruments, or books of the debtor, if a farmer, mechanic, surveyor, clergyman, lawyer, physician, teacher, or professor; the horse, or the team, consisting of not more than two horses or mules, or two yoke of cattle, and the wagon or other vehicle, with the proper harness or tackle, by the use of which the debtor, if a physican, public officer, farmer, teamster, or other laborer habitually earns his living; and to the debtor, if a printer, there shall also be exempt a printing press and the types, furniture, and material necessary for the use of such printing press and a newspaper office connected therewith, not to exceed in all the value of twelve hundred dollars.

Family defined.—SEC. 3073. The word "family," as used in the last section, does not include strangers or boarders lodging with the family.

Personal earnings.—SEC. 3074. The earnings of such debtor for his personal services, or those of his family, at any time within ninety days next preceding the levy, are also exempt from execution and attachment.

Unmarried persons.—SEC. 3075. There shall be exempt to an unmarried person not the head of a family, and to non-residents, their own ordinary wearing apparel and trunk necessary to contain the same.

Persons who have started to leave the State.—SEC. 3076. Where the debtor, if the head of a family, has started to leave this state, he shall have exempt only the ordinary wearing apparel of himself and family, and such other property, in addition, as he may select, in all not exceeding seventy-five dollars in value; which property shall be selected by the debtor and appraised according to the provisions of section two thousand nine hundred and ninety-seven of chapter one of this title, but any person coming into this state with the intention of remaining, shall be considered a resident within the meaning of this chapter.

Purchase money.—SEC. 3077. None of the exemptions prescribed in this chapter shall be allowed against an execution issued for the purchase money of property claimed to be exempt, and on which such execution is levied.

Absconding debtor.—SEC. 3078. Where a debtor absconds and leaves his family, such property shall be exempt in the hands of the wife and children, of either of them.

Liberal construction of the statutes.—The statute granting exemptions require a liberal construction in order to carry out the benevolent intention of the legislature. Yet parties must bring themselves within the spirit of the provisions before they can claim exemptions under them. 1 Iowa, 435; 22 Iowa, 137.

Who is not the head of a family.—An unmarried man who works a farm on shares with his brother, the brother's wife keeping house for him, but he having the supervision of the house, and procuring and furnishing the necessaries for house keeping and living, is not the head of a family within the meaning of the exemption act. 11 Iowa, 226.

Habitual use of team: what is.—If a person abandon one employment and procures a team, or a part of a team (intending to complete it), for the purpose of using the same in good faith, to earn for himself a livelihood, that is such an habitual use of the team in contemplation of the statute as to exempt the same from levy, whether the party claiming the benefit of the law, has an opportunity of using the property much or little. He must, in such a case, make a beginning, and if his new character as a teamster is shown, the property which he honestly intends to use in that capacity to earn for himself a living, should be as effectually shielded from levy and sale during that period, as if he had used it for a whole year. 13 Iowa, 122.

The debtor may dispose of exempt property.—A person owning exempt property, has a right to dispose of the same by sale, and if he attempts to do so, but before the sale is made effectual in law, it is levied upon, he will not thereby lose his rights under the exemption law, but may insist on the same. 13 Iowa, 122.

No waiver of exemption rights.—A waiver of exemption laws, contained in a promissory note, will not, when judgment is obtained on the note, entitle the plaintiff to have an execution levied on the property exempt from execution. 20 Iowa, 376.

Exemption of earnings.—The statute exempting from execution the earnings of a debtor for his personal services and those of his family, for ninety days preceding the levy, does not authorize the holding of the earnings subsequently accruing by garnishing the employer of the debtor. In such a case the employer is not liable under garnishment, unless at some subsequent time, there should be due from such employer to the debtor an indebtedness for more than ninety days' labor. 22 Iowa, 137.

Turning out exempt property.—If the debtor voluntarily surrender, or turn out exempt property to the officer, this would be a waiver of his exemption rights thereto, and he would be estopped thereby from afterward asserting such claim. 30 Iowa, 574.

Personal property in the hands of widow exempt.—The Code further provides in reference to the estate of deceased persons as follows:

SECTION 2371. When the deceased leaves a widow, all property which in his hands as the head of a family would be exempt from execution, after being inventoried and appraised, shall be set apart to her and be exempt in her hands as in the hands of the decedent.

Homestead exemption.—To enable the officer to fully understand his duty, it is deemed advisable to set forth the homestead laws in full, which are as follows:

Exempt.—SECTION 1988. Where there is no special declaration of the statute to the contrary, the homestead of every family whether owned by the husband or wife, is exempt from judicial sale.

Head of family defined.—SEC. 1989. A widow or widower, though without children, shall be deemed a family while continuing to occupy the house used as such at the time of the death of the husband or wife.

Conveyance of.—SEC. 1990. A conveyance or encumbrance by the owner is of no validity unless the husband and wife, if the owner is married, concur in and sign the same joint instrument.

Liable for taxes.—SEC. 1991. The homestead is liable for taxes accruing thereon, and, if platted as hereinafter directed, is liable only for such taxes, and subject to mechanic's liens for work, labor, or material, done or furnished exclusively for the improvement of the same, and the whole or a sufficient portion thereof may be sold to pay the same.

For debts contracted previous to purchase.—SEC. 1992. The homestead may be sold on execution for debts contracted prior to the purchase thereof, but it shall not in such case be sold except to supply the deficiency remaining after exhausting the other property of the debtor liable to execution.

When contract stipulates it may be sold.—SEC. 1993. The homestead may be sold for debts created by written contract, executed by the persons having the power to convey and expressly stipulating that the homestead is liable therefor, but it shall not in such case be sold except to supply the deficiency remaining after exhausting the other property pledged for the payment of the debt in the same written contract.

Extent of.—SEC. 1994. The homestead must embrace the house used as a home by the owner thereof, and if he has two or more houses thus used by him at different times and places, he may select which he will retain as his homestead.

SEC. 1995. It may contain one or more lots or tracts of land, with the buildings thereon, and other appurtenances, subject to the limitations contained in the next section, but must in no case embrace different lots and tracts unless they are contiguous, or unless they are habitually and in good faith used as part of the same homestead.

SEC. 1996. If within a town plat it must not exceed one-half an acre in extent, and if not within a town plat it must not embrace in the aggregate more than forty acres. But if, when thus limited, in either case its value is less than five hundred dollars, it may be enlarged till its value reaches that amount.

SEC. 1997. It must not embrace more than one dwelling house, or any other buildings except such as are properly appurtenant to the homestead as such; but a shop or other building situated thereon, and really used and occupied by the owner in the prosecution of his own ordinary business, and not exceeding three hundred dollars in value, may be deemed appurtenant to such homestead.

Who may select, and have platted and recorded.—SEC. 1998. The owner, or the husband or wife, may select the homestead, and cause it to be marked out, platted, and recorded, as provided in the next section. A failure in this respect does not leave the homestead liable, but the officer having an execution against the property of such a defendant, may cause the homestead to be marked off, platted, and recorded, and may add the expense thence arising to the amount thus embraced in his execution.

SEC. 1999. The homstead shall be marked off by fixed and visible monuments, and in giving the description thereof, the direction and distance of the starting point from some corner of the dwelling house shall be stated. The description and plat shall then be recorded by the recorder in a book to be called the "homestead book," which shall be provided with a proper index.

May be changed.—SEC. 2000. The owner may, from time to time, change the limits of the homestead by changing the metes and bounds, as well as the record of the plat and description, or may change it entirely, but such changes shall not prejudice conveyances or liens made or created previously thereto, and no such change of the entire homestead, made without the concurrence of the husband or wife, shall affect his or her right, or those of the children.

New homestead exempt.—SEC. 2001. The new homestead, to the extent in value of the old, is exempt from execution in all cases where the old or former homestead would have been exempt, but in no other, nor in any greater degree.

Disagreement: how settled.—SEC. 2002. When a disagreement takes place between the owner and any person adversely interested, as to whether any land or buildings are properly a part of the homestead, the sheriff shall, at the request of either party, summon nine disinterested persons having the qualification of jurors. The parties then, commencing with the owner of the homestead, shall in turn strike off one juror each and shall continue to do so until only three of the number remain. These shall then proceed as referees to examine and ascertain all the facts of the case, and shall report the same with their opinion thereon to the next term of the court from which the execution or other process may have issued.

SEC. 2003. If either party fail to strike off jurors in the manner directed in the last section, the sheriff may strike off such jurors.

SEC. 2004. The court may also, in its discretion, refer the whole matter, or any part, of it, back to the same referees, or to others to be selected in the same manner, or as the parties otherwise agree, giving them directions as to the report that is required of them.

SEC. 2005. When the court is sufficiently possessed of the facts of the case, it shall make its decision, and may, if expedient, direct the homestead to be marked off anew, or a new plat and description to be made and recorded, and may take any farther step in the premises which, in its discretion, it may deem proper for attaining the objects of this statute. It shall also award costs as nearly as may be in accordance with the practice observed in other cases.

Change of circumstances.—SEC. 2006. The extent or appurtenances of the homestead as thus established, are liable to be called in question in like manner, whenever a change in value or circumstances will justify such new proceeding.

Survivor to occupy.—SEC. 2007. Upon the death of either husband or wife, the survivor may continue to possess and occupy the whole homestead until it is otherwise disposed of according to law.

Disposal of: what deemed descent.—SEC. 2008. The setting off of the distributive share of the husband or wife in the real estate of the deceased, shall be such a disposal of the homestead as is contemplated in the preceding section. But the survivor may elect to retain the homestead for life in lieu of such share in the real estate of the deceased; but if there be no such survivor,. the homestead descends to the issue of either husband or wife, according to the rules of descent, unless otherwise directed by will, and is to be held by such issue exempt from any antecedent debts of their parents or their own.

When sold.—SEC. 2009. If there is no such survivor or issue, the homestead is liable to be sold for the payment of any debts to which it might at that time be subjected if it had never been held as a homestead.

Devise of.—SEC. 2010. Subject to the rights of the surviving husband or wife as declared by law, the homestead may be devised like other real estate of the testator.

What is a homestead.—The homestead is the house used as a home. To be the homestead it must be used as a home, a place to abide in, a place for the family.

When it is thus used and occupied, it becomes the homestead, and not before; and a portion of the building used as a home may be exempt, and another portion not. Where a house was a three-story building, erected on a half-lot, and the cellar and first floor were designed as a business house, and the second and third floor as a residence by the owner, and his family, but had been previously rented in part for offices, it was held that the cellar and first floor of the building were liable to be seized and sold on execution, and that the soil, and second and third stories were exempt. 1 Iowa, 435; 4 Iowa, 373.

The homestead is for the family.—The homestead belongs not alone to the husband, but is wisely set apart by the law for the benefit of the family, and is not to be taken from them by law. 1 Iowa, 512; 6 Iowa, 30.

Value and extent of homestead.—Under the Code, the value of the homestead is not limited, but the extent of ground is. 4 Iowa, 368; 12 Iowa, 516.

Liable for antecedent debts.—The homestead is liable for antecedent debts, but not till after exhausting all other property of the defendent liable to execution, and the homestead law in force at the time of a contract, enters into and becomes a part of the same, and if the homestead right is acquired and perfected, such right will not be affected or impaired by a repeal of the law. 4 G. Greene, 563; 3 Iowa, 287.

By a parity of reasoning, the same would be true of rights under exemption and appraisement laws which we shall hereafter consider.

The extent of a homestead.—The statute provides that where a homestead is neither a town or a city plat, it must not exceed one-half an acre.

But where a party occupied as a homestead six acres, and the corporate limits of a city were extended so as to embrace it, but the land had never been laid out into streets and alleys, it was held that the homestead was not within the town or city plat, as contemplated by the law, and that the whole six acres could be held as a homestead; and an injunction to restrain a sale by a judgment creditor under such circumstances, was made perpetual. 12 Iowa, 516.

Leasehold property as a homestead.—Leasehold property, as well as a freehold, may be the subject of a homestead right, and in such a case, the right of possession under the lease cannot be assigned by the husband without the wife's consent; but it does not embrace buildings though situate on the same lot which are rented to others. 13 Iowa, 53 and 371.

Interest of a tenant in common as a homestead.—A tenant in common may hold his undivided share of the common premises as a homestead, and he may have more than forty acres set apart to him as a homestead, if its value does not exceed five hundred dollars. 14 Iowa, 49.

When the homestead character attaches.—The homestead character does not attach to property until it is actually used and occupied as a home. A mere intention to occupy, though subsequently carried out, does not make the premises a homestead until actually a residence.

To merely plat and record a tract of ground is not a sufficient occupancy; the use of it by the family is an essential requirement. 14 Iowa, 438 and 527; 10 Iowa, 51; 9 Iowa, 60.

Additions made under verbal contract of purchase.—An addition made to the homestead held under a verbal contract of purchase, followed by actual possession and improvements, is not subject to sale on general execution for a debt contracted subsequent to the possession and improvement, but before actual conveyance.

New homestead from the proceeds of old.—A new homestead acquired with the proceeds arising from the sale of the old one, is also exempt from sale in all cases in which the former homestead would have been exempt, and the owner has a right not only to change his homestead from one tract or lot of land to another owned by him at the time he acquired the homestead, but to sell his homestead and with the proceeds of such sale, acquire a new homestead exempt from execution to the value of the old one, but if he should not with the proceeds of such sale acquire a new homstead, such proceeds would be liable to be taken in satisfaction of his debts. 18 Iowa, 4, 36; 14 Iowa, 570.

Temporary absence does not affect the right.—Nor does the homestead lose its character as such, if left for a mere temporary purpose; the occupation under such circumstances is regarded as actual; but if there has been an actual abandonment, it is like any other property, and an actual removal from the homestead with no intention of returning, is a waiver of any right, though no new homestead be acquired. 14 Iowa, 524; 18 Iowa, 4.

Right of election—and waiver of rights.—If parties occupying a homestead at the time of a judicial sale have another place which they prefer as a homestead, they must do some act to cause this to be elected, otherwise that which they occupy at the time will be treated as such. 9 Iowa, 509.

A widower and his mother a family.—A widower without children who buys the property as a homestead, and who removes to and actually resides on the premises with his mother, can hold the homestead; the homestead of every family is exempt, but it is not necessary that the owner should be the head of a family. 11 Iowa, 104; Code, Sec. 1988.

It may be sold for taxes, and on mortgage foreclosure.— The homestead can be sold for taxes; on mechanic's liens for work, labor or material furnished, to make improvements on the same; and also on a mortgage foreclosure where the parties interested have united in the execution of the mortgage; but not till other property mortgaged, or pledged in the same instrument, for the payment of the debt, is exhausted; and it is also liable to satisfy a judgment for the purchase money, as this is considered an indebtedness prior to the acquisition of the homestead. 14 Iowa, 377, 387, 5.7; 16 Iowa, 149; 13 Iowa, 594; 11 Iowa, 183; 17 Iowa, 510; 23 Iowa, 208; 18 Iowa, 252.

The foregoing is, perhaps, sufficient to guide the officer in such cases. Of course, it is not within the proper scope of this treatise to consider the law fully, relating to homesteads, but only so far as is necessary to guide the officer in the discharge of his duty.

VI. SALE UNDER EXECUTION.

The Code provides for a sale of property under execution, as follows:

Notice of sale.—SECTION 3079. The sheriff must give four weeks' notice of the time and place of selling real property, and three weeks' notice of personal property.

How given.—SEC. 3080. Notice shall be given by being posted up in at least three public places of the county, one of which shall be at the place where the last district court was held. In addition to which, in the case of the sale of real estate, or where personal property to the amount of two hundred dollars or upwards is to be sold, there shall be two publications of such notice, in some newspaper printed in the county, if there be one. In constables' sales, there shall be no newspaper publication, and the notice shall be posted in three public places of the township of the justice, and one of them at his office door; the time of such notice shall be two weeks.

Penalty for selling without notice.—SEC. 3081. An officer selling without the notice above prescribed, shall forfeit one hundred dollars to the defendant in execution, in addition to the actual damages sustained by either party; but the validity of the sale is not thereby affected.

How made.—SEC. 3082. The sale must be at public auction, between nine o'clock in the forenoon, and four o'clock in the afternoon, and the hour of the commencement of the sale must be fixed in the notice.

SEC. 3083. When there are no bidders, or when the amount offered is grossly inadequate, or when from any cause the sale is prevented from taking place on the day fixed, the sheriff may postpone the sale for not more than three days, without being required to give any farther notice thereof; but he shall not make more than two such postponements, and such postponement shall be publicly announced when the sale should have taken place.

SEC. 3084. When the property sells for more than the amount required to be collected, the overplus must be paid to the defendant, unless the officer have another execution in his hands, on which said overplus may be rightfully applied.

SEC. 3085. If the property levied on sell for less than sufficient for that purpose the plaintiff may order out another execution, which shall be credited with the amount of the previous sale. The proceedings under this second sale, shall conform to those hereinbefore prescribed.

SEC. 3086. When property is unsold for want of bidders, the levy still holds good; and if there be sufficient time, it may again be advertised, or the execution returned and one issued commanding the officer to sell the property, describing it, previously levied on, to which a clause may be added, that if such property does not produce a sum sufficient to satisfy such execution, the officer shall proceed to make an additional levy, on which he shall proceed as on other executions or the plaintiff may, in writing filed with the clerk or justice, abandon such levy upon paying the costs thereof. In which case execution may issue with the same effect as if none had been issued.

SEC. 3087. If the defendant is in actual occupation and possession of any part of the land levied on, the officer having the execution, shall, at least twenty days previous to such sale, serve the defendant with written notice stating that the execution is levied on said land, and mentioning the time and place of sale; and sales made without the notice required in this section, may be set aside, on motion made at the same or the next term thereafter.

SEC. 3088. At any time before nine o'clock, A. M., of the day of the sale, the defendant may deliver to the officer a plan of division of the land levied on, subscribed by him, and in that case, the officer shall sell, according to said plan, so much of the land as may be necessary to satisfy the debt and costs, and no more. If no such plan is furnished, the officer may sell without any division.

SEC. 3089. When the purchaser fails to pay the money when demanded, the plaintiff or his attorney may elect to proceed against him for the amount; otherwise the sheriff shall treat the sale as a nullity, and may sell the property on the same day, or after a postponement as above authorized.

SEC. 3090. When any person shall purchase at a sheriff's sale, any real estate on which the judgment upon which the execution issued was not a lien at the time of the levy, and which fact was unknown to the purchaser, the court shall set aside such sale on motion, notice having been given to the debtor, as in case of action, and a new execution may be issued to enforce the judgment, and upon the order being made to set aside the sale, the sheriff or judgment creditor shall pay over to the purchaser the purchase money; said motion may also be made by any person interested in the real estate.

SEC. 3091. Money levied upon may be appropriated without being advertised or sold. The same may be done with bank bills, drafts, promissory notes, or other papers of the like character, if the plaintiff will receive them at their par value, as cash, or if the officer can exchange them for cash at that value.

SEC. 3092. When a judgment has been obtained against the executor of one deceased, *or against the decedent in his lifetime*, which the personal estate of the deceased is insufficient to satisfy, the plaintiff may file his petition in the office of the clerk of the court where the judgment is a lien, against the executor, the heirs and devisees of real estate (if such there be), setting forth the facts, and that there is real estate of the deceased, describing its location and extent and praying the court to award execution against the same.

SEC. 3093. The person against whom the petition is filed shall be notified by the plaintiff to appear on the first day of the term, and show cause, if any he have, why execution should not be awarded.

SEC. 3094. The notice shall be served and returned in the ordinary manner, and the same length of time shall be allowed for appearance as in civil actions, and service of such notice on non-resident defendants may be had in such cases by publication.

SEC. 3095. At the proper time, the court shall award the execution, unless sufficient cause be shown to the contrary.

SEC. 3096. The non-age of the heirs and devisees shall not be deemed such sufficient cause.

SEC. 3097. Mutual judgments, the executions on which are in the hands of the same officer may be set off, the one against the other; except that the costs shall not be so set off, unless the balance of cash actually collected on the large judgment is sufficient to pay the costs of the judgments, and such costs shall be paid therefrom accordingly.

SEC. 3098. When real property has been levied upon, if the estate is less than a leasehold, having two years of an unexpired term, the sale is absolute.

SEC. 3099. When the estate is of a larger amount, the property is redeemable, as hereinafter prescribed.

No. 82.

NOTICE OF SHERIFF'S SALE.

Notice is hereby given: That by virtue of a ... execution, directed to me from the clerk of the .... Court of .... county, Iowa, on a judgment obtained in said court on the ... day of ...., 18.., in favor of ..., as plaintiff, and against ..., as defendant, for the sum of .... dollars and .... cents, and costs taxed at $...., and accruing costs, I have levied upon the following real estate,(or personal property or both), as the property of said defendant, to satisfy said execution, to-wit: [here describe the property]; and will offer the same for sale to the highest bidder for cash in hand, on the .... day of ...., A. D. 18.., in front of the court-house door in ...., at the hour of .. o'clock, .. M.. of said day, when and where due attendance will be given by the undersigned, (or if personal property state the place of sale according to the fact).

Dated at ...., 18...

...., *Sheriff of said county.*

9

Time of notice and publication.—It will be observed that the statute requires four weeks' notice to be given of the sale of real estate, and three weeks' notice of personal property; and in case of the sale of real estate or personal property of the amount of two hundred dollars and upward, two publications of the notice is required in some newspaper of the county, if there be one.

It is not necessary that the notice be published four weeks previous to the sale; two publications in a daily paper at any time before the sale would be sufficient.

But in every case there should be one of such notices posted up in three different places in the county, one of which should be at the place where the last District Court was held.

The notice should fix the time and place of sale, but where the notice fixed the time as between the hours of two and five o'clock in the afternon, it was held, under a former statute, that a valid sale might be made under such a notice, as it would not be presumed that the officer sold after the time directed by the statute, and that it would be presumed until the contrary appeared, that the officer did his duty; but under the Code such a sale would in any event be good so far as the purchaser would be concerned. 4 G. Greene, 510.

Sale valid without notice.—The statute provides, that a sale without such notice, shall not affect the validity of the sale, but the officer in such a case forfeits one hundred dollars, beside actual damages sustained by either party. Code, Sec. 3081.

Notice to defendant.—The statute requires notice to be given to the defendant of a levy on land, where he is in the actual possession of the same, or any part thereof. This notice is required to be in writing, and should be served on the defendant at least twenty days previous to the sale, and should state that the execution is levied on the land describing it, and the time and place of sale; and sales made without this notice may be set aside on motion made at the same, or the next term thereafter.

The notice to the defendant may be in the following form:

NOTICE TO DEFENDANT OF LEVY.

No. 83.

STATE OF IOWA, } ss.
...... County, }

To ....:

You are hereby notified that by virtue of an execution to me directed, issued out of the clerk's office of the .... Court of the State of Iowa, in and for .... county, upon a judgment rendered in said court, in favor of ...., against you for the sum of .... dollars debt, and .... costs, I have levied upon the following real estate, to-wit: [here describe the property], of which you are in the actual occupation and possession; and that on the .... day of ...., 18.., at the front door of the court house in said county, at .... o'clock, .. M., of said day I will offer the same for sale to the highest bidder at public auction, to satisfy said execution, with all legally accruing costs.

Dated this .... day of ...., 18...

A.... B...., *Sheriff of said county.*

When the sale is absolute.—If the estate is less than a leasehold, having two years of unexpired term, the sale shall be absolute, and when it is of larger amount, it is redeemable as we shall hereafter notice.

Provision of the Revision of 1860.—The Revision of 1860 provided for the sale of all property on execution only after appraisement, and for two-thirds of its appraised value, except where the property had been conveyed by the debtor to hinder or delay collection or defraud creditors, and except that if the defendant elected to have it sold subject to redemption before a levy, and filed his election in writing with the clerk of the court issuing the writ, the sheriff should in this case sell the same subject to redemption. Rev., Secs. 3360, 3371.

The right not impaired by repeal of statute.—The rights of a debtor under these provisions to have real estate sold on appraisement, cannot be impaired by the provisions of the Code, for a sale without appraisement and with right of redemption, where the debt on which the judgment was rendered, was contracted while the provisions of the Revision of 1860 were in force, and before the Code took effect, and the officer should in such cases proceed to appraise in making sales on execution, and sell the lands for not less than two-thirds of the appraised value, as provided by the Revision. Rev., Secs. 3360, 3370, 3371, and 4 G. Greene, 563; 3 Iowa, 287; 10 Iowa, 470; 11 Iowa, 284; 1 How. S. C. R. 311; 2 Id., 608; 3 Id., 707.

In cases of appraisement.—The Code provides for the appraisement of property in certain cases, as follows:

How done and amount it must sell for.—SEC. 3100. Personal property levied upon and advertised for sale on execution, must be appraised before sale by two disinterested householders of the neighborhood, one of whom shall be chosen by the execution debtor, and the other by the plaintiff, or in case of the absence of either party, or if either or both parties neglect or refuse to make choice, the officer making the levy shall choose one or both, as the case may be, who shall forthwith proceed to return to said officer a just and true appraisement, under oath, of said property, if they can agree; and in case they cannot agree, they shall choose another disinterested householder, and with his assistance they shall complete such appraisement, and the property shall not be sold for less than two-thirds of said valuation; provided the same shall be offered for three successive days at the same place and hour of day as advertised, and if no offer equal to two-thirds the value thereof be made, then it shall be lawful to sell said property for one-half of said valuation.

OATH TO APPRAISERS.

No. 84.

You, and each of you, do solemnly swear, (or affirm,) that you will make a just and true appraisement of each and every article of personal property now here shown you for that purpose, according to the best of your knowledge and ability. So help you God.

The above may be administered orally to the appraisers.

APPRAISEMENT AND RETURN.

No. 85.

STATE OF IOWA, } ss.
........County, }

We, the undersigned, householders of said county, having been duly selected and sworn by A B, sheriff of said county, to make a just and true appraisement of the personal property hereinafter described, do certify and return to said officer, that we have made the appraisement as follows:

One bay horse appraised at........................	$150.00
One covered buggy, appraised at....................	125.00
One ditching machine, appraised at..................	80.00
Total value..............................	$355.00

Witness our hands this .... day of ...., 18..

FEES:—

C D, six hours,	.75	C.... D....,	Appraisers.
E F, six hours,	.75	E.... F....,	
G H, six hours,	.75	G.... H....,	

Appraisement of real estate.—The provisions of the Revision in reference to appraisement are obscure and indefinite, as for instance in reference to the amount of liens, and who should determine the amount of them.

The interests of the defendant to be appraised.—The interest of the defendant only in the real estate should be appraised, and where the property is subject to prior liens, the appraisement should be of the interest of the defendant therein, which is the balance found by deducting such prior liens, from two-thirds of the appraised value. 16 Iowa, 469.

If the interest is an equitable one.—Where the interest of the defendant in the real estate is only equitable, and not an absolute one, the value thereof should be appraised accordingly; and the safer practice would seem to be, where there are claims and interests of an indefinite and uncertain character, and some uncertainty exists as to whether they constitute proper liens, or superior equities to the estate, to merely appraise the interest of the defendant, and not attempt to fix the amount of said claims as prior liens, and appraise the estate accordingly.

APPRAISEMENT AND OATH.

No. 86.

STATE OF IOWA, } ss.
.... County. }

We, the undersigned appraisers, selected to value the property hereafter described, which was levied upon by ...., sheriff of .... county, Iowa, by virtue of an execution issued out of the clerk's office of the .... Court, in favor of ...., and against the property of ...., do here report that we have valued said property according to its fair value at this time, and that the schedule, hereto annexed, contains a correct inventory of said property, and that the values therein affixed to each article respectively are the fair values thereof at this time, namely:

Schedule of property appraised. [Here insert list of property.]

Signed this .... day of ...., A. D. 18..

...., } *Appraisers.*
...., }

STATE OF IOWA, } ss.
.... County. }

We, ..., being duly sworn, depose and say that the foregoing appraisement made by us, shows the fair value of the property in the above schedule described, at this time, as we believe.

...., } *Appraisers.*
...., }

Sworn to before me, and subscribed in my presence, by the said ...., this .... day of ...., A. D., 18..

...., *Sheriff.*

VII. RIGHT OF REDEMPTION ON EXECUTION SALES.

The Code provides in relation to redemption, and the sheriff's duty, as follows:

REDEMPTION.

Officer to execute deed or certificate.—SEC. 3101. If the property sold is not subject to redemption, the sheriff must execute a deed therefor to the purchaser; but if the same is subject to redemption, he shall execute to such purchaser a certificate containing a description of the property and the amount of money paid by such purchaser, and stating that unless redemption is made within one year thereafter according to law, he or his heirs or assigns, will be entitled to a deed for the same.

By defendant when.—SEC. 3102. The defendant may redeem real property at any time within one year from the day of sale as herein provided, and will, in the meantime, be entitled to the possession of the property. But in no action where the defendant has taken an appeal from the circuit or district court, or stayed execution on the judgment, shall he be entitled to redeem.

When by creditors.—SEC. 3103. For the first six months after such sale, his right to redeem is exclusive; but if no redemption is made by him at the end of that time, any creditor of the defendant whose demand is a lien upon such real estate, may redeem the same at any time within nine months from the day of sale. ' But a mechanic's lien, before judgment thereon, is not of such character as to entitle the holder to redeem.

Entitled to assignment.—SEC. 3120. A creditor redeeming as above contemplated, is entitled to receive an assignment of the certificate issued by the sheriff to the original purchaser as hereinbefore directed.

Sale in parcels.—SEC. 3121. When the property has been sold in parcels, any distinct portion may be redeemed by itself.

Tenants in common.—SEC. 3122. When the interests of several tenants in common have been sold on execution, the undivided portion of any or either of them may be redeemed separately.

Defendant may transfer right.—SEC. 3123. The rights of a defendant in relation to redemption are transferable, and the assignee has the like power to redeem.

Deed made to whom.—SEC. 3124. If the defendant or his assignee fail to redeem, the sheriff must, at the end of the year, execute a deed to the person who is entitled to the certificate as hereinbefore provided, or to his assignee. If the person entitled be dead, the deed shall be made to his heirs, but the property will be subject to the payment of the debts of the deceased in the same manner as if acquired during his lifetime.

When evidence of title to be recorded.—SEC. 3125. The purchaser of real estate at a sale on execution, need not place any evidence of his purchase upon record until twenty days after the expiration of the full time of redemption. Up to that time, the publicity of the proceedings is constructive notice of the rights of the purchaser, but no longer.

Deeds imply regularity.—SEC. 3126. Deeds executed by a sheriff in pursuance of the sales contemplated in this chapter, are presumptive evidence of the regularity of all previous proceedings in the case, and may be given in evidence without preliminary proof.

SHERIFF'S REDEMPTION CERTIFICATE.

No. 87.

To whom it may concern:

I, ..., sheriff of .... county, Iowa, hereby certify that by virtue of a .... execution to me directed, dated ......, A. D. 18.., and issued out of the clerk's office of the .... Court of the state of Iowa, in and for .... county, upon a judgment ...., rendered in said court on the .... day of ...., A. D. 18.., in favor of ...., and against ...., for the sum of .... dollars debt, and .... dollars costs, I did, on the .... day of ...., A. D. 18.., levy on the following described real estate, to-wit: [here describe the real estate], as the property of the said .... to satisfy the said execution, amounting to .... dollars debt, and .... dollars costs, together with interest and accruing costs thereon; that I gave four weeks' notice of the time and place of selling said real property, under said execution, by posting up printed notices thereof at three public places in said county, one of which was at the court house in ...., where the last District Court was held, and by causing two publications of said notice to be made in the ...., a newspaper printed at ...., in said county, immediately before the time of sale, that in pursuance of the notice of sale aforesaid, in conformity to law and by virtue of said execution, I did, on the .... day of ...., A. D. 18.., at .... o'clock in the ....noon of said day, at ...., expose and offer the said real estate for sale at public auction, and the said .... then and there bid the sum of .... dollars for the same ...., and that being the highest and best bid offered for said real estate, the same was then and there openly struck off and sold to the said .... for the sum of .... dollars, who then and there paid the amount of said bid to me in cash.

Now, unless redemption is made within one year after the date of said sale, according to law, the said ... ., his heirs and assignees, will be entitled to a deed for the said real estate sold as aforesaid, and described as follows, to-wit: [Here describe the real estate sold].

In witness whereof I have hereunto set my hand this .... day of ...., A. D. 18...

A.... B...., *sheriff of* .... *county, Iowa.*

SHERIFF'S DEED.

No. 88.

This indenture, made the .... day of ...., A. D. 18.., by and between ...., sheriff of .... county, Iowa, of the first part, and ...., of the county of ...., in the State of ...., of the second part, witnesseth: That whereas, by virtue of a .... execution, directed to ...., the then acting sheriff of .... county, dated the .... day of ...., A. D. 18.., and issued out of the clerk's office of the .... Court of the State of Iowa, in and for .... county, under the seal of said court upon a ......, rendered in said .... Court, on the .... day of ...., A. D. 18.., in favor of ...., and against ...., for the sum of .... dollars and .... cents, debt, and .... dollars and .... cents, costs, the said ...., sheriff as aforesaid, did, on the .... day of ...., A. D. 18.., levy upon the real estate hereafter described, as the property of the said ...., defendant, to satisfy the said execution, amounting to .... dollars and .... cents, debt, and .... dollars and .... cents, costs, together with interest and accruing costs; and whereas, the said ...., sheriff as aforesaid, gave four weeks' notice of the time and place of selling said real estate under said execution, by posting up .... notices thereof at three public places in said .... county, one of which was at the court house in ...., where the last District Court was held, and by causing two publications of said notice to be made in the ...., a newspaper printed at ...., in said county, immediately preceding the day of sale. [If there be no newspaper published in the county, so state the fact; and if there was an appraisement of the property, here insert the facts in the form hereafter suggested].

And whereas, the said ...., as sheriff aforesaid, in pursuance of the notice of sale aforesaid, in conformity to law, and by virtue of said execution, ..., did, on the .... day of ...., A. D. 18.., at the hour of .... o'clock, in the ....noon of said day, at ...., expose and offer for sale at public auction the real estate hereinafter described, and then and there sell the same at public auction to ...., for the sum of ... dollars, he being the highest and best bidder therefor. Whereupon the said sheriff, after receiving the said sum of money from said purchaser, made and delivered him a certificate of sale as directed by law; and whereas, the time of redemption having expired without any redemption being made: (or in case of redemption by a creditor, or an assignment of the certificate, so state the fact, and insert the redemptioner's or assignee's name as grantee).

Now therefore, this indenture witnesseth, that in consideration of the premises, and of the said sum of .... dollars so bid and paid as aforesaid, the receipt whereof is hereby acknowledged, I, the said ...., sheriff as aforesaid, party of the first part, do hereby sell and convey unto the said ...., party of the second part, his heirs and assigns forever, the following described real estate, situated in the county of ...., and State of Iowa, (being the same real estate hereinbefore referred to), to-wit: [Here describe the real estate]. To have and to hold the said real estate, with all the appurtenances thereunto belonging, to the said ...., his heirs and assigns forever, as fully and absolutely as the said party of the first part, by virtue of the premises, might and could sell and convey the same.

In witness whereof, the said party of the first part has hereunto set his hand this .... day of ...., A. D. 18...

...., *sheriff of .... county.*

STATE OF IOWA, }
.... County. } SS.

Be it remembered, that on this .... day of ...., A. D. 18.., before the undersigned ...... in and for said county, personally appeared ...., sheriff of .... county, Iowa, to me personally known to be the identical person whose name is subscribed to the foregoing deed as grantor, and acknowledged the execution thereof to be his voluntry act and deed as said sheriff, for the purposes therein mentioned.

[SEAL.] Witness my hand and seal, the day and year last above written.

....

Deed on appraisement or on sale of lease-hold interest.—If a sale is made after appraisement, or is of a a lease-hold interest of less than two years unexpired term, the sale is absolute and the deed should be executed at once to the purchaser, and the facts relating to the appraisement, if the same was appraised, should be recited in the deed immediately after the recital of the notices of the time and place of sale, and may be in the following form:

AND WHEREAS, for the purpose of ascertaining the value of said real estate, E F, and G H, two disinterested freeholders of the neighborhood, were on the .... day of ...., 18.., chosen according to law, as appraisers of the value thereof, and then made and delivered to said sheriff, an appraisement thereof in writing, duly signed and sworn to by them, and from which it appeared that they appraised the value thereof at $....:

Now therefore, (concluding as in the last form.)

In case of sale after appraisement.—The part of the above form relating to redemption, should of course be omitted, and the deed should show a sale for at least two-thirds of the appraised value.

VIII. REVIVOR OF JUDGMENTS.

On this subject so far as relates to the duty of the sheriff, the Code provides:

Death of plaintiff: how execution may issue.—SEC. 3130. The death of one or all the plaintiffs shall not prevent an execution being issued, but on such execution the clerk shall indorse the death of such of them as are dead, and if all be dead, the names of the personal representatives, or the last survivor, if the judgment passed to the personal representatives, or the names of the survivor's heirs, if the judgment was for real property.

Officer's duty.—SEC. 3131. The sheriff, in acting upon an execution indorsed as provided in the last section, shall proceed as if the surviving plaintiff or plaintiffs, or the personal representatives or heirs, were the only plaintiffs in the execution, and take bonds accordingly.

IX. PROCEEDINGS AUXILIARY TO EXECUTION.

On proceedings auxiliary to execution, the statutes further provide, that the sheriff may be appointed a receiver of the property of the judgment debtor; and he and the sureties on his official bond, are liable in such cases for the faithful discharge of his duties as such. Code, Secs. 3141, 3143.

X. DECISIONS RELATING TO SHERIFFS.

Presumptions.—In regard to sheriff's sales it has been held, that it is to be presumed that the sale was regularly conducted, and that a sheriff's sale under an execution made after seventy days from the *teste* thereof, would be an irregularity only and not render the sale void. 20 Iowa, 431; 21 Iowa, 97, 291.

But a prior levy, undisposed of, renders a sale of the property upon a subsequent levy under execution irregular. 21 Iowa, 135.

An attorney cannot adjourn a sale.—A sheriff has no power to authorize an attorney to adjourn a judicial sale, and a sale made in pursuance of such an adjournment is invalid. 27 Iowa, 348.

Inadequacy of price.—Inadequacy of price would not be sufficient to set aside a judicial sale where there was no fraud in the transaction. 25 Iowa, 456.

Presumptions in favor of the officer.—We have already observed, that the officer is presumed to do his duty; and where the return showed that a sale of two lots was made upon an execution, and it did not appear that they were sold separately, it was held, that it was to be presumed that the officer did his duty in that respect, and that although the fact that two lots were sold on execution *en masse*, might be available to defeat the sale to the execution plaintiff, it may well be questioned whether it could be, as against a third party after the expiration of the time of redemption, and the execution and delivery of a sheriff's deed. 24 Iowa, 204.

The return of the officer to the writ is *prima facie* evidence of the facts therein stated. 9 Iowa, 140.

Sale en masse.—A sale *en masse* of lands by the sheriff on execution was set aside, where it apeared that it was sold for less than one-sixth of the value of the land, and pending litigation. 26 Iowa, 283.

But a sheriff's sale will not be set aside on the ground of a sale *en masse*, where it appears that the land was first offered in forty-acre tracts by the sheriff, and that no bids were made for any portion thus offered. 27 Iowa, 468.

Discretion of the officer.—As to the time, place and manner of sale and its adjournment, the sheriff is invested with a sound discretion. He should never forget that he is for many purposes the agent of both parties in the execution of the power with which the law invests him. His discretion must be exercised with a fair and impartial attention to the interests of all concerned, and where on the day first fixed for a sale there are no bidders, or where the amount bid is grossly inadequate, he should ordinarily postpone the sale, especially where he is requested to do so by the debtor, and if he does not, it will be set aside upon a seasonable application; but censurable conduct on the part of the sheriff, as in changing the day of sale without reason, and in showing ill will to the debtor, is not sufficient ground for setting aside a sale, when it is not shown that the purchaser was connected with it. 16 Iowa, 519.

Failure to pay bid.—Upon the failure of the successful bidder at a judicial sale to pay the amount of his bid, the plaintiff or his attorney may elect to proceed against him for the amount, otherwise the sheriff shall treat the sale as a nullity, and may sell the property on the same day or after a postponement as authorized by statute. The sheriff cannot on a subsequent day accept an unsuccessful bid and convey the property without a re-sale. 16 Iowa, 519.

Computing time of redemption.—In computing time of redemption of real estate from sale under execution, the first, or day of sale, should be excluded, and the right of redemption exists until the last moment of the same day of the next year. 23 Iowa, 527.

XI. INDORSEMENT OF LEVY, AND RETURN.

The sheriff should, as before remarked, indorse the levy on the execution at the time of making the same, and it may be in the following form:

INDORSEMENT OF LEVY.

No. 89.

STATE OF IOWA, }
......County, } ss.

I, A B, sheriff of said county, hereby certify, that by virtue of the within execution I have this day levied upon the property described in the annexed inventory, as the property of the defendant:

INVENTORY.

[Here describe the property, whether real or personal.]
Dated this....day of....18...

A.... B...., *Sheriff.*

The return of an execution.—The return of the officer to an execution should show every act done by him by virtue of the execution, with the dates, amounts, etc.

The return should be indorsed on, or attached to the execution, and may be in the following form:

RETURN TO AN EXECUTION.

No. 90.

STATE OF IOWA }
...... County. } ss.

I, A B, sheriff of .... county, Iowa, hereby certify and return that I received the within (or annexed) execution on the .... day of ...., A. D. 18.., at .... o'clock in the ....noon; that by virtue thereof I did on the .... day of ...., A. D. 18.., levy upon the property of the said ...., defendant therein described as follows, to-wit: [describe property]. And after making said levy I gave .... weeks' notice of the time and place of selling said .... property, by posting up printed notices thereof in three public places within my county, one of which was at the place where the last District (or Circuit) Court was held; and by causing two publications of said notice to be made in the ...., a newspaper printed at ...., in said county of ...., immediately before said sale; that on the .... day of ...., A. D. 18.., twenty days before said sale, I served the said ...., who was in the actual possession of said .... property, with written notice, stating that I had levied on said .... property by virtue of this execution, and mentioning the time and place of said sale, a copy of which is attached hereto, and marked Exhibit "A," and made a part of this return. [If there has been an appraisement of property, here state the facts and attach the return of the appraisers as a part of the return, marked Exhibit ..].

And further certify and return that, in pursuance of said notice, I did, on the .... day of .... A. D. 18.., at .... o'clock in the ....noon of said day, that being the time appointed for said sale at ...., expose to sale at public auction the property aforesaid, to the highest and best bidder for cash, and then and there sold [here describe the property sold], to ...., for the sum of .... dollars, he being the highest and best bidder therefor, who then and there paid to me the said sum of .... dollars bid by him; whereupon I executed to the said ...., a certificate of purchase, (or a deed), in due form of law for the said .... estate; and that I have said moneys now in court, to render unto the said ...., (or, in case of payment to plaintiff of amount due him, so state), as by this writ I am commanded.

A.... B ..., *sheriff of .... County.*

RETURN OF SHERIFF'S FEES.

FEE BILL:

Serving execution	$ 1.20
Serving notice of sale.....	.50
Copy....................	.20
Posting notices	1.40
Mileage.................	2.10
Publication	7.00
Selling property..........	....
Per cent.................	....
Certificate...............	....
Total....	$ ....

A.... B...., *Sheriff.*

Modified to suit other cases. The above form can be modified to suit the case of a levy on, and sale of, personal property on appraisement, or other facts in the case.

CHAPTER XIII.

OF REPLEVIN; OR ACTION FOR THE RECOVERY OF SPECIFIC PERSONAL PROPERTY.

I. PROVISIONS OF THE STATUTE.

The Code provides for the recovery of specific personal property; directs what the petition must contain; and requires that where immediate possession is desired, the plaintiff shall execute a bond with sureties to be approved by the clerk.

It further provides:

Clerk to issue orders.—SECTION 3230. The clerk shall thereupon issue an order, under his hand and seal of the court, directed to the sheriff, requiring him to take the property therein described and deliver the same to the plaintiff. And where the petition shows that the property has been wrongfully removed into another county from the one in which the action is commenced, the order may issue from the county whence the property was so wrongfully taken, and may be served in any county where the property may be found in the same manner and with like effect as is in the county where suit is brought.

Order follow property.—SEC. 3231. When any of the property is removed to another county after the commencement of the action, counterparts of the proper order may issue on the demand of the plaintiff to such other county, and may be executed upon such goods found in such county, and farther orders and the necessary counterparts thereof may issue as often as may be necessary.

ORDER—EXECUTION OF.

Execution of: duty of officers.—SEC. 3332. The sheriff must forthwith execute the order by taking possession of the property therein mentioned, if it is found in the possession of the defendant, or of his agent, or of any other person who obtained possession thereof from the defendant, directly or indirectly, after the order was placed in the sheriff's hands, for which purpose he may break open any dwelling house or other enclosure, having first demanded entrance and exhibited his authority, if required.

Defendant examined to discover property.—SEC. 3233. When it appears by affidavit that the property claimed has been disposed of, or concealed so that the order cannot be executed, the court or judge may compel the attendance of the defendant, and examine him on oath as to the situation of the property, and punish a willful obstruction or hindrance, or disobedience of the order of the court in this respect as in case of contempt.

Property delivered to plaintiff. SEC. 3234. The sheriff having taken the property, or any part thereof, shall forthwith deliver the same to the plaintiff.

Defendant may prevent delivery.—SEC. 3235. At any time before the actual delivery to the plaintiff, the defendant may stay all proceedings under the aforesaid order and retain the property in his own possession, by executing a bond to the plaintiff, with sureties to be approved by the clerk or sheriff, conditioned that he will appear in and defend the action, and deliver the property to the plaintiff if he recover judgment therefor in as good condition as it was when the action was commenced, and that he will also pay all costs and damages that may be adjudged against him for the taking or detention of the property.

Must let plaintiff inspect property.—SEC. 3236. But when the property is so retained by the defendant, he shall permit the sheriff and plaintiff to inspect the same; and if the plaintiff so request, the sheriff shall cause the property to be examined and appraised by two sworn appraisers, chosen by the parties to the action, or in their default, by the sheriff himself, in the manner provided for other cases of appraisement; and he shall return their appraisement with the execution.

Return of order.—SEC. 3237. The sheriff must return the order on or before the first day of the trial term, and shall state fully what he has done thereunder. If he has taken any property he shall describe particularly the same. And if he has taken a bond from the defendant as provided in the preceding section, he shall file the same with his return.

II. BOND FOR RETAINING THE PROPERTY, AND PROCEEDINGS IN THAT CASE.

The bond provided for by the statute to enable the defendant to retain the property may be in the following form.

BOND.

No. 91.

Know all men by these presents: That we, C D, principal, and E F and G H, sureties, are held and firmly bound unto I J, in the sum of .... dollars.

The condition of this obligation is such, that whereas A B, sheriff of .... county, Iowa, by virtue of a writ issued by the clerk of the .... Court of said county, in a certain cause wherein the said I J, is plaintiff, and the said C D, is defendant, and to said sheriff directed and delivered, requiring him to take the property therein described, to-wit: [Here describe each article of property,] and deliver the same to said plaintiff; and whereas the said C D, desires to retain possession of said property:

Now therefore, if the said C D, will appear in and defend said action and deliver said property to said plaintiff if he recover judgment therefor, in as good a condition as it was when said action was commenced, and will also pay all costs and damages that may be adjudged against him for the taking or detention of said property, then this obligation to be void, otherwise to be and remain in full force and virtue.

Dated this .... day of ...., 18..

C.... D...., *Principal.*

E.... F...., } *Sureties.*
G.... H.... }

Who to approve the bond.—The bond may be approved by the clerk or sheriff, and when approved by the sheriff, it may be in the following form:

No. 92.

I hereby approve of the within bond and the sureties thereto.

Dated this....day of....18..

A ... B...., *Sheriff.*

Amount of bond and appraisement.—The amount of the bond should be twice the value of the property taken or sought to be taken, and when the property is so retained by the defendant he must permit the sheriff and plaintiff to inspect the same, and if the plaintiff requests it, the sheriff should cause the property to be examined and appraised by two sworn appraisers chosen by the parties to the action, or in case of their default, by the sheriff, in the manner provided for other cases of appraisement, and he is required to return their appraisement with the writ.

Summons, oath and report.—The form of summons and oath may be the same as No. 73 and 74, and of their report, the same as in cases of appraisement on execution, as to which see form No. 86.

The appraisement a guide.—The appraisement may be a guide to the sheriff in fixing the amount of the bond; and in case there is no appraisement the sheriff should fix the penalty of the bond in double the value of the property, according to his best information and judgment.

III. SHERIFF'S RETURN.

No. 93.

SHERIFF'S RETURN.

STATE OF IOWA, } ss.
.... County. }

I, A B, sheriff of said county, hereby certify and return, that

I received the within writ for service on the .... day of ...., 18.., that on the same day, (or some other day), by virtue thereof I took possession of the following property in said county, described in said writ, to-wit: [Here give a particular description of the property taken,] and forthwith delivered the same to C D, the plaintiff therein named pursuant to the command thereof, and now return said writ duly executed.

Dated this .... day of ...., 18..

A.... B...., *Sheriff.*

If all the property is not found.—If all the property cannot be found, the return to the writ should show that fact, and the above form can be modified to suit that case.

RETURN WHERE THE DEFENDANT HAS GIVEN BOND.

No. 94.

STATE OF IOWA, ...County, } ss.

I, A B, sheriff of said county, hereby certify and return, that I received the within writ for service on the .... day of ...., 18..; that on the .... day of ...., 18.., by virtue thereof I took possession of the property therein described, (or if a portion of the same, so state and particularly describe it), in said county; that on the same day, (or any other day, naming it), the said C D, the defendant therein named, for the purpose of staying further proceedings under said writ, and retaining possession of said property, executed a bond to the said E F, plaintiff therein named, with sureties approved by me, (or in case the bond and sureties are approved by the clerk, so state), in a penal sum of double the value of said property as appraised by two sworn appraisers chosen by said parties, (or by me, they having failed to choose said appraisers), which bond is hereto annexed and returned, marked "Exhibit A," with the written return of said appraisers made to me, hereto annexed and marked "Exhibit B."

Whereupon I released said property and delivered the same to the defendant, and I now return this writ with my doings in the premises as aforesaid.

Dated this .... day of ...., 18...

A.... B...., *Sheriff.*

IV. DIRECTIONS OF THE STATUTES.

The statute directs the officer charged with the execution of the writ, to take possession of the property if found in the possession of the defendant or his agent, or any other person who obtained possession thereof directly or indirectly from the defendant after the writ was placed in the sheriff's hands.

The officer is justified in obeying the commands of the writ, if genuine and regular on its face. This rule applies to all process. Conk. Tr., 247, 1 Ed.

Verdict of the jury on the trial.—The Code provides that on the trial of the action the jury must assess the value of the property, as also damages for the taking or detention, whenever by their verdict there will be a judgment for the recovery or return of the property; and when requested to do so by either party, they must find the value of each article thereof.

The Code further provides:

Form of judgment.—SECTION 3239. The judgment shall determine which party is entitled to the possession of the property, and shall designate his right therein and if such party have not the possession thereof, shall also determine the value of the right of such party, which right shall be absolute as to an adverse party having no right in such property, and shall also award such damages to either party as he may be entitled to for illegal detention of such property.

Execution: form of.—SEC. 3240. The execution shall require the sheriff to deliver the possession of the same, particularly describing it, to the party entitled thereto, and may, at the same time, require the sheriff to satisfy any costs, damages, or rents and profits, with interest, recovered by the same judgment, out of the property of the party against whom it was rendered subject to execution, and the value of property for which judgment was recovered to be specified therein, if a delivery thereof cannot be had, and shall in that respect be deemed an execution against property.

Plaintiff's option as to what he will take.—SEC. 3241. If the party found to be entitled to the property, be not already in possession thereof by delivery under the provisions of this chapter, or otherwise, he may, at his option, have execution for the specific delivery of the property, or for the value thereof as determined by the jury. And if any article of the property cannot be obtained on execution, he may take the remainder with the value of the missing articles.

Judgment on bond.—SEC. 3242. When property for which a bond has been given, as hereinbefore provided, is not forthcoming to answer the judgment, and the party entitled thereto elects to take judgment for the value thereof, such judgment may be entered against the principal and sureties in the bond.

When property has been concealed.—SEC. 3243. When it appears by the return of the officer, or by the affidavit of the plaintiff, that any specific property which has been adjudged to belong to one party, has been concealed or removed by the other, the court or a judge may require him to attend and be examined on oath respecting such matter, and may enforce its order in this respect as in the case of contempt.

SEC. 3245. A money judgment taken under the provisions of this chapter in lieu of property exempt from execution, shall also be, to the same extent, exempt from execution and from all set-off or diminution either by the adverse party or by any other person, and such exemption may, at the option of the party, be stated in the judgment.

CHAPTER XIV.

PROPERTY TAKEN FOR INTERNAL IMPROVEMENT.

I. PROVISIONS OF THE CODE.

The Code provides for the taking of private property for works of internal improvement, and for its condemnation for this purpose as follows:

MANNER OF CONDEMNATION.

Sheriff to summon jury.—SECTION 1244. If the owner of any real estate, necessary to be taken for either of the purposes mentioned in the three preceding sections, refuse to grant the right of way, or other necessary interest in said real estate required for such purposes, or, if the owner and the corporation cannot agree upon the compensation to be paid for the same, the sheriff of the county in which said real estate may be situated, shall, upon the application of either party, appoint six disinterested freeholders of said county, not interested in a like question, who shall inspect said real estate and assess the damages which said owner will sustain by the appropriation of his land for the use of said corporation, and make report in writing to the sheriff of said county, and if said corporation shall, at any time before it enters upon said real estate for the purpose of constructing said railway, pay to said sheriff for the use of said owner, the sum so assessed and returned to him as aforesaid, it may construct and maintain its railway over and across such premises.

Jury to assess damages.—SEC. 1245. The application to the sheriff shall be in writing, and the freeholders appointed shall be the commissioners to assess all damages to the owners of real estate in said county, and said corporation, or the owner of any land therein, may, at any time after their appointment, have the damages assessed in the manner herein prescribed by giving the other party five days notice thereof in writing, specifying therein the day and hour when such commissioner will view the premises, which shall be served in the same manner as original notices.

Minor or insane owner.—SEC. 1246. If the owner of any lands is a minor, insane, or other person under guardianship, the guardian of such minor, insane, or other person, may, under the direction of the circuit judge, agree and settle with said corporation for all damages by reason of the taking of such lands for any of the purposes aforesaid, and may give valid conveyances of such land.

Notice to non-resident owner.—SEC. 1247. If the owner of such lands is a non-resident of the county in which the same are situate, no demand of the right of way, or other purpose for which such lands are desired, shall be necessary, except the publication of a notice which may be in the following form:

NOTICE.—For the appropriation of lands for railway purposes. To (here name each person whose land is to be taken or affected,) and all other persons having any interest in, or owning any of the following real estate, [here describe the land by its congressional numbers in tracts not exceeding one-sixteenth of a section, or, if the land consists of lots in a town or city, by the numbers of the lot and block.] You are hereby notified that the . . . . has located its railway over the above described real estate, and desires the right of way over the same, to consist of a strip or belt of land . . feet in width, through the center of which the center line of said railway will run, together with such other land as may be necessary for bermes, waste banks and borrowing pits, and for wood and water stations, (or desires the same for the purposes mentioned in sections twelve hundred and forty-two, and twelve hundred and forty-three of this chapter, as the case may be) and unless you proceed to have the damages to the same appraised on or before . . . day of . . . . , A. D., 18 . , (which time must be at least four weeks after the first publication of the notice,) said company will proceed to have the same appraised on the . . . day of . . . . , (which must be at least eight weeks after the first publication of the notice), at which time you can appear before the appraisers that may be selected.

. . . . Railway Company.

By . . . . attorney, or . . . . agent.

Notice published.—SEC. 1248. Said notice shall be published in some newspaper in the county, if there be one, if there is none, then in a newspaper published in the nearest county through which the proposed railway is to run, for at least eight successive week, prior to the day fixed for the appraisement at the instance of the corporation.

Appraisement: how made and returned.—SEC. 1249. At the time fixed in either aforesaid notices, the appraisement may be made and returned in tracts larger than forty acres, and all the lands appearing of record to belong to one person, and lying in one tract, may be included in one appraisement and return, unless the agent or attorney of the corporation, or the commissioners, has actual knowledge that the tract does not belong wholly to the person in whose name it appears of record; and in case of such knowledge, the appraisement shall be made of the different parcels, as they are known to be owned.

Where dwelling house, garden, or orchard is affected.—SEC. 1250. If it appears from the finding of the commissioners that the dwelling house, out-houses, orchard or garden, of the owner of any land taken will be otherwise injuriously affected by any dam or reservoir to be constructed under section twelve hundred and forty-two of this chapter, such dam shall not be erected until the question of such overflowing or other injury has been determined upon appeal in favor of the corporation,

Talesmen.—SEC. 1251. In case of the death, absence, neglect, or refusal, of any of said freeholders to act as commissioners as aforesaid, the sheriff shall summon other freeholders to complete the panel.

Costs: how paid.—SEC. 1252. The corporation shall pay all the costs of the assessment made by the commissioners and those occasioned by the appeal, unless on the trial thereof a less amount of damages is awarded than was allowed by the commissioners.

Commissioners' report may be recorded.—SEC. 1253. The report of the commissioners, where the same has not been appealed from, and the amount of damages assessed and costs have been deposited with the sheriff, or, if an appeal is taken and the amount of damages assessed on the trial thereof has been paid to the sheriff, may be recorded in the record of deeds in the county where the land is situate, and such record shall be presumptive evidence of title in the corporation to the property so taken, and shall constitute constructive notice of the rights of such corporation therein.

APPEALS.

How taken.—SEC. 1254. Either party may appeal from such assessment of damages to the circuit court within thirty days after the assessment is made, by giving the adverse party, or, if such party is the corporation, its agent or attorney, and the sheriff, notice in writing that such appeal has been taken; the sheriff shall thereupon file a certified copy of so much of the appraisement as applies to the part appealed from, and said court shall thereupon take jurisdiction thereof and try and dispose of the same as in actions by ordinary proceedings. The land owner shall be plaintiff and the corporation defendant.

Not to delay work if amount assessed is deposited with sheriff.—SEC. 1255. An appeal shall not delay the prosecution of the work upon said railway, if said corporation pays or deposits with the sheriff the amount assessed by the commissioners; said sheriff shall not pay such deposit over to the person entitled thereto after the service of notice of an appeal, but shall retain the same until the determination thereof.

When barred.—SEC. 1256. An acceptance by the land owner of the damages awarded by the commissioners shall bar his right to appeal.

Trial of: judgment.—SEC. 1257. On the trial of the appeal, no judgment shall be rendered except for costs; the amount of damages shall be ascertained and entered of record, and, if no money has been paid or deposited with the sheriff, the corporation shall pay the amount so ascertained, or deposit the same with the sheriff before entering upon the premises.

SEC. 1258. If, on the trial of the appeal, the damages awarded by the commissioners are increased, the corporation shall pay or deposit with the sheriff the whole amount of damages awarded before entering on, or, in any manner whatever, using or controlling the premises. And said sheriff, upon being furnished with a certified copy of such assessment, may remove said corporation, its agents, servants, or contractors, from said premises unless the amount of the assessment is forthwith paid or deposited with him.

SEC. 1259. If the amount of the damages awarded by the commissioners is decreased on the trial of the appeal, the amount assessed on the trial of such appeal only shall be paid the land owners.

NON-USER.

By railway corporations of right of way.—SEC. 1260. In any case where a railway, constructed in whole or in part, has ceased to be operated or used for more than ten years, or in any case where the construction of a railway has been commenced, and work on the same has ceased for more than ten years, and the same remains unfinished, it shall be deemed and taken that the corporation or person thus in default has abandoned all right and privilege over so much as remains unfinished as aforesaid.

How right of way may be condemned.—SEC. 1261. In every such case of abandonment, any other corporation may enter upon such abandoned work, or any part thereof, and acquire the right of way over the same, and the right to any unfinished work or grading found thereon and the title thereto, by proceeding in the manner provided, and conforming in all particulars as near as may be to the provisions of this chapter; but parties who have previously received compensation in any form for the right of way on the line of such abandoned railway, which has not been refunded by them, shall not be permitted to recover the second time, but the value of such road-bed and right of way, excluding the work done thereon, when taken for a new company, shall be assessed to the former company or its legal representative.

STATE MAY CONDEMN.

How done and for what purpose.—1271. Whenever in the opinion of the governor, the public interest requires the construction of any drains, sewers, or other conveniences for the benefit of the penitentiary, hospitals for the insane, or any other institutions of the state, upon or across lands being private property, the same proceedings may be had in the name of the state as provided in this chapter, and for that purpose the state shall be considered a person, and the proceedings shall be conducted by the district attorney of the district in which the land is situated whenever directed by the governor, or, the governor may appoint some other person for that purpose.

Damages: how certified and paid.—SEC. 1272. Whenever the amount of the damages contemplated in the preceding section is finally determined, the sheriff or clerk, as the case may be, shall certify the amount thereof to the governor, who shall, by an order indorsed thereon, direct the payment of the same, and the auditor of state shall issue a warrant on the treasury for the amount, which shall be paid with any money not otherwise appropriated. When the money is paid to the sheriff or person entitled thereto, the state, through its proper agent or officer, may enter on the premises and construct the desired work.

II. MANNER OF SUMMONING APPRAISERS AND APPRAISEMENT.

The sheriff in this case may summon appraisers in the same manner provided for an appraisement of property on execution, and the form of appraisement and the oath used for that purpose, with the change which will be suggested, can be used in cases under the above provisions. See form No. 86. For form of summons, see No. 73.

APPLICATION FOR THE APPOINTMENT OF APPRAISERS.

No. 95.

To the Sheriff of .... county, Iowa :

You are hereby required to appoint six disinterested freeholders of said county, not interested in a like question, to inspect the following described real estate, to-wit: [Here insert a description of the land to be condemned,] and assess the damages the owner thereof will sustain by reason of the taking, holding and condemnation thereof, by the .... railway company, in the construction and operation of its railway over the same.

C D, *owner*, (or .... Railway Company,
By ...., Attorney,) (*or Agent*).

The application may be made by either party interested.

FORM OF NOTICE OF ASSESSMENT OF DAMAGES.

No. 96.

To C.... D...., (the owner of the land, or the .... Railway Company, as the case may require.)

You are hereby notified that the commissioners appointed by the sheriff of .... county, Iowa, for that purpose, will, on the .... day of ...., 18.., at .. o'clock, .. M., view and inspect the lands owned by you, (or me,) and described as follows: [Here describe the lands to be condemned], and assess the damages that will be sustained by you (or me, as the case may be,) by reason of the taking, holding and condemnation of the same by the .... Railway Company, for the purpose of constructing and operating its railroad across said land, (or for the location, construction and convenient use of its railway on, across or near said land.

.... Railway Company,

By its Attorney (or Agent, or C D, owner of said land, as the case may be.)

Report of the Appraisers.—The report of the appraisers should be made to the sheriff in writing.

FORM OF APPRAISERS' REPORT.

No. 97.

STATE OF IOWA, }
..... County, } ss.

To A.... B...., Sheriff of said county:

We, the undersigned, appraisers appointed by you to inspect the following described real estate: [Here describe the lands], and assess the damages the owner thereof will sustain, by reason of the taking, holding and condemnation thereof by the .... Railway Company, for the operation, construction and convenient use of its railway, (or for a right of way, or for wood and water stations, or for dams and reservoirs, etc., as the case may be,) on or over said land, do hereby report thereon, as follows:

Having been first duly sworn as such appraisers, we, on the .... day of ...., 18.., at .. o'clock, .. M., of said day, proceeded to inspect said real estate, and thereupon assessed said damages at the sum of $....

Dated this .... day of 18..

C.... D....,
E.... F....,
G.... H....,
I .... J....,
K.... L....,
O.... P...., } *Appraisers.*

FEES—

C.... D...., one day, $2.00.
C.... D...., five miles, .50.
E.... F...., one day, 2.00.
E.... F...., six miles, .60.

Non-Resident owners.—In the case of non-resident owners, a form of notice is given in the Code for publication; and the commissioners could proceed in that case to appraise the damages of the several owners, as specified in the notice, and reference in their report might be made to this notice for a description of the land to be condemned, and the assessment of the damages of each owner for his land appropriated, made in one report, and the notice aforesaid might be attached thereto.

Session laws.—Chapter 34 of the Session Laws of 1874, provide additional powers and duties for the sheriff, as follows:

Quarry or mine owners may have public way established.—SECTION 1. *Be it enacted by the General Assembly of the State of Iowa*, That any person, co-partnership, joint-stock association, or corporation, owning, leasing, or possessing any lands having thereon or thereunder any coal, stone, lead, or other mineral, may have established over the land of another a public way from any stone-quarry, coal, lead, or other mine, to any railway or highway, not exceeding (except by the consent of the owner of the land to be taken) fifty feet in width. When said road shall be constructed, it shall, when passing through inclosed lands, be fenced on both sides by the person or corporations causing said road to be established,

Proceedings to condemn right of way.—SEC. 2. If the owner of any real estate, necessary to be taken for the purposes mentioned in this act, refuse to grant the right of way, or if such owner and the person, partnership, joint-stock association, or corporation seeking to have such way established, cannot agree upon the compensation to be paid for the same, the sheriff of the county in which said real estate may be situated shall, upon the application of either party, appoint six disinterested freeholders of the county, not interested in a like question, who shall inspect said real estate, and assess the damage which said owner will sustain by the appropriation of said land for such public way, and make a report in writing to the sheriff of said county, and if the applicant for such public way shall at any time before entering upon said real estate, for the purpose of constructing such way, pay to said sheriff, for the use of said owner, the sum so assessed and returned to him, as aforesaid, said highway may be at once constructed and maintained over and across said premises.

Code applied to this act.—SEC. 3. In proceeding under this act, the application to the sheriff, the duty of commissioners, the time and manner of assessing the damages, the giving of notice thereof to residents and non-residents, the power of guardians to settle and convey, the making and returning of appraisement, the selection of talesmen, the payment of the costs of assessment, the report of the commisioners, the recording thereof, the right of appeal, the proceedings relating thereto, the result of non-user, the rights and duties as to the other highways, are and shall be the same as provided in the sections of the code numbered twelve hundred and forty-five to and including twelve hundred and sixty-eight, and the provisions of all of said sections, so far as applicable, are declared to be a part of this act, except that the report of the commissioners, and record thereof, shall confer no title to the applicant for the land taken for the highway, but shall be presumptive evidence of the establishment of such way.

Persons condemning may establish railway.—SEC. 4. Any owner, lessee, or possessor of lands having coal, stone, lead, or other mineral thereon, who has paid the damages assessed for highways established under this act, may construct, use, and maintain a railway on such way, for the purpose of reaching and operating any quarry or mine on such land, and of transporting the products thereof to market. In the giving of the notices required by this act, the applicant shall state whether a railway is to be constructed and maintained on the way sought to be established; and if it be so stated the jury shall consider that fact in the assessment of damages.

CHAPTER XV.

THE FORECLOSURE OF CHATTEL MORTGAGES.

I. SHERIFF'S DUTY ON CHATTEL MORTGAGE FORECLOSURE.

The Code provides for a sale of personal property under chattel mortgages, as follows:

Of personal property: how foreclosed.—SECTION 3307. Any mortgage of personal property to secure the payment of money only, and where the time of payment is therein fixed, may be foreclosed by notice and sale as hereinafter provided, unless a stipulation to the contrary has been agreed upon by the parties, or may be foreclosed by action in the proper court.

Notice.—SEC. 3308. The notice must contain a full description of the property mortgaged, together with the time, place and terms of the sale.

Service: on whom.—SEC. 3309. Such notice must be served on the mortgagor, and upon all purchasers from him subsequent to the execution of the mortgage, and all persons having recorded liens upon the same property which are junior to the mortgage, or they will not be bound by the proceedings.

Return.—SEC. 3310. The service and return must be made in the same manner as in the case of the original notice by which civil actions are commenced, except that no publication in the newspapers is necessary for this purpose, the general publication directed in the next section being a sufficient service upon all the parties in cases where service is to be made by publication.

Notice of sale.—SEC. 3311. After notice has been served upon the parties, it must be published in the same manner, and for the same length of time as is required in cases of the sale of like property on execution, and the sale shall be conducted in the same manner.

Title to purchaser.—SEC. 3312. The purchaser shall take all the title and interest on which the mortgage operated.

Bill of sale.—SEC. 3313. The sheriff conducting the sale shall execute to the purchaser a bill of sale of the personal property, which shall be effectual to carry the whole title and interest purchased.

Evidence of service perpetuated.—SEC. 3314. Evidence of the service and publication of the notice aforesaid, and of the sale made in accordance therewith, together with any postponement or other material matter, may be perpetuated by proper affidavits thereof.

SEC. 3315. Such affidavits shall be attached to the bill of sale, and shall then be receivable in evidence to prove the facts they state

Validity of sales.—SEC. 3316. Sales made in accordance with the above requirements, are valid in the hands of a purchaser in good faith, whatever may be the equities between the mortgagor and mortgagee.

Contest: how effected.—SEC. 3317. The right of the mortgagee to foreclose, as well as the amount claimed to be due, may be contested by any one interested in so doing, and the proceeding may be transferred to the district or circuit court, for which purpose an injunction may issue if necessary.

Deeds of trust.—SEC. 3318. Deeds of trust of real or personal property may be executed as securities for the performance of contracts, and shall be considered as, and foreclosed like mortgages,

Notice.—The notice required by the foregoing provisions, may be in the following form:

SHERIFF'S NOTICE OF SALE OF MORTGAGED PROPERTY.

No. 98.

To C D, (and if there are subsequent purchasers or parties having liens on the property insert their names here.)

You are hereby notified, that by virtue of a chattel mortgage of the following described personal property, to wit: [here insert a full description of the mortgaged property,] executed by you the said C D, to E F, to secure to said E F, the sum of $...., (or to secure the payment of a promisory note executed by said E F, to said C D, for the sum of $...., and interest at .... per cent,) and the costs and expenses of a foreclosure; which mortgage, (and note in case a note was given,) bears date .... 18.., and which mortgage was recorded in the office of the recorder of .... county, Iowa, on the .... day of ...., 18.., in book .. of mortgages, page .., will be foreclosed by a sale of said mortgaged property, or so much thereof as will be necessary to satisfy said mortgage, at public auction at ...., in said county, on the .... day of .... 18.., at .... o'clock .. M., of said day.

Said sale will be conducted by the undersigned, sheriff of said county, by virtue of said mortgage.

Dated this .... day of ..... 18..

A ... B...., *sheriff of .... county, Iowa.*

Service of notice.—The notice of sale should be served on the mortgagor, and all purchasers from him subsequent to the execution of the mortgage, and on all persons having recorded liens upon the same property which are junior to the mortgage lien, and the service and return should be made in the same manner as in case of original notices by which civil actions are commenced; and in addition thereto, notice should be posted up in at least three public places in the county, one of which should be at the place where the last District Court was held; and where personal property to the amount of two hundred dollars or upward is to be sold, there should be two publications of the notice in a newspaper in the county, if there be one.

Evidence perpetuated by affidavits.—The notice with the service, including the posting thereof and publication, may be perpetuated by affidavits.

Evidence.—The bill of sale and affidavits attached are receivable in evidence to prove the facts they state.

FORM OF BILL OF SALE.

No. 99.

Know all men by these Presents :

That, whereas, on the .... day of ...., 18.., C D, executed and delivered to E F, a certain chattel mortgage on the following described personal property, to-wit: [Here insert a description of the property], to secure the payment of $...., and interest at .... per cent. and the expenses of a foreclosure of the same, (or the payment of a promissory note of the said C D, for $...., and interest at .... per cent. of even date of said mortgage,) which mortgage was duly filed for record in the office of the recorder of .... county, State of Iowa, where said property was situated on the .... day of ...., 18.., and recorded in the office of said recorder, in book .... of mortgages, page ... ; and, whereas, on the .... day of ...., 18.., said sum secured, (or some portion thereof, stating it,) remaining due and unpaid, the notice of the sale of said property hereto attached was duly served on the said C D, (and if on others, here name them,) and by posting a copy of the same in three public places in said county, one of which was at the place where the last District Court was held, at least three weeks previous to the time of said sale, (and in case the property is of the value of two hundred dollars, add: by two publications thereof in a newspaper published in said county, previous to said sale) ; and, whereas, said sum so secured (or some part of it,) remained due and unpaid at the time fixed for the sale of said property in said notice, I then and there sold said property at public auction to ...., he being the highest bidder therefor, for the sum of $....

Now, therefore, I, A B, sheriff of said county, in consideration of the premises, and of said sum of $...., in hand paid by the said ...., do hereby sell and convey unto the said ...., all the right, title and interest of the said C D, (and also all other parties having claims to, or junior liens on said property, and on whom notice was served,) in and to said property, on which said mortgage operated.

Witness my hand, this .... day of ...., 18..

A.... B...., *sheriff of .... county, Iowa.*

How to apply the Proceeds.—After satisfaction of the mortgage, the balance, if any, should be paid to the mortgagor, unless the sheriff should have notice of the intervening rights of other parties.

It is easy to conceive of cases where other parties would be entitled to the residue. In such cases the sheriff would be acting as agent for both parties or all parties interested; and when he has acted in good faith and with ordinary prudence, he will be protected, otherwise he might be liable for damages.

Where the mortgage fixes the time and place of notice of sale, it should be observed in making the sale, by the sheriff.

CHAPTER XVI.

INJUNCTION CASES.

I. THE SHERIFF'S DUTIES.

The duties of the sheriff in proceedings by injunction are generally confined to the service of the original notice and the writ, and sometimes the service of attachments for contempts in disregarding the mandates of the writ.

The service of the writ.—The service of the writ of injunction is made by reading the original writ to the defendant and giving him a copy thereof, and the return should show these facts, and the time and place of service. Miller's Pleading and Prac., 666.

Sheriff's disobedience of the writ.—For a disobedience of the commands of such process the sheriff may be punished for a contempt of court.

RETURN OF SERVICE.

No. 100.

STATE OF IOWA, } ss.
........County, }

I, A B, sheriff of said county, hereby certify and return, that I received the within writ for service on the .... day of ...., 18.., and that I served the same personally on C D, the defendant therein named, on the .... day of ...., 18.., at ...., in said county, by reading the same to him, and by then and there delivering to him personally, a copy of said writ.

FEES:
Mileage $....
Service ....
Copy.. ....

A.... B...., *sheriff of said county.*

CHAPTER XVII.

SUBPŒNAS.

I. HOW SERVED—RETURN.

How served.—The most common process the sheriff is called upon to serve is the subpœna. Service is made by reading the same to the witness, personally, and by leaving a copy with him, if demanded, and by tendering to him his fees for one day's attendance, and traveling fees if required; or, in case the witness cannot be found, it may be served by leaving a copy thereof at the usual place of residence of the witness, with the fees and traveling expenses above mentioned; but in this last case the witness is not liable for a contempt, until it is shown that said copy came into the hands of the witness together with said fees. Code, Secs. 3674, 3676.

II. FURTHER PROVISIONS OF THE CODE.

When witness conceals himself.—SEC. 3677. If a witness conceal himself, or in any manner attempt to avoid being personally served with a subpœna, any sheriff or constable having the subpœna may use all necessary and proper means to serve the same, and for that purpose may break into any building or other place where the witness is to be found, having first made known his business and demanded admission.

FORM OF RETURN.

No. 101.

STATE OF IOWA, }
......County, } ss.

I, A B, sheriff of said county, hereby certify and return, that I received this subpœna for service on the .... day of ...., 18.., and that I served the same on C D, the witness therein named, at ...., on the .... day of ...., 18.., by reading the same to him, and by then and there leaving a copy thereof with him personally, he having demanded the same; and that no fees were required by said witness; (or, if witness fees were required, so state, and whether paid or not, and if paid, how much.)

Dated ...., 18...

A.... B...., *Sheriff.*

RETURN WHERE COPY IS LEFT.

No. 102.

STATE OF IOWA, ... County. } SS.

I, A B, sheriff, etc., hereby certify and return, etc., and that after diligent search said witness was not found, and that on the .... day of ...., 18.., I left a copy of said subpoena at the dwelling house of the said C D, in .... in said county, that being the usual place of residence of the said C D, with E D, wife of the said C D, and that I also then and there, left with the said E D, the sum of $...., as the fees of said witness.

Dated .... day of ...., 18...

A.... B...., *Sheriff.*

CHAPTER XVIII.

OF CERTIORARI.

SERVICE OF WRIT.

The writ of certiorari must be served the same as an original notice, except that the original writ should be left with the defendant and a return of service made upon a copy thereof. Code, Sec. 3220.

The forms given, for returns on notices, may be changed to suit the required returns in cases of certiorari.

CHAPTER XIX.

WRIT OF HABEAS CORPUS.

HOW AND BY WHOM SERVED.

Who may serve it.—This writ may be served by the sheriff, or by any person appointed for that purpose, in writing, by the court or judge by whom it is issued or allowed. Code, Sec. 3460.

Mode of service.—The proper mode of service is to leave the original with the defendant and preserve a copy thereof on which to make a return of service. Code, Sec. 3461.

If the defendant cannot be found, or if he has not the plaintiff in his custody, the service may be made on any person having the plaintiff in his custody, in the same manner and with the same effect as though he had been made defendant therein. Code, Sec. 3462.

The Code further provides:

Power of officer when defendant is concealed.—SECTION 3463. If the defendant conceal himself, or refuse admittance to the person attempting to serve the writ, or if he attempt wrongfully to carry the plaintiff out of the county or the state, after the service of the writ as aforesaid, the sheriff, or the person who is attempting to serve, or who has served the writ as above contemplated, is authorized to arrest the defendant, and bring him, together with the plaintiff, forthwith before the officer or court before whom the writ is made returnable.

Arrest.—SEC. 3464. In order to make such arrest, the sheriff or other person having the writ, possesses the same power as is given to a sheriff for the arrest of a person charged with a felony.

SEC. 3465. If the plaintiff can be found, and if no one appears to have the charge or custody of him, the person having the writ may take him into custody, and make return accordingly. And to get possession of plaintiff's person in such cases, he possesses the same power as is given by the last section for the arrest of the defendant.

Want of form.—SEC. 3466. The writ of habeas corpus must not be disobeyed for any defects of form or misdescription of the plaintiff or defendant, provided enough is stated to show the meaning and intent of the writ.

Penalty for eluding writ.—SEC. 3467. If the defendant attempt to elude the service of the writ of habeas corpus, or to avoid the effect thereof by transferring the plaintiff to another, or by concealing him, he shall, on conviction, be imprisoned in the penitentiary or county jail not more than one year, and fined not exceeding one thousand dollars. And any person knowingly aiding or abetting in any such act shall be subject to the like punishment.

Refuse to give copy of process.—SEC. 3468. An officer refusing to deliver a copy of any legal process by which he detains the plaintiff in custody, to any person who demands such copy, and tenders the fees therefor, shall forfeit two hundred dollars to the person so detained.

When to issue.—SEC. 3469. The court or judge to whom the application for the writ is made, if satisfied that the plaintiff would suffer any irreparable injury before he could be relieved by the proceedings as above authorized, may issue a precept to the sheriff, or any other person selected instead, commanding him to bring the plaintiff forthwith before such court or judge.

Evidence.—SEC. 3470. When the evidence aforesaid is farther sufficient to justify the arrest of the defendant for a criminal offense committed in connection with the illegal detention of the plaintiff, the precept must also contain an order for the arrest of the defendant.

How served.—SEC. 3471. The officer or person to whom the precept is directed, must execute the same by bringing the defendant, and also the plaintiff if required, before the court or judge issuing it, and thereupon the defendant must make return to the writ of habeas corpus in the same manner as if the ordinary course had been pursued.

Examination.—SEC. 3472. The defendant may also be examined and committed or bailed or discharged, according to the nature of the case.

RETURN TO HABEAS CORPUS.

No. 103.

STATE OF IOWA, } ss.
.... County. }

I, A B, sheriff of said county, hereby certify and return, that I received the original writ of habeas corpus of which the within is a copy, for service on the .... day of ...., 18.., and that on the same day, (or some other day, naming it,) I served the same on C D, the defendant therein named at ...., in said county, by leaving with said C D, said original writ.

Dated this .... day of ...., A. D. 18...

A.... B...., *Sheriff.*

RETURN WHERE SERVICE IS MADE ON ANOTHER PARTY.

No. 104.

STATE OF IOWA, } ss.
.......County. }

I, A B, sheriff of said county, hereby certify and return, that I received the original writ of habeas corpus, of which the within is a copy, for service, on the .... day of ...., 18.., and that on the .... day of ...., 18.., at ...., in said county, I served the same on E F, the person who had the plaintiff in his custody, by leaving with him said original writ.

Dated, ..., 18..

A.... B...., *Sheriff.*

CHAPTER XX.

WRIT OF MANDAMUS.

SERVICE AND RETURN.

The service and return of a writ of mandamus may be the same as in case of habeas corpus, and the forms given in that case will be sufficient guide to the officer in the case of mandamus.

CHAPTER XXI.

COMMITMENT FOR INSANITY.

SHERIFF'S DUTY.

On the finding of a jury that a person charged with a crime is insane, the Code provides as follows:

If insane.—SECTION 4624. If the jury find the defendant insane, the proceedings on the indictment shall be suspended until he becomes sane, and the court, if it deem his discharge dangerous to the public peace or safety, may order that he be in the meantime committed by the sheriff to the Iowa Insane Hospital, and that upon his becoming sane, he be delivered by the superintendent of the hospital to the sheriff.

Bail: released.—SEC. 4625. The commitment of the defendant, as provided in the last section, exonerates his bail, or entitles a person authorized to receive the property of the defendant, to a return of the money he may have deposited instead of bail.

Detained in hospital.—SEC. 4626. If the defendant be received into the hospital he must be detained there until he becomes sane. When he becomes sane, the superintendent of the hospital must give notice of that fact to the sheriff and the district attorney of the proper district. The sheriff must thereupon, without delay, bring the defendant from the hospital, and place him in the proper custody until he be brought to trial or judgment, as the case may be, or be legally discharged.

Expenses.—SEC. 4627. The expense of sending the defendant to the hospital, bringing him back, and any other expense incurred, are to be paid in the first instance by the county from which he was sent, but the county may recover from the estate of the defendant, if he have any, or from a relative, or another county, town, township, or city, bound to provide for or maintain him elsewhere.

SEC. 4628. Sheriffs, for delivering persons found to be insane, under the provisions of this chapter, are entitled to the same fees therefor as are allowed for conveying convicts to the penitentiary.

CHAPTER XXII.

OF THE SERVICE OF OTHER PROCESS.

Other notices, orders and process than those we have mentioned are sometimes required to be served by the sheriff, such as notices of appeal, of motions, to tenants, etc. But the mode of service is usually pointed out by the statute relating to those matters.

The provisions of the Code relating to service of notices of motions, are as follows:

SERVICE.

Service: how made.—SECTION 2916. Notices and copies of motions mentioned in this chapter, my be served by any one who would be authorized to serve an original notice.

SEC. 2917. The service shall be on each of the parties adverse to the motion, if more than one, or on an attorney of record of such party.

SEC. 2918. The service may be personal on such party or attorney, or may be made in the same manner as is provided for the service of the original notice in civil actions; or it may be served on the attorney by being left at his office with any person having the charge thereof.

Return.—SEC. 2919. Any officer authorized to serve any notice, shall serve at once the same and make prompt return to the party who delivered the same to him, and a failure to do so shall be punished as a disobedience of the process of the court.

SEC. 2920. The return of proof of service must state the manner in which it was made.

When court may direct manner of service.—SEC. 2921. When the party has no known place of abode in this state, and no attorney in the county where the action is pending, or where the parties, plaintiffs or defendants, are numerous, the court or judge may direct the mode of serving notices, and on whom they shall be served.

SERVICE OF NOTICES IN OTHER CASES—EXECUTIONS.

Notices: how served.—SEC. 3214. The service of all notices of appeal, or in any way growing out of such rights or connected therewith, and all notices in the supreme court, shall be in the way provided for the services of like notices in the circuit or district court, and they may be served by the same person and returned in the same manner, and the original notice of the appeal must be returned immediately after service to the office of the clerk of the district or circuit court, where the suit is pending.

Executions: Form of.—SEC. 3215. Executions issued from the supreme court shall be the same as those from the district or circuit court and attended with the same consequences, and shall be returnable in the same time.

CHAPTER XXIII.

SHERIFF'S DUTY IN RELATION TO CRIMES.

I. RELATING TO ARRESTS.

May summon the power of the county.—The sheriff and his deputies, as we have already observed, are conservators of the peace, and in order to preserve the same or prevent crime, or arrest any person guilty thereof, or lawfully charged therewith, or to execute any lawful process, may call any person to their aid, and when necessary in the discharge of their duty in this respect, may summon the *posse comitatus*, or power of the county. Code, Sec. 340.

Provision of the Code relating to arrests.—The Code particularly defines what an arrest is, and how and by whom it may be made, and what should be done on arrests, as follows:

OF ARREST ON PRELIMINARY EXAMINATION.

Complaint.—SECTION 4185. When complaint is made before a magistrate of the commission of some designated public offense, triable on indictment in the county in which such magistrate has local jurisdiction, and charging some person with the commission thereof, he may issue a warrant for the arrest of such person. The complaint may be in form substantially the same as provided in section four thousand six hundred and sixty-three of chapter fifty-two of this title.

Warrant: form of.—SEC. 4186. The warrant of arrest on a preliminary information, must be substantially in the following form:

COUNTY OF . . .
THE STATE OF IOWA,

To any peace officer in the State:

Preliminary information upon oath having been this day laid before me that the crime of (designating it,) has been committed, and accusing A B thereof:

You are, therefore, commanded forthwith to arrest the said A B, and bring him before me at (naming the place,) or in case of my absence or inability to act, before the nearest or most accessible magistrate in this county.

Dated at . . , this . . day of . . , A. D. 18 .

C . . D . . , *Justice of the Peace,*
(or as the case may be.)

Subpœna as witnesses E . . F . . and G . . H . .

SEC. 4187. The warrant must specify the name of the defendant, and if it be unknown to the magistrate, may designate him by any name. It must also state, by name or general description, an offense which authorizes the magistrate to issue the warrant, the time of issuing it, and the county, city, town, township, or village where it was issued, and must be signed by the magistrate with his name of office.

Directed.—SEC. 4188, It must be directed to "any peace officer in the state."

If offense is a misdemeanor.—SEC. 4189. If the offense stated in the warrant be a misdemeanor, the magistrate issuing it must make an indorsement on the warrant as follows; "Let the defendant, when arrested, be admitted to bail in the sum of . . dollars, if he desires to give bail," and fix in the indorsement the amount in which bail may be taken.

How served.—SEC. 4190. The warrant of arrest may be delivered to any peace officer for execution, and executed in any county in the state.

If offense be felony.—SEC. 4191. If the offense stated in the warrant be a felony, the officer making the arrest must take the defendant before the magistrate who issued it at the place mentioned in the command thereof, or, in the event of his absence or inability to act, before the nearest or most accessible magistrate in the county in which it was issued.

Bail in case of misdemeanor.—SEC. 4192. If the offense stated in the warrant be a misdemeanor, and the defendant be arrested in another county, the officer must, upon being required by the defendant, take him before a magistrate or the clerk of the district court of the same county in which he was arrested, for the purpose of giving bail, and the magistrate or clerk before whom he is taken in such county, must take bail from him accordingly for his appearance at the district court of the county in which the warrant was issued, on the first day of the next term thereof.

Order for discharge of defendant.—SEC. 4193. On taking bail in the case provided for in the preceding section, the magistrate or clerk taking such bail must make on the warrant an order signed by him with his name of office, for the discharge of the defendant, substantially as follows:

COUNTY OF (here name the county:)
THE STATE OF IOWA.

To (here state the name of the officer who has the defendant in custody, with the addition of his name of office, thus A, B., sheriff of . . county, according to the truth:)

The defendant named in the warrant of arrest in your custody, under the authority thereof, for the offense therein designated, having given sufficient bail to answer the same, by the undertaking herewith delivered to you, you are commanded forthwith to discharge him from custody, and without unnecessary delay deliver this order, together with the said undertaking of bail, to the clerk of the district court of . . county, on or before the first day of the next term thereof.

Dated at . . , this . . day of . . , A. D., (or as the case may be.)

. . . . , *Justice of the Peace,*
(Or as the case may be.)

And must deliver the warrant with the order thereon, together with the undertaking of bail, to the officer having the defendant in custody, who shall forthwith discharge the defendant from arrest and without unnecessary delay, and on or before the first day of the next term of the court at which the defendant is required to appear, deliver or transmit by mail or otherwise the warrant, with the order thereon, together with the undertaking of bail, to the clerk of the court at which the defendant is required to appear, who shall forthwith file the same in his office; and the magistrate who issued the warrant shall return to the clerk the affidavits of the informant, and his witnesses upon which the warrant was issued, on or before the first day of the next term of the court, and the clerk shall, when the affidavits are returned by the magistrate, file the same in his office, with the warrant and undertaking of bail.

If bail be not given.—SEC. 4194. If bail be not forthwith given by the defendant as provided in the two preceding sections, the magistrate or clerk must re-deliver to the officer the warrant, and the officer must take the defendant before the magistrate who issued it, at the place mentioned in the command thereof, or, if he be absent or unable to act, before the nearest or most accessible magistrate in the county in which the warrant was issued.

Proceedings after arrest.—SEC. 4195. In all cases when the defendant is arrested, he must be taken before the magistrate or clerk without unnecessary delay, and the officer must at the same time deliver to the magistrate or clerk the warrant with his return thereon, indorsed and subscribed by him in his name of office.

SEC. 4196. If the defendant be taken before a magistrate in the county in which the warrant was issued, other than the magistrate who issued it as hereinbefore provided, the affidavits on which the warrant was issued must be sent to such magistrate, or if they cannot be procured, the informant and his witnesses must be subpœnaed to make new affidavits.

BY WHOM AND HOW MADE.

What is.—SEC. 4197. Arrest is the taking of a person in custody in a case, and in the manner authorized by law.

By whom.—SEC. 4198. An arrest may be made by a peace officer, or by a private person.

With warrant.—SEC. 4199. A peace officer may make an arrest in obedience to a warrant delivered to him.

Without by peace officer.—SEC. 4200. A peace officer without a warrant may make an arrest:

1. For a public offense committed or attempted in his presence;

2. Where a public offense has in fact been committed, and he has reasonable ground for believing that the person to be arrested has committed it.

By private person.—SEC. 4201. A private person may make an arrest:

1. For a public offense committed or attempted in his presence;

2. When a felony has been committed, and he has reasonable ground for believing that the person to be arrested has committed it.

Magistrate may orally order arrest.—SEC. 4202. A magistrate may orally order a peace officer, or a private person, to arrest any one committing, or attempting to commit a public offense in the presence of such magistrate, which order shall authorize the arrest.

When made.—SEC. 4203. An arrest may be made on any day, or at any time of the day or night.

How to be made.—SEC. 4204. The person making the arrest must inform the person to be arrested of the intention to arrest him, of the cause of the arrest, of his authority to make it, and that he is a peace officer, if such be the case, and require him to submit to his custody, except when the person to be arrested is actually engaged in the commission of, or attempt to commit, the offense, or flies immediately after its commission, and if acting under the authority of a warrant, he must give information thereof, and show the warrant if required.

When resisted.—SEC. 4205. When the arrest is being made by an officer under the authority of a warrant, after information of the intention to make the arrest, if the person to be arrested either flee or forcibly resist, the officer may use all necessary means to affect the arrest.

May break and enter premises.—SEC. 4106. To make an arrest, if the offense be a felony, a private person, if any public offense, a peace officer acting under the authority of a warrant, or without a warrant, may break open a door or window of a house in which the person to be arrested may be, or in which they have reasonable grounds for believing he is, after having demanded admittance and explained the purpose for which admittance is desired.

In order to get out.—SEC. 4207. Any person who has lawfully entered a house for the purpose of making an arrest under the provisions of the preceding section, may break open the door or window thereof if detained therein, when necessary for the purpose of liberating himself; and an officer may do the same, when necessary for the purpose of liberating a person who, acting in his aid, and by his command, lawfully entered for the purpose of making an arrest, and is detained therein.

Refuses to assist in making arrest.—SEC. 4208. Any person making an arrest, may orally summon as many persons as he deems necessary to aid him in making the arrest, and all persons failing to obey such summons shall be guilty of a misdemeanor.

Arrest: how made.—SEC. 4209. An arrest is made by an actual restraint of the person to be arrested, or by his submission to the custody of the person making the arrest.

Force.—SEC. 4210. No unnecessary force or violence shall be used in making an arrest.

How treated.—SEC. 4211. A person arrested is not to be subjected to any more restraint than is necessary for his detention.

May take weapons from persons arrested.—SEC. 4212. He who makes an arrest may take from the person arrested all offensive weapons which he may have about his person, and must deliver them to the magistrate before whom he is taken, to be disposed of according to law.

Escape.—SEC. 4213. If a person, after being arrested, either by a peace officer without a warrant, or by a private person, escape, or be rescued, the person from whose custody he escaped or was rescued, may immediately pursue and retake him in any part of the state, and for that purpose may, if necessary, break open the door or window of a house in which he may be, or in which he has reasonable ground to believe he is, after having stated his purpose and demanded admittance, and when the person escaping or rescued was in custody under a warrant or commitment, this may be done at any time under the original warrant or commitment.

Arrest by bystander.—SEC. 4214. A peace officer may take before a magistrate a person who, being engaged in a breach of the peace, is arrested by a bystander and delivered to him.

When arrest is by private person.—SEC. 4215. A private person who has arrested another for the commission of an offense, must, without unnecessary delay, take him before a magistrate or deliver him to a peace officer.

SEC. 4216. A private person who makes an arrest and delivers the person arrested to a peace officer, must also accompany the officer before the magistrate.

By officer with warrant.—SEC. 4217. An officer making an arrest in obedience to a warrant, shall proceed with the person arrested as commanded by the warrant, or as provided by law.

When without warrant.—SEC. 4218. When an arrest is made without a warrant, whether by a peace officer or a private person, the person arrested shall, without unnecessary delay, be taken before the nearest or most accessible magistrate in the county in which the arrest is made; and the grounds on which the arrest was made shall be stated to the magistrate by affidavit, subscribed and sworn to by the person making the statement before the magistrate, in the same manner as upon a preliminary information, as nearly as may be.

HEARING BEFORE MAGISTRATE.

Magistrate may order information to be filed.—SEC. 4219. If the magistrate believes from the statements in the affidavit that the offense charged is triable in the county in which the arrest was made, and that there is sufficient ground for a trial or preliminary examination, as the case may require, and that it will not be inconvenient for the witnesses on the part of the state that such trial or preliminary examination should be had before him, he shall proceed as if the person arrested had been brought before him on arrest under a warrant, and if the case be one within his jurisdiction to try and determine, shall order an information to be filed against him.

May order hearing to take place before another magistrate.—SEC. 4220. If the magistrate believes from the statements in the affidavit that the offense charged is triable in the county in which the arrest is made, and that there is sufficient ground for a trial or preliminary examination, and that it will be more convenient for the witnesses on the part of the state that such trial or examination should be had before some other magistrate, he shall, by a written order by him signed with his name of office, commit the person arrested to a peace officer, to be by him taken before such magistrate in the same county who has jurisdiction to try or examine the charge as the case may require, and as shall be convenient for the witnesses on the part of the state, and deliver the affidavit and the order of commitment to the peace officer, who shall proceed with the person arrested as directed by the order; and such magistrate, when the person arrested is brought before him, shall proceed as on an arrest under a warrant, and, if the case be within his jurisdiction to try and determine, shall order an information to be filed against the person arrested.

When the offense is triable in another county.—SEC. 4221. If the magistrate believes from the statements in the affidavit that the offense charged is triable in a county different from that in which the arrest is made, and that there is sufficient ground for a trial or preliminary examination, he shall, by a written order by him signed with his name of office, commit the person arrested to a peace officer, to be by him taken before a magistrate in the county in which the offense is triable, who has jurisdiction to make either preliminary examination into the charges, or try and determine the same, as the case may require, and, if the offense be a misdemeanor only triable on indictment, shall fix in the order the amount of bail which the person arrested may give for his appearance at the district court of the county in which the offense is indictable, on the first day of the next term thereof, to answer an indictment.

Bail: commitment: discharge..—SEC. 4222. If bail be given as provided in the preceding section, it may be either before the magistrate making the order, or the magistrate in the county in which the offense is triable before whom he is taken under the order, or a magistrate of any county through which he passes in going from the county in which the arrest was made to that in which the offense is triable, or the clerk of the district court of either of said counties; and, when given, the magistrate or clerk taking the same shall make on the order of commitment an order for the discharge of the person arrested from custody, who shall forthwith be discharged accordingly, and to transmit by mail or otherwise, to the clerk of the district court of the county at which the person arrested is bound to appear, on or before the first day of the next term thereof, and as soon as it can be conveniently done after taking the bail, the affidavits, the order of commitment and discharge, together with the undertaking of the bail, who shall file the same together in his office.

SEC. 4223. If bail be not given as provided in the last two sections, before the magistrate in the county in which the arrest was made, or if the offense charged is a misdemeanor, triable on information, the magistrate must deliver the affidavits and the order of commitment to a peace officer, who shall proceed with the person arrested as directed by the order, or provided by law; and the magistrate in the county in which the offense is triable, when the person arrested is brought before him, shall proceed as on an arrest under a warrant, and if the case be within his jurisdiction to try and determine, shall order an information to be filed against the person arrested.

Officer having person in custody to take him before magistrate.—SEC. 4224. In the cases contemplated in the last three sections, the officer having the person arrested in custody, under the order, shall take him before the proper magistrate in the county in which the offense is triable, which is most convenient for the witnesses on the part of the state, unless, in case of a misdemeanor triable on indictment as hereinbefore provided, the person arrested desires to give bail, in which case he shall take him before the most convenient magistrate in the county in which the offense with which he is charged is triable, or any county through which he passes in going from the county in which the arrest was made to the county in which the offense is triable, or before the clerk of the district court of either of said counties for the purpose of giving bail.

Officer's return how made.—SEC. 4225. In all cases, the peace officer, when he takes a person committed to him under an order as provided in this chapter before a magistrate, or clerk of the district court, either for the purpose of giving bail, if bail be taken, or for trial or preliminary examination, must make his return on such order, and sign such return with his name of office, and deliver the same to the magistrate or clerk.

Same as common law.—The foregoing provisions in relation to arrests are in harmony with the general rules of the common law. 4 Black., 292; Foster's Com. Law, 311; Chit. Crim. Law, 15.

What constitutes an arrest.—To constitute an arrest the officer should take the defendant into his custody. And this at common law required that the party be actually touched by the officer, or confined in a room, or submit himself by words and actions to the custody of the officer.

When a party may be arrested.—The arrest may be

made in the day or night time and on Sundays as well as other days, and if the party is liable on a criminal charge, the court will not inquire into the manner of arrest though the party be arrested in a foreign State. 3 East., 157; 9 Barn. & Cress., 446.

Directions of the warrant and exceeding authority.—The officer should not arrest the wrong person on the warrant or he will be a trespasser, and if the warrant is defective, or the officer exceeds his lawful authority under it, he is not protected by it.

When a dwelling house may be broken open.—Under the provisions of the statute there must be at least a reasonable ground for believing that the party to be arrested is in the house, to justify either a private person or an officer to break it open, even after a demand of admittance and explanation of the cause for which the admittance is desired.

When justified—though the party is not found.—If the party for the purpose of making an arrest in good faith, and upon reasonable grounds of belief of the presence of a party sought to be arrested is within, he would be justified, in breaking open a dwelling house, even though the party sought be not in the house, or be acquitted on the trial; and according to the principles of the common law, if an officer was killed by a party resisting his entrance into a house to make an arrest, and there was no reasonable grounds for believing the party to be arrested was within the house at the time, and he was not within, and the officer did not act in good faith, it would be justifiable homicide; while on the other hand the killing of the party resisting under such circumstances would be murder, or at least manslaughter in the officer. 4 Black., 288.

The same would probably be true under the provisions of the statute.

An arrest without warrant.—In case a party is arrested by a private person, or by an officer without a warrant, the person arrested should be taken without unnecessary delay before the nearest and most accessible magistrate and the grounds of the arrest stated in an affidavit to the magistrate.

II. THE OFFICER'S DUTY ON SEARCH WARRANTS.

Closely related to arrests in many respects is the duty of the officer on search warrants.

The following are the provisions of the Code on the subject:

By whom served.—SECTION 4637. A search warrant may in all cases be served by any of the officers mentioned in its direction, but by no other person except in aid of the officer, on his requisition, he being present and acting in its execution.

Officer may break open doors.—SEC. 4638. The officer may break open any outer or inner door or window of a house, or any part of the house, or anything therein to execute the warrant, if, after notice of his authority and purpose, he be refused admittance.

SEC. 4639. He may break open any outer or inner door or window of a house for the purpose of liberating a person, who, having entered to aid him in the execution of the warrant, is detained therein, or, when necessary, for his own liberation.

Must be served in day time.—SEC. 4640. The magistrate must insert a direction in the warrant, that it be served in the day time unless the affidavit be positive that the property is on the person, or in the place to be searched; in which case, he may insert a direction that it may be served at any time of the day or night.

Return: in what time.—SEC. 4641. A search warrant must be executed and returned to the magistrate by whom it was issued within ten days after its date. After the expiration of such time, the warrant, unless executed, is void.

Officer receipt for property.—SEC. 4642. When the officer takes any property under the warrant, he must give a receipt for the property taken, specifying it in detail, to the person from whom it was taken or in whose possession it was found, or, in the absence of the person, he must leave it in the place where he found the property.

Return with inventory.—SEC. 4643. The officer must forthwith return the warrant to the magistrate, and at the same time deliver to him a written inventory of the property taken, made publicly or in the presence of the person from whose possession it was taken and of the applicant for the warrant, if they be present, verified by the affidavit of the officer at the foot of the inventory and taken before the magistrate, to the following effect: "I, the officer by whom the annexed warrant was executed, do swear that the above inventory contains a true and detailed account of all the property taken by me on the warrant."

Officer must not exceed authority.—SEC. 4651. A peace officer who in executing a search warrant willfully exceeds his authority, or exercises it with unnecessary severity, is guilty of a misdemeanor.

SEC. 4652. When a person charged with a felony is supposed by the magistrate before whom he is brought, to have upon his person a dangerous weapon or anything which may be used as evidence of the commission of the offense, the magistrate may direct him to be searched in his presence, and the weapon or other thing to be retained, subject to his order, or the order of the court in which the defendant may be tried.

SEC. 4653. When any officer, in the execution of a search warrant, shall find any stolen or embezzled property, or shall seize any other things, for which a search is allowed by this chapter, all the property and things so seized, shall be safely kept by the direction of the court or magistrate, so long as shall be necessary for the purpose of being produced as evidence on any trial; and as soon as may be afterwards, all such stolen and embezzled property shall be restored to the owner thereof, and all other things seized by virtue of such warrant shall be destroyed, under the direction of the court or magistrate.

III. OF THE DISPOSAL OF PROPERTY STOLEN OR EMBEZZLED.

Held by officer.—SECTION 4654. When property alleged to have been stolen or embezzled, comes into the custody of a peace officer, he must hold the same subject to the order of the magistrate authorized by the next section to direct the disposal thereof.

Delivered to owner.—SEC. 4655. On satisfactory proof of title by the owner of the property, the magistrate before whom the information is laid, or who shall examine the charge against the person accused of stealing or embezzling the same, may order it to be delivered to the owner, on his paying the reasonable and necessary expenses incurred in the preservation and keeping thereof, to be certified by the magistrate. The order shall entitle the owner to demand and receive the property.

SEC. 4656. If the property stolen or embezzled come into the custody of a magistrate, it must be delivered to the owner on satisfactory proof of his title, and on his paying the necessary expenses incurred in its preservation, to be certified as before provided.

SEC. 4657. If the property stolen or embezzled has not been delivered to the owner, the court before which a conviction is had, may, on proof of his title, order restoration.

When not claimed.—SEC. 4558. If the property stolen or embezzled be not claimed by the owner before the expiration of six months from the conviction of the person stealing or embezzling it, the magistrate or other officer having it in his custody, must, on payment of the necessary expenses incurred for its preservation, deliver it to the auditor of the county to be applied under the direction of the board of supervisors thereof for the benefit of the poor of the county.

Officer give receipts for property.—SEC. 4659. When the money or other property is taken from the defendant arrested upon a charge of a public offense, the officer taking it shall, at the time, give duplicate receipts therefor, specifying particularly the amount of money and the kind of property taken; one of which receipts he must deliver to the defendant, and the other he must forthwith file with the clerk of the district court of the county where the depositions and statements are to be sent by the magistrate.

To follow the directions of the warrant.—The officer in the execution of a search warrant should carefully follow its directions if he would be protected by it.

He cannot search other than the person or house described in the warrant.

House of a company.—If the warrant describes a house to be searched as the house of a company, it will not authorize the officer to search a house of an individual member of the company;

and if goods be described in general terms as goods, wares, and merchandise, without any specification of their character, quality, number or weight, or any other circumstance tending to describe or distinguish them, it is not such a particular description of the property as is required by the statute and the constitution, of which the officer should take notice, and he would be liable as a trespasser in the execution of such a warrant, and the property could be replevied. Constitution Art. 1, Sec. 8; Code, Sec. 4631–4636; 33 Iowa, 134; 34 Iowa, 128.

Warrant regular.—If the warrant is issued by a proper magistrate and regular on its face, and the person and place are particularly described in it, it is a sufficient justification to the officer to execute the process according to the command thereof and in the manner pointed out by the statute.

RETURN OF SERVICE.

No. 105.

STATE OF IOWA, } ss.
......County, }

I, A B, sheriff of said county, hereby certify and return, that I received the within warrant for service on the .... day of ...., 18.., and that by virtue thereof, on the same day (or at any other time,) I made search on the person of C D, named therein to be searched, (or in the house situated, etc., described therein,) at ...., in said county, for the property described therein, and found the same, and forthwith took possession thereof (or a portion of the same, describing it,) and that the following is a true inventory of the same, then and there made publicly (or in the presence of the said C D, and the applicant for the warrant, if such was the fact,) by me to-wit:

INVENTORY.

One gold hunter case Elgin watch;
One pistol, six shooter;
One United States 5-20 bond of $1,000;
One large sole-leather trunk.
[If all the property should not be found, so state the fact.]
Dated this....day of....18..

A ... B...., *Sheriff.*

OATH OF OFFICER TO THE RETURN.

No. 106.

STATE OF IOWA, } ss.
.... County. }

I, A B, being duly sworn, depose and say that I am sheriff of said county; that I executed the annexed search warrrant as said officer; that the return thereon made by me is true; and that the inventory contained in said return, contains a true and detailed account of all property taken by me on said warrant.

A.... B....

Subscribed and sworn to by said A B, before me this .... day of .... 18..

E.... F...., *Justice of the Peace.*

CHAPTER XXIV.

BENCH WARRANTS ON INDICTMENTS AND AFTER FINAL JUDGMENT.

I. WHERE AND HOW SERVED.

The provisions of the Code in reference to bench warrants on indictment, are as follows:

Where served.—SECTION 4324. The bench warrant may be served in any county in the state.

Proceedings.—SEC. 4325. If the defendant, when arrested, be brought before a magistrate, or the clerk of the district court of the same county in which it was issued, or another county, for the purpose of giving bail, the same proceedings must be had, in all respects, as if he had been arrested on a warrant of arrest, issued by a magistrate on a preliminary information, as nearly as may be.

Indictment against a corporation.—SEC. 4326. The process upon an indictment against a corporation shall be a notice; which shall be issued by the clerk at any time after the filing of the indictment in his office, on the application of the district attorney. The notice shall be under the seal of the court, and shall substantially, notify the defendant of the finding of the indictment, of the nature of the offense charged, and that he must forthwith appear and answer the same. It may be served by any peace officer in any county in the state on any officer or agent of the defendant, by reading the same to him and leaving with him a copy thereof. It shall be returned to the clerk's office without delay, with proper evidence of its service; and, from and after two days from the time of making such service, the defendant shall be considered in court, and thereafter shall be considered to be present to all proceedings had on the indictment.

Defendant arraigned.—SEC. 4327. As soon as practicable after an indictment is found, the defendant must be arraigned thereon, unless he waive the same; but where a corporation is defendant, arraignment shall not be required.

If for felony or misdemeanor.—SEC. 4328. If the indictment be for a felony, the defendant must be personally present, but if for a misdemeanor only, his personal appearance is unnecessary, and he may appear upon arraignment by counsel.

If in custody.—SEC. 4329. When he is in custody, the court must direct the officer in whose custody he is to bring him before it to be arraigned, and the officer must do so accordingly.

If on bail.—SEC. 4330. If the defendant has been discharged on bail, or has deposited money instead thereof, and does not appear for arraignment when his personal appearance is necessary, the court, in addition to the forfeiture of the undertaking of bail, or of the money deposited, may, on motion of the district attorney, make an order directing the clerk to issue a bench warrant for his arrest, and fix the amount in which bail will be taken if the offense be bailable.

II. BENCH WARRANTS FOR FINAL JUDGMENT.

The provisions of the Code in relation to the service of bench warrants, issued for the arrest of a defendant failing to appear to receive the judgment of the court, are as follows:

Service.—SECTION 4501. The bench warrant may be served in any county in the state.

SEC. 4502. Whether the bench warrant be served in the county where it was issued, or in another county, the officer must arrest the defendant and bring him before the court, or commit him to the officer mentioned in the warrant according to the command thereof.

III. ATTACHMENTS AND WARRANTS.

Attachments or warrants may be issued by the order of the court for contempts, as for failure to answer interrogatories, for disobedience of a judgment or order of the court in certain cases, etc., etc.

The service in such cases should be according to the command of the warrant, and the return made according to the facts in the case.

IV. EXECUTION OF JUDGMENT IN CRIMINAL CASES.

The provisions of the Code in relation thereto are as follows:

OF EXECUTION.

Copy of judgment furnished officer.—SECTION 4512. When a judgment of imprisonment, either in the penitentiary or county jail is pronounced, a certified copy of the entry thereof in the record book, must be forthwith furnished to the officer whose duty it is to execute the same, who shall proceed and execute it accordingly, and no other warrant or authority is necessary to justify or require its execution.

Commitment of defendant.—SEC. 4513. If the judgment be imprisonment, or a fine and imprisonment until it be satisfied, the defendant must forthwith be committed to the custody of the proper officer, and by him detained until the judgment be complied with, or the defendant discharged by due course of law.

By whom executed.—SEC. 4514. When the judgment is imprisonment in the county jail of the county in which the trial is had, or a fine and that the defendant be imprisoned in such county jail until it be satisfied, the judgment must be executed by the sheriff of that county. In all other cases, when the judgment is imprisonment, the sheriff of the county, in which the trial was had, must deliver the defendant to the proper officer in execution of the judgment.

SEC. 4515. If the judgment be imprisonment, or a fine and imprisonment until it be satisfied, in the county jail of the county in which the trial was not had, the sheriff of the county in which the trial was had, shall deliver a certified copy of the entry of the judgment, together with the body of the defendant, to the keeper of the jail or prison in which the defendant is to be imprisoned, and take his receipt therefor on a duplicate copy of such entry, which he must forthwith return to the clerk of the court in which the judgment was rendered, with his return thereon.

Officer's authority in committing.—SEC. 4516. The sheriff or his deputy, while conveying the defendant to the proper prison, has the same authority to require the assistance of any citizen of the state in securing the defendant, and retaking him if he escape, as if the sheriff were in his own county; and every person who neglects or refuses to assist the sheriff when so required shall be punishable as if the sheriff were in his own county.

Return.—SEC. 4517. An officer executing a judgment of imprisonment shall make a written return of the execution of such judgment forthwith after such execution, and file the same with the clerk of the court, by which the judgment was rendered.

Execution for fine.—SEC. 4518. Upon a judgment for a fine, a writ of execution may be issued as upon a judgment in a civil case.

How judgment for abatement of nuisance enforced.—SEC. 4519. When the judgment is for the abatement or removal of a nuisance, or for anything other than the payment of money by the defendant, a certified copy of the entry of such judgment, delivered to the sheriff of the proper county, shall authorize and require him to execute such judgment, and he shall return the same with his doings under the same thereon indorsed to the clerk of the court in which the judgment was rendered within seventy days after the date of the certificate of such certified copy, unless it be a judgment of imprisonment, which is hereinbefore provided for,

RETURN TO JUDGMENT EXECUTION.

No. 107.

STATE OF IOWA, }
.... County. } ss.

I, A B, sheriff of said county, do hereby certify and return that I received the within certified copy of judgment entry for service on the .... day of ...., 18.., and by virtue thereof forthwith committed C D, the defendant therein named, to the jail of said county, as required by said judgment.

Witness my hand this ....day of ...., 18...

A.... B...., *Sheriff.*

RETURN WHERE DEFENDANT IS COMMITTED TO THE PENITENTIARY.

No. 108.

STATE OF IOWA }
...... County. } ss.

I, A B, sheriff of said county, hereby certify and return,

that I received the within certified copy of judgment entry, for service on the .... day of ...., 18.., and by virtue thereof, I forthwith conveyed C D, the defendant therein named, to the penitentiary at ...., Iowa, and delivered the said defendant to ...., warden of said penitentiary, with a duplicate of said transcript of judgment, on the .... day ...of 18.., and at the same time took a receipt from said warden of said delivery, hereon indorsed, and herewith returned to the clerk of the District Court of said county.

Dated this .... day of ...., 18...

A.... B...., *Sheriff.*

WARDEN'S RECEIPT.

No. 109.

STATE OF IOWA,
......County, } ss.

I, M H, warden of the penitentiary of said State at ...., in said county, hereby certify that I received from A B, sheriff of .... county, in said State, C D, the defendant named in the within certified copy of judgment entry, for imprisonment in said penitentiary, on the .... day of ...., 18.., at said penitentiary, and at the same time and place I also received from said sheriff a duplicate copy of said certified judgment entry.

Witness my hand this .... day of ...., 18...

M.... H...., *Warden.*

The receipt.—The receipt should, with the return, be indorsed on the certified copy, and the whole should be by the sheriff returned to the clerk of the court where the judgment was rendered.

V. ABATEMENT OF NUISANCE.

RETURN ON THE ABATEMENT OF A NUISANCE.

No. 110.

STATE OF IOWA,
..... County, } ss.

I, A B, sheriff of said county, hereby certify and return, that I received the within certified copy of judgment entry for execution on the .... day of ...., 18.., by [here state the acts required to be done by the judgment, and done by the sheriff by virtue thereof,] at ...., in said county, and I now return said process duly executed, to the clerk of the court where said judgment was rendered, duly executed.

Dated this ....day of ...., 18...

A.... B...., *Sheriff.*

VI. OTHER AND MINOR DUTIES.—SUMMARY.

The sheriff is required to serve requisitions issued by the Auditor of State; Code, Sec. 74; to cause a notice to be delivered to one of the judges of election in each precinct, of the number of jurors apportioned for the ensuing year to his precinct; to summon jurors to appear before the court on the precept of the clerk; Code, Sec. 237; to serve the warrant of a coroner; Code, Sec. 362; and cause to be published the proclamation of the Governor of a general election. Code, Sec. 578.

CHAPTER XXV.

JAILS, PRISONERS, ETC.

1. HIS DUTY AS KEEPER OF THE JAIL AND PRISONERS.

Has charge of the jail.—The sheriff has charge and custody of the jail or other prison of his county, and the prisoners in the same; and is required to receive those lawfully committed thereto, and keep them himself or by his deputy or jailor, until discharged by law.

The provisions of the Code in relation to these duties are as follows:

Jails: for what used.—SECTION 4723. The common jails now erected, or which may hereafter be erected in the several counties in this state, in charge of the respective sheriffs, are to be used as prisons:

1. For the detention of persons charged with an offense, and duly committed for trial or examination;

2. For the detention of persons who may be duly committed to secure their attendance as witnesses on the trial of any criminal cause;

3. For the confinement of persons pursuant to sentence upon conviction for any offense, and of all other persons duly committed for any cause authorized by law;

4. The provisions of this section extend to persons detained or committed by authority of the courts of the United States, as well as the courts and magistrates of this state.

Keeper's duty.—SEC. 4724. It is the duty of the keeper of the jail of the county to see that the same is constantly kept in a cleanly and healthy condition, and he must pay strict attention to the personal cleanliness of all the prisoners in his custody as far as may be. Each prisoner must be furnished daily with as much clean water as may be necessary for drink and for personal cleanliness, and with a clean towel and shirt once a week, and must be served three times each day with wholesome food, which must be well cooked, and in sufficient quantity.

Sheriff's duty.—SEC. 4725. The sheriff of the county must keep a true and exact calendar of all prisoners committed to any prison under his care, which calendar must contain the names of all persons who are committed, their place of abode, the time of their commitment, the time of their discharge, the cause of commitment, the authority that committed them, and description of their persons, and when any prisoner is liberated, such calendar must state the time when, and the authority by which such liberation took place; and if any person escape, it must state particularly the time and manner of such escape.

Calendar for District Court.—SEC. 4726. At the opening of each term of the district court within his county, the sheriff must return a copy of such calendar under his hand to the judge of such court; and if any sheriff neglect or refuse so to do, he shall be punished by fine not exceeding one hundred dollars.

What furnished prisoners.—SEC. 4727. The keeper of each jail must furnish necessary bedding, clothing, fuel, and medical aid for all prisoners under his charge, and keep an accurate account of the same.

When jail takes fire.—SEC. 4728. Whenever, by reason of any jail being on fire, or any building contiguous or near to a jail being on fire, there be reason to apprehend that the prisoners confined in such jail may be injured or endangered thereby, the sheriff or keeper of such jail may, at his discretion, remove such prisoners to some safe and convenient place, and there confine them so long as may be necessary to avoid such danger.

To report prisoners at each session of District Court.—The calendar of prisoners and certificate of the sheriff to a copy thereof required by the foregoing provisions may be in the following form:

No. 111.

CALENDAR AND CERTIFICATE.

To the District Court .... County, ... Term, 18..

The following is a copy of the calendar of prisoners imprisoned in the jail of said county, to-wit:

PRISON CALENDAR, ... COUNTY, IOWA.

NAME.	RESIDENCE.	DESCRIPTION.					Cause of commitment.	Time of commitment.	By whom committed.	Time discharged.	By whom discharged.	Remarks.
		Age.	Height.	Hair.	Complexion.	Peculiarities.						
....	....	.	.	.	..	..	..	..	..	..	..	.
....	....	.	.	.	..	..	..	..	..	..	..	.
....	....	.	.	.	..	..	..	..	..	..	..	.
....	....	.	.	.	..	..	..	..	..	..	..	.
....	....	.	.	.	..	..	..	..	..	..	..	.
....	....	.	.	.	..	..	..	..	..	..	..	.
....	....	.	.	.	..	..	..	..	..	..	..	.
....	....	.	.	.	..	..	..	..	..	..	..	.
....	....	.	.	.	..	..	..	..	..	..	..	.
....	....	.	.	.	..	..	..	..	..	..	..	.
....	....	.	.	.	..	..	..	..	..	..	..	.

STATE OF IOWA, }
.... County. } ss.

I, ..., sheriff of said county, hereby certify that the foregoing is a copy of the calendar of all prisoners committed to the jail of said county, under my care since ....

Dated this .... day of ...., 18..

...., *Sheriff.*

The Code further provides as follows:

II. INSPECTORS OF JAILS.

Who constitute.—SECTION 4729. In each county of this state the judge of the circuit court and district attorney are inspectors of the jails respectively, and have power, from time to time, to visit and inspect the same, and inquire into all matters connected with the government, discipline, and police of such prisons.

Their duty.—SEC. 4730. It is the duty of such inspectors to visit and inspect such prisons twice each year, and at the next district court which is thereafter held in their county, to present to such court on the first day of its sitting, a detailed report of the condition of such prisons at the time of such inspection.

Report.—SEC. 4731. Such report must state the number of persons confined in such prison, and for what cause respectively, the number of persons usually confined in one room, the distinction, if any, usually observed in the treatment of the prisoners, the evils, if any, found to exist in such prisons; and particularly whether any provisions of this chapter have been violated or neglected, and the cause of such violation or neglect.

Right to inspect: given fully.—SEC. 4732. The keepers of such prisons shall admit the said inspectors, or any of them, into any part of such prisons, to exhibit to them on demand, all the books, papers, documents, and accounts pertaining to the prison or to the prisoners confined therein, and to render them every other facility in their power to enable them to discharge the duties above prescribed.

May swear officers.—SEC. 4733. For the purpose of obtaining the necessary information to enable them to make such reports as is above required in this chapter, the said inspectors have power to examine on oath, to be administered by either of them, any of the officers of such prison, or any of the prisoners therein.

Refractory prisoners.—SEC. 4734. If any person confined in any jail upon a conviction or charge of any offense, is refractory or disorderly, or if he willfully destroy or injure any article of bedding, or other furniture, door, or window, or any other part of such prison, the sheriff of the county, after due inquiry, may chain and secure such person, or cause him to be kept in solitary confinement not more than ten days for any one offense; and during such solitary confinement he must be fed with bread and water only, unless other food is necessary for the preservation of his health.

SEC. 4735. All charges and expenses of safe keeping and maintaining convicts and persons charged with public offenses and committed for examination or trial to the county jail, shall be paid from the county treasury, the accounts therefor being first settled and allowed by the board of supervisors; except prisoners committed or detained by the authority of the courts of the United States, in which cases the United States must pay such expenses to the county.

III. TO KEEP ACCURATE ACCOUNTS.

The sheriff, by the provisions of the above statutes is required to keep accurate accounts of all proper charges, and expenses of maintaining the prisoners which should be paid by the county, except the expenses of keeping prisoners committed by the United States courts, which should be paid by the United States.

Accounts for keeping the prisoners should be properly made out and presented to the board of supervisors of the county for allowance, and if found correct and just should be allowed and settled by them.

IV. IMPRISONMENT AT HARD LABOR, AND DUTY TO PRISONERS.

In relation thereto the Code provides:

May be required to labor.—SECTION 4736. Any able-bodied male person over the age of sixteen years, and not over the age of fifty years, now or hereafter confined in any jail in this state, under the judgment of any court of record or of any other tribunal authorized to imprison for the violation of any law, ordinance, by-law, or police regulation, may be required to labor during the whole or part of the time of his sentence, as hereinafter provided, and such court or other tribunal, when passing final judgment of imprisonment, whether for non-payment of fine or otherwise, shall have the power to determine, and shall determine, whether such imprisonment shall be at hard labor or not.

SEC. 4737. Such labor may be on the roads, streets, or public highways, on or about public buildings or grounds, or at such other places in the county, where confined, and during such reasonable time of the day as the person having charge of the prisoners may direct, and not exceeding eight hours per day.

SEC. 4738. In case the sentence be for the violation of any of the statutes of the state, the sheriff of the county where the imprisonment is, shall superintend the performance of the labor herein contemplated, and shall furnish the tools and material, if necessary, to work with at the expense of the county in which the convict is confined, and such county shall be entitled to his earnings.

SEC. 4739. When the imprisonment is pursuant to the judgment of any court, police court, police magistrate, mayor, or other tribunal of any incorporated city or town, for the violation of any ordinance, by-law, or other regulation, the marshal shall superintend the performance of the labor herein contemplated, and shall furnish the tools and materials if necessary, at the expense of the city or town requiring the labor, and such city or town shall be entitled to the earnings of its convicts.

SEC. 4740. The officer having charge of any convicts, for the purpose specified in this chapter, may use such means as, and no more than, are necessary to prevent escape, and if any convict attempt to escape, either while going from or returning to the jail, or while at labor, or at any time, or if he refuse to labor, the officer having him in charge, after due inquiry, may, to secure such person, or to cause him to labor, use the means authorized by section four thousand seven hundred and thirty-four of this chapter; *provided*, such punishment shall be inflicted within the jail or the jail enclosure for refusal to work, and shall not be considered as any part of the time for which the prisoner is sentenced,

Prisoners credited for labor.—SEC. 4741. For every day's labor performed by any convict under the provisions hereof, there shall be credited on any judgment for fine and costs against him, the sum of one dollar and fifty cents, and no person shall be entitled to the benefits of the law providing for the liberation of poor convicts, if, in the opinion of the sheriff, the judgment may be satisfied by the labor of the person as herein authorized.

Cruel treatment of prisoners.—SEC. 4742. If any officer or other person treat any prisoner in a cruel and inhuman manner, he shall be punished by fine not exceeding one thousand dollars, or by imprisonment in the county jail not exceeding twelve months, or by both such fine and imprisonment.

Duty of officer in charge of prisoners.—SEC. 4743. The officer having such prisoner in charge shall protect him from insult and annoyance, and communication with others while at labor, and going to and returning from the same, and he may use such means as are necessary and proper therefor; and any person persisting in insulting, and annoying, or communicating with any prisoner, after being commanded by such officer to desist, shall be punished by a fine not exceeding ten dollars, or by imprisonment not exceeding three days.

CHAPTER XXVI.

SHERIFF'S DUTY TO ATTEND ON COURTS.

To attend courts and appoint bailiffs.—The Code provides that the sheriff shall attend on the District and Circuit Courts of his county, and while either remains in session, he shall be allowed the assistance of such number of bailiffs as either court may direct. The bailiffs shall be appointed by the sheriff and shall be regarded as deputy sheriffs, and for whose acts the sheriff shall be responsible. Code, Sec. 341.

May require bond of bailiff.—The sheriff may require bonds of his bailiffs, and they may perform any act in the name of the sheriff, which could lawfully be done by the sheriff.

Duty to preserve order and silence.—Among the duties of the sheriff, and his deputies and bailiffs in attendance on the courts are to preserve order and silence in court, and prevent anything which interferes with the proper business of the court; and on the opening and adjournment of the court from day to day, to proclaim the fact publicly.

The following forms may be used for that purpose:

ON OPENING COURT.

No. 112.

Hear ye! hear ye! hear ye! The District Court of .... county is now in session.

ON ADJOURNMENT.

No. 113.

Hear ye! The District Court of .... county is adjourned till to-morrow morning at 9 o'clock.

ON OPENING COURT AFTER ADJOURNMENT.

No. 114.

Hear ye! The District Court of .... county is now in session pursuant to its adjournment.

Other duties of the sheriff and bailiffs.—It becomes the duty of the sheriff or his deputies, or bailiffs, under the direction of the court to take charge of witnesses excluded from the court during the trial of a cause; to bring in witnesses required on a trial, who are absent from court; to serve bench warrants and attachments that may be ordered by the court; to take charge of the trial jury; to attend on the grand jury; and to wait upon and obey the lawful orders of the court in all matters.

Judicial notice.—The court will take judicial notice of the sheriff and of all officers of the court. 7 Iowa, 56.

CHAPTER XXVII.

LIABILITY OF SHERIFF AND HIS DEPUTIES.

Technical objections disregarded.—The sheriff, as well as his sureties on his official bond, are liable for a breach of official duty; for non-performance as well as mal-performance thereof; and courts will disregard objections to bonds purely technical, and hold such undertakings invalid only upon the most cogent and satisfactory grounds.

A bond good as a voluntary obligation.—And the bond of a public officer, though not good as a statutory undertaking, may be good as a voluntary obligation, and an action at common law will lie thereon. 8 Iowa, 129 and 553.

Sureties not liable after the expiration of the term.—Sureties are not liable on the official bond of an officer, for the acts of the officer committed after the expiration of the term for which he was elected, and after the time allowed by law for the person elected as his successor to qualify, although such may not have qualified, and the former incumbent may have continued to act as such officer. 10 Iowa, 39.

Liability to damages on sale without levy and notice.—The officer is liable for damages sustained by a sale of land without a levy and the notice of sale required by law, if the plaintiff is thereby deprived of his title. 3 G. Greene, 246.

Sureties when not liable for money.—But where money is intrusted to a sheriff, which should be paid to the clerk, the sureties on the sheriff's bond are not liable therefor. Nor would they be liable for any act of the sheriff before they became sureties. 4 G. Greene, 117.

Sureties liable in other cases.—But the sureties would be liable for money in the hands of the officer by virtue of his office at the time the bond was given, and the sheriff and his sureties would be liable for all damages for failure to take a bond required by law, or where the bond taken was not sufficient in form or amount, or the obligors not responsible, if he did not exercise proper prudence and judgment in the matter, and took no oath as to their responsibility, or where he neglects to serve process or make a proper return thereof, or makes a false return, or where he levies on property exempt from execution. 20 Iowa, 260; 11 Iowa, 158.

Sureties on substituted bond: when not liable.—The sureties on a substituted bond are not liable for moneys coming into the hands of a principal prior to the execution of such bond and during the existence of a prior bond, for which the substituted bond was given. 22 Iowa, 360.

Liability of principal.—The principal is liable in all cases for a failure to do his official duty to all parties damaged thereby.

Statute of limitations.—All actions, however, against an officer growing out of a liability incurred by doing an act in an official capacity or by omission of an official duty, including the non-payment of money collected on execution, must be brought within three years after their causes accrue and not afterward. Code, Sec. 2529.

Judgments on motions.—A judgment against a sheriff may be obtained on motion by the plaintiff in an execution, for the recovery of money or property collected on execution. Code, Sec. 2906.

May perform the duty of constables.—The sheriff may perform any of the duties required of a constable, and when any process from a justice's court is delivered to him for service it is his duty to serve it the same as the constable. Code, Sec. 3632.

CHAPTER XXVIII.

FEES AND COMPENSATION.

I. GENERAL PROVISIONS.

On this subject the Code provides:

Sheriff.—SECTION 3788. The sheriff is entitled to charge and receive the following fees:

For attending the supreme court, to be paid out of the amount appropriated for contingent expenses of such court, two dollars per day;

For serving any order or notice and making return thereof, for the first person served, fifty cents; for each additional person served, twenty-five cents; and for each warrant two dollars and mileage, and all necessary expenses as sworn to by the sheriff;

For each copy of such order, warrant, or notice, when required, for each hundred words, ten cents;

For serving any order or warrant, and calling to his aid when necessary to serve the same the power of the county, one dollar and fifty cents;

Each commitment to prison, twenty-five cents;

Discharge from same, twenty-five cents;

Attending with a person before a court or judge when required, for each day, besides mileage, one dollar;

Copy of a paper required by law, when made by him, for each hundred words, ten cents;

For serving and returning subpœna for each person, twenty cents;

Calling a jury in each case, ten cents;

Summoning a grand or trial jury, for each panel, including mileage, to be paid out of the county treasury, eight dollars;

Traveling fees in other cases required by law, going and returning, per mile, five cents;

Selling land or other property on execution, for each day, one dollar;

Making and executing a deed for land sold on execution, one dollar;

Summoning a jury in cases of forcible entry and detainer, including mileage, one dollar and fifty cents;

Serving an execution or order for the partition of real estate, or assignment of dower, two dollars;

For taking each bond required by law, twenty-five cents;

For summoning a jury to assess the damages to the owner of lands taken for any work of internal improvements, and attending upon them, including mileage, five dollars;

If such case occupies more than one day for each day, or fraction thereof, one dollar and fifty cents;

For serving each attachment, one dollar;

For time necessarily employed in making an inventory of property attached or levied upon, per day, one dollar;

For collecting and paying over money, on the first two hundred dollars, or part thereof, three per cent.;

On the next three hundred dollars or part thereof, two per cent;

On all excess over five hundred dollars, one per cent;

But where the property is purchased by the plaintiff in execution, or where money is collected without sale of property, one-half of the above rates;

For returning any order, warrant, or notice not served, five cents;

For receiving a prisoner on surrender by bail, twenty-five cents;

For taking new bail or bond, twenty-five cents;

For dieting a prisoner, for each day, fifty cents; and for dieting a prisoner in conveying him to state prison or jail outside of his county, one dollar per day;

For conveying each convict to the penitentiary, and as full compensation therefor, sixteen cents for each mile traveled, to be computed from the county seat where the conviction took place by the most direct route of travel; the same to be paid out of the county treasury.

Salary.—SEC. 3789. The sheriff is also entitled for attending district and circuit court and delivering notices, including mileage, and for other services for which no compensation is allowed by law, such annual salary in each county with a population of ten thousand inhabitants, not less than fifty dollars;

In each county with a population of fifteen thousand inhabitants, not less than one hundred and fifty dollars;

In each county with a population of twenty thousand inhabitants or over, not less than two hundred dollars.

In criminal cases.—SEC. 3790. In all criminal cases where the prosecution fails, or where the money cannot be made from the person liable to pay the same, the facts being certified by the clerk or justice as far as their knowledge extends, and verified by the affidavit of the sheriff, the fees allowed by law in such cases shall be audited by the county auditor, and paid out of the county treasury.

Fees on seizure of intoxicating liquors.—SEC. 3807. A constable or other officer who serves any warrant for the seizure of intoxicating liquors shall be allowed:

For such service, one dollar;

For the removal and custody of such liquor, his reasonable expenses;

For the destruction of such liquor under the order of the court his reasonable expenses, and one dollar;

For posting and leaving notices, in such cases, one dollar.

II. FOR CARRIAGE HIRE IN CERTAIN CASES.

The Code provides as follows for carriage hire:

Carriage hire.—SECTION 3820. Every officer or person who shall arrest any person with a warrant or order issued by any court or officer, or who shall be required to convey a prisoner from a place distant from the county jail to such jail on an order of commitment, shall be allowed to charge as fees, which shall be collectable the same as other fees in criminal cases, besides the fees allowed by law, whatever sums such officer or person shall actually and necessarily pay for carriage hire in so conveying such person to jail.

III. FURTHER FEES.

Further fees are provided for by Secs. 3822 and 3825, of the Code:

On sales made by him in pursuance of Chapter Three, of Title Eleven of the Code, four per cent on the amount.

For conveying an insane person to the insane hospital on the warrant of the insane commissioners, at the rate of three dollars per day for the time necessary and actually employed, and mileage the same as in other cases for like services.

For putting up an advertisement when not otherwise provided for. (See Sec. 3838.) Twenty-five cents.

For delivering defendants, found to be insane by a jury, to the insane asylum, under the provisions of Chapter 49, of the Code, sheriffs are entitled to the same compensation as is allowed for conveying convicts to the penitentiary, *i e.* 16 cents for each mile traveled, to be computed from the county seat where the conviction took place, by the most direct route of travel.

When the sheriff performs the ordinary duties of the constable he does so, not as constable, but as sheriff, and he would undoubtedly be authorized to charge therefor sheriff's fees.

CHAPTER XXIX.

OF COUNTY SUPERVISORS.

I. PROVISIONS OF THE CODE.

The Code provides in reference to county supervisors as follows:

Number: election.—SECTION 294. The board of supervisors in each county shall consist of three persons, except where the number may heretofore have been, or hereafter be, increased in the manner provided by section two hundred and ninety-nine of this chapter. They shall be qualified electors, and be elected by the qualified voters of their respective counties, and shall hold their office for three years.

When elected.—SEC. 295. At the general election in each year, there shall be at least one supervisor elected in each county, who shall not be a resident of the same township with either of the members holding over, and who shall continue in office three years.

Meetings of.—SEC. 296. The members of the board shall meet at the county seat of their respective counties, on the first Mondays of January, April, June, September, and the first Monday after the general election in each year, and such special meetings as are provided for by law.

Quorum.—SEC. 297. A majority of the board of supervisors shall be a quorum to transact business, but should a division take place on any question when only two members of the board are in attendance, the question shall be continued until there is a full board of supervisors.

Resignation.—SEC. 298. The absence of any supervisor from the county for six months in succession shall be a resignation of his office.

Number: how increased.—SEC. 299. The board of supervisors of any county may, and when petitioned to do so by one-fourth of the electors of said county shall, submit to the qualified voters of the county at any regular election, the question, "Shall the number of supervisors be increased to five," or "seven," as the board shall elect in submitting the question. If the majority of the votes cast shall be for the increase of the number, then, at the next ensuing election for a supervisor, the requisite additional supervisors shall be elected, whose terms of office shall be determined by lot in such a manner that one-half of the additional members shall hold their office for three years, and one-half for two years. In any county where the number of supervisors has been increased to "five" or "seven," the board of supervisors, on the petition of one-fourth of the legal voters of the county, shall submit to the qualified voters of the county, at any regular election the question, "Shall the number of supervisors be reduced to five," or "three?" If a majority of the votes cast shall be for the decrease, then the board of supervisors shall be reduced to the number indicated by such vote, and thereafter there shall be annually elected the number requisite to keep the board full.

Chapter 39, of the Session Laws of the Fifteenth General Assembly (1874), further provides as follows:

Board may establish supervisor districts.—SECTION 1. That the board of supervisors of each county may at their regular meeting in June, A. D. 1874, divide their respective counties, by townships, into a number of supervisor districts, corresponding to the number of supervisors in their respective counties.

How constituted.—SEC. 2. Such districts shall be as nearly equal in population as possible, and shall each embrace townships as nearly contiguous as practicable, each of which said districts shall be entitled to one member of such board, to be elected by the electors of said district.

Election of, from unrepresented districts.—SEC. 3. In case such division, or any subsequent division, shall be found to leave any district or districts without a member of such board of supervisors, then at the next ensuing general election a supervisor shall be elected by and from such district having no member of such board; and, if there be two such districts or more, then the new member or members of said board shall be elected by and from the district or districts having the greater population according to the last state census, and so on till each of said districts have one member of such board.

Re-districting.—SEC. 4. Any county my be re-districted, as provided by the preceding sections of this act, once in each and every two years, and not oftener, and nothing herein contained shall be construed or have the effect to lengthen or diminish the term of office of any member of such board.

Organization and powers of the board.—The following are the provisions of the Code in reference to the organization and powers of the board:

Organization: powers.—SECTION 300. The board of supervisors, at their first meeting in every year, shall organize by choosing one of their number as chairman, who shall preside at ail the meetings of the board during the year. Every chairman of the board of supervisors shall have power to administer an oath to any person concerning any matter submitted to the board or connected with their powers.

Special meetings.—SEC. 301. Special meetings of the board of supervisors shall be held only when requested by a majority of the board, which request shall be in writing, addressed to the county auditor, and shall specify the object for which such special meeting is desired. The auditor shall thereupon fix a day for such meeting, not later than ten days from the day of the filing of the petition with him, and shall immediately give notice in writing to each of the supervisors personally, or by leaving a copy thereof at his residence, at least six days before the day set for such meeting. The notice shall [illegible]he time and place where the meeting will be held and the object of it, as sta[illegible] petition; and at such special meeting no business other than that so designat[illegible]he petition and notice shall be considered or transacted. The auditor shall also give public notice of the meeting by publication in not exceeding two newspapers published in the county, or, if there be none, by causing notice of the same to be posted on the front door of the court house of the county, and in two other public places therein, one week before the time set therefor.

Failure of duty.—SEC. 302. If any supervisor shall neglect or refuse to perform any of the duties which are, or shall be, required of him by law as a member of the board of supervisors, without just cause therefor, he shall, for each offense, forfeit one hundred dollars.

Powers.—SEC. 303. The board of supervisors at any regular meeting shall have the following powers, to-wit:

Chairman.—1. To appoint one of their number chairman, and also a clerk in the absence of the regular officers;

Adjourn.—2. To adjourn from time to time, as occasion may require;

County property.—3. To make such orders concerning the corporate property of the county as they may deem expedient;

Settle accounts.—4. To examine and settle all accounts of the receipts and expenditures of the county, and to examine, settle, and allow all just claims against the county unless otherwise provided for by law;

Buildings.—5. To build and keep in repair the necessary buildings for the use of the county and of the courts;

To insure.—6. To cause the county buildings to be insured in the name of the county, or otherwise, for the benefit of the county as they shall deem expedient, and in case there are no county buildings, to provide suitable rooms for county purposes;

Change boundaries.—7. To sell off, organize, and change the boundaries of townships in their respective counties, designate and give names thereto, and define the place of holding the first election;

Ferries.—8. To grant licenses for keeping ferries in their respective counties as provided by law;

Purchase real estate for county.—9. To purchase for the use of the county, any real estate necessary for the erection of buildings for county purposes, to remove or designate a new site for any county buildings required to be at the county seat, when such removal shall not exceed the limits of the village or city at which the county seat is located;

Control officers.—10. To require any county officer to make a report, under oath, to them on any subject connected with the duties of his office, and to require any such officers to give such bonds, or additional bonds, as shall be reasonable or necessary for the faithful performance of their several duties; and any such officer who shall neglect or refuse to make such report or give such bonds within twenty days after being so required, may be removed from office by the board by a vote of a majority of the members elected;

County agents.—11. To represent their respective counties, and to have the care and management of the property and business of the county in all cases where no other provision shall be made;

School fund.—12. To manage and control the school fund of their respective counties as shall be provided by law;

Highways.—13. To appoint commissioners to act with similar commissioners duly appointed in any other county or counties, and to authorize them to lay out, alter, or discontinue any highway extending through their own and one or more other counties; subject to the ratification of the board;

Fix compensation.—14. To fix the compensation of all services of county and township officers not otherwise provided for by law and to provide for the payment of the same;

Submit to vote.—15. To authorize the taking of a vote of the people for the re-location of the county seat as provided by law;

Highways.—16. To alter, vacate, or discontinue any state or territorial highway within their respective counties;

17. To lay out, establish, alter, or discontinue any county highway heretofore or now laid out, or hereafter to be laid through or within their respective counties, as may be provided by law;

Bridges.—18. To provide for the erection of all bridges which may be necessary, and which the public convenience may require within their respective counties, and to keep the same in repair;

Bounty.—19. To determine what bounties, in addition to those already provided by law, if any, shall be offered and paid by their county on the scalps of such wild animals taken and killed within their county as they may deem it expedient to exterminate. But no such bounty shall exceed five dollars.

Poor house.—20. To purchase for the use of the county any real estate necessary for the erection of buildings for the support of the poor of such county and for a farm to be used in connection therewith;

Poor.—21. To have and exercise all the powers in relation to the poor given by law to the county authorities;

Rules.—22. To make such rules and regulations, not inconsistent with law, as they may deem necessary for the government of their body, the transaction of business, and the preservation of order;

Canvassers.—23. The board of supervisors shall constitute the board of county canvassers;

Submit to vote: buildings: bridges.—24. It shall not be competent for said board of supervisors to order the erection of a court-house, jail, poor-house, or other building or bridge, where the probable cost will exceed five thousand dollars, nor the purchase of real estate for county purposes exceeding two thousand dollars in value, until a proposition therefor shall have been first submitted to the legal voters of the county, and voted for by a majority of all voting for and against such proposition, at a general election, notice of the same being given for thirty days previously in a newspaper, if one is published in the county. * * * See Code, page 53.

II. PROCEEDINGS OF THE BOARD TO BE PUBLISHED.

The Code provides in relation thereto as follows:

Proceedings published.—SECTION 304. They shall cause to be made out and published immediately after each regular or special meeting of the board, in at least one newspaper, if there be one in the county, and if not, by posting on the court-house door, a schedule of the receipts and expenditures of the county, which shall state the names of all claimants, the amount claimed, the amount allowed, for what purpose allowed, and a full statement of the amounts of the treasurer's accounts at the last settlement as on his balance sheet, or account-current in making such settlement.

Majority of whole board required.—SEC. 305. No tax shall be levied, no contract for the erection of any public buildings entered into, no settlement with the county officers made, no real estate purchased or sold, no new site designated for any county buildings, no change made in the boundaries of townships, and no money appropriated to aid in the construction of highways and bridges, without a majority of the whole board of supervisors voting therefor and consenting thereto.

Newspapers: how selected.—SEC. 307. The board of supervisors shall, at its January session of each year, select two newspapers published within the county, or one, if but one be published therein, having the largest circulation in the county where published, in which the proceedings of said board shall be published at the expense of the county, and in counties having eighteen thousand inhabitants, a paper printed in a foreign language, if published in said county, shall also be selected, in which such proceedings shall be published; and the auditor shall furnish such papers selected a copy of such proceedings for that purpose; *provided*, That the cost of such publication shall not exceed one-third the rate allowed by law for legal advertisements.

III. BOOKS TO BE KEPT BY THE BOARD.

Books kept.—SEC. 308. The board is authorized and required to keep the following books:

Minute book.—1. A book to be known as the "minute book," in which shall be recorded all orders and decisions made by them, except those relating to highways. All orders for the allowance of money from the county treasury, shall state on what account and to whom the allowance is to be made, dating the same, and numbering them consecutively through each year;

Highway record.—2. A book to be known as the "highway record," in which shall be recorded all proceedings and adjudications relating to the establishment, change, or discontinuance of highways;

Warrant book.—3. A book to be known as the "warrant book," in which shall be entered in the order of their issuance, the number, date, amount, name of drawee of each warrant drawn on the treasury, and the number of warrants as directed in relation to the minute book.

IV. SUBMISSION OF CERTAIN MATTERS TO A VOTE OF THE PEOPLE.

To borrow money: and other matters.—SECTION 309. The board of supervisors may submit to the people of the county at any regular election, or at any special one called for that purpose, the question whether money may be borrowed to aid in the erection of any public buildings; whether any species of stock, not now prohibited by law, shall be permitted to run at large, and at what time it shall be prohibited; and the question of any other local or police regulation not inconsistent with the laws of the state. And when the warrants of a county are at a depreciated value, they may in like manner submit the question whether a tax of a higher rate than that provided by law shall be levied; and in all cases when an additional tax is laid in pursuance of a vote of the people of any county for the special purpose of repaying borrowed money, or constructing, or aiding to construct, any highway or bridge, such special tax shall be paid in money, and in no other manner.

Mode of submission.—SEC. 310. The mode of submitting such questions to the people shall be the following: the whole question, including the sum desired to be raised, or the amount of tax desired to be levied, or the rate per annum, and the whole regulation, including the time of its taking effect or having operation, if it be of a nature to be set forth, and the penalty for its violation, if there be one, shall be published at least four weeks in some newspaper printed in the county. If there be no such newspaper, the publication shall be by being posted up in at least one of the most public places in each township in the county, and in addition, in at least five among the most public places in the county one of them being the door of the court house, for at least thirty days prior to the time of taking the vote. All such notices shall name the time when such question will be voted upon, and the form in which the question shall be taken, and a copy of the question submitted, shall be posted up at each place of voting during the day of election.

To levy a tax.—SEC. 311. When a question so submitted involves the borrowing, or the expenditure of money, the proposition of the question must be accompanied by a provision to lay a tax for the payment thereof, in addition to the usual taxes, as directed in the following section, and no vote adopting the question proposed will be of effect unless it adopt the tax also.

SEC. 312. The rate of tax shall in no case be more than one per cent. on the county valuation in one year. When the object is to borrow money for the erection of public buildings as above provided, the rate shall be such as to pay the debt in a period not exceeding ten years. When the object is to construct, or to aid in constructing, any highway or bridge, the annual rate shall not be less than one mill on the dollar valuation, and any of the above taxes becoming delinquent shall draw the same interest with the ordinary taxes.

To make levy continuous.—SEC. 313. When it is supposed that the levy of one year will not pay the entire amount, the proposition and the vote must be to continue the proposed rate from year to year, until the amount is paid.

To record vote, etc.—SEC. 314. The board of supervisors, on being satisfied that the above requirements have been substantially complied with, and that a majority of the votes cast are in favor of the proposition submitted, shall cause the proposition, and the result of the vote to be entered at large in the minute book, and a notice of its adoption to be published for the same time and in the same manner as above provided for publishing the preliminary notice, and from the time of entering the result of the vote in relation to borrowing or expending money, and from the completion of the notice of its adoption in the case of a local or police regulation, the vote and the entry thereof on the county records shall be in full force and effect.

Propositions may be rescinded.—SEC. 315. Propositions thus adopted, and local regulations thus established, may be rescinded in like manner and upon like notice by a subsequent vote taken thereon, but neither contracts made under them, nor the taxes appointed for carrying them into effect, can be rescinded.

When they must submit questions.—SEC. 316. The board shall submit the question of the adoption or rescission of such a measure when petitioned therefor by one-fourth of the voters of the county, unless a different number be prescribed by law in any special case.

Record is evidence of regularity.—SEC. 317. The record of the adoption or rescission of any such measure shall be presumptive evidence that all the proceedings necessary to give the vote validity have been regularly conducted.

When tax exceeds amount sought.—SEC. 318. In case the amount produced by the rate of tax proposed and levied exceeds the amount sought for the specific object, it shall not therefore be held invalid, but the excess shall go into the ordinary county funds.

Fund must be kept separate.—SEC. 319. Money so raised for such purposes is specially appropriated and constitutes a fund distinct from all others in the hands of the treasurer, until the obligation assumed is discharged.

V. OATH OF OFFICE, AND SUMMARY.

Oath.—It will be seen by reference to the general provisions of the Code and the Constitution contained in Chapter One, that although supervisors are not required to give bonds, still they are required to take an oath of office to support the Constitution of the United States, and of the State of Iowa, and to perform the duties of the office according to the best of their ability. Const., Sec. 5, Art. 1.

SUMMARY OF OTHER PROVISIONS.

The limits of this treatise forbid any full or exhaustive treatment of the powers, duties, liabilities and responsibilities of the board of supervisors. The statutes relating thereto may be found in many chapters of the Code, of which in addition to those already given, we can only give a general summary.

They should provide for a place for holding courts in the county; Code, Sec. 173; furnish the county surveyor with a record book; Code, Sec. 379, 381; divide the county into townships and establish the boundaries thereof; Code, Sec. 379, 381; divide townships in certain cases; Code, Sec. 384; designate the place for holding elections therein; Code, Sec. 385; order election of township collectors and approve their bonds; Code, Sec. 400, 401; levy a tax to defray the expense of the township board of health; Code, Sec. 420; assess the expense of platting lands by the auditor in certain cases, and order the same to be paid out of the county treasury, and assess the lots *pro rata* therewith. Code, Sec. 560.

Divide townships into precincts.—They may divide the townships into election precincts and number or name them; Code, Secs. 603, 604; they should provide each election precinct with a ballot box, and a lock and key thereto; Code, Sec. 614 ; fix the compensation of deputy county officers, in case the principal officer receives a salary, and is compelled, by the pressure of business, to employ a deputy; Code, Sec. 771; levy taxes upon the assessed value of taxable property at their September session; Code, Sec. 796; may exempt from taxation except for State purposes, an amount not exceeding $500 for each acre of forest trees, less than three years old, planted and suitably cultivated in timber, or for each one mile, and a proportionate exemption for each one-fourth mile, of shade trees along the highway, or for each acre of fruit trees not more than three years old; Code, Sec. 799, Laws 1874, Ch. 45; to classify property for taxation; Code, Sec. 870; to settle with the county treasurer on his going out of office, and see that his books are correctly balanced, before being passed into the hands of the treasurer elect; Code, Secs. 831, 917; to establish, vacate or alter highways; Code, Sec. 921; and to cause highways to be re-surveyed, platted and recorded, where the field-notes of the original survey have been lost, or where the original survey or record was defective, or its location cannot be determined; Code, Sec. 964; to grant licenses for toll bridges; Code, Sec. 1003; to license ferries, and prescribe rates of ferriage; Code, Secs. 1011–1012; and the license must be entered on the records and contain the rates of toll allowed; Code, Sec. 1019; cause to be entered a statement of railroad property; Code, Sec. 1321; fix the location of railroad bridges over certain streams, and impose terms and conditions thereon; Code, Sec. 1031; construct drains and change any water course in certain cases; Code, Sec. 1207; order the removal of a pauper to the county of his settlement; Code, Sec. 1357; order relief furnished paupers to be paid out of the county treasury; Code, Sec. 1363; establish a poor-house, and make contracts and prescribe rules in relation thereto; Code, Sec. 303; levy a tax for the support of the poor, let out the use of the poor-house farm and the support of the poor for a period not exceeding three years; Code, Secs. 1381, 1382; and remit the taxes on property destroyed by fire or tornado; Code, Sec. 800, amended by Session Laws, 1874, Chap. 66.

County board of equalization.—The board of supervisors constitute a county board of equalization, and must equalize the assessments of the several townships of their county at their regular meeting in June in each year, substantially as the State board equalize assessments among the several counties of the State. Code, Sec. 831.

Bridges.—They have power to aid in the construction of bridges in certain cases, but only at the rate of forty dollars a lineal foot; but cannot exceed a total of fifteen thousand dollars. Code, Sec. 303.

CHAPTER XXX.

THE RECORDS.

I. THE AUDITOR TO MAKE RECORDS.

The county auditor is required to record all proceedings of the board in proper books provided for that purpose.

The minute book.—The board is required to keep a minute book, in which the auditor should record all orders and decisions made by the board, except those relating to highways.

ENTRY OF MINUTES.

No. 115.

THE COUNTY AUDITOR'S OFFICE, ... *County, State of Iowa, January* ...., 18..

The supervisors of .... county, Iowa, met at the office of the auditor of said county, this .... day of January, 18..

Present: H S, supervisor holding over, and G G B, J A C, W J B, and J S, supervisors elected at the last general election, and C C, auditor.

The supervisors elect were then duly qualified by taking and subscribing an oath of office as required by law, and proceeded to draw lots for their terms of office, whereupon W J B and G G B each drew for the term of three years from the first day of January, 18.., and J A C and J S, for the term of two years each, from the first day of January, 18...

The board was thereupon duly organized by the election of J A C, permanent chairman of said board.

The following proceedings were then had:

On motion, standing committees were appointed as follows:

On Highways and Bridges—G.... G.... B....

On Finance—W.... J.... B....

On Paupers—H.... S....

On Swamp Lands—G.... G.... B....

On Public Buildings—H.... S....

On Claims—H.... S...., J.... A.... C...., G.... G....
On Equalization—J.... S....
On School Fund—J.... A.... C...., J.... S ...
On Official Bond—J.... A.... C....
On the Poor House—J.... S....
On Salaries—W.... J.... B....

The following rules and regulations of the board were then adopted, to-wit: [Here insert any rules, regulations, or order of business that may be adopted].

The board then adopted the following classification and schedule of average valuation of personal property therein designated to aid the assessors, to-wit: [Here copy the schedule of average valuation].

And thereupon the board proceeded to fix the amount of the official bonds of county and township officers as follows:

County Treasurer's bond....	$100,000
County Coroner's bond......................	500
County Surveyor's bond....................	1,000
County Auditor's bond..........	10,000
County Sheriff's bond......................	10,000
County Superintendent's bond..............	1,000
Justice of the Peace's bond................	1,000
Constable's bond..........................	500
Assessor's bond...................	1,000
Collector's bond........	10,000

[This last should be in double the amount of tax to be collected by them.]

Whereupon the committee on official bonds made a report in favor of the approval of the following official bonds, and the sureties thereon, to-wit:

J H D—	County	Treasurer elect	$100,000
V C W—	"	Coroner elect..............	500
J H J—	"	Surveyor elect....	1,000
C C—	"	Auditor elect..............	10,000
A J B—	"	Sheriff elect...............	10,000
A B—	"	Superintendent elect.... ...	1,000
R D—		Justice of the Peace .... Tp.	500
S D P—		Constable.......... "	500
J B McQ—		Assessor........... "	1,000
E V M—		Collector, ... Tp....	6,000

And thereupon, on motion, said report was adopted, and said bonds with the sureties thereto were approved.

And thereupon said officers, having taken and subscribed an official oath on said bonds, were duly qualified for said several officers respectively as required by law.

The following claims were then taken up for action thereon by the board and were duly considered and orders made thereon as follows:

No. Claim.	Name of Claimant.	Nature of Claim,	Amount.	Amount allowed.	When allowed.
1	J. . G. . McG.	Services as Comm'r of Insanity	20 00	20 00	Jan. 4, 1874.
2	E. . B. . C. .	" Supt. of Sch.	22 00	00 00	. . " . " .
3	E. . B	" attending pauper . .	5 00	5 00	. . " . " .
4	R. . D	" J. P., State v. Gill . .	9 00	9 00	. . " . " .
5	A. . J. . G. .	" Township Trustee . .	4 00	4 00	. . " . " .
6	H. O. . F. .	" Const., State v. Gill .	12 00	12 00	. . " . " .
7	V. . C. . W. .	" Cor. in case of B, dec'd	9 00	9 00	. . " . " .
8	V. . C. . W, .	" Township Clerk . . .	15 00	15 00	. . " . " .
9	S. . D. . P. .	" Const., State v. Hay .	7 50	n't al'd	. . " . " .
10	E. . B	" Med. attend. Pauper .	22 00	20 00	. . " . " .

In the matter of the petition of N H, to reduce his assessment: J S, committee on equalization reports against granting the petition; whereupon said report was adopted, and said petition was denied.

The matter of the appointment by A J B, sheriff, of D W, as his deputy, duly made and certified in writing to the board, came up for approval:

Whereupon it appearing that a deputy sheriff is necessary, and that he has given the requisite bond to his principal, and that he has duly taken and subscribed an official oath on said appointment, the board on motion duly approved of said appointment.

In the matter of the petition of P S, for the erection of a bridge at .... Ford, on the South Fork of the Maquoketa river in .... township; the committee report in favor of the same, and recommend that the contract therefor, be let to the lowest bidder under seal, to be built according to the plan and draft thereof made, and also reported by said committee; and that the sum of $.... be appropriated therefor, out of the bridge fund, to be drawn on the order of the bridge committee. Said report was adopted.

The foregoing forms are probably adequate to illustrate the mode in which the record may be kept, and can be varied to suit almost any record required to be made.

II. THE HIGHWAY BOOK.

The board of supervisors are also required to keep a book to be known as, "The Highway Book," in which must be recorded all proceedings, and adjudications relating to the establishment, change or vacation of highways. And any order made or action taken in relation to highways shall be entered, distinguishing between those made by the auditor, and those made by the board of supervisors.

The highway record may be in the following form.

No. 116. HIGHWAY BOOK.

AUDITOR'S OFFICE, *County of* ...., *State of Iowa*, ..., 18..

In the matter of the petition of .... and others, for the location of a highway in .... township, in said county:

The petition in the above case having been this day presented to the undersigned, auditor of said county, describing the location, and the commencement and terminus of the proposed highway, and a bond having been presented by the petitioners for the payment of the costs and expenses herein, and duly approved by me, F M B is appointed a commissioner to view said proposed highway on the .... day of ...., 18.., and report to me on the expediency thereof on or before the ... day of ...., 18..

C.... C...., *Auditor.*

OFFICE OF THE COUNTY AUDITOR OF .... *County, Iowa*, ..., 18..

In the matter of the petition of ...., and others, for the location of a highway in .... township, in said county:

The report of F M B, commissioner appointed herein by me, the undersigned, auditor of said county, to view and report to me the expediency of the proposed highway, having this day been made in favor of the expediency and of the establishment thereof, and he having also reported an accurate survey thereof, accompanied with his field-notes of the survey, and a plat thereof; I hereby appoint the .... day of ...., 18.., as the day when further action will be taken in the premises.

C ... C...., *Auditor.*

OFFICE OF THE AUDITOR OF .... *County, Iowa*, ..., 18..

In the matter of the petition of ...., and others, for the location of a highway, in .... township, in said county.

It appearing to the undersigned, auditor of said county, that due notice of this proceeding, and that all claims for damages, by reason of the establishment of said highway, and all objections thereto, must be filed in this office before this time, has been duly served on each owner and occupier of lands in the proposed highway, and abutting on the same, and duly published as required by law, and that J T, an owner of lands as aforesaid, has filed in writing in this office, a claim for damages by reason of the establishment of this road, in the sum of $....; [if there are other claims, here state them.] Now, therefore, I, the said auditor, do appoint T S, G L and E V M, disinterested electors of said county, to view the ground on the .... day of ...., 18.., and report upon the amount of damages sustained by the said claimants, within thirty days from this date.

C.... C...., *Auditor.*

AUDITOR'S OFFICE, ... *County, Iowa, June* ...., 18..

JUNE SESSION OF BOARD OF SUPERVISORS—4TH DAY.

Report of the Committee on Highways:

In the matter of the petition of .... and others, for the location of a highway in ... township, in said county:

The appraisers appointed herein by the auditor to view the ground, and report on the damage sustained by ...., by reason of the establishment of said proposed highway, having appraised his damages and reported, and filed the same, in which said damages are appraised at $...., we recommend the establishment of said highway as reported by the commissioner appointed herein, on the payment of said damages and costs, and expenses therein.

Whereupon, the said board having heard testimony and examined the petition for and the remonstrance against said road, on motion said report was adopted, and said road ordered to be established as reported by said commissioner, and platted by him on the payment of said damages, and the costs and expenses herein incurred within thirty days from this date.

And it was further ordered, that this case be continued until the next September session, of this board for final action.

SESSION OF THE BOARD OF SUPERVISORS, SEPT. .., 18.., 6TH DAY.

In the matter of the petition of ...., and others, for the location of a highway in .... township, in said county:

It appearing to the board that the conditions for the establishment of this highway, made at the last session of the board, have been complied with, and that all damages and costs, and expenses incurred herein, have been fully paid, it is ordered by the board, that said highway, as located by the commissioner appointed herein, be unconditionally established, and that the report of said commissioner with his plat, and field-notes of the survey and location of said highway be entered on the records by the auditor; which is done accordingly to-wit:

STATE OF IOWA, }
.... County. } ss.

To ...., auditor of said county:

The undersigned having been appointed a commissioner to view, and if thought necessary, locate a certain highway in said county, petitioned for by [name of petitioner] and others, and known as [name the road], would report as follows: That, having been duly sworn, he found upon examination that it was expedient, and necessary, for the accommodation of the public, that the highway should be located as petitioned for.

Therefore, with the assistance of [name the surveyor] as surveyor, [name the chainmen] as chainmen, [name the axmen] as axmen, who were all duly sworn, your commissioner proceeded on the day set therefor, to-wit: the .... day of ...., A. D. 18.., to lay out and locate said highway, and to distinguish the same by the proper marks, mounds and stakes, in the manner prescribed by law, and in accordance with the field-notes and plat of survey of the highway, which are hereto annexed, and which are made part of this report.

Your commissioner is of the opinion that the highway will be of great convenience and utility to the public, and would hereby recommend its establishment.

All of which is respectfully submitted.

F.... M.... B...., *Commissioner.*

PLAT OF THE PROPOSED ROAD.

Township 83 *N.*, *Range* 3 *W.*, *5th P. M.*

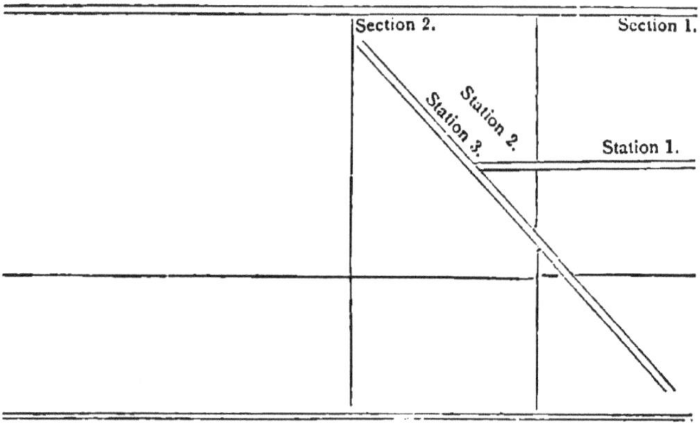

Section 2.
Section 1.
Station 2.
Station 3.
Station 1.

FIELD-NOTES OF PROPOSED ROAD.

STATION.	COURSE.	DISTANCE.	REMARKS.
1	West..	80 chains	At qr. cor. in E. side, Sec. 1, T. 83, R. 3, W. 5th P. M.
2	"	15 chains, 3 links .	At qr. cor. in W. side, Sec. 1, T. 83, R. 3, W. 5th P. M.
3	. . .	. . . .	At center of Anamosa and Rome roads . . . .

F . . M . . B . . , *Commissioner and County Surveyor.*

Final action by the Auditor.—If no objections, or claims for damages, on account of the proposed highway are made after the service of the notice required by the statute, and on or before noon of the day fixed for filing the same, and the auditor is satisfied that the provisions of the statute have been complied with, he is required to proceed with the matter, and establish such highway himself, as recommended by the commissioner, on the payment of the expenses of the proceedings within ten days.

If such costs are not paid within ten days, the auditor is required to report his action in the premises to the board of supervisors, at their next session, who may affirm the action of the auditor, or establish such highway at the expense of the county.

If the auditor establishes the highway, the record would, of course, be the same as above, except that part relating to the action of the board; instead of which the record may be in the following form:

No. 117. RECORD OF ESTABLISHMENT BY AUDITOR.

AUDITOR'S OFFICE, ... *County*, ..., 18..

In the matter of the petition, etc.

Now to-wit: ...., 18.., being the time fixed on or before which any objections to, or claim for damages in consequence of the establishment of this road should be filed, and no objections thereto, nor claim for damages therein, being filed in this office; it comes on for a hearing before the auditor of said county. And it appearing to said auditor, that the notice required by the statute has been duly served on the parties interested, and published as required by law, and that all of the provisions of the law relating to the establishment of the highway have been complied with, said highway is ordered to be established, on the payment of the costs herein incurred, amounting to $...., within ten days from this date, [if said costs should be paid at the time, the auditor could state the fact thus: and said costs being now paid said highway is unconditionally established as located by the report of the commissioner herein appointed, and the plat and field-notes of his survey thereof.]

C.... C...., *Auditor.*

To which, in case the costs should be paid as provided by law, there should be annexed a record of the report, plat, and field-notes of the commissioner as given above.

FEES IN LAYING OUT ROADS.

For laying out public highways.—SECTION 3824. The following fees shall be paid persons engaged in laying out and changing highways:

Commissioners for each day, two dollars;

Surveyor for each day, four dollars;

Chain carriers, markers, and other assistants, for each day, one dollar and fifty cents.

If the highway extends into more than one county, such expenses when so adjudged shall be paid by the several counties in proportion to the length of time occupied on the highway in each county.

The road record and form book.—The forms above furnished could be printed in a proper book for that purpose, with suitable blanks, and thus place the complete records in each case together, and secure system and uniformity in the records of road cases, and thereby save much labor and time on the part of the county auditor.

Sets of the above forms could be repeated, and both for final action by the board, and the auditor; and if either acted, the form adapted to the action of the other, could remain blank; or the sets of forms for the different cases could be placed separate, in different parts of the book. This plan is quite common in the recorder's office for the record of deeds, that are uniform in their general forms, and also in the clerk's office for the entry of judgments and decrees that may be made uniform, as in case of common defaults on notes, and on notes with foreclosure of mortgages given to secure the same.

This plan would tend to secure accuracy and order where much informality, and want of accuracy and order usually prevails.

III. WARRANT BOOK.

What it should contain.—The warrant book required to be kept, generally consists, so far as I have observed, of a book in which blank county warrants are printed with printed blank "stubs" for each warrant, for entering in the order of their issuance the number of the warrant with the date, amount, and name of the payee, as directed and required by law.

IV. RECORD BOOK OF OFFICIAL BONDS.

What it should contain.—In this book should be recorded the official bonds of all officers whose bonds are approved by the board. Code, Sec. 683.

V. HIGHWAY PLAT BOOK.

Required to be kept by auditor.—This book is required to be kept by the auditor, and on which he is required to plat all the hghways of the county, and all that may be legally established. Code, Sec. 967.

VI. OFFICIAL BONDS.

How approved.—We have already noticed that official bonds of county, and some township officers, should be approved by the board of supervisors. This should be done by an action of the board thereon. But in addition thereto the chairman of the board should indorse upon the bonds, his certificate of said approval by the board. For a form in such cases, see form for indorsement on the clerk's bond, No. 3.

CHAPTER XXXI.

POWERS, DUTIES, LIABILITIES, RESPONSIBILITY AND COMPENSATION.

I. DECISIONS RELATING TO THEIR POWERS, DUTIES AND LIABILITIES.

To employ an attorney.—The board of supervisors has power to employ an attorney, or attorneys, to prosecute or defend in a criminal case, properly belonging to the duties of the district attorney; and the board having power to act in such a case, may devolve the performance of the duty on a committee of its own members, to carry out such a contract of employment. 32 Iowa, 15.

Erection of public buildings.—They may order the erection of a public building the cost of which does not exceed $5,000, and may also order the purchase of grounds on which to erect the same, the cost of which does not exceed $2,000.

The cost of the building and grounds are not to be estimated together. Code, Sec. 303; 32 Iowa, 200.

Contract for county.—A resolution of the board of supervisors offering a bounty to each volunteer enlisting in the military service, to the credit of the county, "under the present call or to fill any call that might thereafter be made," is unlimited as to the time of enlistment, or as to the calls under which made. The fact that one-half of the bounty was to be paid at a fixed date, would not affect the rule. Nor would the fact that no distinct quota was specifically assigned to the county, affect the right of the claimant to recover, if each township had assigned to it the number of men necessary to be furnished by it, and the enlistment in question was credited to a particular township. 32 Iowa, 530.

Equalization of assessments.—The board has power to equalize assessments of townships, cities and incorporated towns of their county; they may add to, or deduct from, the valuation of any township such percentage as may be necessary to equalize the same, and its discretionary action in this respect cannot be reviewed on certiorari. 30 Iowa, 531.

Misdemeanor in office.—The ordering of the erection of a bridge at a cost of more than $5,000, without first submitting a proposition therefor to the voters of the county, is the doing of an act prohibited by statute, and renders the members of the board voting for the order indictable for a misdemeanor. 30 Iowa, 238; Code, Sec. 303.

Publication of laws and proceedings.—Where laws have once been published in a newspaper, selected therefor by the board, according to law, and which was then the only newspaper published in the county, the board have not the power at its January session in the following year, to order their publication again in another paper, established subsequently to the first.

And it seems that if no paper is published in the county, at the time when the board is by law to make the selection, it cannot subsequently order them published in a paper subsequently established.

But as to the publication of the proceedings of the board, their publication may be ordered at any session of the board.

But the proprietor of a newspaper has no such private or personal interest in the publication of such laws and proceedings as that he can in his own name maintain an action to compel by mandamus, the board to order such publication in his paper. 23 Iowa, 199.

To determine the circulation.—The power to determine the circulation of papers in each case is conferred upon the board, and in doing this, they are not confined to the affidavits filed by the respective proprietors of newspapers, but all other practicable sources of information are open to them. *Smith v. Yoran, et al.*, (Board of Sup.,) Sept. T. Sup. Ct., (not yet published.)

Power in reference to bridges.—The board is invested with power to erect all bridges in the county, which may be necessary, and which the public convenience may require; and may levy a tax for that purpose not exceeding three mills on the dollar. The statute giving cities and incorporated towns the control of bridges within the city or town does not oust the county of the right to erect free bridges across a river on a public highway within the limits of the city or incorporated town. And the appropriation of $7,000 out of the swamp land money belonging to the county to aid in the construction of a bridge, by authority of a vote of the electors of a county imposes no restriction upon the powers of the board of supervisors to make an additional appropriation. 21 Iowa, 119.

Lease with offer to sell: what is not acceptance.—A lease of a certain building for use as a court house, entered into between the board of supervisors and the owners of said building, contained the stipulation that, "the county shall have the privilege of purchasing the property hereby leased, at any time during the existence of the lease for $12,000." The board afterward, in accordance with law, ordered the question of the purchase of said building to be submitted to a vote of the people of the county, which was accordingly done, and their vote regularly given in the affirmative, and was so declared and entered by the board. In an action afterward brought by the owners of said property, to compel the specific performance of the contract, which it was claimed had been made complete by the aforesaid action of the board and the people, the petition averred the foregoing facts: It was *held:*

1. That the facts alleged did not constitute a complete contract of sale enforceable in a court of equity.

2. That the effect of the vote of the people was merely to authorize, not require, the board to make the purchase at the price stipulated, and that until they should contract by accepting the offer, pursuant to the authority conferred upon them, there was no consummation of the same. 22 Iowa, 491.

Fraud in the submission of questions.—In order to avoid on the ground of fraud the result of a submission to the voters of the county a question involving the purchase of a public building, there must be some showing of artifice to conceal material facts peculiarly within the knowledge of the board of supervisors ordering such submission, and not open to, or attainable by others. 22 Iowa, 492.

Proposition to levy a tax.—A submission by the board to the voters of the county of a question involving the expenditure of money in the purchase of a public building is of no effect unless accompanied by a proposition to levy a tax for the payment thereof, and the adoption of the same, together with the proposition of expenditure. 12 Iowa, 155.

Power to grade roads.—The board has power to grade and improve the public roads, and to contract therefor. 32 Iowa, 181.

Appeal.—An appeal lies from an order of the board refusing to allow a claim, or establishing a private road, and the taking of land for a private road is unconstitutional. 25 Iowa, 540; 15 Iowa, 256; 19 Iowa, 29.

Road record.—The establishment of a road will not be held invalid on the ground that the petition therefor does not sufficiently state the commencement and terminus of the road when these are made sufficiently certain by the record plat and survey; nor because it asks for "the appointment of a commissioner to open a road," instead of, "the establishment of a road." 26 Iowa, 223; 24 Iowa, 362; 19 Iowa, 124.

Counties not liable for their officers.—Counties and other *quasi* corporations are generally not liable to private actions for the neglect of their officers in respect to highways, unless the statute has by express provision created the liability; nor for an injury caused by a defective culvert or small bridge which it was the duty of the officers of the road district to keep in repair. 26 Iowa, 264.

When liable for unsafe condition of bridges.—In analogy to the liability of municipal corporations with respect to their streets, it has been held that counties were liable for the unsafe condition of county bridges proper, that is, bridges built by the county authorities in the exercise of their statutory power and duty, and over which they had exercised jurisdiction. 26 Iowa, 264; 16 Iowa, 339.

Duty of repairing roads not imposed.—The duty of repairing roads is not imposed by statute upon the county as a corporation, but upon the respective road districts, and for the default of the road districts or its officers, the county is not liable. 26 Iowa, 264.

The record as evidence.—Where a road was established upon condition that the damages awarded should be paid within a certain time, and the record showed they were paid, but not the time when, they will be presumed to have been paid within the time prescribed. And it will be presumed that the notices required by law were duly posted. 25 Iowa, 232; 24 Iowa, 362; 19 Iowa, 133.

Field-notes and plat.—The directions of the statute relating to mile-posts, and other monuments, and the making of field-notes and plats, are directory; and a failure to comply therewith by the surveyor, will not render the proceedings void. 24 Iowa, 362; 9 Iowa, 583.

Certiorari.—Proceedings in the establishment of a road will not be annulled on *certiorari*, unless it is shown that the board has exceeded its jurisdiction, or is acting illegally. 7 Iowa, 248.

Highways in cities and towns.—Special acts conferring upon cities and incorporated towns the power to regulate and improve the lanes and alleys, and regulate the width of sidewalks; and that the lanes and alleys and the roads leading from the city or town for one mile, shall constitute one road district, do not affect the power given the board to establish roads throughout the county. And the establishment of a road more than 66 feet wide is irregular, but not void. It can be corrected on appeal, but cannot be attacked collatterally. 20 Iowa, 248.

Cannot establish a road beyond the terminus.—The commissioners have no power to lay out a highway beyond the terminus named in the notice and petition, and a report establishing such an extension is null and void. 18 Iowa, 525.

The appraisers cannot allow for benefits.—In the assessment of damages in the location of a road, the appraisers cannot take into account any advantage or benefit that may result to the owner by reason of the establishment of the road, as that it would tend to drain and improve the land. 32 Iowa, 254.

The Session Laws of 1874, provide additional powers and duties for the board of supervisors, as follows:

In each county where coal and other minerals are mined they may appoint a person practically acquainted with mining, as inspector of mines whose duty is prescribed by the statute. Sess. Laws, 1874, Chap. 31.

They may make an appropriation to aid in the support of the Teachers Normal Institute. Session Laws, 1874, Chap. 57. And they may remit the penalty and interest on the payment of taxes that have remained due and uncollected for four years. Sess. Laws, 1874, Chap. 29.

II. RESPONSIBILITY OF THE OFFICE.

Special duty.—The office of supervisors is a highly honorable and responsible one. They are the legally constituted guardians of the rights and interests of the county, and it is made their special duty to inquire into, and investigate the accounts of the county officers and particularly those having charge of the finances of the county.

In the discharge of this important duty they should exercise at least a reasonable diligence, and require the accounts of these officers to be rendered to them in a clear and business-like-way, and to examine and scrutinize these accounts closely.

Owing to the neglect of this duty, in some cases, large losses have resulted to counties in this State.

The law contemplates, and the people expect, and demand, a faithful discharge of this duty on the part of supervisors, and the neglect of the same, tends to general looseness, and want of order and system on the part of the officer.

It frequently occurs that petitions are presented to the board, and claims are made, against the county in relation to which the board has no jurisdiction. Of this class are petitions to reduce the assessment of individuals. The Code provides that parties aggrieved by assessments, may apply to the township board of equalization, which is composed of the township trrustees, and meet for this purpose on the first Monday of April, in each year. The board of supervisors has no power to act in such cases, and the practice leads to trouble and vexation on the part of the board. They might be thus unprofitably occupied during the whole year.

III. COMPENSATION.

Provisions of the statute.—The statute provides for the compensation of supervisors as follows:

SEC. 3791. The members of the board of supervisors shall each receive four dollars for each day actually in session, and two dollars and fifty cents per day, exclusive of mileage, when not in session but employed on committee service, and six cents per mile for every mile traveled in going to and from said session of the board: *provided*, that in counties having a population as shown by the last preceding census of less then ten thousand they shall not receive compensation for more than twenty days in one year; and in counties having a population of more than ten thousand, but less than thirty thousand, for more than thirty days in the year; and in counties having a population of thirty thousand or over, not more than forty days in one year.

CHAPTER XXXII.

THE AUDITOR.

I. HIS DUTY.

Closely related to the duties of the board of supervisors are the duties of the auditor.

The general provisions of the Code in reference to those duties are as follows:

Duties of.—SECTION 320. The county auditor shall:

1. Record all the proceedings of the board in proper books provided for that purpose;

2. Make full entries of all their resolutions and decisions on all questions concerning the raising of money, and for the allowance of money from the county treasury;

3. Record the vote of each supervisor on any question submitted to the board, if required by any member present;

4. Sign all orders issued by the board for the payment of money, and record in a book provided for the purpose, the reports of the county treasurer of the receipts and disbursements of the county;

5. Preserve and file all accounts acted upon by the board, with their action thereon, and perform such special duties as are or may be required of him by law;

6. Designate upon every account on which any sum shall be allowed by the board, the amount so allowed, and the charges for which the same was allowed;

7. Deliver to any person who may demand it, a certified copy of any record or account in his office on payment of his legal fees therefor.

When to sign warrants.—SEC. 321. The auditor shall not sign or issue any county warrant except upon the recorded vote or resolution of the board of supervisors authorizing the same, except for jury fees, and every such warrant shall be numbered, and the date, amount, and number of the same, and the name of the person to whom issued, shall be entered in a book to be kept by him in his office for the purpose.

School fund.—SEC. 322. Whenever the auditor of any county shall receive from the state auditor, notice of the apportionment of school moneys to be distributed in the county, he shall file the same in his office and transmit a certified copy thereof to the county treasurer, and he shall also lay a certified copy thereof before the board at its next regular meeting.

Court house.—SEC. 323. The county auditor shall have the general custody and control of the court house in each county respectively, subject to the direction of the board of supervisors.

Report to secretary of state.—SEC. 324. The county auditor shall report to the secretary of state the name, office, and term of office of every county officer elected or appointed, within ten days after their election and qualification, and the secretary of state shall record the same in a book to be kept for that purpose in his office.

Who eligible.—SEC. 325. The clerk of the district court and county recorder shall each be eligible to the office of county auditor, and may discharge the duties of both offices.

Cannot be treasurer.—SEC. 326. The offices of county auditor and county treasurer shall not be united in the same person. The auditor and his deputy are prohibited from acting as attorney, either directly or indirectly, in any matter pending before the board of supervisors.

Oath of any receiver of public money before credit given.—SEC. 73. When a county treasurer or other receiver of public money, seeks to obtain credit on the books of the auditor's office for payment made to the treasurer, before giving such credit the auditor shall require him to take and subscribe an oath that he has not used, loaned or appropriated any of the public money for his private benefit, nor for the benefit of any other person.

Requisition to officer to account.—SEC. 74. In those cases where the auditor is authorized to call upon persons or officers for information, or statements, or accounts, he may issue his requisition therefor in writing to the person or officer called upon, allowing reasonable time, which having been served as a notice in a civil action by the sheriff of the county in which the person or officer called upon resides, and returned to the auditor with the service indorsed thereon, shall be evidence of the making of the requisition therein expressed.

II. SUMMARY OF OTHER DUTIES.

To deliver the session laws.—It is his duty to deliver to each county officer and the mayor of each incorporated town and city, and to each justice, constable, trustee, member of a town and city council, township clerk and assessor a copy of the general laws of each session of the legislature of the State furnished him by the Secretary of State, and to sell and dispose of any of the balance of said laws that may be furnished him, and be required by others; to report annually on the fifteenth day of November, of copies of said laws sold and the number on hand, and the amount paid into the State or county treasury on account of such sales, and charge such State or county treasurer with the amount; and he is required to deliver to his successor in office the copies remaining on hand. And he is further to distribute the Code to certain officers. Code, Secs. 40, 41, 42; Sess. Laws 1874, Chap. 15.

Census.—He is required to forward to the Secretary of State on or before the first day of September on the year of taking of the census, an abstract of the census returns, and upon the failure of the township assessor to take the census, he is required to appoint some suitable person to take the same. Code, Secs. 114, 117.

To provide for grand and trial jurors.—He is required to apportion the number of jurors to be selected in each election precinct as near as practicable in proportion to the number of votes polled therein at the last general election, and deliver a statement thereof to the sheriff and at least twenty days prior to the first day of any term of court at which a jury is to be selected, the auditor or his deputy must write out the names on the lists of grand and trial jurors, which have not been previously drawn as jurors, during the year, on separate ballots, and the clerk of the District Court or his deputy, and the sheriff having compared said ballots with the list and corrected the same if necessary, shall place the same in a box to be provided for that purpose. Code, Secs. 236, 240.

Special meeting of supervisors.—When a special meeting of the board of supervisors is required and requested by a majority of the board, in writing addressed to the auditor, it is his duty to fix a day for such meeting not later than ten days from the filing of the petition with him, and he is required to immediately give notice in writing to each of the supervisors personally, or by leaving a copy thereof at his residence at least six days before the time fixed for said meeting.

The notice must state the time and place of meeting, and the object of it as stated in the petition. Code, Sec. 301.

To make a duplicate tax list.—In counties where township collectors are elected, he is required to make out duplicate tax lists for each township, and deliver the same with the original to the county treasurer. Code, Sec. 402.

To cause plats of land to be made in certain cases.—In case the original owner or proprietor of any sub-division of land, has sold any part thereof and has failed, or neglected to file a plat, as provided by law, the county auditor is required to notify such owner, or proprietor, and if he fail to file said plat for thirty days, the auditor is required to cause a plat thereof to be made and filed for record, which shall have the same effect as if made by the proprietor or proprietors thereof. Code, Sec. 568.

And whenever any congressional sub-division of lands of forty acres or less, is owned by two or more persons in severalty, and the description of one or more parcels thereof are in the opinion of the auditor not sufficiently certain and accurate for the purpose of assessment and taxation, he may cause the same to be platted and said plat recorded, as required in relation to plats of towns and cities. Code, Sec. 569.

To furnish two poll-books.—He is required to prepare and furnish to each precinct two poll-books, having each of them a sufficient column for the number of voters, and sufficient blank leaves to contain the entries of the oaths, certificates and returns of elections, and also all books, blanks and material necessary to carry out the provisions of the law in reference to registration of voters. Code, Sec. 615. And he is required to send a messenger to the percincts where the returns of elections have not been made on the fourth day after the election. Code, Sec. 634.

In case of a tie vote.—In case of a tie vote between two or more persons, it is the duty of the auditor to notify said persons to appear at his office on a day named in the notice, and within twenty days from the election, and determine by lot which of them is to be declared elected. Code, Sec. 643. And it is the further duty of the auditor in such cases to notify the board of canvassers, or in case of their absence or inability to act, the recorder and sheriff of such lot, and of the day fixed therefor. Code, Sec. 644.

To transmit abstract of votes.—He is required to seal up, direct and transmit the abstract of votes cast in the county for senator and representative, where the district is composed of more than one county, duly certified by the county canvassers to the secretary of State and to the auditor of each other county in the district, who should file the same in his office. Code, Sec. 546.

To file and record official bonds.—He is required to file and record in a book to be kept by him for that purpose in his office, and to be known as the "record book of official bonds," the official bonds of all county officers, including justices of the peace and constables, and keep an index of said book, in which, under the title of each office he shall enter the names of each principal and his sureties, and the date of the filing of the bond. Code, Sec. 683.

To be clerk of the court in contested elections.—The auditor shall be clerk of the court on the trial of contested elections; and he is required to keep the papers and records of the proceedings in the election book in a manner similar to the record of proceedings in the District Court, except when the auditor is a party, in which case the board should appoint a suitable person as clerk, whose appointment should be recorded.

And he may issue subpœnas for witnesses in such cases, at any time after notice of trial is served. Code, Secs. 396 and 704.

In cases of removal or suspension from office.—In case of a trial and judgment of removal or suspension from office of any county or township officer, a copy thereof should be certified to the county auditor, and he should cause it to be entered in the election book.

If the proceedings relate to a justice of the peace, and he is removed from office, the auditor should notify the proper township trustees or clerk of the removal. Code, Secs. 754 and 779.

He may appoint a deputy.—It will be seen by reference to the statute relating to deputies in the first chapter of this volume, that the auditor may appoint a deputy, for whose acts he is responsible. But in all cases the appointment of a deputy must receive the approval of the board of supervisors. For the proper forms and requirements for this purpose, reference may be had to those furnished for the clerk in such cases.

To notify the township clerk of certain vacancies.—Whenever a vacancy occurs in the office of a justice of the peace, or constable, more than thirty days prior to any general election, the auditor should immediately notify the clerk of the township in which the vacancy exists thereof; and the auditor may approve the bond of a justice of the peace or constable, appointed by the township trustees of any township to fill a vacancy, on the recommendation of the sufficiency of the sureties upon such bond, signed by any member of the board of supervisors. Code, Secs. 794 and 795.

III. HIS DUTY RELATING TO REVENUE.

To make out and transmit abstracts.—The auditor is required, on or before the third Monday of June in each year, to make out and transmit to the auditor of State an abstract of the real and personal property in his county, in which he shall set forth:

1. The number of acres of land in his county, and the aggregate value of the same, exclusive of town lots, returned as corrected by the board of equalization.
2. The aggregate value of real property in each town in the county returned by the assessor, as corrected by the county board of equalization.
3. The aggregate value of personal property in his county.
4. An abstract of the aggregate value and number of cattle, the aggregate value and number of horses, the aggregate value and number of mules, the aggregate value and number of swine over six months old, as the same are returned by the assessors of his county. Code, Sec. 833.

To make assessment conform to requirements of the State board of equalization.—It is the duty of the auditor, on the receipt of the statement from the State board of equalization, to add to, or deduct from, the valuation of each parcel of real estate in his county, the percentage required by the State board, rejecting all fractions of fifty cents or less, in the result, and counting all over fifty cents as one dollar; and before the first Monday of November, in each year, transcribe the assessments of the several townships into a book to be provided at the expense of the county, properly ruled, and headed with distinct columns, in which shall be entered the names of the tax payers, descriptions of the lands, number of acres and values, value of personal property, and each description of tax, with a column for polls, and one for payments. Code, Sec. 837.

The consolidated tax.—All taxes which are uniform throughout any civil township or independent school district shall be formed into a single tax, and entered upon the tax list in a single column, and denominated a consolidated tax, and each tax receipt shall show the percentage levied for each separate fund. Code, Sec. 838.

His duty relating to the tax book.—The board of supervisors are required at their meeting in September in each year, to levy the requisite tax for the current year, and record the same in a proper book; and it is the duty of the auditor, as soon as practicable thereafter, to complete the list, by carrying out in a column by itself, the consolidated tax, highway tax, polls, and irregular tax, if any be levied, and the total taxes, and after adding up each column of said taxes, he shall in his abstract, at the end of each township, incorporated town or city list, apportion the consolidated tax among the respective funds to which it belongs, according to the number of mills levied for each of said funds, showing a summary of the total amount of each distinct tax. Code, Sec. 839.

To correct errors.—He may correct any clerical or other error in the assessment, or tax book, and when such correction affecting the amount of tax is made after the books have passed into the hands of the treasurer, he shall charge the treasurer with all sums added to the several taxes, and credit him with any deductions therefrom, and report the same to the supervisors. Code, Sec. 841.

To designate on the books land sold.—Before the tax books are placed in the hands of the treasurer for collection of the taxes thereon, it is the duty of the auditor to designate thereon each piece or parcel of real estate previously sold for taxes and not redeemed, by writing in a plain manner opposite to each piece the word "sold." Code, Sec. 842.

What the tax books should show.—He is required to make an entry upon the tax list, showing what it is, and for what county and year, and deliver it to the county treasurer on or before the first day of November, taking his receipt therefor. Code, Sec. 843.

To certify statement to the Auditor of State.—At the same time he is required to furnish the Auditor of State a certified statement, showing the aggregate valuation of lands, town property, and personal property in the county, each by itself, and also the aggregate amount of each separate tax as shown by said tax book. Code, Sec. 844.

To keep accounts with the treasurer.—The auditor is required to keep full and complete accounts with the county treasurer, and with each separate fund or tax by itself, in each of which accounts he shall charge him with the amounts in his hands at the opening of such accounts, whether it be delinquent taxes, notes, cash, or other assets belonging to such funds, the amount of each tax for each year when the tax book is received by him, and all additions to each tax, or fund, whether by additional assessments, interest, or delinquent taxes, the amounts received for peddlers' licenses, and other items, and shall credit the treasurer on proper vouchers, for money disbursed, for double and erroneous assessments, including all improper and illegal assessments, a correction or remission of which causes a diminution of the tax, and for unavailable taxes, or such as have been properly and legally assessed, but which there is no prospect of collecting. Code, Sec. 869.

The manner of keeping accounts.—The manner and form of keeping these accounts may be the same as suggested for the county treasurer, in treating of that officer. It is evident that a cash book and a ledger are all the books required for this purpose, and the accounts will be but a duplicate of the treasurer's accounts. The theory of the law is, that the auditor at all times has the amounts received by the treasurer from all sources; and at stated, and short intervals, when he examines his vouchers for money paid out, he has an accurate account of the condition of the various funds in the hands of the treasurer, and of the condition of the finances of the county.

To attend tax sales.—The auditor is required to attend all sales of real property for taxes made by the treasurer, and to make a record thereof in a book to be kept by him for that purpose, in the same manner as is required of the treasurer, and if he fail to attend any sale of lands, as aforesaid, either in person, or by a competent deputy, he is liable to a fine of not less than fifty, nor more than three hundred dollars. Code, Secs. 882-884.

Not to purchase at tax sales.—Any county auditor who shall be, directly or indirectly, concerned in the purchase of any real property sold for the payment of taxes, is liable to a penalty of not more than one thousand dollars, and all such sales are void. Code, Sec. 885.

To issue certificates of redemption.—The auditor is required, upon the application of any party, to redeem any lands sold for the payment of taxes, and upon being satisfied that said party has a right to redeem the same, and upon the payment of the proper amount, to issue to such party a certificate of redemption, setting forth the facts of sale substantially as contained in the certificate of sale, the date of redemption, the amount paid, and by whom redeemed; and he shall make the proper entries in the book of sales in his office, and give immediate notice thereof to the treasurer. Code, Sec. 891.

IV. RELATING TO THE LOCATION, ALTERATION, OR VACATION OF HIGHWAYS.

To appoint a commissioner, when.—On the presentation of a petition for the location, alteration or vacation of a highway, he may approve the bond required by law for the payment of the costs, and appoint a commissioner to examine into the expediency of the proposed highway, or the alteration or vacation thereof, and on the filing of the commissioner's report in favor of the same, he must appoint a day, not less than 60 nor more than 90 days distant, when the matter will be acted upon. Code, Secs. 923, 924, 934.

Failure to examine or report.—The time for the commissioner to commence the examination, shall be fixed by the auditor, and if the commissioner fails to commence the examination at the time fixed therefor, or if he fails to report as provided by law, the auditor may fix another day, or extend the time of making such report, or may appoint another commissioner. Code, Sec. 935.

Where no objections or claim for damages are filed.—If no objections, or claims for damages, are filed on or before noon of the day fixed for filing the same, and contained in the notice served and published as required by the statute, and the auditcr is satisfied that the provisions of the statute in relation to the proposed highway have been complied with, he should proceed to establish the highway as recommended by the commissioner, upon the payment of costs; but if the auditor is satisfied that the notice has not been served and published as required by law, he must appoint another day and cause such notice to be served, and published as provided by the statute, and thereafter proceed as before stated. Code, Secs. 937, 938.

All proceedings to be entered in the highway book.—Any order made, or action taken, in the establishment of a highway should be entered in the highway book, distinguishing between those made or taken by the auditor, and those by the board of supervisors; and after the highway has been finally established, the plat and field-notes must be recorded by the auditor, and he should certify the same to the township clerk who shall certify the same to the road supervisors, and the supervisor of highways shall be directed by him to have the same opened and worked, allowing a reasonable time to enable the owners of land to erect the necessary fences adjoining the new highway, and where crops have been planted, or sown before the highway is finally established, the opening of the same shall be deferred until the crop is harvested. Code, Secs. 949, 950, Chap. 19, Sess. Laws, 1874.

The form of record in road cases.—The forms for keeping the records in road cases, both where final action is had before the board of supervisors, and also by the auditor, has already been furnished, when treating of supervisors, and also other directions in relation thereto.

Appeal and other matters.—The bonds required on appeals from the final decision of the board in relation to highways, must be approved by the auditor, and he is required on appeal to file a transcript of the papers, and proceedings of the board, in the office of the clerk of the Circuit Court;

to give notice by publication, or posting notices of the re-survey of lands, where the survey was defective or the field-notes lost, and in case said re-survey is approved by the board of supervisors, to record the same. Code, Secs. 960, 961.

To plat all highways.—It is his duty to cause every highway to be platted in a book to be obtained for that purpose, and known as the "Highway Plat Book," and have all changes in, or additional highways legally established, immediately entered upon said plat book, with appropriate references to the files in which the papers relating to the same may be found; to furnish the township clerks a certified copy of said plat book so far as the same relates to their respective townships, and the auditor is required to notify said clerks of all changes made in the plat book, so far as they relate to their townships respectively. Code, Secs. 965, 966, 967, 968.

Statement of railroad property.—He is required to transmit a statement of railroad property lying in each city, town, township, or lesser taxing district through which the railroad runs, to the city council or trustees of such city, incorporated town, township, or lesser taxing district. Code, Sec. 1321.

V. TO PERFORM VARIOUS OTHER DUTIES.

He is required to keep a military register; issue warrants for the expenses of taking insane persons to the insane hospital; Code, Sec. 1010; collect expenses for keeping insane persons in certain cases, from their relations; Code, Sec. 1433; cause the return of justices of the peace in relation to estrays to be published; Code, Sec. 1468; subscribe for one copy of a newspaper in which estray notices are published; Code, Sec. 1469; enter in the estray book the warrant issued, and the affidavit of the taker-up of lost goods; Code, Sec. 1514; and fix a day and cause notice to be published of the application of a person to sell intoxicating liquors; Code, Sec. 1529.

VI. DUTY RELATING TO THE SCHOOL FUND.

To apportion the school tax and interest.—It is the duty of the auditor on the first Monday of April, and the fourth

Monday of September, in each year, to apportion the county school tax, together with the interest of the permanent school fund, to which the county is entitled, and all other money in the hands of the county treasurer, and belonging in common to the schools of his county and not included in any previous apportionment, among the several sub-districts therein, in proportion to the number of persons therein between five and twenty years of age, as shown by the report of the county superintendent, filed with him for the year immediately preceding; and he should immediately notify the president of each the sum to which his district is entitled by said apportionment, and is required to issue his warrant for the same to accompany said notice, which warrant is required to be signed also by the president of the district, and countersigned by the secretary, in whose favor the same is drawn, and will then authorize the district treasurer to draw the amount from the county treasurer. Code, 1781–2.

To certify the appointment or election of County Superintendent.—He is required to forward to the Superintendent of Public Instruction a certificate of the election or appointment and qualification, and on the second Monday in February and August in each year, transmit to the Auditor of State a report of the interest of the school fund then in the hands of the county treasurer, and not included in any previous apportionment, and also the amonnt of said interest unpaid. Code, Secs. 1781, 1782, 1783.

To report delinquents and make abstracts.—He must report delinquents, who fail to pay interest on amounts due the school fund to the district attorney, examine titles, and make and preserve abstracts of titles to lands given in security for money borrowed of the permanent school fund, and approve the security therefor, in cases where he grants applications for loans. Code, Sec. 1864.

To report money received and paid out.—He is required at each meeting of the board of supervisors, to give them a full statement of all money received for, and loaned out of, the school fund, and submit to their examination all notes, mortgages and abstracts of title, connected therewith. Code, Sec. 1866.

Liable on his bond, etc.—He is liable on his official bond for amounts loaned where the security is insufficient; he may give certificates to debtors of the school fund of the amount due from them; publish notices of the time when debts become due to the school fund; keep an account of the school fund with the county treasurer; report annually to the Auditor of State the sales of school lands, and also when the school fund on hand cannot be loaned. Code, Secs. 1872, 1877, 1881, 1883.

For failure to perform duty.—For a failure or neglect to perform any of the duties required of him relating to the school fund, the auditor is liable to a fine of not less than one and not more than five hundred dollars. Code, Sec. 1878.

VII. TRANSFER AND INDEX BOOKS.

The provisions of the Code, in reference to transfer and index books, are as follows:

TRANSFER AND INDEX BOOKS.

County auditor to keep.—SECTION 1948. The county auditor shall keep in his office, books for the transfer of real estate, which shall consist of a transfer book, index book, and book of plats.

Form of.—SEC. 1949. Said transfer book shall be ruled and headed substantially after the following form; and entries thereupon shall be in numerical order beginnig with section one.

SECTION NO. ...., TOWNSHIP ...., RANGE ....

Grantee.	Grantor.	Date of instrument.	Description.	Page of Plats.
......	....	......	....	......
......	....	......	....	......
......	....	......	....	......
......	....	......	....	......
......	....	......	....	......

THE INDEX BOOK THUS:

NAMES OF GRANTEES.	PAGES OF TRANSFER BOOK.
....	....
....	....
....	....
....	....
....	....

Book of plats: how ruled and kept.—Sec. 1950. The auditor shall so keep the book of plats as to show the number of lot and block, or township and range, divided into sections and sub-divisions as occasion may require, and shall designate thereon each piece of land or town lot, and mark in pencil the name of the owner thereon in a legible manner. Said plats shall be lettered or numbered so that they may be conveniently referred to by the memoranda of the transfer book, and shall be drawn on a scale of not less than four inches to the mile.

Entries by auditor in index and transfer book.—Sec. 1951. Whenever a deed of unconditional conveyance of real estate is presented, the auditor shall enter in the index book, in alphabetical order, the name of the grantee, and opposite thereto the number of the page of the transfer book on which such transfer is made; and upon the transfer book he shall enter in the proper columns, the name of the grantee, the name of the grantor, date of instrument, the character of the instrument, the description of the property, and the number or letter of the plat on which the same is marked.

Indorse deed.—Sec. 1952. After the auditor has made the entries contemplated in the preceding section, he shall indorse upon the deed the following words: "Entered for taxation this . . . day of . . . A. D . . . . ," with the proper date inserted, and sign his name thereto.

Cannot be filed for record until indorsed.—Sec. 1953. The recorder shall not file for record any deed of real property, until the proper entries have been made upon the transfer books in the auditor's office and indorsed upon the deed.

Auditor correct.—Sec. 1954. The auditor shall correct the transfer books from time to time, as he shall find them incorrect.

VIII. FEES AND COMPENSATION OF THE AUDITOR.

The provisions of the Code in reference to fees and compensation of the county auditor are as follows:

Fees.—Section. 3797. The county auditor shall be entitled to charge and receive the following fees;

For recording each bond required to be by him recorded, fifty cents;

For transfers made in the transfer books, for each deed, twenty-five cents;

For issuing certificate of redemption of land sold for taxes, twenty-five cents;

For each certificate issued by the treasurer for lands sold for non-payment of taxes, fifteen cents.

Render account of fees to supervisors: additional compensation.—Sec. 3798. Such auditor shall enter in a book kept for that purpose, all fees contemplated in the preceding section received by him, and shall render to the board of supervisors at each session, an account verified by affidavit, stating the amount of fees received and from what source derived, and the said board shall allow him such additional compensation as is deemed just and proper.

Session Laws 1874.—Additional duties are imposed on the auditor by the laws of 1874, as follows:

He is required to furnish to any State institution in his county, and to each justice of the peace and township clerk of his county, a copy of the Code and take a receipt therefor; and in case the number of Codes he may have on hand are not sufficient therefor, he is authorized to draw upon the Secretary of State to supply the deficiency. Sess. Laws, 1874, Chap. 15. He is also required to issue warrants to jurors on the certificate of the clerk of the amounts due them as jurors, without the same being audited by the board of supervisors. Session Laws, 1874, Chap. 16.

CHAPTER XXXIII.

THE TREASURER.

I. THE IMPORTANCE OF—HIS ELECTION—QUALIFICATION.

The importance of the office.—The office of the county treasurer is one of the most important and responsible of the county officers.

He has charge of the revenues of the county, and is its financial agent.

Election and qualification, etc.—The provisions of the Code relating to his election qualification, removal, suspension, appointment of deputies, additional security, vacancies, criminal acts, and the publication of official notices, may be found in Chapter One; and directions and forms relating to several of these matters have been given in treating them in connection with the office of the clerk.

II. GENERAL DUTIES.

Provisions relating to his duties.—The Code provides:

To receive funds.—SECTION 327. The treasurer shall receive all money payable to the county, and disburse the same on warrants drawn and signed by the county auditor and sealed with the county seal, and not otherwise; and shall keep a true account of all receipts and disbursements, and hold the same at all times ready for the inspection of the board of supervisors.

When no funds.—SEC. 328. When the warrant drawn by the auditor on the treasurer is presented for payment, and not paid for want of money, the treasurer shall indorse thereon a note of that fact and the date of presentation, and sign it, and thenceforth it shall draw interest at the rate of six per cent.; and when a warrant which draws interest is taken up, the treasurer is required to indorse upon it the date and amount of interest allowed, and such warrant is to be considered as canceled, and shall not be re-issued.

Warrants when divided.—SEC. 329. When a person wishing to make a payment into the treasury, presents a warrant of an amount greater than such payment, the treasurer shall cancel the same and give the holder a certificate of the overplus, upon the presentation of which to the county auditor, he shall file it and issue a new warrant of that amount and charge the treasurer therewith, and such certificate is transferable by delivery, and will entitle the holder to the new warrant, which, however, must be issued in the first drawee's name.

Warrant book.—SEC. 330. The treasurer shall keep a book ruled so as to contain a column for each of the following items in relation to the warrants drawn on him by the auditor, the number, date, drawee's name, when paid, to whom, original amount, and interest paid on each.

Keep separate accounts.—SEC. 331. The treasurer shall keep a separate account of the several taxes for state, county, school, and highway purposes, opening an account between himself and each of those funds, charging himself with the amount of the tax, and crediting himself with the amounts paid over severally, and with the amount of delinquent taxes when legally authorized so to do.

Warrants canceled.—SEC. 332. The warrants returned by the treasurer shall be compared with the warrant book, and the word "canceled" be written over the minute of the proper numbers in the warrant book, and the original warrant be preserved for at least two years.

Returns of.—SEC. 333. The treasurer is required to make weekly returns to the auditor of the number, date, drawee's name, when paid, to whom paid, original amount, and interest, as kept in the book before directed.

Accounts each term.—SEC. 334. A person re-elected to, or holding over the office of treasurer, shall keep separate accounts for each term of his office.

When county bonds are issued.—His duty when county bonds are issued is provided for as follows:

Disposition of bonds.—SECTION 290. Whenever bonds, issued under this chapter, shall be duly executed, numbered consecutively and sealed, they shall be delivered to the county treasurer, and his receipt taken therefor, and he shall stand charged on his official bond with all bonds delivered to him and the proceeds thereof, and he shall sell the same, or exchange them, on the best available terms for any legal indebtedness of the county, outstanding on the first of January, 1872, [January, 1874, by Session Laws 1874, Chap. 9], but in neither case for a less sum than the face value of the bonds, and all interest accrued on them at the date of such sale or exchange. And if any portion of said bonds are sold for money, the proceeds thereof shall be applied exclusively for the payment of liabilities existing against the county at and before the date above named. When they are exchanged for warrants and other legal evidence of county indebtedness, the treasurerer shall at once proceed to cancel such evidence of indebtedness, by indorsing on the face thereof the amount for which they were received, the word "canceled," and the date of cancellation. He shall also keep a record of bonds sold or exchanged by him by number, date of sale, amount, date of maturity, the name and post office address of purchasers, and, if exchanged, what evidences of indebtedness were received therefor, which record shall be open at all times for inspection by the public. Whenever the holder of any bond shall sell or transfer it, the purchaser shall notify the treasurer of such purchase, giving at the same time the number of the bond transferred and his post office address; and every such transfer shall be noted on the record. The treasurer shall also report, under oath, to the board at each regular session, a statement of all bonds sold or exchanged by him since the preceding report, and the date of such sale or exchange; and, when exchanged, a list or description of the county indebtedness exchanged therefor, and the amount of accrued interest received by him on such sale or exchange, which latter sum shall be charged to him as money received on bond fund, and so entered by him on his books; but such bonds shall not be exchanged for any indebtedness of the county except by the approval of the board of supervisors of said county.

Tax levied to pay bonds.—SEC. 291. The board of supervisors shall cause to be assessed and levied each year upon the taxable property of the county, in addition to the levy authorized for other purposes, a sufficient sum to pay the interest on outstanding bonds issued in conformity with the provisions of this chapter accruing before the next annual levy, and such proportion of the principal, that at the end of three years the sum raised from such levies shall equal at least twenty per cent. of the amount of bonds issued; at the end of five years at least forty per cent. of the amount; and at and before the date of maturity of the bonds, shall be equal to the whole amount of the principal and interest; and the money arising from such levies shall be known as the bond-fund, and shall be used for the payment of bonds and interest-coupons, and for no other purpose whatever; and the treasurer shall open and keep in his books a separate and special account thereof, which shall at all times show the exact condition of said bond-fund.

How paid or redeemed.—SEC. 292. Whenever the amount in the hands of the treasurer belonging to the bond-fund, after setting aside the sum required to pay interest maturing before the next levy, is sufficient to redeem one or more bonds, he shall notify the owner of such bond or bonds that he is prepared to pay the same, with all interest accrued thereon, and if not presented for payment or redemption within thirty days after the date of such notice, the interest on such bonds shall cease, and the amount due thereon shall be set aside for its payment whenever presented. All redemptions shall be made in the exact order of their issuance, beginning at the lowest or first number; and the notice herein required shall be directed to the post-office address of the owner, as shown by the record kept in the treasurer's office.

III. HIS DUTY RELATING TO TAXES.

Duplicate tax lists.—The Code provides in relation thereto as follows:

Auditor's duty.—SECTION 402. The auditor, in counties where township collectors are elected, shall make out a duplicate tax list of each township, and deliver the same, with the original, to the county treasurer.

Treasurer's duty: powers of collector.—SEC. 403. The county treasurer shall deliver to each township collector in the county, as soon as he has qualified, such duplicate tax list of his township, and take his receipt therefor, specifying the total amount of the tax charged in such list, and charge the same over to each township collector in a book to be kept for that purpose; and such duplicate tax list, when so made out and delivered to the township collectors, may be used as an execution, and shall be sufficient authority for them to collect the taxes therein charged in any township in the county by distress and sale or otherwise, as now provided by law for the collection of taxes by the county treasurer; and the county treasurer shall not receive or collect any of the taxes charged in any duplicate tax list so delivered, except the tax of non-residents of the township, until the same has been returned to him as hereinafter provided. The said county treasurer shall procure for and deliver to each township collector with said tax list, a tax receipt-book, with a blank margin or stub, upon which the said township collector shall enter the number and date of the tax receipt given to the tax-payer, the amount of tax and by whom paid, which said tax receipt-book shall be returned to the county treasurer, with the said duplicate tax list, as hereinafter provided.

Duty of township collectors thereupon.—The Code further provides that the collectors shall give notice of the reception of said tax list, and proceed to collect the taxes, and make monthly statements to the county treasurer, and pay over to him monthly the amounts collected by them, which matters we shall hereafter have occasion to consider more fully when treating of township collectors. Code, Sec. 404.

Treasurer's duty relative to unpaid taxes.—The Code provides:

Unpaid taxes.—SECTION 408. After the return of said duplicate tax lists and settlement as provided above, the county treasurer shall receive, receipt for, and collect any unpaid taxes in the county, and shall proceed to advertise and sell all the real estate in the county upon which the taxes have not been paid, for the unpaid taxes thereon as provided by law.

When there is failure to collect.—SEC. 409. If any of the taxes mentioned in the tax list shall remain unpaid, and the collector shall not be able to collect the same, he shall deliver to the county treasurer an account of the taxes so remaining due; and upon making oath before the county auditor, or in case of his absence, before any justice of the peace, that the sums mentioned in such account remain unpaid, and that he has not, upon diligent inquiry, been able to discover any goods or chattels belonging to or in the possession of the person charged with or liable to pay such sums, whereon he could levy the same, he shall be credited by the county treasurer with the amount thereof, but such oath and credit shall only be presumptive evidence of the correctness thereof.

Liability.—SEC. 410. Such collector and his sureties shall be liable for the loss by theft or otherwise, of any money collected by him and in his possession.

Taxes collected for a township board of health.—The taxes levied by the board of supervisors on any township to provide for the expenses of the board of health of the township, the treasurer is required to collect with the other taxes and pay over to the township clerk. Code, Sec. 420.

He is required to pay over to the treasurer of municipal corporations.—All moneys received by him arising from taxes levied belonging to such corporation on or before the first day of March in each year, and such moneys as the treasurer receives after that time for delinquent taxes belonging to such corporation, he is required to pay to the treasurer thereof when demanded. Code, Sec. 498.

The collection of the taxes generally.—For the purpose of presenting the treasurer's duties in relation to taxes generally, it is deemed advisable to copy the provisions of the Code in reference thereto, which are as follows:

To enter taxes unpaid for previous years: sale void.—SECTION 845. The treasurer, on receiving the tax book for each year, shall enter upon the same in separate columns, opposite each parcel of real property or person's name, on which, or against whom any tax remains unpaid for ether of the preceding years, the year or years for which such delinquent tax so remains due and unpaid. And any sale for the whole or any part of such delinquent tax, not so entered, shall be invalid.

Treasurer to collect: illegality in proceedings.—SEC. 846. The treasurer, after making the above entry, shall proceed to collect the taxes, and the list shall be his authority and justification against any illegality in the proceedings prior to receiving the list; and he is also authorized and required to collect, as far as practicable, the taxes remaining unpaid on the tax books of previous years.

Notice when land has been sold.—SEC. 847. Each county treasurer shall, when any person offers to pay taxes on any real estate marked "sold," notify such person that such property has been sold for taxes, and inform him for what taxes said property was sold, and at what time said sale was effected.

To certify amount required to pay taxes and redeem: compensation for.—SEC. 848. The county treasurer shalll certify, in writing, the entire amount of taxes and assessments due upon any parcel of real estate, and all sales of the same for unpaid taxes or assessments shown by the books in his office, with amount required for redemption from the same, if still redeemable, whenever he shall be requested so to do by any person having any interest in said real estate, and paid or tendered his fees for such certificate at the rate of fifty cents for the first parcel in each township, incorporated town, or city, and ten cents for each subsequent parcel in the same township, town or city. Each description in the tax list shall be reckoned a parcel in computing the amount of such fees.

Effect of certificate.—SEC. 849. Such certificates, with the treasurer's receipt showing the payment of all the taxes therein specified, and the auditor's certificate of redemption from the tax sales therein mentioned, shall be conclusive evidence for all purposes and against all persons, that the parcel of real estate in said certificate and receipt described, was, at the date thereof, free and clear of all taxes and assessments, and sales for taxes or assessments, except sales whereon the time of redemption had already expired, and the tax purchaser had received his deed.

Treasurer liable for error.—SEC. 850. For any loss resulting to the county, or any sub-division thereof, or to any tax-purchaser, or tax-payer, from an error in said certificate or receipt, the treasurer and his sureties shall be liable on his official bond.

May assess property omitted.—SEC. 851. The county treasurer shall assess any real property subject to taxation, which may have been omitted by the assessor, board of equalization, or county auditor, and collect taxes thereon, and in such cases he is required to note opposite the tract or lot assessed, the words, "by treasurer;" *provided*, that such assessment shall be made within two years after the tax list shall have been delivered to him for collection, and not afterwards.

Owner to have property omitted assessed.—SEC. 852. In all cases where real property subject to taxation shall not have been assessed by the township assessor or other proper officer, the owner thereof, by himself or his agent, shall have the same properly assessed by the treasurer and to pay the taxes thereon; and no failure of the owner to have such property assessed, or to have the errors in the assessment corrected, and no irregularity, error, or omission in the assessment of such property, shall affect in any manner the legality of the taxes levied thereon, or affect any right or title to such real property which would have accrued to any party claiming or holding under and by virtue of a deed executed by the treasurer as provided for by this title, had the assessment of such property been in all respects regular and valid.

Taxes when lien.—SEC. 853. All taxes upon real estate shall, as between vendor and purchaser, become a lien upon such real estate on and after the first day or November in each year.

Warrants received for taxes.—SEC. 854. Auditor's warrants shall be received by the county treasurer in full payment of state taxes, and county warrants shall be received at the treasury of the proper county for the ordinary county tax, but money only shall be received for the school tax. Highway taxes may be discharged and highway certificates of work done received as provided by law.

Currency received for taxes.—SEC. 855. The county treasurers are authorized and required to receive in payment of all taxes by them collected, together with the interest and principal of the school fund, treasury notes issued as legal tender by the government of the United States, and the notes issued by the banks organized under, and in accordance with, the conditions of the act of the congress of the United States entitled, "An act to provide a national currency secured by a pledge of United States stocks, and to provide for the redemption thereof," approved February 25, 1863.

Same received by treasurer of state.—SEC. 856. The treasurer of state is hereby required to receive of the several county treasurers the above mentioned notes, in payment of any claims the state may have against any county for any part af the permanent school fund, or for any taxes due the state; and the state treasurer shall pay out said notes in redemption of outstanding auditor's warrants.

DISTRESS AND SALE.

When and how made.--SEC. 857. No demand of taxes shall be necessary, but it is the duty of every person subject to taxation to attend at the office of the treasurer, unless otherwise provided, at some time between the second Monday of November and the first day of February, and pay his taxes; and if any one neglects to pay them before the first day of February following the levy of the tax, the treasurer is directed to make the same by distress and sale of his personal property, not exempt from taxation, and the tax-list alone shall be sufficient warrant for such distress.

Notice of sale given: expenses: proceeds.—SEC. 858. When the treasurer distrains goods, and the owner shall refuse to give a good and sufficient bond for the delivery of said goods on the day of sale, he may keep them at the expense of the owner, and shall give notice of the time and place of their sale within five days after the taking, in the manner constables are required to give notice of the sale of personal property under execution; and the time of sale shall not be more than twenty days from the day of taking, but he may adjourn the sale from time to time, not exceeding five days in all, and shall adjourn at least once when there are no bidders, and in case of adjournment he shall put up a notice thereof at the place of sale. Any surplus remaining above the taxes, charges of keeping, and fees for sale, shall be returned to the owner, and the treasurer shall, on demand, render an account in writing of the sale and charges.

Deputies: compensation: delinquent taxes.—SEC. 859. Immediately after the taxes become delinquent, each county treasurer shall proceed to collect the same by distress and sale of the personal property of the delinquent tax-payers, in the manner prescribed in the preceding section, and for this purpose he shall, within sixty days after the taxes become delinquent, appoint one or more deputies to aid and assist him in collecting the delinquent taxes in his county. Each deputy so appointed, shall receive as a compensation for his services, and expenses, the sum of five per cent. on the amount of all delinquent taxes collected and paid over by him, which percentage he shall collect from the delinquent, together with the whole amount of delinquent taxes and interest; and in the discharge of his duties as such assistant collector, should it become necessary to make the delinquent taxes by distress and sale, he shall be entitled to receive the same compensation, in addition to the five per cent. provided for in this section, as constables are entitled to receive for the sale of property on execution. But this section sha'l not apply, so far as it authorizes the appointment of deputies, to any county in which township collectors of taxes are elected, and the owners or agents of land that has been sold for delinquent taxes shall have the same privilege and extension of time for paying taxes as other tax payers whose land has not been so sold.

When treasurer is resisted.—SEC. 860. If the treasurer, or his deputy, be resisted or impeded in the execution of his office, he may require any suitable person to assist him therein, and if such person refuse the aid, he shall forfeit a sum not exceeding ten dollars to be recovered by civil action in the name of the county, and the person resisting shall be liable as in the case of resisting the sheriff in the execution of civil process.

Taxes certified to treasurer of any other county.—SEC. 861. In all cases of delinquent taxes, in any county where the person upon whose property the same were levied, shall have removed into another county of the state, leaving no property within the county where the taxes were levied, out of which the same can be made, the treasurer of the county where said taxes are delinquent, shall make out a certified abstract of said taxes as they appear upon the tax-book, and forward the same to the treasurer of the county in which the person resides, or has property, who is owing said taxes, whenever the treasurer transmitting said abstract has reason to believe that said taxes can be collected thereby.

Force and effect of.—SEC. 862. The treasurer forwarding, and the one receiving, said abstract, shall each keep a record thereof, and upon the receipt and filing of said abstract in the office of the treasurer to whom the same is sent, it shall have the full force and effect of a levy of taxes in that county, and the collection of the same shall be proceeded with in the same manner provided by law for the collection of other taxes.

Penalty.—SEC. 863. The officer collecting taxes so certified into another county, shall, in addition to the penalties provided by law on delinquent taxes, assess and collect the further penalty of twenty per cent. on the whole amount of such taxes, inclusive of the penalties thereon.

Return made.—SEC. 864. The officer receiving said abstract, shall, whenever in his opinion the taxes are uncollectable, return the abstract with the indorsement thereon of "uncollectable," and in case said taxes are collected, the officer receiving the same shall transmit the amount to the treasurer of the county where said taxes were levied, less the penalty provided by section eight hundred and sixty-three of this chapter.

DELINQUENT—LIEN—PENALTY.

When delinquent: liens on property.—SEC. 865. On the first day of February, the unpaid taxes, of whatever description, for the preceding year shall become delinquent and shall draw interest as hereinafter provided; and taxes upon real property are hereby made a perpetual lien thereon against all persons except the United States and this state, and taxes due from any person upon personal property shall be a lien upon any real property owned by such person or to which he may acquire a title. The treasurer is authorized and directed to collect the delinquent taxes by the sale of any property upon which the taxes are levied, or any other personal or real property belonging to the person against whom the taxes are assessed.

Penalty after delinquent.—SEC. 866. The treasurer shall continue to receive taxes after they become delinquent, untill collected by distress and sale; but if they are not paid before the first day of March, he shall collect, in addition to the tax of each tax-payer so delinquent, as a penalty for non-payment, at the rate of one per cent. a month on the amount of the tax for the first three months, two per cent. for the second three months, and three per cent. a month thereafter. But the penalty provided by this section shall not be construed to apply, and shall not apply, upon taxes levied by order of any court to pay judgments on city or county bonded indebtedness, and upon such taxes no other penalty than the interest which such judgments draw shall be collected

MISCELLANEOUS.

Form of receipt: effect of.—SEC. 867. The treasurer shall, in all cases, make out and deliver to the tax-payer a receipt, stating the time of payment, the description and assessed value of each parcel of land, and the assessed value of personal property, the amount of each kind of tax, the interest on each, and costs, if any, giving a separate receipt for each year; and he shall make the proper entries of such payments on the books of his office. Such receipt shall be in full of the party's taxes for that year, but the treasurer shall receive the full amount of any county, state, or school tax, whenever the same is tendered, and give a separate receipt therefor.

Treasurer apportion consolidated tax and make report.—SEC. 868. The treasurer of each county shall, on or before the tenth day of each month, apportion the consolidated tax of each civil township or independent school district in his county, collected during the preceding month, among the several funds to which it belongs, according to the number of mills levied for each fund contained in said consolidated tax, and having entered the amount of tax for each fund, including other taxes collected during the preceding month, upon his cash account, he shall report the amount of each distinct tax to the county auditor, who shall charge him up with the same.

Auditor keep accounts: each fund kept separate.—SEC. 869. The county auditor shall keep full and complete accounts with the county treasurer, with each separate fund or tax by itself, in each of which accounts he shall charge him with the amounts in his hands at opening of such account, whether it be delinquent taxes, notes, cash, or other assets belonging to such fund, the amount of each tax for each year when the tax book is received by him, and all additions to each tax or fund, whether by additional assessments, interest or delinquent taxes, amount received for peddlers' licenses or other items, and shall credit the treasurer on proper vouchers, for money disbursed, for double and erroneous assessments, including all improper and illegal assessments, the correction or remission of which causes a diminution of the tax, and for unavailable taxes, or such as have been properly and legally assessed, but which there is no prospect of collecting.

Treasurer to refund taxes when directed by supervisors.--SEC. 870. The board of supervisors shall direct the treasurer to refund to the tax-payer, any tax, or any portion of a tax, found to have been erroneously or illegally exacted or paid, with all interest and costs actually paid thereon, and in case any real property subject to taxation shall be sold for the payment of such erroneous tax, interest or costs as above mentioned, the error or irregularity in the tax may at any time be corrected as above provided, and shall not affect the validity of the sale, or the right or title conveyed by the treasurer's deed, if the property was subject to taxation for any of the purposes for which any portion of the taxes for which the land was sold was levied, and the taxes, were not paid before the sale and the property had not been redeemed from sale.

TAX SALE.

When and how made.—SEC. 871. On the first Monday in October in each year, the county treasurer is required to offer at public sale at his office, all lands, town lots, or other real property on which taxes of any description for the preceding year or years shall remain due and unpaid, and such sale shall be made for and in payment of the total amount of taxes, interests, and costs, due and unpaid on such real property.

Notice: what to contain.—SEC. 872. The notice to be given of such sale shall state the time and place thereof, and contain a description of the several parcels of real property to be sold for the delinquent taxes of the preceding year, and such real property as has not been advertised for the taxes of previous years, and on which the taxes remain due and delinquent, and the amount of taxes and amount of interests and costs against each tract, and the name of the owner, when known, or person, if any, to whom taxed.

How published.—SEC. 873. The county treasurer shall give such notice by causing the same to be published once in each week for three successive weeks, the last publication to be at least one week prior to the day of sale, in some newspaper printed in such county, if any such there be, or if not, then in the nearest newspaper in this state having a general circulation in such county; and also by causing a copy of such notice to be posted on the door of the county court house at least four weeks before the day of sale. But no newspaper shall be selected unless it has two hundred regular weekly subscribers, and has been regularly printed and published for at least three months preceding the fifteenth of September of said year in the same county, and has had at least twenty actual subscribers in the county wherein the delinquent property is situated, for at least three months preceding the fifteenth of September of that year. And in all cases where the treasurer may doubt the qualifications of any paper as above fixed, he shall require proof thereof by the affidavit of the publisher.

Cost of publication: notice filed.—SEC. 874. The treasurer shall charge and collect, in addition to the taxes and interest, a sum not exceeding twenty cents on each tract of real property advertised for sale, which sum shall be paid into the county treasury, and the county shall pay the costs of publication, but in no case shall the county be liable for more than the amount charged to the delinquent lands for advertising, and if the treasurer cannot procure the publication of said notice for that sum, or, if for any other reason the treasurer is unable to procure the publication of said notice, he shall post up written notices of said sale in four of the most public places in his county four weeks before sale, and notice so given shall have the same effect as though the same had been published in a newspaper. In that case he shall, before making such sale, file in the office of the auditor of his county, a copy of said notice with his certificate indorsed thereon, setting forth that said notice had been posted up in four of the most public places in his county four weeks before the sale, which certificate shall be subscribed by him and sworn to before said auditor, and shall be presumptive evidence of the facts therein stated.

Hour and place of sale.—SEC. 875. The county treasurer shall, at his office, on the day of the sale, at the hour of ten o'clock in the forenoon, offer for sale, separately, each tract or parcel of real property advertised for sale, on which the taxes and costs shall not have been paid.

Purchaser: homestead liable.—SEC. 876. The person who offers to pay the amount of taxes due on any parcel of land, or town lot, for the smallest portion of the same is to be considered the purchaser, and when such purchaser shall designate the portion of any tract of land or town lot for which he will pay the whole amount of taxes assessed against any such tract or lot, the portion thus designated shall, in all cases, be considered an undivided portion. In all cases where the homestead is listed separately as a homestead, it shall be liable only for the taxes thereon.

Sale continued.—SEC. 877. The treasurer shall continue the sale from day to day as long as there are bidders, or until the taxes are all paid.

Re-sale.—SEC. 878. The person purchasing any parcel or part thereof, shall forthwith pay to the treasurer the amount of taxes and costs charged thereon, and on failure to do so, the said parcel shall at once again be offered as if no such sale had been made. Such payment may be made in the same funds receivable by law in payment of taxes.

Owner may pay before sale.—SEC. 879. Any person owning or claiming lands, or town lots, advertised for sale as aforesaid, may pay to the county treasurer, at any time before the sale thereof, the taxes due thereon, with interest, cost of advertising, and all the costs which may have accrued up to the time of such payment.

Letters and figures used: informality: effect of.—SEC. 880. In all advertisements for the sale of real property for taxes, and in entries required to be made by the county auditor, treasurer, or other officer, letters and figures may be used as they have been heretofore, to denote townships, ranges, sections, parts of sections, lots, blocks, date, and the amount of taxes, interest, and costs. And no irregularity or informality in the advertisement shall affect in any manner the legality of the sale, or the title to any real property conveyed by the treasurer's deed under this chapter, but, in all cases, the provisions of this chapter shall be sufficient notice to owners of the sale of their property.

Certificate of publication.—SEC. 881. The treasurer shall obtain a copy of said advertisement, together with a certificate of the due publication thereof, from the printer or publisher of the newspaper in which the same shall have been published, and shall file the same in the office of the county auditor, and such certificate shall be substantially in the following form:

I, A B, publisher (or printer) of the . . a . . newspaper printed and published in the county of . . . , and state of Iowa, do hereby certify that the foregoing notice and list were published in said newspaper once in each week for three successive weeks, and the last of which publications was made on . . day of . . . , A D 18 . , and that copies of each number of said paper in which said notice and said list were published, were delivered by carrier or transmitted by mail to each of the subscribers to said paper, according to the accustomed mode of business in this office.

A . . B . . ,
Publisher (or printer) of the . .

STATE OF IOWA, }
. . . . COUNTY, } SS.

The above certification of publication was subscribed and sworn to before me by the above named A B, who is personally known to me to be the identical person described therein, on the . . day of . . , A. D, 18 . .

C. . D. . ,
County Auditor, . . . County, Iowa.

Auditor to attend sales: duty: treasurer to keep record.—SEC. 882. The county auditor shall attend all sales of real property for taxes made by the treasurer, and make a record thereof in a book to be kept by him for that purpose, therein describing the several parcels of real property on which the taxes and costs were paid by the purchaser, as they are described in the list or advertisement on file in his office, stating in separate columns the amount as obtained from the treasurer's tax list, of each kind of tax, interest, and costs for each tract or lot, how much and what part of each tract or lot was sold, to whom sold, and date of sale. The treasurer shall also keep a book of sales, in which, at the time of sale, he shall make the same records. He shall also note in the tax-list, opposite the description of the property sold, the fact and date of such sale.

Sale adjourned.—SEC. 883. When all the parcels of real property advertised for sale shall have been offered, and a portion thereof shall remain unsold for want of bidders, the treasurer shall adjourn the sale to some day not exceeding two months from the time of adjournment, due notice of which day shall be given at the time of adjournment, and also by keeping a notice thereof posted in a conspicuous place in the treasurer's office; but no further advertisement shall be necessary. On the day fixed for the re-opening of the sale, the same proceedings shall be had as provided hereby for the sale commencing on the first Monday of October. And further adjournments shall be made from time to time, not exceeding two months, and the sales shall be thus continued until the next regular annual sale, or until all the taxes shall have been paid.

Penalty on auditor and treasurer for failure of duty.—SEC. 884. If any treasurer or auditor shall fail to attend any sale of lands as required by this chapter, either in person or by competent deputy, he shall be liable to a fine of not less than fifty nor more than three hundred dollars, to be recovered by an action in the district court against the treasurer or auditior, as the case may be, and his bondsmen. And if such officer or deputy shall sell, or assist in selling any real property, knowing the same to be not subject to taxation, or that the taxes for which the same is sold have been paid, or shall knowingly and willfully sell, or assist in selling, any real property for payment of taxes to defraud the owner of such real property, or shall knowingly and willfully execute a deed for property so sold, he shall be liable to a fine of not less than one thousand nor more than three thousand dollars, or to imprisonment not exceeding one year, or to both fine and imprisonment, and to pay the injured party all damages sustained by any such wrongful act, and all such sales shall be void.

SEC. 885. If any county treasurer or auditor shall hereafter be, either directly or indirectly, concerned in the purchase of any real property sold for the payment of taxes, he shall be liable to a penalty of not more than one thousand dollars, to be recovered in an action in the district court, brought in the name of the county against such treasurer or auditor, as the case may be, and his bondsmen; and all such sales shall be void.

Sale at any other time.—SEC. 886. If, from neglect of officers to make returns, or from any other good cause, real property cannot be duly advertised and offered for sale on the first Monday of October, the treasurer shall make the sale on the first

Monday of the next succeeding months in which it can be made, allowing time for the publication as provided in this chapter.

CERTIFICATE OF PURCHASE.

How made: what contain.—SEC. 887. The county treasurer shall make out, sign, and deliver to the purchaser of any real property sold for the payment of taxes as aforesaid, a certificate of purchase, describing the property on which the taxes and costs were paid by the purchaser, as the same was described in the records of sales, and also how much and what part of each tract or lot was sold, and stating the amount of each kind of tax, interest, and costs for each tract or lot for which the same was sold, as described in the records of sales, and that payment had been made therefor. If any person shall become the purchaser of more than one parcel of property, he may have the whole included in one certificate, but each parcel shall be separately described.

Certificate assignable.—SEC. 888. The certificate of purchase shall be assignable by indorsement, and an assignment thereof shall vest in the assignee, or his legal representative, all the right and title of the original purchaser; and the statement in the treasurer's deed of the fact of the assignment shall be presumptive evidence of such assignment. In case said certificate is assigned, then the assignment of said certificate shall be placed on record in the office of the county treasurer in the register of tax sales.

When purchaser pays subsequent taxes.—SEC. 889. The county treasurer shall also make out, sign, and deliver to the purchaser of any real property sold for taxes aforesaid, duplicate receipts for any taxes, interest, and costs, paid by said purchaser, after the date of said purchase for any subsequent year or years, one of which receipts said purchaser shall present to the county auditor, to be by him filed in his office, and a memorandum thereof entered on the register of sales. And if he neglect to file such duplicate receipt with the auditor before the redemption, such tax shall not be a lien upon the land, and the person paying such tax shall not be entitled to recover the same of the owner of such real estate.

REDEMPTION.

How effected.—SEC. 890. Real property, hereafter sold under the provisions of this chapter, may be redeemed at any time before the right of redemption is cut off, as herein after provided, by the payment to the county auditor of the proper county, to be held by him subject to the order of the purchaser, of the amount for which the same was sold and twenty per centum of such amount immediately added as a penalty, with ten per cent. interest per annum on the whole amount thus made from the day of sale, and also the amount of all taxes, interest, and costs paid for any subsequent year or years, and a similar penalty of twenty per centum added as before on the amount of the payment for each subsequent year, with ten per cent. interest per annum on the whole of such amount or amounts from the day or days of payment, unless such subsequent taxes shall have been paid by the person for whose benefit the redemption is made, which fact may be shown by the treasurer's receipt; and provided further, that such penalty for the non-payment of the taxes of any such subsequent year or years shall not attach, unless such subsequent tax or taxes shall have remained unpaid until the first day of March after they become due, so that they have become delinquent, nor shall any of said penalties apply in the cases mentioned in the last clause of section eight hundred and sixty-six of this chapter.

Certificate of redemption.—SEC. 891. The county auditor shall, upon application of any party to redeem any real property sold under the provisions of this chapter, and being satisfied that such party has a right to redeem the same, and upon the payment of the proper amount, issue to such party a certificate of redemption, setting forth the facts of the sale substantially as contained in the certificate of sale, the date of the redemption, the amount paid, and by whom redeemed, and he shall make the proper entries in the book of sales in his office, and shall immediately give notice of such redemption to the county treasurer. Such certificate of redemption shall then be presented to the treasurer, who shall countersign the same and make the proper entries in the books of his office, and no certificate of redemption shall be held as evidence of such redemption without such signature of the treasurer.

Minors and lunatics.—SEC. 892. If real property of any minor or lunatic is sold for taxes, the same may be redeemed at any time within one year after such disability is removed, in the manner specified in the following section, or such redemption may be made by the guardian or legal representative under section eight hundred and ninety, at any time before the delivery of the deed.

How redeemed after deed made.—SEC. 893. Any person entitled to redeem lands sold for taxes after the delivery of the deed, shall redeem the same by an equitable action in a court of record, in which all persons claiming an interest in the land derived from the tax sale, as shown by the record, shall be made defendants, and the courts shall determine the rights, claims, and interest of the several parties, including liens for taxes and claims for improvements made on the land by the person claiming under the tax title. And no person shall be allowed to redeem land sold for taxes in any other manner after the service of the notice provided for by the next section, and the execution and delivery of the treasurer's deed.

EXECUTION OF DEED—NOTICE GIVEN.

Before deed is made notice to be given: what contain: how served.—SEC. 894. After the expiration of two years and nine months after the date of sale of the land for taxes, the lawful holder of the certificate of purchase may cause to be served upon the person in possession of such land or town lot, and also upon the person in whose name the same is taxed, if such person resides in the county where the land is situated, in the manner provided by law for the service of original notices, a notice signed by him, his agent, or attorney, stating the date of sale, the description of the land or town lot sold, the name of the purchaser, and that the right of redemption will expire and a deed for said land be made, unless redemption from such sale be made within ninety days from the completed service thereof. Service may be made upon non-residents of the county by publishing the same three times in some newspaper printed in said county, and if no newspaper is printed in said county, then in the nearest newspaper published in this state. But any such non-resident may file with the treasurer of the county a written appointment of some resident of the county where his lands or lots are situated as agent upon whom service shall be made and in such case, personal service of said notice shall be made upon said agent. Service shall be deemed completed when an affidavit of the service of said notice, and of the particular mode thereof, duly signed and verified by the holder of the certificate of purchase, his agent, or attorney, shall have been filed with the treasurer authorized to execute the tax-deed. Such affidavit shall be filed by said treasurer, and entered upon the records of his office, and said record or affidavit shall be presumptive evidence of the completed service of notice herein required, and, until ninety days after the service of said notice, the right of redemption from such sale shall not expire. Any person swearing falsely to any fact or statement contained in said affidavit, shall be deemed guilty of perjury and punished accordingly. The cost of serving said notice, whether by publication or otherwise, together with the cost of the affidavit, shall be added to the redemption money.

When deed shall be made.—SEC. 895. Immediately after the expiration of ninety days from the date of service of the written notice hereinbefore provided, the treasurer then in office shall make out a deed for each lot or parcel of land sold and remaining unredeemed, and deliver the same to the purchaser upon the return of the certificate of purchase. The treasurer shall demand twenty-five cents for each deed made by him on such sales, but any number of parcels of land bought by one person may be included in one deed, if desired by the purchaser.

Form of.—SEC. 896. Deeds executed by the treasurer shall be substantially in the following form:

Know all men by these presents, that whereas the following described real property, viz; [here follows the description], situated in the county of . . . , and State of Iowa, was subject to taxation for the year (or years) A. D. . . : and whereas the taxes assessed upon said real property for the year (or years) aforesaid remained due and unpaid at the date of the sale hereinafter named; and whereas, the treasurer of said county did, on the . . . day of . . . , A. D. 18 . . , by virtue of the authority in him vested by law, at (an adjourment of) the sale begun and publicly held on the first Monday of . . . , A. D. 18 . . , expose to public sale at the office of the county treasurer in the county aforesaid, in substantial conformity with all the requisitions of the statute in such case made and provided, the real property above described, for the payment of the taxes, interest and costs then due and remaining unpaid on said property; and whereas, at the time and place aforesaid, A B, of the county of . . . , and State of . . . , having offered to pay the sum of . . . dollars and . . . cents, being the whole amount of taxes, interest, and costs then due and remaining unpaid on said property, for [here follows the description of the property sold] which was the least quantity bid for; and payment of said sum having been by him made to said treasurer, said property was stricken off to him at that price; and whereas, the said A B did, on the . . . day of . . . , A. D. 18 . . , duly assign the certificate of the sale of the property as aforesaid, and all his right, title, and interest to said property to E F, of the county of . . . , and state of . . . : and whereas, by the affidavit of . . . . , filed in said treasurer's office on the . . . day of . . . , A. D. . . . , it appears that due notice has been given more than ninety days before the execution of these presents to . . . . and . . . . , of the expiration of the time of redemption allowed by law; and whereas, three years have elapsed since the date of said sale, and said property has not been redeemed therefrom as provided for by law.

Now, therefore, I, C D, treasurer of the county aforesaid, for and in consideration of said sum to the treasurer paid as aforesaid, and by virtue of the statute in such case made and provided, have granted, bargained, and sold, and by these presents do grant, bargain, and sell unto the said A B (or E F), his heirs and assigns, the real property last hereinbefore described, to have and to hold unto him the said A B (or E F), his heirs and assigns forever: subject, however, to all the rights of redemption provided by law. In witness whereof, I, C D, treasurer as aforesaid, by virtue of the authority aforesaid, have hereunto subscribed my name on this . . . day of . . . , 18 . . .

STATE OF IOWA, }
. . . COUNTY. } SS.

I hereby certify that before me . . . . in and for said county, personally appeared the above named C D, treasurer of said county, personally known to me to be the treasurer of said county at the date of the execution of the above conveyance, and to be the identical person whose name is affixed to and who executed the above conveyance as treasurer of said county, and acknowledged the execution of the same to be his voluntary act and deed as treasurer of said county, for the purposes therein expressed.

Given under my hand [and seal] this . . day of . . A. D, 18 . .

. . . .

EFFECT OF DEED.

Vests title in purchaser.—SEC. 897. The deed shall be signed by the treasurer in his official capacity, and acknowledged by him before some officer authorized to take acknowledgments of deeds; and, when substantially thus executed and recorded in the proper record of titles to real estate, shall vest in the purchaser all the right, title, interest, and estate of the former owner in and to the land conveyed, and also all the right, title, interest, and claim of the state and county thereto, and shall be presumptive evidence in all the courts of this state, in all controversies and suits in relation to the rights of the purchaser, his heirs or assigns, to the land thereby conveyed, of the following facts:

1. That the real property conveyed was subject to taxation for the year or years stated in the deed;

2. That the taxes were not paid at any time before the sale;

3. That the real property conveyed had not been redeemed from the sale at the date of the deed;

4. That the property had been listed and assessed;

5. That the taxes were levied according to law;

6. That the property was duly advertised for sale;

7. That the property was sold for taxes as stated in the deed. And it shall be conclusive evidence of the following facts:

1. That the manner in which the listing, assessment, levy, notice, and sale were conducted was in all respects as the law directed;

2. That the grantee named in the deed was the purchaser;

3. That all the pre-requisites of the law were complied with by all the officers who had, or whose duty it was to have had, any part or action in any transaction relating to or affecting the title conveyed, or purporting to be conveyed, by the deed, from the listing and valuation of the property up to the execution of the deed, both inclusive, and that all things whatsoever required by law to make a good and valid sale, and to vest the title in the purchaser, were done, except in regard to the points named in this section, wherein the deed shall be presumptive evidence only.

And in all controversies and suits involving the title to real property claimed and held under and by virtue of a deed executed substantially as aforesaid by the treasurer, the person claiming title adverse to the title conveyed by such deed, shall be required to prove, in order to defeat the said title, either that the said real property was not subject to taxation for the year or years named in the deed, that the taxes had been paid before the sale, that the property had been redeemed from the sale according to the provisions of this chapter, and that such redemption was had or made for the use and benefit of persons having the right of redemption under the laws of this state, or, that there had been an entire omission to list or assess the property, or to levy the taxes, or to give notice of the sale, or to sell the property: but no person shall be permitted to question the title acquired by a treasurer's deed without first showing that he, or the person under whom he claims title, had title to the property at the time of the sale, or that the title was obtained from the United States or this state after the sale, and that all taxes due upon the property have been paid by such person, or the person under whom he claims title as aforesaid; *provided*, that in any case where a person had paid his taxes, and through mistake in the entry made in the treasurer's books or in the receipt, the land upon which the taxes were paid was afterwards sold, the treasurer's deed shall not convey the title; *provided further*, that in all cases where the owner of lands sold for taxes shall resist the validity of such tax title, such owner may prove fraud committed by the officer selling the same, or in the purchaser, to defeat the same, and if fraud is so established such sale and title shall be void.

Previous sales not affected by Code.—SEC. 898. The provisions of this title shall not affect sales heretofore made, or tax deeds given in pursuance of sales made before the taking effect of this code.

SALES WRONGFULLY MADE.

County to hold purchaser harmless.—SEC. 899. When, by mistake or wrongful act of the treasurer, land has been sold on which no tax was due at the time, or whenever land is sold in consequence of error in describing such land in the tax receipt, the county is to hold the purchaser harmless by paying him the amount of principal and interest and costs to which he would have been entitled had the land been rightfully sold, and the treasurer and his bondsmen will be liable to the county to the amount of his official bond; or the purchaser, or his assignee, may recover directly of the treasurer, in an action brought to recover the same in any court having jurisdiction of the amount, and judgment shall be against him and his bondsmen; but the treasurer or his bondsmen shall be liable only for his own or his deputies' acts.

Interest acquired by purchaser in school or university land.—SEC. 900. Whenever any school or university land, bought on a credit, is sold for taxes, the purchaser at such tax sale shall only acquire the interest of the original purchaser in such lands, and no sale of any such lands for taxes shall prejudice the rights the state or university therein, or preclude the recovery of the purchase money or interest due thereon; and in all cases where real estate is mortgaged or otherwise encumbered to the school or university fund, the interest of the person who holds the fee shall alone be sold for taxes, and in no case shall the lien or interest of the state be affected by any sale of such encumbered real estate made for taxes.

When land not subject to taxation is sold.—SEC. 901. Whenever it shall be made to appear to the satisfaction of the county treasurer, either before the execution of a deed for real property sold for taxes, or if the deed be returned by the purchaser, that any tract or lot was sold which was not subject to taxation, or upon which the taxes had been paid previous to the sale, he shall make an entry opposite such tract or lot on the record of sales, that the same was erroneously sold, and such entry shall be evidence of the fact therein stated. And in such cases the purchase money shall be refunded to the purchaser as provided by this chapter.

LIMITATIONS OF ACTIONS.

When action must be brought.—SEC. 902. No action for the recovery of real property sold for the non-payment of taxes shall lie, unless the same be brought within five years after the treasurer's deed is executed and recorded as above provided; *provided*, that where the owner of such real property sold as aforesaid, shall, at the time of such sale be a minor or insane, or convict in the penitentiary, five years after such disability shall be removed shall be allowed such person, his heirs or legal representatives to bring their action.

Acts of officers in fact valid.—SEC. 903. In all suits and controversies involving the question of title to real property held under and by virtue of a treasurer's deed, all acts of assessors, treasurers, auditors, supervisors, and other officers *de facto* shall be deemed and construed to be of the same validity as acts of officers *de jure*.

When assessed to wrong person.—SEC. 904. No sale of real property for taxes shall be considered invalid on account of the same having been charged in any other name than that of the rightful owner, if the said property be in other respects sufficiently described.

Certified copies of books evidence.—SEC. 905. The books and records belonging to the offices of the county auditor and county treasurer, or copies thereof, properly certified, shall be deemed sufficient evidence to prove the sale of any real property for taxes, the redemption thereof, or the payment of taxes thereon.

PEDDLERS.

Amount of tax.—SEC. 906. A tax for state purposes shall be levied upon peddlers of merchandise not manufactured in this state, for a license to peddle throughout the state for one year as follows: upon each peddler of watches or jewelry, or either of them, thirty dollars; upon each peddler of clocks, fifty dollars; upon each peddler of dry goods, fancy articles, notions, or patent medicines, as follows: upon each peddler thereof, ten dollars; upon each peddler who pursues his occupation with a vehicle drawn by one animal, twenty-five dollars; if drawn by two, and less than four, fifty dollars: if drawn by four or more animals, seventy-five dollars.

Wholesale dealers exempt.—The foregoing section was amended by the 15th General Assembly, Sess. Laws 1874, Chap. 62, as follows:

"*Provided, however*, That nothing in this section shall apply to wholesale dealers in any of the above enumerated articles, who use wagons for the delivery of goods sold at wholesale prices and by the box or package."

License: how obtained.—SEC. 907. Such license may be obtained from the auditor of the county upon paying the proper tax to the treasurer thereof, and may issue for a less period than one year for the proportionate amount of tax, and all such licenses shall state the date of the expiration of the same; and any person so peddling without a license, or after the expiration of his license, is guilty of a misdemeanor, and the person actually peddling is liable, whether he be the owner of the goods or not. Upon conviction of peddling without a license as aforesaid, the offender shall forfeit and pay to the county treasurer, in addition to the fine imposed upon him for the misdemeanor, double the amount of license for one year as fixed by section nine hundred and six of this chapter.

PROVISIONS FOR THE SECURITY OF THE REVENUE.

County responsible for State tax.—SEC. 908. Each county is responsible to the state for the full amount of tax levied for state purposes, excepting such amounts as are certified to be unavailable, double, or erroneous assessments, as hereinafter provided.

When treasurer is defaulter.—SEC. 909. If any county treasurer prove to be a defaulter to any amount of state revenue, such amount shall be made up to the state within the next three coming years by additional levies, in such manner as to annual amounts as the board of supervisors may direct. In such cases the county can have recourse to the official bond of the treasurer for indemnity.

Interest on warrants: how receipted.—SEC. 910. When interest is due and allowed by the treasurer of any county, or the state treasurer, on the redemption of auditor's warrants, or county warrants, the same shall be receipted on the warrants by the holder of the same, with the date of the payment, and no interest shall be allowed by the auditor of state or board of supervisors, except such as is thus receipted.

Penalty for discounting warrants.—SEC. 911. If the state treasurer, or any county treasurer, discount auditor's warrants at less than the amount due thereon, either directly or indirectly, or through third persons, they shall be liable to a fine not exceeding one thousand dollars, to be prosecuted as other fines.

Penalty for loaning public money.—SEC. 812. County treasurers shall be liable to a like fine for loaning out, or in any manner using for private purposes, state or county funds in their hands, and the state treasurer shall be liable to a fine of not more than ten thousand dollars for a like misdemeanor, to be prosecuted by the attorney-general in the name of the state.

PAYMENTS BY COUNTY TREASURER.

Supervisors to settle with treasurer.—SEC. 913. At their regular meetings in January and June of each year, the board of supervisors shall make a full and complete settlement with the county treasurer, and they shall make and certify to the auditor of state, all credits to the treasurer for double or erroneous assessments, and unavailable taxes, also all dues for state revenue, interest, or delinquent taxes, sales of land, peddler's licen es, and other dues, if any; also the amounts collected for these several items, and revenues still delinquent, each year to itself. Said reports shall be forwarded by mail.

When, and how payments made to treasurer of state.—SEC. 914. The treasurer of each county shall, on or before the fifteenth day of each month, prepare a sworn statement of the amount of money in his hands on the first day of that month belonging to the state treasury, and forward the same by mail to the auditor of state, and he shall, each year, unless otherwise directed by the state auditor, pay into the state treasury, on or before the fifteenth day of March, all the money due the state remaining in his hands on the first day of March, and on or before the fifteenth day of November, all the money due the state remaining in his hands on the first day of November; he shall also, at any time when directed by the auditor of state, forthwith pay into the state treasury, or to the treasurer of any county, or to any bank incorporated under the laws of this state, or any national bank in this state, any or all the money due the state and remaining in his hands. In case the treasurer of any county shall fail to prepare and forward the statement required in this section, he shall forfeit and pay for each and every failure a sum not less than one hundred nor more than five hundred dollars, to be recovered in an action brought in the name of the state auditor, against him and his bondsmen, in any court of record.

When payments made through banks.—SEC. 915. The state auditor may require any county treasurer to make his payment through any other county treasurer, or through any bank chartered by the laws of this state, or any national bank in this state; but no charge shall be made against the state by said bank on said amounts to exceed one-fourth of one per cent. for transportation; and any payments made in pursuance of such requirements by the auditor shall be a release to the county of its liabilities to the amount so paid.

Duty of auditor of state and supervisors.—SEC. 916. The state auditor shall make and transmit to each county auditor, on the first day or May of each year, a statement of the county treasurer's account with the state treasurer, which account shall be submitted by said auditor to the board of supervisors at their next meeting and if they find the same to be incorrect in any particular, they shall forthwith certify the facts in relation to the same to the auditor of state.

Treasurer to settle with supervisors.—SEC. 917. When a county treasurer goes out of office, he shall make a full and complete settlement with the board of supervisors, and deliver up all books, papers, moneys, and all other property appertaining to the office, to his successor, taking his receipt therefor. The board of supervisors shall make a statement, so far as state dues are concerned, to the auditor of state, showing all charges against the treasurer during his term of office, and all credits made, the delinquent taxes and other unfinished business charged over to his successor, and the amount of money paid over to his successor, showing to what year and to what account the amount so paid over belongs. They shall also see that the books of the treasurer are correctly balanced before passing into the possession and control of the treasurer elect.

State treasurer keep funds separate: state and county to account.—SEC. 918. The state treasurer shall keep each distinct fund coming into his possession as public money, in a separate apartment of his safe, and, at each quarterly settlement with the state auditor, he shall count each fund in the presence of the auditor to see if the same agrees with the balance found on the books. The total amount acknowledged to belong to each fund shall be exhibited before the count. County treasurers shall account with such persons as the board of supervisors may direct in like manner, and a report of such accounting shall be made to the board at their next meeting, by the person so appointed by them.

Penalty for failure to perform duty.—SEC. 919. If any county auditor, or county treasurer, or other officer, shall neglect or refuse to perform any act or duty specifically required of him by any provision of this title, such officer shall be deemed guilty of a misdemeanor and indicted therefor; and, being found guilty, shall be fined in any sum not exceeding one thousand dollars, for the payment whereof his bondsmen shall also be liable; and he and his bondsmen shall also be liable to an action on his official bond for the damages sustained by any person through such neglect or refusal.

IV. SUMMARY OF OTHER STATUTES.

He is required to collect taxes on railroad property and pay the same over to the persons or corporations entitled to receive them; Code, Sec. 1321; to collect of the proper parties accounts for clothing furnished blind pupils sent from the county to the College for the Blind, and pay the same into the state treasury; Code, Sec. 1678; and to collect accounts for clothing furnished to the deaf and dumb, sent from his county to the Deaf and Dumb Asylum, and pay the same into the State treasury. Code, Sec. 1695.

In counties having two county seats.—The Session Laws of 1874, Chap. 46, provides for the collection of taxes in counties having two county seats, that in counties divided into two districts for the collection of taxes, and where there are two county seats, for the sale of lands and property for delinquent taxes, in each collection district, shall be *sold* at the county seat, or place where the taxes for each district are collected, and the deputy treasurer and the recorder or his deputy, at such county seat or place, shall do and perform all the duties required of the treasurer and auditor of such county. The records of such sales, and all matters and things pertaining to the same, shall be kept by and in the office of, the deputy treasurer and the recorder, or his deputy, as is required to be kept by the treasurer and auditor. All property sold under the provisions of this act shall be redeemed of the recorder or his deputy, and the certificate of redemption so issued shall be countersigned by the deputy treasurer, and the deputy treasurer and recorder or his deputy shall be authorized and empowered to do and perform all the duties in relation to such redemption as required of the treasurer and auditor of the county. At the expiration of the time for the redemption, as required by sections 890, 891, 892, 893, 894, 895, of the Code, the deputy treasurer is authorized to make, execute, acknowledge, and deliver good and sufficient deeds to the purchaser or holder of the sale-certificate, and to do and perform all other acts and duties required by law of the treasurer of the county in regard to the same.

Remission of penalty and interest on delinquent personal tax.—The Session Laws of 1874, Chap. 29, provides that in all cases where the county treasurer in any county in this State has neglected for the term of four years, or more, to bring forward the delinquent taxes on personal property on the tax-books, as required in section 845 of the Code, or has for four years, or more, neglected to collect said tax by distress and sale of personal property or real estate, upon which said tax is a lien, it shall be the duty of the board of supervisors of the county to remit all of the penalties and interest that may have accrued on such delinquent taxes, on the payment by the person liable for the same of the original amount of such tax.

Taxation of capital.—The Session Laws of 1874, Chap. 60, provides that the paid-up capital of all savings banks organized and doing business shall be subject to the same rates of taxation and rules of valuation as other taxable property, by the revenue laws of the State, which taxes shall be levied on and paid by the banks and not the individual stockholders. The franchise of such banks, the savings and funds deposited therein, and the mortgages and securities, wherever the same are invested, are not to be taxed, but are expressly exempted therefrom, and may be omitted from assessments of the bank required by the revenue laws of this State.

V. SCHOOL DISTRICT TAX.

The provisions of the Code in reference to school district taxes are as follows:

Pay over taxes to appropriate officer.—SECTION 1784. The county treasurer shall, on the first Monday in April of each year, pay over to the treasurer of the district the amount of all school district tax which shall have been collected and shall render him a statement of the amount uncollected, and shall pay over the amount in his hands quarterly thereafter. He shall also keep the amount of tax levied for school-house purposes, separate in each sub-district, where such levy has been made directly upon the property of the sub-district making the application, and shall pay over the same quarterly to the township treasurer for the benefit of such sub-district. He shall, in all counties wherein independent districts are organized, keep a separate account with said independent districts, in which the receipts shall be daily entered, which books shall at all times be open to the inspection and examination of the district board of directors, and shall pay over to the said independent districts the amount of school taxes in his possession on the order of the board, on the first day of each and every month.

To notify president of school board quarterly.—SEC. 1785. On the first day of each quarter, the county treasurer shall give notice to the president of the school board of each township in his county of the amount collected for each fund; and the president of each board shall draw his warrant, countersigned by the secretary, upon the county treasurer for such amount, who shall pay the amount of such taxes to the treasurers of the several school boards only on such warrants.

VI. THE SCHOOL FUND.

To pay therefrom amounts loaned by the auditor.—The treasurer is required to pay from the permanent school fund the amounts loaned by the auditor on presentation of a copy of the notes given therefor, duly certified by the auditor, and retain said certified copy as his voucher, and immediately upon receiving or paying out any moneys belonging to the school fund to enter a correct account thereof on proper books kept by him for the purpose; and in all cases where money is received distinguishing between principal and interest, and he is required to keep an account showing all money due the school fund, whether principal or interest, and distinguishing the amount of each and from whom due; and his books should at all times present a clear and intelligible statement of the school fund in his hands; and said books shall at all times be open to the inspection and examination of any householder or tax-payer in the county. Code, Secs. 1864, 1876.

Normal Institutes.—The Session Laws of 1874, Chap. 57, provides for the holding of Teachers' Normal Institutes, and defraying expenses thereof. County superintendents are obliged to return to the county treasurer all fees received from such institutes, and unexpended balances of State appropriations, which is to be known as the "institute fund." The inference is that this fund should be kept by the treasurer, separate from other funds, in his accounts, although there are no positive directions requiring it.

Penalty for neglect of duty.—Any treasurer failing or neglecting to perform any of the duties required of him, relating to the school fund is liable to a fine of not less than one nor more than five hundred dollars, to be recovered of him and his bondsmen. Code, Sec. 1878.

VII. PROCEEDS OF UNCLAIMED PROPERTY.

Provisions for the sale of.—The Code provides for the sale of unclaimed property by warehousemen and carriers, and that the surplus, after the payment of their charges and the expenses of sale, be disposed of as follows:

DISPOSITION OF PROCEEDS.

Surplus over charges to be deposited in county treasury.—SECTION 2181. After the charges due and unpaid on the property, and the expenses and costs of sale have been taken out of the proceeds, the excess in the hands of the agent or person who was in charge thereof, shall be by him forthwith deposited with the county treasurer of the county where the goods were sold, subject to the order of the owner, said ownership being properly authenticated under oath, and such person shall take from such treasurer a receipt for such money, and deposit the same with the county auditor. He shall also file with the county treasurer a schedule of the property, with the name of the consignee or owner, if known, of each piece of property sold, the sum realized from the sale of each separate package, describing the same, together with a copy of the advertisement as hereinbefore provided, and a full statement of the receipts of the sale, and the amount disbursed to pay charges, costs, and expenses of sale, all of which shall be under the oath of the party or his agent, which schedule, statement, oath, and advertisement shall all be filed and preserved in the treasurer's office, for the inspection of any one interested in the same.

Duty of treasurer.—SEC. 2182. Should the owner of the property sold not make a demand upon the county treasurer for any money that may be in the treasury to his credit, according to the provisions of this chapter, the sum so unclaimed shall be accounted for by the county treasurer, and placed to the credit of the county in the next subsequent settlement made by the treasurer with the county; and should the money or any part thereof, remain unclaimed during the period of one year, it shall then be paid into the school fund, to be distributed as other funds may be by law, which may be raised by tax on other property of the county. But nothing herein contained shall be a bar to any legal claimant from prosecuting and proving his claim for such money at any time within ten years, and, the claim being within that period prosecuted, it shall be paid out of the county treasury in which it was originally placed without interest.

VIII. KEEPING ACCOUNTS.

An important duty.—In the discharge of his many important duties he is required to keep accurate accounts with the county, and with each of the various funds.

Owing to the magnitude of these several funds, these several accounts should be kept with system, accuracy and neatness, and in such a manner that the treasurer can at any time render to the board of supervisors, or any other person, entitled thereto a clear balance sheet, showing the exact condition of each fund or tax, and the accounts between himself and the county, and thereby the financial condition of the county.

The necessary books of his office.—The necessary books of his office are as follows:

1. The tax books, or lists.
2. A warrant book, for the register of warrants paid.
3. A receipt book, containing printed blank receipts for taxes, with the proper stubs.
4. A book to register tax sales.
5. A cash book.
6. A ledger.

Although there are many other books usually found in use in the treasurer's office, it is believed that the above are all that are essential.

On the cash book could be made the daily entries of all cash received and paid out, or in case of the numerous receipts for taxes paid the treasurer, at the close of business each day, foot the amount of tax receipts for the different funds, and debit himself with the county, and credit the different funds with the amount received. The stubs of the printed tax receipts may contain a memorandum of the amounts received of the different taxes and funds, with which the treasurer should keep an account; and it would be an easy matter to take the necessary items from these stubs, for a proper entry on the cash book, and post them in proper places on the ledger.

The following forms for keeping the accounts and books have been prepared by an accountant, and are recommended to treasusers, as the most simple, and convenient method of keeping them:

1874.		CASH ACCOUNT.	DR.
Jan.	1	To received of L. S., ex-Treasurer, as follows, viz:	
		County Fund........................	$3,837 74
		Bridge Fund........................	4,555 50
		Anamosa Corporation................	54 73
		State Fund.........................	110 65
		Clay Township Road Fund............	15 81
		School District Township of Cass.......	117 21
		Permanent School Fund.............	889 28
		School Fund interest, account.........	1,196 75
			$10,777 67
Jan.	1	*To balance brought down*...............	$10,777 67
	3	To Permanent School Fund, received of O. T. Day....	300 00
	3	To Permanent School Fund, received of S. M. Graves.......................	120 00
	5	To Permanent School Fund, received of N. Potter..........................	380 00
	10	To County Fund, received of J. C. Deitz, clerk, sheriff's fees...............	100 00
	10	To County Fund, received of J. C. Deitz, clerk, costs, State *v.* Johnson......	100 00
	10	To County Fund, received of J. C. Deitz, clerk, jury fees	6 00
	20	To Permanent School Fund, received of G. Ellis............................	140 00
	20	To School Fund, interest on account, rec'd of E. Ackerman....	15 00
	20	To School District Township of Cass.....	285 90
			$12,224 57
Feb.	1	*To balance brought down*..............	$12,224 57
	10	To Permanent School Fund, received of J Bender..........................	350 00
	10	To School Fund, interest account, rec'd of J. Ellis.......................	14 00
	25	To Permanent School Fund, received of Wm. Paul.................	500 00
	25	To School District Township of Cass, rec'd per taxes collected in February ...	1,000 14
			$14,088 71

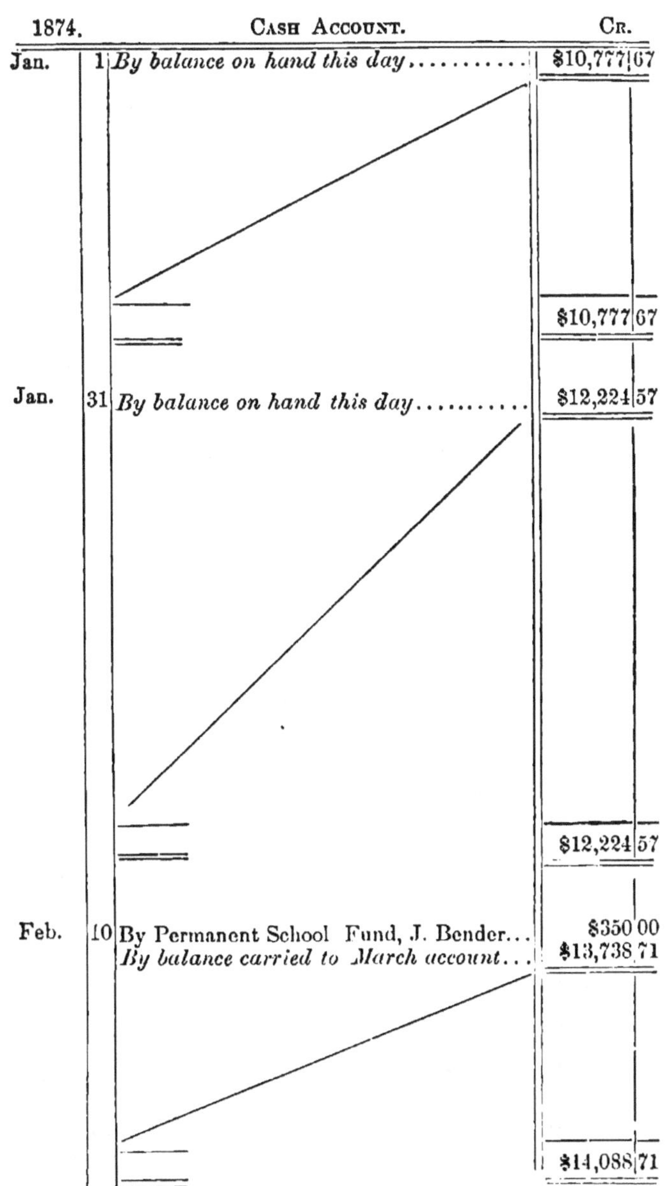

1874.		Cash Account.	Cr.
Jan.	1	*By balance on hand this day*	$10,777 67
			$10,777 67
Jan.	31	*By balance on hand this day*	$12,224 57
			$12,224 57
Feb.	10	By Permanent School Fund, J. Bender...	$350 00
		By balance carried to March account...	$13,738 71
			$14,088 71

1874.		CASH ACCOUNT.	DR.	
March	1	*To Bal. on hand this day*	$13,738	71
	5	To Sch. Fund Int. acc't A. Fulton.......	30	45
	20	To Permanent School Fund rec'd of J. Warren	700	00
	31	To School Dist. Tp. of Cass, rec'd Taxes collected March	613	95
			$15,083	11
April	1	*To Balance on hand this day*..........	$14,383	11
	10	To Permanent Sch. Fund rec'd of C. Hines	400	00
	15	To School Fund Int. acc't rec'd of W. Dunning..................	30	60
	30	To School District Tp. of Cass rec'd for taxes collected April.............	226	22
			$15,039	96
May	1	*To Balance on hand May* 1............	$14,739	93
	6	To Permanent School Fund rec'd of A. Mershon..................	500	00
	20	To Sch. Fund Int. acc't rec'd of R. Lewis.	105	50
	25	To Sch. Fund Int. acc't rec'd of J. Doe...	205	00
	31	To Sch. District Tp. of Cass, taxes collected May........................	73	71
			$15,624	14
June	1	*To Bal. on hand this day*	$15,374	14
	1	To County Fund Taxes collected to date .	20,380	36
	1	Bridge Fund Taxes collected to date	3,801	89
	1	To Anamosa Corporation Taxes collected to date	2,533	86
	1	To State Fund Taxes collected to date ..	14,000	00
	1	To Clay Tp. Road Fund Taxes collected to date..................	174	83
	1	To School District Tp. of Cass, Auditor's appr. Mar. 6, '74	314	00
	31	To Permanent Sch. Fund rec'd of R. Life	700	00
			$57,279	08
July	1	*To Balance on hand this day*	$23,012	83

1874.		Cash Account.	Cr.	
March	20	By Permanent School Fund of Wm. Hill .	$ 700	00
		By carried to April acc't	14,383	11
			$15,083	11
April	10	By Permanent School Fund, J. Jones	$ 300	00
		By Balance carried to May acc't	14,739	93
			$15,039	93
May	5	By Permanent School Fund, D. Fall.....	$ 250	00
		By Balance carried to June acc't.......	15,374	14
			$15,624	14
June	1	By County Fund p'id C'nty W'rr'nts to date	$11,998	11
		By Bridge Fund paid Bridge Warrants to date..............................	3,629	59
		By Anamosa Corporation paid W. S. Benton, Treasurer to date............	2,129	03
		By State Fund paid State Treasurer to date	12,194	08
		By Clay Tp. Road Fund paid Tp. Clerk ..	190	64
		By Sch. Dist. Tp. of Cass paid Treasurer .	1,990	00
		By Sch. Dist. Tp. of Cass paid Treasurer, (apportionment of Auditor)	314	00
	25	By Permanent School Fund, J. Ellis.	600	00
		By Sch. Fund Int. acc't paid Dist. Tp. Cass	314	00
		By Sch. Fund Int. acc't paid Dist. Tp. Fairview........	326	80
		By Sch. Fund Int. acc't paid Dist. Tp. Hale	220	00
		By Sch. Fund Int. acc't paid Dist Tp. Jackson........	140	00
		By Sch. Fund Int. acc't p'd Dist. Tp. Wayne	220	00
		By Balance carried down	23,012	83
			$57,279	08

1874.		County Fund.	Dr.
June	1	To C. B. 4	$11,998 11
July	1	*To Balance*	12,425 99
			$24,424 10

1874.		Bridge Fund.	Dr.
June	1	To C. B. 4	$3,629 59
July	1	*To Balance*	4,727 80
			$8,357 39

1874.		Anamosa Corporation.	Dr.
June	1	To C. B. 4	$2,129 03
July	1	*To Balance*	459 56
			$2,588 59

1874.		State Fund.	Dr.
June	1	To C. B. 4	$12,194 08
July	1	*To Balance*	1,916 57
			$14,110 65

1874.		Clay Township Road Fund.	Dr.
June	1	To C. B. 4	$190 64
			$190 64

1874.		COUNTY FUND.	CR.	
Jan.	1	By C. B. 1	$3,837	74
Jan.	10	By C. B. 1	206	00
June	1	By C. C. 3	20,380	36
			$24,424	10
July	1	*By Balance*	$12,425	99

1874.		BRIDGE FUND.	CR.	
Jan.	1	By C. B. 1	$4,555	50
June	1	By C. B. 3	3,801	89
			$8,357	39
July	1	*By Balance*	$4,727	80

1874.		ANAMOSA CORPORATION.	CR.	
Jan.	1	By C. B. 1	$54	73
June	1	By C. B. 3	2,533	86
			$2,588	69
July	1	*By Balance*	$459	56

1874.		STATE FUND.	CR.	
Jan.		By C. B. 1	$110	65
June		By C. B. 3	14,000	00
			$14,110	65
July	1	*By Balance*	$1,916	57

1874.		CLAY TOWNSHIP ROAD FUND.	CR.	
Jan.	1	By C. B. 1	$15	81
June	1	By C. B. 3	174	83
			$190	64

1874.		SCH. DISTRICT TOWNSHIP OF CASS.	DR.
June	1	To C. B. 4	$1,990 00
June	25	To C. B. 4	314 00
		To Balance	327 13
			$2,631 13

1844.		PERMANENT SCHOOL FUND.	DR.
Feb.	10	To C. B. 1	$350 00
March	20	To C. B. 4	700 00
April	10	To C. B 4	300 00
May	5	To C. B. 4	250 00
June	25	To C. B. 4	600 00
		To Balance	2,779 28
			$4,979 28

1874.		Sch. District Township of Cass.	Cr.	
Jan.	1	By C. B. 1	$117	21
Jan.	20	By C. B. 1	285	90
Feb.	25	By C. B. 1	1,000	14
March	31	By C. B. 3	613	95
April	30	By C. B. 3	226	22
May	30	By C. B. 3	73	71
June	1	By C. B. 3	314	00
			$2,631	13
July	1	*By Balance*	$327	13

1874.		Permanent School Fund.	Cr.	
Jan.	1	By C. B. 1	$889	28
Jan.	3	By C. B. 1	300	00
Jan.	3	By C. B 1	120	00
Jan.	5	By C. B. 1	380	00
Jan.	20	By C. B. 1	140	00
Feb.	10	By C. B. 1	350	00
Feb.	25	By C. B. 1	500	00
March	20	By C. B. 1	700	00
April	10	By C. B. 1	400	00
May	6	By C. B. 1	500	00
June	30	By C. B. 1	700	00
			$4,979	28
July	1	*By Balance*	$2,779	28

1874.		School Fund Interest Account.	Dr.	
June	25	To C. B. 4	$860	80
June	25	To C. B. 4	360	00
		To Balance	376	50
			$1597	30

1874.		Cash Account.	Dr.	
Jan.	1	To C. B. 1	$10,777	67
		To Balance	10,777	67
Jan.	20	To C. B. 1	1,446	90
			$12,224	57
Feb.	1	*To Balance*	$12,224	57
Feb.	25	To C. B. 1	1,864	14
			$14,088	71
March	1	*To Balance*	$13,738	71
March	31	To C. B. 3	1,344	40
			$15,083	11
April	1	*To Balance*	$14,383	11
April	30	To C. B. 3	656	82
			$15,039	93
May	1	*To Balance*	$14,739	93
May	31	To C. B. 3	884	21
			$15,624	14

1874.		School Fund Interest Account.	Cr.
Jan.	1	By C. B. 1....	$1,196 75
Jan.	20	By C. B. 1............................	15 00
Feb.	10	By C. B. 1............................	14 00
March	5	By C. B. 3........	30 45
April	15	By C. B. 3..	30 60
May	20	By C. B. 3....	105 50
May	25	By C. B. 3............................	205 00
			$1,597 30
July	1	*By Balance*.........................	$376 50

1874.		Cash Account.	Cr.
Jan.	1	*By Balance*.........................	$10,777 67
Jan.	31	*By Balance*.........................	$12,224 57
			$12,224 57
Feb.	10	By C. B. 2............................	$350 00
March	1	*By Balance*.........................	13,738 71
			$14,088 71
March	31	By C. B. 4............................	$700 00
March	31	*By Balance*.........................	14,383 11
			$15,083 11
April	30	By C. B. 4............................	$300 00
April	30	*By Balance*.........................	14,739 93
			$15,039 93
May	5	By C. B. 4........................	$250 00
May	31	*By Balance*............	15,374 14
			$15,624 14

1874.		Cash Account.	Dr.	
June	1	To Balance........	$ 15,374	14
	30	To C. B. 4....	41,904	94
			$ 57,279	08
July		*To Balance*.......	$ 23,012.83	

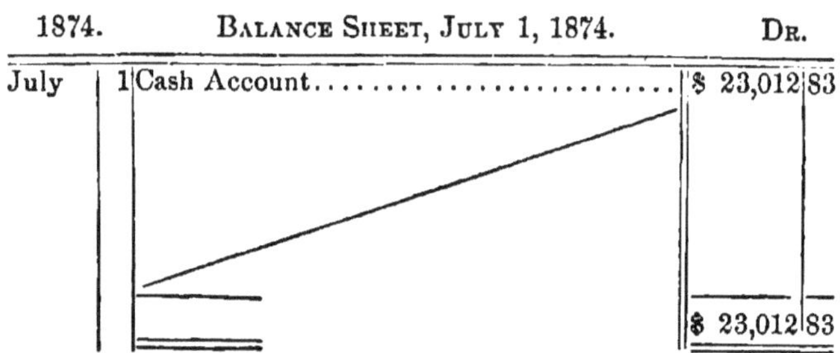

1874.		Balance Sheet, July 1, 1874.	Dr.	
July	1	Cash Account.......	$ 23,012	83
			$ 23,012	83

1874.		Cash Account.	Cr.	
June	30	By C. B. 4..................................	$ 34,266	25
	31	*By Balance*....	23,012	83
			$ 57,279	08

1874.		Balance Sheet, July 1, 1874.	Cr.	
July	1	County Fund..........................	$ 12,425	99
		Bridge Fund	4,727	80
		Anamosa Corporation.	459	56
		State Fund....	1,916	57
		School District Township Cass..........	327	13
		Permanent School Fund................	2,779	28
		School Fund Interest Account	376	50
			$ 23,012	83

IX. DECISIONS ILLUSTRATING HIS DUTIES AND LIABILITIES.

His liability fixed by his official bond.—The duties and responsibilities of the county treasurer are fixed by his official bond, and from it the measure of liability incurred by him in the preservation and disposal of the money received by him, as treasurer, is to be ascertained and determined.

He is only required to exercise reasonable diligence, and care, in the preservation and disposal of the public money, and if money is stolen from the treasury of the county, without any want of reasonable care, and diligence on the part of the treasurer, in the care and preservation of said money, he is not liable therefor. 5 Iowa, 149.

The tax list and warrant, his justification.—The tax list and warrant for its collection are sufficient authority and justification to the treasurer for the collection of the taxes in the mode prescribed by law, and he cannot be made liable as a wrong-doer, in consequence of any illegality in the proceedings prior to his receiving the tax list, even when the list in question is not for the collection of the ordinary State and county revenue, but for a tax levied for a special purpose and in a particular manner, as to pay the subscription of the county to the stock of a railroad company. 8 Iowa, 193.

Illegality of the tax, no defense for not accounting.—In an action against the treasurer and his sureties upon his official bond, the defendants cannot set up the illegality of the assessment as an excuse for not accounting for and paying over the taxes which have been paid without objection by the tax payers, and received by the treasurer by virtue of his office; and where the bond is for the faithful discharge of all duties "now or hereafter required of his office by law," it constitutes no defense to an action upon it, that a part of the money sued for came into his hands under a law prepared subsequently to the execution of the bond. 14 Iowa, 170.

Statute of limitation: when it applies.—The failure of the treasurer to pay over and account to the county or State for the revenue in his hands is the omission of an official duty within the meaning of the statute, and an action for such failure must be commenced within three years, or it will be barred by the statute of limitation. 17 Iowa, 223.

County not liable for wrongful acts of officers.—The general principle rendering a master liable for the tortious acts of his servant committed in his service, does not apply to the wrongful acts of the officers of a municipal corporation who are elected for a definite term, during which they are restrained and governed only by the statutes which prescribe their duties, which statutes, by presumption of law, are known to, and which by the exercise of a reasonable diligence may be practically understood by, every one who may have business with them; and a county is not liable to a tax payer for moneys fraudulently collected by the treasurer, as taxes, and appropriated to his own use. 18 Iowa, 199.

Sureties on a substituted bond: when not liable.—The sureties upon a substituted official bond, are not liable for moneys which came into the hands of the principal prior to the execution of the bond, and during the existence of a prior bond for which the substituted bond was given. 22 Iowa, 360.

Treasurer liable for partial taxes received.—The treasurer is liable on his bond, for moneys received by him in partial payment of taxes. 21 Iowa, 84.

Treasurer not responsible for acts of a book-keeper: when.—The treasurer is not liable for the acts or defalcations of a book-keeper, or assistant in his office, employed by, and acting under, the direction of the board of supervisors of his county. 34 Iowa, 317; 16 Illinois, 81.

Term of office limited to two years: consequences of holding over.—The term of office of a county treasurer is for two years and until his successor is elected and qualified, but a failure to qualify, creates a vacancy in the office, which should be filled by appointment. And where a treasurer was re-elected and continued in office during a second term, without being re-qualified, it was held

1. That after the time fixed for qualification he did not legally hold over, but remained treasurer *de facto* only.

2. That the sureties on the bond executed by him when qualified for his first term, were not liable for his mis-feasance or nonfeasance in office after the expiration of that term. 10 Iowa, 39.

Sureties only liable for acts during term.—Sureties on official bonds are liable only for acts done during the term for which the bond was given, even when the principal holds over after the expiration of that term. 10 Iowa, 39.

X. FEES AND COMPENSATION.

What the Code provides in reference thereto.—SECTION 3793. Each county treasurer shall receive for his services the following compensation:

1. Two per cent of all money collected by him as taxes due any incorporated city or town, to be paid out of the same;

2. Three per cent of all taxes collected by him for all other tax funds, to be paid out of the county treasury;

3. All fees now allowed him, exclusive of his annual salary;

4. For each certificate of purchase issued for land sold for non-payment of taxes, thirty-five cents;

5. For mileage by the nearest traveled route when paying money into the State treasury or national bank, when required by law, ten cents for each mile, counting one way;

6. Such additional compensation as the board of supervisors may deem proper. When the aggregate amount of the compensation authorized by this section, exceeds fifteen hundred dollars, exclusive of what is received under the following section and the fourth sub-division hereof, the excess shall be paid into the county treasury for the use of the county, except that in counties having two county-seats, such aggregate compensation shall not exceed two thousand dollars. But the compensation for clerks necessary for the proper transaction of the business shall be paid by the county.

Give information relative to taxes, when.—SEC. 3794. The county treasurer shall, if applied to by letter, enclosing thirty cents value in postage stamps, asking for information of the amount of taxes upon any specified parcel or parcels of land in his county, answer the same correctly by mail, giving direct answers to all inquiries in such letter respecting the amount and interest of the unpaid taxes, as the same appears from the tax-books in his office.

If the total of such land specified in any one letter exceeds three hundred and twenty acres, then such treasurer is not bound to answer such letter unless it contains, besides the thirty cents above provided, ten cents in addition for every one hundred and sixty acres, when the total acres specified in such letter exceed the said three hundred and twenty acres; but the aggregate fees thus charged shall in no case exceed the sum of fifty cents: and upon the return to the treasurer of the letter or a copy thereof so sent by him, with the amount due as shown by such letter, such treasurer shall pay such taxes and return a receipt therefor by mail.

Penalty for failure.—SEC. 3795. Any treasurer who shall neglect for twenty days after the receipt of any such letter with money enclosed as aforesaid, to answer the same fully as required in the preceding section, or who shall directly or indirectly receive or be concerned in receiving any greater compensation for the serv-

mentioned in the preceding section than is therein provided, shall forfeit to the person aggrieved, for each offense the sum of fifty dollars, which may be recovered in a civil action in any court having jurisdiction.

Render account of money received as compensation to supervisors.—SEC. 3796. The county treasurer shall enter in a book kept for that purpose, all moneys received by him for services rendered, designating for what the same was received, and shall render an account verified by affidavit to the board of supervisors at each session thereof, stating fully all money so received and from what source derived and any excess to which he would be entitled under the preceding section over and above the sum therein limited, shall be paid into the county treasury.

CHAPTER XXXIV.

THE RECORDER.

I. HIS ELECTION, DEPUTIES, ETC.

Provisions of the statute relating to his election, etc. —It will be observed by reference to the provisions of the Code, contained in the first chapter of this treatise, that the recorder is elected in each even-numbered year; that he should give an official bond and qualify like the clerk at the same time; that he may appoint a deputy, from whom he is required to take a bond, and for whose acts he is responsible; and that the general provisions of the statute in reference to removal, vacancies and misdemeanors in office, apply to him, as well as to the other county officers.

The forms relating to these matters may be found in this treatise, relating to the clerk.

II. HIS DUTIES.

General provisions.—The Code provides in relation thereto as follows:

Duties of.—SECTION 335. The recorder shall keep his office at the county seat, and he shall record at length, and as speedily as possible, all instruments in writing which may be delivered to him for record in the manner directed by law.

Treasurer eligible.—SEC. 336. The same person may be eligible to, and hold the office of county recorder and county treasurer; *provided*, the number of inhabitants in such county does not exceed ten thousand.

On the vacation of a town or city plat.—On the vacation of a town or city plat, or any addition thereto, as provided by Chap. 12 of the Code, he is required to write in plain letters, across the plat so vacated, the word "vacated," and also to make a reference on the same, to the volume and page in which the instrument of vacation is recorded.

Other records and books required.—Beside the records and necessary books required by the foregoing provisions of the statute, the Code further provides as follows:

Conditional sales: when invalid.—SECTION 1922. No sale, contract, or lease, wherein the transfer of title or ownership of personal property is made to depend upon any condition, shall be valid against any creditor or purchaser of the vendee, or lessee in actual possession obtained in pursuance thereof, without notice, unless the same be in writing, executed by the vendor or lessor, acknowledged and recorded the same as chattel mortgages.

Mortgages must be recorded.—SEC. 1923. No sale or mortgage of personal property, where the vendor or mortgagor retains actual possession thereof, is valid against existing creditors or subsequent purchasers, without notice, unless a written instrument conveying the same is executed, acknowledged like conveyances of real estate, and filed for record with the recorder of the county where the holder of the property resides.

Recorder to keep entry book or index.—SEC. 1924. The recorder must keep an entry book or index for instruments of the above description, having the pages thereof ruled, so as to show in parallel columns, in the manner hereinafter provided in case of deeds for real property:

1. The mortgagors or vendors;
2. The mortgagees or vendees;
3. The date of the filing of the instrument;
4. The date of the instrument itself;
5. Its nature;
6. The page and book where the record is to be found.

To make note of day and hour of filing, etc.—SEC. 1925. Whenever any written instrument of the character above contemplated is filed for record as aforesaid, the recorder shall note thereon the day and hour of filing the same, and forthwith enter in his entry book all the particulars required in the preceding section, except the sixth; and from the time of said entry, the sale or mortgage shall be deemed complete as to third persons, and have the same effect as though it had been accompanied by the actual delivery of the property sold or mortgaged.

Must record.—SEC. 1926. The recorder shall, as soon as practicable, record such instrument, and enter in his entry book in its proper place, the page and book where the record may be found.

Beside the foregoing provisions, the Code further provides for the indexing and recording of instruments relating to real property, as follows:

Instrument affecting recorded.—SECTION 1941. No instrument affecting real estate, is of any validity against subsequent purchasers for a valuable consideration, without notice, unless recorded in the office of the recorder of the county in which the land lies as hereinafter provided.

SEC. 1942. It shall not be deemed lawfully recorded, unless it has been previously acknowledged or proved in the manner herein prescribed.

Recorder to keep index of records.—SEC. 1943. The recorder must keep an entry book or index, the pages of which are so divided as to show in parallel columns:

1. The grantors;
2. The grantees;
3. The time when the instrument was filed;
4. The date of the instrument;
5. The nature of the instrument;
6. The book and page where the record thereof may be found;
7. The description of the land conveyed.

To make entries on instrument and in index.—SEC. 1944. The recorder must indorse upon every instrument properly filed in the office for record, the time when it was so filed, and shall forthwith make the entries provided for in the preceding section, except that of the book and page where the record of the instrument may be found, and, from that time, such entries shall furnish constructive notice to all persons of the rights of the grantee conferred by such instrument.

Arranged alphabetically.—SEC. 1945. The entries in such entry book, shall show the names of the respective grantors and grantees arranged in alphabetical order.

Must be recorded.—SEC. 1946. Every such instrument shall be recorded, as soon as practicable, in a suitable book to be kept by the recorder for that purpose; after which he shall complete the entries aforesaid, so as to show the book and page where the record is to be found.

Deeds of town lots recorded in separate books.—SEC. 1947. The recorder shall record all deeds, mortgages, and other instruments affecting town lots in cities or villages, the plats whereof are recorded in separate books from those in which other conveyances of real estate are recorded.

Cannot file until indorsed.—SEC. 1953. The recorder shall not file for record any deed of real property, until the proper entries have been made upon the transfer books in the auditor's office and indorsed upon the deed.

III. DECISIONS RELATING TO RECORDER.

Directions of the statutes to be strictly observed.—Although matters relating to the effect of instruments thus recorded, or to the neglect, or mistake in properly indexing and recording, so far as third parties are concerned, do not properly come within the proper scope of this treatise, yet, it may be proper to observe that the directions of the statute in reference thereto, should be strictly observed by the recorder.

The property should be correctly referred to in the index.—It has been repeatedly held that the property described, or referred to in the index, is the extent of the notice imparted by the record. 11 Iowa, 261; 13 Iowa, 570; 14 Iowa, 269.

An acknowledgment by an interested party.—An acknowledgment of a conveyance, taken and certified by a person interested as grantee, should not be recorded; a record thereof is not constructive notice to a subsequent purchaser. 20 Iowa, 231.

His liability for omission of duty.—The importance of a faithful discharge of the duty of recorder, in respect to proper entries on the index book, will be apparent, when it is understood that he is liable to any party that may be injured by the omission of this duty; and it is evident from the decisions above referred to, and the general principles of the law, that he with his sureties, would be liable on his official bond, for all such neglect of duty, whereby any damage should result to any person.

IV. BOOK ENTITLED "COPIES OF ORIGINAL ENTRIES."

The Code provides in reference thereto as follows:

Books of original entries.—SECTION 3703. The recorder in each of the several counties in this state, shall cause to be procured a book, entitled "copies of original entries" to be kept as a record in his office, in which shall be copied a list of the original entries of land within his county, with name of the person or persons entering the same and the date of such entry, for which he shall receive a reasonable compensation, to be audited and allowed by the board of supervisors of his county.

Copies of.—SEC. 3704. Said book, containing a copy of such entries, when compared with the originals, and certified to as true copies by the register of the land office at which such original entries were made, shall be deemed a matter of record, and certified copies thereof under the hand of said recorder may be received and read in evidence in all the courts in this state, with like effect as other certified copies of orignal papers recorded in his office.

V. EVIDENCE.

Certified copy of his records as evidence.—It will be observed by reference to a general provision of the Code, Section 3702, contained in Chapter One, that certified copies of any records in his office, are evidence of equal credibility with the original record.

RECORDER'S CERTIFICATE.

No. 118.

STATE OF IOWA, }
.... County. } ss.

I, R D, recorder of said county, hereby certify that the

foregoing writing is a copy from the original record in my office, and of the whole thereof.

Dated this .... day of ...., 18..

R.... D...., *Recorder.*

Abstracts.—By reason of the familiarity of the recorder with the records of his office, as well as his usual competency and skill, he is frequently called upon to furnish abstracts of the title to land in his county.

Abstracts not an official act.—His acts in this respect are usually not official, and his certificates of the correctness thereof, would be of no value as evidence. Nor would his sureties on his official bond, be liable for any damages arising from any error or mistake in such abstract.

Abstract.—The value of such an abstract and certificate, would depend upon the skill and integrity of the party making the same, whether prepared by the recorder, or any other person.

No. 119.

ABSTRACT.

S. W. qr. S. W. qr. Sec. 10, *Tp.* 84, *N. R.* 3, *W. of 5th P. M.*

Grantors.	Grantees,	Date of instrument.	Date of filing.	Character of instrument.	Book.	Page.	Remarks.
United States	John Doe .	Mar. 10, '50.	. . . . . .	Patent . .	.	.	. . . . .
John Doe .	Richard Roe	April 5, '54	April 10, '54.	W'rr'ty d'd	5	140	. . . . .
Richard Roe	John Dunn .	May 7, '60.	May 8, '60.	"	10	420	. . . . .
J. Dunn, *et ux*	Enoch Grubb	June 1, '74.	June 1, '74.	"	20	502	. . . . .
John Doe ·	James Mann	April 20, 50.	April 20, '50.	Mortgage .	5	210	Satisfied in full, J'ly 1, 51,
J. Dunn, *et ux*	Richard Roe	May 7, '60.	May 8, '60.	"	12	25	Satisfied in full, M'y 8, '62

VI. FEES AND COMPENSATION OF THE RECORDER.

In addition to office, stationery and books to be furnished by the county, the recorder is entitled to the following fees, as provided by the Code:

Fees.—SECTION 3792. The recorder shall be entitled to charge and receive the following fees:

For recording each instrument containing four hundred words, fifty cents;

For every additional hundred words, or fraction thereof, ten cents.

In addition to which he is entitled to ten cents for every one hundred words for making a copy of the records of his office, and certifying the same. Code, Sec. 3819.

VII. ADDITIONAL DUTIES.

The Session Laws of 1874 provide further in relation to the Recorder:

Not to admit plats of city or town unless free from incumbrance.—Whenever any person or corporation shall lay out any parcel of land into town or city lots, such proprietor shall procure a certified statement from the recorder of deeds, that the title in fee to said land is in such proprietor, and that the same is free from every incumbrance, which shall be filed with the recorder of deeds before the plat of the said town or city lots shall be admitted to record or of any validity. Session Laws 1874, Chap. 25.

In counties having two county seats: to attend tax sales.—Where there are two county seats, the recorder or his deputy must attend the sale of lands for delinquent taxes. Sess. Laws 1874, Chap. 46.

Duties relating to savings banks.—These are fully set forth in Chap. 60, Session Laws of 1874.

CHAPTER XXXV.

THE SURVEYOR.

I. ELECTION—QUALIFICATION, ETC.

It will be seen by reference to the general provisions of the Code, in the first chapter of this treatise, that the surveyor is elected at the general election in each odd-numbered year, and of course holds his office for the term of two years, unless there should be a vacancy for some of the causes provided by the statute.

Qualification: deputy, etc.—Those statutes also provide for the qualification, appointment of deputy, etc. For the requisite forms, and directions in such cases, reference may be had to these subjects set forth in treating of the office of the clerk.

Increasing importance of the office.—The office of county surveyor is growing in importance and responsibility, and is likely to advance in these respects, with the improvement and increase in value of our real estate.

Important private interests frequently depend on the skill and integrity of the surveyor; and in view of this, it becomes his duty to acquire a practical and scientific knowledge of the profession, and an acquaintance with the rules and instructions furnished to surveyors of our public lands, at the time of the original survey thereof.

II. HIS DUTIES GENERALLY.

Provisions of the Code.—The Code provides in reference to the duties of the surveyor as follows:

Duties.—SECTION 369. The county surveyor shall make all surveys of land within his county which he may be called upon to make, and his surveys shall be held as presumptively correct.

SEC. 370. The field-notes and plats made by the county surveyor shall be transcribed into a well bound book under the supervision of the surveyor, when desired by a person interested and at his expense.

Field-notes.—SEC. 371. Previous to making any survey, he shall furnish himself with a copy of the field-notes of the original survey of the same land, if there be any in the office of the county auditor, and his survey shall be made in accordance therewith.

Corners.—SEC. 372. He is required to establish the corners by taking bearing trees and noting particularly their course and distance, but if there be no trees within reasonable distance, the corners are to be marked by stones firmly placed in the earth, or by mounds.

Rules.—SEC. 373. In the re-survey and sub-divisions of lands by county surveyors, their deputies, or other persons, the rules prescribed by acts of congress and the instructions of the secretary of the interior, shall be in all respects followed.

Plat and copy evidence.—SEC. 374. The county surveyor shall, when requested, furnish the person for whom the survey is made with a copy of the field-notes and plat of the survey, and such copy certified by him, and also a copy from the record, certified by the county auditor, with the seal, shall be presumptive evidence of the survey, and of the facts herein required to be set forth, and which are stated accordingly, between those persons who join in requesting it, and any other person then concerned, who has reasonable notice that such a survey is to be made and the time thereof.

Book furnished.—SEC. 375. The board of supervisors is required to furnish a substantial, well bound book, in which the field-notes and plats made by the county surveyor may be recorded.

Plat: what to show.—SEC. 376. The plat and record shall show distinctly of what piece of land it is a survey; at whose personal request it was made, the names of the chainmen, and that they were approved and sworn by the surveyor, and the date of the survey; and the courses shall be taken according to the true meridian, and the variation of the magnetic needle from the true meridian stated.

Chainmen.—SEC. 377. The necessary chainmen and other persons must be employed by the person requiring the survey done, unless otherwise agreed; but the chainmen must be disinterested persons and approved of by the surveyor, and sworn by him to measure justly and impartially to the best of their knowledge and ability.

Administer oaths.—SEC. 378. County surveyors, when establishing defaced or lost land corners or lines, may issue subpœnas for witnesses and administer oaths to them, and all fees for service of officers and attendance of witnesses shall be the same as in proceedings before justices of the peace.

OATH TO CHAINMEN.

No. 120.

You, and each of you, do solemnly swear that you will, as chainmen, measure justly and impartially, the land now about to be surveyed, to the best of your knowledge and ability. So help you God.

Subpœnas for witnesses.—When it becomes necessary to issue subpœnas for witnesses, to establish defaced or lost corners, or lines, the usual form of subpœnas from Justices' Courts may be used, signed by the surveyor, and served in the same manner as subpœnas from said courts.

No. 121. OATH TO WITNESS TO ESTABLISH CORNER.

You, and each of you, do solemnly swear (or affirm,) that you will true answers make to such questions as may be put to you, touching the lost corner at the .... corner of the .... quarter of section .., township .., north (or south,) range .., west of the 5th principal meridian. So help you God.

Fees of officers and witnesses.—The fees of officers and witnesses on such investigations, are the same as in proceedings before justices of the peace; which would be fifty cents a day for the witnesses, and for travel each way five cents a mile; and for the constable, in serving the subpœnas, fifteen cents for each person served, beside mileage going and returning, five cents, a mile. These fees should be paid by the party requesting the survey.

III. EVIDENCE.

Certificate of the surveyor.—The certificate of the surveyor to the plat and field-notes, may be in the following form:

No. 122. SURVEYOR'S CERTIFICATE.

STATE OF IOWA, }
.... County. } ss.

I, A B, surveyor of said county, hereby certify that the foregoing is a copy of the plat and field-notes of land surveyed by me, for C D and E F, who joined in requesting it. Said survey was made on the .... day of ...., 18..

Dated this .... day of ...., 18..

A.... B...., *Surveyor.*

Copy of the field-notes and plat as evidence.—The Code provides in reference to a certified copy of the plat and field-notes as follows:

Field-notes and plats.—SECTION 3701. A copy of the field-notes of any surveyor, or a plat made by him and certified under oath as correct, may be received as evidence to show the shape or dimensions of a tract of land, or any other fact whose ascertainment requires only the exercise of scientific skill or calculation.

IV. RULES AND INSTRUCTIONS.

Rules to be observed by surveyors.—It will be observed that by the provisions of Section 373 of the Code, the surveyor in the re-survey and sub-divisions of lands, the rules prescribed by acts of congress, and the instructions of the Secretary of the Interior, shall in all respects be followed. It is, therefore, important for surveyors to know what these acts and instructions are. No surveyor can properly discharge his duty, without a knowledge of the original method of surveying our public lands.

Instructions of the Secretary of the Interior.—The following are the more important instructions of the Secretary of the Interior, relating to the original survey of the public lands, adopted February 12, 1855, and Approved by act of Congress, May 30th, 1862.

These instructions were a revision of earlier surveying instructions of the Department; and the original surveys of Iowa, and other Western States, were made in accordance with them.

System of Rectangular Surveying.—1. The public lands of the United States are ordinarily surveyed into rectangular tracts, bounded by lines conforming to the cardinal points.

2. The public lands are laid off, in the first place, into bodies of land of six miles square, called *townships*, containing as near as may be, 23,040 acres. The townships are sub-divided into thirty-six tracts, called sections, of a mile square, each containing, as near as may be, 640 acres. Any number or series of contiguous townships, situate north or south of each other, constitute a range.

The law requires that the lines of the public surveys shall be governed by the true meridian, and that the townships shall be *six miles square*—two things involving in connection a mathematical impossibility—for, strictly to conform to the meridian necessarily throws the township out of square, by reason of the convergency of meridians, and hence, by adhering to the true meridian, results the necessity of departing from the strict requirements of law, as respects the precise area of townships, and the sub-divisional parts thereof, the townships assuming something of a trapezodial form, which inequality develops itself more and more as such, the higher the latitude of the surveys. It is, doubtless, in view of these circumstances, that the law provides (see section 2, of the act of May 18, 1796,) that the sections of a mile square shall contain the quantity of six hundred and forty acres, *as nearly as may be*; and, moreover, provides, (see section 3, of the act of 10th of May, 1800,) in the following words: "And in all cases where the exterior lines of the townships thus to be sub-divided into sections or half-sections, shall exceed, or shall not extend six miles, the excess or deficiency shall be specially noted, and added to or deducted from the western or northern ranges of sections or half-sections in such township, according as the error may be in running the lines from east to west, or from south to north; the sections and half-sections bounded on the northern and western lines of such townships, shall be sold as containing only the quantity expressed in the returns and plats, respectively, and all others as containing the complete legal quantity."

The accompanying diagram, marked "A," will serve to illustrate the method of running out the exterior lines of townships, as well on the *north* as on the *south* side of the base line; and the order and mode of sub-dividing townships will be found illustrated in the accompanying specimen field-notes, conforming with the township diagram "B." The method here presented is designed to insure a full compliance with all the requirements, meaning, and intent of the surveying laws as, it is believed, is practicable.

The section lines are surveyed from *south* to north on true meridans, and from *east* to west in order to throw the excesses or deficiencies in measurement on the north and west sides of the township, as required by law.

3. The townships are to bear numbers in respect to the base line either north or south of it; and the tiers of townships, called "ranges," will bear numbers in respect to the meridian line, according to their relative position to it, either on the east or west.

4. The thirty-six sections into which a township is sub-divided are numbered, commencing with number *one* at the *northeast* angle of the township, and proceeding west to number six, and thence proceeding east to number twelve, and so on, alternately, until the number thirty-six, in the southeast angle.

5. Standard Parallels, (usually called correction lines,) are established at stated intervals, to provide for or counteract the error that otherwise would result from the convergency of meridians, and also to arrest error arising from inaccuracies in measurements on meridian lines, which, however, must ever be studiously avoided. On the *north* of the principal base line, it is proposed to have these standards run at distances of every *four* townships, or twenty-four miles, and on the *south* of the principal base, at distances of every *five* townships, or thirty miles.

Of measurements, chaining and marking.—1. Where uniformity in the variation of the needle is not found, the public surveys must be made with an instrument operating independently of the magnetic needle. Burts' Improved Solar Compass, or other instrument of equal utility, must be used of necessity in such cases; and it is deemed best that such instrument should be used under all circumstances.

Where the needle can be relied on, however, the ordinary compass may be used in sub-dividing and meandering.

2. The township lines, and the sub-division lines, will usually be measured by a two-pole chain of thirty-three feet in length, consisting of fifty links, and each link being seven inches and ninety-two hundredths of an inch long. On uniform and level ground, however, the four-pole chain may be used. Your measurements will, however, always be represented according to the four-pole chain of one hundred links. The deputy surveyor must also have with him a measure of the standard chain, wherewith to compare and adjust the chain in use, from day to day, with punctuality and carefulness; and must return such chain to the Surveyor-General's office for examination when his work is completed.

Of tally pins.—3. You will use eleven tally pins made of steel, not exceeding fourteen inches in length, weighty enough towards the point to make them drop perpendicularly, and having a ring at the top, in which is to be fixed a piece of red cloth, or something else of conspicuous color, to make them readily seen when stuck in the ground.

Process of chaining.—4. In measuring lines with a two-pole chain, every five chains are called "a tally," because at that distance the last of the ten tally pins with which the forward chainman set out will have been stuck. He then cries "tally;" which cry is repeated by the other chainman, and each registers the distance by slipping a thimble, button, or ring of leather, or something of the kind, on a belt worn for that purpose, or by some other convenient method. The hind chainman then comes up, and having counted in the presence of his fellow the tally pins which he has taken up, so that both may be assured that none of the pins have been lost, he then takes the forward end of the chain, and proceeds to set the pins. Thus the chainmen alternately change places, each setting the pins that he has taken up, so that one is forward in all the odd, and the other in all the even tallies. Such procedure, it is believed, tends to insure accuracy in measurement, facilitates the recollection of the distances to objects on the line, and renders a miss-tally almost impossible.

Leveling the chain and plumbing the pins.—5. The length of every line you run is to be ascertained by precise horizontal measurement, as nearly approximating to an air line as is possible in practice upon the earth's surface. This all important object can only be attained by a rigid adherence to the three following observances:

(1.) Ever keeping the chain *stretched* to its utmost degree of tension on even ground.

(2.) On uneven ground, keeping the chain not only stretched as aforesaid, but horizontally *leveled*. And when ascending and descending steep ground, hills, or mountains, the chain will have to be *shortened* to one-half its length, (and sometimes more,) in order accurately to obtain the true horizontal measure.

(3.) The careful plumbing of the tally pins, so as to attain precisely the *spot* where they should be stuck. The more uneven the surface, the greater the caution needed to set the pins.

Marking lines.—6. All lines on which are to be established the legal corner boundaries are to be marked after this method, viz: Those trees which may intercept your line must have two chops or notches cut on each side of them, without any other marks whatever. These are called "*sight trees*," "*line trees*," or "*station trees*."

A sufficient number of other trees standing nearest to your line, on either side of it, are to be blazed on two sides diagonally, or quartering towards the line, in order to render the line conspicuous, and readily to be traced, the blazes to be opposite each other, coinciding in direction with the line where the trees stand very near it, and to approach nearer each other the further the line passes from the blazed trees. Due care must ever be taken to have the lines so well marked as to be readily followed.

On trial or random lines.—The trees are not to be blazed, unless occasionally from indispensable necessity, and then it must be done so guardedly as to prevent the possibility of confounding the marks of the trial line with the *true*. But bushes and limbs of trees may be lopped, and *stakes* set on the trial or random line at every *ten* chains to enable the surveyor on his return to follow and correct the trial line, and establish therefrom the *true line*. To prevent confusion, the temporary stakes set on the trial or random lines must be *pulled up* when the surveyor returns to establish the true line.

Insuperable objects on line: witness points.—7. Under circumstances where your course is obstructed by impassable obstacles, such as ponds, swamps, marshes, lakes, rivers, creeks, etc., you will prolong the line across such obstacles by taking the necessary right-angle off-sets; or, if such be inconvenient, by a traverse or trigonometrical operation, until you regain the line on the opposite side. And in case a north and south, or a true east and west line is regained in advance of any such obstacle you will prolong and mark the line back to the obstacle so passed, and state all the particulars in relation thereto in your field-book. And at the intersection of lines with both margins of impassable obstacles you will establish a *witness point*, (for the purpose of perpetuating the intersections therewith,) by setting a post, and giving in your field-book the course and distance therefrom to two trees on opposite sides of the line, each of which trees you will mark with a blaze and notch facing the post; but on the margins of navigable water-courses, or navigable lakes, you will mark the trees with the proper number of the fractional section, township, and range.

The best marking tools adapted to the purpose must be provided for marking neatly and *distinctly* all the letters and figures required to be made at corners; and, the deputy is to have always at hand the necessary implements for keeping his marking irons in order; for which purpose a rat-tail file and a small whetstone will be found indispensable.

Establishing corner boundaries. – To procure the faithful execution of this portion of a surveyor's duty is a matter of the utmost importance. After a true coursing, and most exact measurements, the corner boundary is the consummation of the work, for which all the previous pains and expenditures have been incurred. If, therefore, the corner boundary be not perpetuated in a permanent and workman-like manner, the *great aim* of the surveying service will not have been attained. A boundary corner, in a timbered country, is to be a *tree*, if one be found at the precise spot; and if not, a *post* is to be planted thereat; and the position of the corner post is to be indicated by trees adjacent, the angular bearings and distances of which from the corner are facts to be ascertained and registered in your field book. (See article, "Bearing Trees.")

In a region where stone abounds, the corner boundary will be a small *monument of stones* alongside of a single marked stone for a township corner, and a single stone for all other corners.

In a region where timber is not near, and stone not found, the corner will be a *mound of earth*, of prescribed size, varying to suit the case.

The following are the different points for perpetuating corners, viz:

1. For township boundaries, at intervals of every six miles.
2. For section boundaries, at intervals of every mile, or 80 chains.
3. For quarter-section boundaries, at intervals of every half mile, or 40 chains.

Exceptions, however, occur on east and west lines, as explained hereafter.

[The half quarter-section boundary is not marked in the field, but is regarded by the law as a point intermediate between the half-mile or quarter-section corners. See act of 24th of April, 1820, entitled "an act making further provision for the sale of the public lands," which act refers to the act of Congress passed on the 11th of February, 1805, entitled "an act concerning the mode of surveying the public lands of the United States," for the manner of ascertaining the corners and contents of half quarter-sections. The sub-division of the half quarter-section into quarter quarter-sections is authorized by "an act supplementary to the several laws for the sale of the public lands." Approved, April 5, 1832.]

4. *Meander Corner Posts* are planted at all those points where the township or section lines intersect the banks of such rivers, bayous, lakes, or islands, as are by law directed to be meandered.

The courses and distances on meandered navigable streams govern the calculations wherefrom are ascertained the true areas of the tracts of land (sections, quarter-sections, etc.,) known to the law as *fractional*, and binding on such streams.

Manner of establishing corners by means of posts.—Township, section, or mile corners, and quarter-section or half-mile corners, will be perpetuated by planting a post at the place of the corner, to be formed of the most durable wood of the forest at hand.

The posts must be set in the earth by digging a hole to admit them *two feet* deep, and must be very securely rammed in with earth, and also with stone, if any be found at hand. The portion of the post which protrudes above the earth must be *squared* off sufficiently smooth to admit of receiving the marks thereon, to be made with appropriate marking irons, indicating what it stands for. Thus the sides of *township corner posts* should be square at least *four inches*, (the post itself being *five* inches in diameter,) and must protrude *two feet*, at least, above the ground; the sides of *section corner posts* must be square at least *three inches*, (the post itself being *four* inches in diameter, and protrude *two feet* from the ground; and the *quarter-section corner posts* and *meander corner posts* must be *three inches wide*, presenting *flattened* surfaces, and protruding two feet from the ground.

Where a township post is a corner common to *four* townships, it is to be set in the earth diagonally, thus:

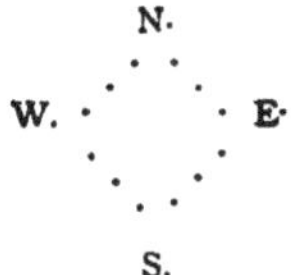

On each surface of the post is to be marked the number of the particular township, and its range, which it faces. Thus, if the post be a common boundary to four townships—say *one* and *two*, south of the base line, of range *one*, west of the meridian; also to townships *one* and *two*, south of the base line, of range *two*, west of the meridian, it is to be marked thus:

From N. to E.	R. 1 W. T. 1. S. S. 31.	From E. to S.	1 W. 2 S. 6
From N. to. W.	2 W. 1 S. 36	From W. to S.	2 W. 2 S. 1

These marks are not only to be distinctly but neatly cut into the wood, at least the eighth of an inch deep; and to make them yet more conspicuous to the eye of the anxious explorer the deputy must apply to all of them *a streak of red chalk*.

Section or mile posts, being corners of sections, and where such are common to *four* sections, are to be set diagonally in the earth, (in the manner provided for township corner posts;) and on each side of the squared surfaces, (made smooth as aforesaid, to receive the marks,) is to be marked the appropriate *number* of the particular one of the *four sections*, respectively, which such side *faces;* also on one side thereof are to be *marked* the numbers of its *township* and *range;* and to make such marks yet more *conspicuous*, in manner aforesaid, a streak of *red chalk* is to be applied.

In every township, subdivided into thirty-six sections, there are twenty-five interior section corners, each of which will be *common* to *four* sections.

A quarter-section, or half-mile post, is to have no other mark on it than a ¼ S., to indicate what it stands for.

Notching corner posts.—Township corner posts, common to four townships, are to be notched with *six* notches on each of the four angles of the squared part set to the cardinal points.

All mile posts *on township lines* must have as many notches on them, on two opposite angles thereof, as they are miles distant from the township corners, respectively. Each of the posts at the corners of sections in the interior of a township must indicate by a number of notches on each of its four corners directed to the cardinal points, the corresponding number of miles it stands from the *outlines* of the township. The four sides of the post will indicate the number of the section they respectively face. Should a tree be found at the place of any corner, it will be marked and notched as aforesaid, and answer for the corner in lieu of a post, the kind of a tree and its diameter being given in the field-notes.

Bearing trees.—The position of all corner posts, or corner trees of whatever description that may be established, is to be evidenced in the following manner, viz: From such post or tree the courses must be taken and the distances measured to two or more adjacent trees in opposite directions, as nearly as may be, and these are called "bearing trees." Such are to be distinguished by a large *smooth blaze*, with a *notch* at its lower end, facing the corner, and in the blaze is to be marked the number of the *range*, *township*, and *section;* but at quarter-section corners nothing but ¼ S, need be marked. The letters B. T., (bearing tree,) are also to be marked upon a smaller blaze, directly under the large one, and as near the ground as practicable.

At all township corners, and at all section corners, on range or township lines *four* bearing trees are to be marked in this manner, one in each of the adjoining sections.

At interior section corners, *four* trees, one to stand within each of the four sections to which such corner is common, are to be marked in manner aforesaid, if such be found.

A tree supplying the place of a corner post is to be marked in the manner directed for posts; but if such tree should be a beech, or other *smooth bark tree*, the marks may be made in the *bark*, and the tree notched.

From quarter-section and meander corners, two bearing trees are to be marked, one within each of the adjoining sections.

Where the requisite number of "bearing trees" is not to be found at convenient and suitable distances, such as are found are to be marked as herein directed; but in all such cases of deficiency in the number of bearing trees, (unless, indeed, the boundary itself be a *tree*), a *quadrangular trench*, with sides of *five* feet, and with the angles to the cardinal points, must be spaded up outside the corner, as a center, and the earth carefully thrown on the inside, so as to form a range of earth which will become covered with grass, and present a small square elevation, which in after time will serve to mark, unmistakably, the spot of the corner.

Corner stones.—Where it is deemed best to use stones for boundaries, in lieu of posts, you may, at *any* corner, insert endwise into the ground to the depth of seven or eight inches, a stone, the number of cubic inches in which shall not be less than the number contained in a stone fourteen inches long, twelve inches wide, and three inches thick—equal to five hundred and four cubic inches—the edges of which must be set north and south, on north and south lines, and east and west, on east and west lines; the dimensions of each stone to be given in the field-notes at the time of establishing the corner. The kind of stone should also be stated.

Marking corner stones.—Stones at township corners common to four townships must have *six* notches, cut with a pick or chisel on each edge or side towards the cardinal points; and where used as section corners on the range and township lines, or as section corners in the interior of a township, they will also be notched to correspond with the directions given for notching posts similarly situated.

Posts or stones at township corners on the base and standard lines, and which are common to two townships on the north side thereof, *six* notches on each of the *west*, *north* and *east* sides or edges; and where such stones or posts are set for corners to two townships south of the base or standard, *six* notches will be cut on each of the west, *south* and east sides or edges.

Stones, when used for quarter-section corners, will have ¼ cut on them—on the west side on north and south lines, and on the north side on east and west lines.

MOUNDS.

Whenever bearing trees are not found, mounds of earth, or stone, are to be raised *around posts* on which the corners are to be marked in the manner aforesaid. Wherever a mound of earth is adopted, the same will present a conical shape; but at its base, on the earth's surface a *quadrangular trench* will be dug; by the "trench" (here meant) is to be understood a *spade deep* of earth thrown up from the four sides of the lines *outside* the trench, so as to form a *continuous elevation along its outer edge*. In mounds of earth, common to *four* townships or to *four* sections, they will present the *angles* of the quadrangular trench (diagonally) towards the cardinal points. In mounds, common only to *two* townships or *two* sections the *sides* of the quadrangular trench will *face* the cardinal points. The sides of the quadrangular trench at the base of a township mound are to be *six feet*, the height of mound *three* feet.

At section, quarter-section, and meander corners, the sides of the quadrangular trench at base of mounds are to be *five* feet, and the conical height *two and a half feet*.

Prior to piling up the earth to construct a mound, there is to be dug a spadeful or two of earth from the corner boundary point, and in the cavity so formed is to be deposited a *marked stone*, or a portion of *charcoal*, the quantity whereof is to be noted in the field-book; or in lieu of charcoal or marked stone a charred stake is to be driven twelve inches down into such center point; either of those will be a *witness* for the future, and whichever is adopted, the fact is to be noted in the field-book.

When mounds are formed of *earth*, the spot from which the earth is taken is called the "*pit*," the center of which ought to be, whenever practicable, at a uniform distance and in a uniform direction from the center of the mound. There is to be a "pit" on *each* side of every mound, distant eighteen inches outside of the trench. The trench may be expected hereafter to be covered by tufts of grass, and thus to indicate the place of the mound, when the mound itself may have become obliterated by time or accident.

At meander corners, the "pit" is to be directly on the line, *eight links* further from the water than the mound. Wherever necessity is found for deviating from these rules in respect to the "pits," the course and distance to each is to be stated in the field-books.

Perpetuity in the mound is a great desideratum. In forming it with light alluvial soil the surveyor may find it necessary to make due allowance for the future settling of the earth, and thus making the mound more elevated than would be necessary in a more compact and tenacious soil, and increasing the base of it. In so doing, the relative proportions between the township mound and other mounds is to be preserved as nearly as may be.

The earth is to be pressed down with the shovel during the process of piling it up. Mounds are to be covered with sod, grass side up, where sod is to be had; but in forming a mound, *sod* is *never* to be *wrought up* with the earth, because sod decays, and in the process of decomposing it will cause the mound to become porous, and therefore liable to premature destruction.

Posts in mounds.—Must show above the top of the mound ten or twelve inches, and be notched and marked precisely as they would be for the same corner without the mound.

Mound memorials.—Beside the *charcoal* marked *stone* or *charred stake*, one or the other of which must be lodged in the earth at the point of the corner, the deputy surveyor is recommended to plant *mid way* between each pit and the trench, seeds of some tree, [those of fruit trees adapted to the climate being always to be preferred,] so that, in course of time, should such take root, a small clump of trees may possibly hereafter note the place of the corner. The facts of planting such seed, and the kind thereof, are matters to be truthfully noted in the field-book.

Witness mounds to township or section corners.—If a township or section corner, in a situation where bearing or witness trees are not found within a reasonable distance therefrom, shall fall within a ravine, or in any other situation where the nature of the ground, or the circumstances of its locality, shall be such as may prevent, or prove unfavorable to the erection of a mound, you will perpetuate such corner by selecting in the immediate vicinity thereof, a suitable plot of ground as a site for a bearing or *witness mound*, and erect thereon a mound of earth, in the same manner, and conditioned in every respect, with *charcoal, stone*, or *charred stake* deposited beneath, as above directed; and measure and state in your-field book the distance and course from the position of the true corner of the bearing or witness mound so placed and erected.

Double corners.—Such corners are to be nowhere except on the base and standard lines, whereon are to appear both the corners which mark the intersections of the lines which close thereon, and those from which the surveys start on the north. On these lines, and at the time of running the same, the township, section, and quarter-section corners are to be planted, and each of these is a corner common to *two*, [whether township or section corners,] on the north side of the line, and must be so marked.

The corners which are established on the standard parallel, at the time of running it, are to be known as "standard corners," and, in additon to all the *ordinary* marks, [as herein prescribed,] they will be marked with the letters S. C. Closing corners will be marked with the letters C. C., in addition to other marks.

The standard parallels are designed to be run *in advance* of the contiguous surveys, on the south of them, but circumstances may exist which will *impede* or temporarily delay the *due* extension of the standard; and when, from uncontrollable causes, the *contiguous townships* must be surveyed in advance of the time of extending the standard, in any such event it will become the duty of the deputy who shall afterward survey any such standard, to plant thereon the *double set* of corners, to-wit: the standard corners, to be marked S. C., and the closing ones, which are to be marked C. C.; and to make such measurements as may be necessary to connect the closing corners and complete the unfinished meridianal lines of such contiguous and prior surveys, on the principles herein set forth, under the different heads of "exterior or township lines," and of "diagram B."

You will recollect that the corners, [whether township or section corners,] which are *common* to *two*, (two townships or two sections,) are not to be planted *diagonally*, like those which are common to *four*, but with the flat sides facing the cardinal points, and on which the marks and notches are made as usual. This, it will be perceived, will serve yet more fully to distinguish the standard parallels from all other lines.

The meandering of navigable streams.—1st. Standing with the face looking *down* stream, the bank on the *left* hand is termed the "left bank," and that on the *right* hand the "right bank." These terms are to be universally used to distinguish the two banks of a river or stream.

2d. Both banks of *navigable* rivers are to be meandered by taking the courses and distances of their sinuosities, and the same are to be entered in the field-book.

At those points where either the township or section lines intersect the banks of a navigable stream, posts, or where necessary, *mounds* of *earth*, or *stone*, are to be established at the time of running these lines. These are called "meander corners;" and in meandering you are to commence at one of these corners on the township line, coursing the banks, and measuring the distance of each course from your commencing corner to the next "meander corner," upon the same or another boundary of the same township, carefully noting your intersection with all intermediate meander corners. By the same method you are to meander the opposite bank of the same river.

The crossing distance *between* the *meander corners* on same line is to be ascertained by triangulation, in order that the river may be protracted with entire accuracy. The particulars to be given in the field-notes.

3d. You are also to meander, in manner aforesaid, all *lakes* and deep ponds of the area of twenty-five acres and upward; also navigable bayous; shallow ponds, readily to be drained, or likely to dry up, are not to be meandered.

You will notice all streams of water falling into the river, lake, or bayou you are surveying, stating the width of the same at their mouth; also all springs, noting the size thereof and depth, and whether the water be pure or mineral; also the head and mouth of all bayous; and all islands, rapids, and bars are to be noticed, with intersections to their upper and lower points to establish their exact situation. You will also note the elevation of the banks of rivers and streams, the heights of falls and cascades, and the length of rapids.

4th. The precise relative position of islands, in a township made fractional by the river in which the same are situated, is to be determined trigonometrically—sighting to a flag or other fixed object on the island, from a special and carefully measured base line, connected with the surveyed lines on or near the river bank, you are to form connection between the meander corners on the river to points corresponding thereto, in direct line, on the bank of the island, and there establish the proper meander corners, and calculate the distance across.

5th. In meandering lakes, ponds, or bayous, you are to commence at a meander corner upon the township line, and proceed as above directed for the banks of a navigable stream.

But where a lake, pond, or bayou lies entirely within the township boundaries, you will commence at a meander corner established in sub-dividing, and from thence take the courses and distances of the entire margin of the same, noting the intersection with all the meander corners previously established thereon.

6th. To meander a pond lying entirely within the boundaries of a section, you will run and measure *two* lines thereunto from the nearest section or quarter-section corner on *opposite* sides of such pond, giving the courses of such lines. At *each* of the points where such lines shall intersect the margin of such pond, you will establish a *witness* point, by fixing a post in the ground, and taking bearings to any adjacent trees, or, if necessary, raising a mound.

The relative position of these points being thus definitely fixed in the section, the meandering will commence at one of them, and be continued to the other, noting the intersection, and thence to the beginning. The proceedings are to be fully entered in the field-book.

7th. In taking the connection of an island with the main land, when there is no meander corner in line, opposite thereto, to sight from, you will measure a special base from the meander corner nearest to such island, and from such base you will triangulate to some fixed point on the shore of the island, ascertain the distance across, and there establish a special meander corner, wherefrom you will commence to meander the island.

The field-notes of meanders you will set forth in the body of the field book, according to the dates, when the work is performed, as illustrated in the specimen notes annexed. They are to state and describe particularly the meander corner from which they commenced, each one with which they close, and are to exhibit the meaders of each fractional section separately; following, and composing a part of such notes, will be given a description of the land, timber, depth of inundation to which the bottom is subject, and the banks, current, and bottom of the stream or body of water you are meandering.

9. No blazes or marks of any description are to be made on the lines meandered between the established corners, but the utmost care must be taken to pass no object of topography, *or change therein*, without giving a particular description thereof in its proper place in your meander notes.

OF FIELD-BOOKS.

The *field-notes* afford the elements from which the plats and calculations in relation to the public surveys are made. They are the source wherefrom the description and evidence of locations and boundaries are officially delineated and set forth. They therefore must be a faithful, distinct and minute record of every thing officially done and observed by the surveyor and his assistants, pursuant to instructions, in relation to running, measuring, and marking lines, establishing boundary corners. etc.; and present, as far as possible, a full and complete *topographical* description of the country surveyed, as to every matter of useful information, or likely to gratify public curiosity.

There will be sundry separate and distinct field-books of surveys as follows:

Field-notes of the *meridian* and *base* lines, showing the establishment of the *township section* or mile, and *quarter-section* or half mile, boundary corners thereon; with the crossings of streams, ravines, hills, and mountains; character of soil, timber, minerals, etc.

Field-notes of the "*standard parallels*," or "correction lines," will show the establishment of the township, section, and quarter-section corners, beside exhibiting the topography of the country on line, as required on the base and meridian lines.

Field-notes of the *exterior* lines of *townships*, showing the establishment of corners on lines, and the topography, as aforesaid.

Field-notes of the *sub-divisions of townships* into sections and quarter-sections.

The field-notes must in all cases be taken precisely in the order in which the work is done on the ground, and the *date* of each day's work must follow immediately after the notes thereof. The *variation of the needle* must always occupy a *separate line* preceeding the notes of measurements on line.

The exhibition of every mile of surveying, whether on township or sub-divisional lines, must be *complete in itself*, and be separated by a black line drawn across the paper. The description of the surface, soil, mineral, timber, undergrowth, etc., on *each mile* of line, is to follow the notes of survey of such line, and not be mixed up with them.

No abbreviations of words are allowable, except of such words as are constantly occurring, such as "*sec.* for *Section;*" "*in. diam.*" for *inches diameter;*" "*chs.* for *chains;*" "*lks.*" for "*links;*" "*dist.*" for "*distant,*" etc. Proper names must never be abbreviated, however often their recurrence.

The nature of the subject-matter of the field-book is to form its title page, showing the State or Territory where such survey lies, by whom surveyed, and the dates of commencement and completion of the work. The second page is to contain the names and duties of assistants. Whenever a new assistant is employed, or the duties of any one of them are changed, such facts, with the reasons therefor, are to be stated in an appropriate entry immediately preceding the notes taken under such changed arrangements. With the notes of the *exterior* lines of townships, the deputy is to submit a plat of the lines run, on a scale of two inches to the mile, on which are to be noted all the objects of topography on lines necessary to illustrate the notes, viz: the distances on line at the crossings of streams, so far as such can be noted on the paper, and the direction of each by an arrow-head pointing down stream; also the intersection of line by prairies, marshes, swamps, ravines, ponds, lakes, hills, mountains, and all other matters indicated by the notes, to the fullest extent practicable.

With the instructions for making sub-divisional surveys of townships into sections, the deputy will be furnished by the Surveyor-General with a diagram of the *exterior* lines of the townships to be sub-divided, (on the above named scale,) upon which are carefully to be laid down the measurements of each of the section lines on such boundaries whereon he is to close, the magnetic variation of each mile, and the particular description of each corner. "P. in M." signifies post in mound. And on such diagram the deputy who sub-divides will make appropriate sketches of the various objects of topography as they occur on his lines, so as to exhibit not only the points on lines at which the same occur, but also the direction and position of each between the lines, or within each section, so that every object of topography may be properly completed or connected in the showing.

These notes must be distinctly written out, in language precise and clear, and their figures, letters, words, and meaning are always to be unmistakable. No leaf is to be cut or mutilated, and none to be taken out, whereby suspicion might be created that the missing leaf contained matter which the deputy believed to be to his interest to conceal.

Summary of objects and data required to be noted.—1. The precise length of every line run, noting all necessary off-sets therefrom, with the reason and mode thereof.

2. The kind and diameter of all *bearing trees*, with the course and distance of the same from their respective corners; and the precise relative position of *witness corners* to the *true corners*.

3. The kind of materials, (earth or stone,) of which *mounds* are constructed—the fact of their being conditioned according to instructions—with the course and distance of the *pits* from the center of the mound, where necessity exists for deviating from the *general rule*.

4. *Trees on line*. The name, diameter, and distance on line to all trees which it intersects.

5. Intersections by line of *land objects*. The distance at which the line first intersects and then leaves every *settler's claim and improvement;* prairie, river, creek, or other "bottom;" or swamp, marsh, grove, and windfall, with the course of the same at both points of intersection; also the distances at which you begin to ascend, arrive at the top, begin to descend, and reach the foot of all remarkable hills and ridges, with their courses, and estimated height, in feet, above the level land of the surrounding country, or above the bottom lands, ravines, or waters near which they are situated.

6. Intersection by line of *water objects*. All rivers, creeks, and smaller streams of water which the line crosses; the distance on line at the points of intersection, and

their widths on line. In cases of navigable streams, their widths will be ascertained between the meander corners, as set forth under the proper head.

7. *The land's surface.*—Whether level, rolling, broken, or hilly.

8. *The soil.*—Whether first, second, or third-rate.

9. *Timber.*—The several kinds of timber and undergrowth, in the order in which they predominate.

10. *Bottom lands.*—To be described as wet or dry, and if subject to inundation, state to what depth.

11. *Springs of water.*—Whether fresh, saline, or mineral, with the course of the stream flowing from them.

12. *Lakes and ponds.*—Describing their banks and giving their height, and also the depth of water, and whether it be pure or stagnant.

13. *Improvements.*—Towns and villages; Indian towns and wigwams; houses or cabins; fields or other improvements; sugar-tree groves, sugar-camps; mill-seats, forges, and factories.

14. *Coal* banks or beds; *peat* or turf grounds; *minerals* and *ores*, with particular description of the same as to quality and extent, and all *diggings* therefor; also, *salt* springs and licks. All reliable information you can obtain respecting these objects, whether they be on your immediate line or not, is to appear in the general description to be given at the end of the notes.

15. *Roads and trails*, with their directions, whence and whither.

16. Rapids, cataracts, cascades, or falls of water, with the height of their fall in feet.

17. Precipices, caves, sink-holes, ravines, stone-quarries, ledges of rock, with the kind of stone they afford.

18. *Natural curiosities*, interesting fossils, petrifactions, organic remains, etc., also, all ancient works of art, such as mounds, fortifications, embankments, ditches, or objects of like nature.

19. The *variation* of the needle must be noted at all points or places on the lines where there is found any material *change* of variation, and the position of such points must be perfectly identified in the notes.

20. Beside the ordinary notes taken on line, (and which must always be written down on the spot, leaving nothing to be supplied by memory, the deputy will subjoin at the conclusion of his book, such further description or information touching any matter or thing connected with the township, (or other survey), which he may be able to afford, and may deem useful or necessary to be known—with a *general description* of the township in the *aggregate*, as respects the face of the country, its soil and geological features, timber, minerals, water, etc.

Swamp lands.—By the act of Congress, approved September 28, 1850, swamp and overflowed lands, "unfit for cultivation," are granted to the State in which they are situated. In order clearly to define the quantity and locality of such lands, the field-notes of surveys, in addition to the other objects of topography required to be noted, are to indicate the points at which you enter all lands which are evidently subject to such grant, and to show the distinctive character of the land so noted; whether it is a swamp or marsh, or otherwise subject to inundation to an extent that, without artificial means, would render it "unfit for cultivation." The depth of inundation is to be stated, as determined from indications on the trees where timber exists; and its frequency is to be set forth as accurately as may be, either from your own knowledge of the general character of the stream which overflows, or from reliable information to be obtained from others. The words "unfit for cultivation," are to be employed in addition to the usual phraseology in regard to entering or leaving such swamps,

DIAGRAM A.

EXTERIORS OR TOWNSHIP LINES.

First correction or Standard Line North.

T.4.N.

T.3.N.

T.2.N.

T.1.N.

R.II.W. R.I.W. R.I.E. R.II.E.

True Meridian North

Principal Meridian

Base Line.

marshy, or overflowed lands. It may be that sometime the margin of bottom, swamp, or marsh, in which such uncultivable land exists, is not identical with the margin of the body of land "unfit for cultivation," and in such cases a separate entry must be made for each, opposite the marginal distance at which they respectively occur.

But in cases where lands are overflowed by *artificial* means, (say, by dams for milling, logging, or for other purposes,) you are not officially to regard such overflow, but will continue your lines across the same without setting meander posts, stating particularly in the notes the depth of the water, and how the overflow was caused.

* * * * * * * * *

Exterior or township lines.—The principal meridian, the base line and the standard parallels having been first run, measured, and marked, and the corner boundaries thereon established, according to instructions, the process of running, measuring, and marking the exterior lines of townships will be as follows:

Townships situated north of the base line, and west of the principal meridian.—Commencing at No. 1, (see figures on diagram A), being the southwest corner of township 1, north, range 1, west, as established on the base line, thence north, on a true meridian line, four hundred and eighty chains, establishing the section and quarter-section corners thereon, as per instructions, to No. 2, whereat establish the corner of townships 1 and 2, north, ranges 1 and 2, west; thence east, on a random or trial line, setting *temporary* section and quarter section stakes, to No. 3, where measure and note the distance at which the line intersects the eastern boundary north or south of the *true* or established corner. Run and measure westward, on the true line, (taking care to note all the land and water-crossings, etc., as per instructions,) to No. 4, which is identical with No. 2, establishing the section and quarter-section *permanent corners* on said line. Should it happen, however, that such random line falls short, or overruns in length, or intersects the eastern boundary of the township at more than three chains and fifty links distance from the *true* corner thereon, as compared with the corresponding boundary on the south, (either of which would indicate an important error in the surveying,) the lines must be *retraced*, even if found necessary to remeasure the meridianal boundaries of the township, (especially the western boundary,) so as to discover and correct the error; in doing which the *true corners* must be established and marked, and the *false ones* destroyed and obliterated, to prevent confusion in future; and *all the facts* must be distinctly set forth in the notes. Thence proceed in a similar manner from No. 4 to No. 5, No. 5 to No. 6, No. 6 to No. 7, and so on to No. 10, the southwest corner of township 4, north, range 1, west. Thence north, still on a true meridian line, establishing the mile and half-mile corners, until reaching the *standard parallel* or correction line; throwing *excess* over, or *deficiency* under, *four hundred and eighty chains* on the *last* half-mile, according to law, and at the intersection establishing the "*closing corner*," the distance of which *from* the standard corner must be measured and noted, as required by the instructions. But should it ever so happen that some impassable barrier will have prevented or delayed the extension of the standard parallel along and above the field of present survey, then the deputy will plant, in place, the corner for the township, subject to correction thereafter, should such parallel be extended.

North of the base line, and east of the principal meridian.—Commence at No. 1, being the *southeast* corner of township 1, north, range 1, east, and proceed as with townships situated "north and west," except that the *random* or trial lines will be run and measured *west*, and the *true* lines east, throwing the excess over or deficiency under four hundred and eighty chains on the *west end* of the line, as required by law; wherefore the surveyor will commence his measurement with the length of the deficient or excessive half-section boundary on the west of the township, and thus the remaining measurements will all be *even* miles and half miles.

Important method of sub-dividing.—1. The first mile, both of the south and east boundaries of each township you are required to sub-divide, is to be carefully traced and measured before you enter upon the sub-division thereof. This will enable you to observe any change that may have taken place in the magnetic variation, as it existed at the time of running the township lines, and will also enable you to compare your chaining with that upon the township lines.

2. Any discrepancy, arising either from a change in the magnetic variation or a difference in measurement, is to be carefully noted in the field-notes.

3. After adjusting your compass to a variation which you have thus found, will retrace the eastern boundary of the township, you will commence at the corner to sections 35 and 36, on the south boundary, and run a line due north forty chains, to the quarter-section corner, which you are to establish between sections 35 and 36; continuing due north, forty chains further, you will establish the corner to sections 25, 26, 35, and 36.

4. From the section corner last named, run a *random* line, without blazing, *due east*, for corner of section 25 and 36 in east boundry, and at forty chains from the starting point, set a post for *temporary* quarter-section corner. If you intersect exactly at the corner, you will blaze your random line back, and establish it as the true line; but if your random line intersects the said east boundary either north or south of said corner, you will measure the distance of such intersection, from which you will calculate a course that will run a *true* line back to the corner from which your random started. You will establish the *permanent* quarter-section corner at a point equi-distant from the two terminations of the *true* line.

5. From the corner of sections 25, 26, 35, 36, run due north between sections 25 and 26, setting the quarter-section post as before, at forty chains, and at eighty chains establishing the corner of sections 23, 24, 25, 26. Then run a random *due east* for the corner of sections 24 and 25 in east boundary; setting temporary quarter-section post at forty chains; correcting back, and establishing *permanent* quarter-section corner at the equi-distant point on the *true* line, in the manner directed on the line between sections 25 and 36.

6. In this manner you will proceed with the survey of each successive section in the first tier, until you arrive at the north boundary of the township, which you will reach in running up a random line between sections 1 and 2. If this random line should not intersect at the corner established for sections 1, 2, 35 and 36, upon the township line, you will note the distance that you fall east or west of the same, from which distance you will calculate a course that will run a true line south to the corner from which your random started. Where the closing corner is on the base or standard line, a deviation from the general rule is explained under the head of Diagram "B."

7. The first tier of sections being thus laid and surveyed, you will return to the south boundary of the township, and from the corner of sections 34 and 35, commence and survey the second tier of sections in the same manner that you pursued in the survey of the first, closing at the section corners on the first tier.

8. In like manner proceed with the survey of each successive tier of sections, until you arrive at the fifth tier; and from each section corner which you establish upon this tier, you are to run random lines to the corresponding corners established upon the range line forming the western boundry of the township; setting, as you proceed,

each *temporary* quarter-section post at forty chains from the interior section corner, so as to throw the excess or deficiency of measurement on the extreme tier of quarter-sections contiguous to the township boundary; and, on returning, establish the *true* line, and establish thereon the *permanent* quarter-section corner.

Quarter-section corners, both upon north and south and upon east and west lines, are to be established at a point *equi-distant* from the corresponding section corners, *except* upon the lines closing on the north and west boundaries of the township, and in those situations the quarter-section corners will always be established at precisely *forty chains* to the north or west (as the case may be) of the respective section corners from which those lines respectively *start*, by which procedure the excess or deficiency in the measurements will be thrown, according to law, on the extreme tier of quarter-sections.

Every north and south section line, except those terminating in the north boundary of the township, is to be eighty chains in length.

The east and west section lines, except those terminating on the west boundary of the township, are to be within one hundred links of eighty chains in length; and the north and south boundaries of any one section, except in the extreme western tier, are to be within one hundred links of equal length. The meanders within each fractional section, or between any two meander posts, or of a pond or island in the interior of a section, must close within one chain and fifty links.

Diagram "A" illustrates the mode of laying off township exteriors *north* of the *base* line and *east* and *west* of the principal *meridian*, whether between the base and first standard, or between any two standards; and the same general principles will equally apply to townships *south* of the base line and east and west of the meridian, and between any two standards *south*, where the distances between the base and first standard, and between the standards themselves, are five townships or thirty miles.

Diagram "B" indicates the mode of laying off a *township* into sections and quarter-sections, and the accompanying set of field-notes (marked B,) critically illustrate the mode and order of conducting the survey under every variety of circumstances shown by the topography on the diagram. In townships lying *south* of and *contiguous* to the base or to any standard parallel, the lines between the northern tier of sections will be run *north*, and be made to close as true lines; quarter-section corners will be set at forty chains, and section corners established at the intersection of such section lines with the base or standard, (as the case may be,) and the distance is to be measured and entered in the field-book to the nearest corner on such standard or base.

The mode and order of surveying the *exterior* boundaries of a township are illustrated by the specimen field-notes marked A; and the mode and order of *sub-dividing* a township into sections and quarter-sections are illustrated by the specimen field-notes marked B. The attention of the deputy is particularly directed to these specimens, as indicating not only the method in which his work is to be conducted, but also the order, manner, language, etc., in which his field-notes are required to be returned to the Surveyor-General's office; and such specimen are to be deemed part of these instructions, and any *departure* from their details, without special authority, in cases where the circumstances are analagous in practice, will be regarded as a violation of his contract and oath.

No. 123.

FORM OF FIELD NOTES OF TOWNSHIP LINES.

[A.]

FIELD-NOTES OF TOWNSHIP LINES.

Township 89 *north between Ranges* 29 *and* 30 *W.*

North between sections 13 *and* 18.

Variation 10°

Chains,
8.00. Pond E. and west,
15.00. Leave same.
40.00. Set post for qr. section corner in mound, pit 8 links East.
48.00. Enter timber NW and SE.
54.00. Brook 4 L. wide, NE.
59.50. Same, runs N. W.
68.00. Enter bottom SE.
70.00. Lizzard Fork, Des Moines, 60 L. wide, runs S. E.
71.00. Leave timber SE.
80.00. Set post for corner to sections 7, 12, 13 and 18 in mound, pit 8 links South, last half partly broken, 1st.

North between sections 7 *and* 12.

Variation 10° 15′.

18.00. Leave bottom SE.
40.00. Set post for qr. section corner in mound, pit 8 links East.
80.00. Set post for corner to sections 1, 6, 7, and 12 in mound, pit 8 links south. Surface rolling. Soil first rate,

---

Township 89 *north, between Ranges* 29 *and* 30.

North between sections 1 *and* 6.

Variation 10° 20′

Chains.
40.00. Set post for qr. section corner in mound, pit 8 links East.
63.00, Pond and marsh S. W.
76.00. Over marsh, W. for C., and set post for corner to townships 89 and 90. North, of ranges 29 and 30 W., in mound, pits 10 L. north and south
Surface level; soil wet, 2d rate.
September 3d, 1853.
Measuring chain compared with standard and found correct.
(This township corner is 100 links east of the true corner, which is in marsh.)

Between Townships 89 *and* 90 *N., Range* 29 *W.* 5*th Meridian.*

West between sections 4 *and* 33.

Variation 9° 35′.

Chains.
40.00. Set post for qr. sec. cor. in mound, pit 8 links East.
80.00. Set post for corner to sections 4, 5, 32 and 33 in mound, pit 8 links South,
Surface mostly level; soil first-rate.

Between Townships 89 *and* 90 *N. Range* 29 *W.* 5*th Meridian.*

West between sections 5 *and* 32.

Variation 9° 50′.

Chains.
40.00. Set post for qr. section corner in mound, pit 8 links East.
80.00. Set post for corner to sections 5, 6, 31 and 32 in mound, pit 8 links South. Surface level; soil first rate.

West between sections 6 *and* 31.

Variation 10°.

Chains.
35.00. Pond and marsh N. and S.
37.50. Leave same W. for C.
40.00. Set post for qr. sec. cor. in mound, pit 8 links East.
79.50. Pond and marsh lies S. W., and set post in mound, pits 10 links N. and S., for witness corner to townships 89 and 90 N., ranges 29 and 30 W.
80.50. Intersected range line 4 chains South of post and made witness corner 100 links East of true corner.
Surface level; soil 2d rate.

Township lines surveyed by JOWN W. ELLIS,
U. S. Deputy Surveyor.

No. 124.

FORM OF FIELD-NOTES OF SUB-DIVISION OF TOWNSHIP.

[B.]

Sub-Division
of
Township No. 89, North
of
Range 30, West of 5th Principal Meridian,
Iowa.
Commenced June 28th, 1854.
Finished July 7th, 1854.
By George Berry, Deputy Surveyor.

Measuring chain compared with standard chain and found to be one inch too long and adjusted thereto.

To determine the course of the east boundary of the township I commence (with my compass adjusted at a variation of 9° 30′ east) at the corner of townships 88 and 89, ranges 29 and 30, and run thence north on a blank line; at 39.56 chains, fell 30 links east of quarter-section post; 79.10 chains fell 54 links east of corner to sections 25 and 36, township 89 North, range 30 West.

From corner to townships 88 and 89, ranges 29 and 30, with compass adjusted at a variation of 9° 15′ East, I run west on a blank line along south boundary of section 36, township 89 North, range 30 West, at 39.57 chains fell 13 links north of quarter-section corner; at 79.10 chains fell 30 links north of corner to sections 35 and 36.

North between sections 35 *and* 36.

Variation 9° 50′ *East.*

Chains.
11.00. Leave marsh, bears N. E. and West; unfit for cultivation.
40.00. Set quarter-section post in a mound of earth and sod-pit 8 links East.

40·50. Enter pond of water 2 feet deep, bears N. E. and S. W.
53.00. Leave same; bears N. E. and S. W.
80.00. Set post corner to sections 25, 26, 35 and 36, in mound of earth and sod; pit 8 links south.
Surface undulating; soil, 2d-rate.

East random between sections 25 *and* 36.

Variation 9° 25′ *East.*

80.20. Intersect range line 80 links south of post.

West corrected between sections 25 *and* 36.

Variation 9° 59′ *East.*

5.60. Enter marsh; bears N. W. and S. E.
19.60. Leave wet marsh; bears N. W. and S. E.; unfit for cultivation.
40.10. Set section post in mound, pit 8 links East.
80.20. Section corner.
Surface level, or rather flat; soil 2d-rate, with a fair proportion of sand.

North, between sections 25 *and* 26.

Variation 10° *East.*

40.00. Set quarter-section post in a mound of earth and sod; pit 8 links East.
80.00. Set post, corner to sections 23, 24, 25, and 26, in mound of earth and sod; pit 8 links South, and enter bottom, bears S. E. and N. W.
Surface, undulating; soil, good second-rate.
June 28th, 1854.
Measuring chain compared with standard chain and found correct.

Township 89 *N., R.* 28 *W., 5th Meridian.*

Meander of Des Moines river, up the right bank in Section 7, *from meander corner between Sections* 7 *and* 18.

Variation 10° *East.*

Courses.
N. 3½° E. 11.08 chains.
North 14.00 chains.
N. 26 ° E. 17.50 chains.
N. 12 ° W. 7.25 chains.
N. 34½° W. 5.00 chains.
N. 45 ° W. 5.77 chains.
N. 77 ° W. 5.00 chains.
S. 74 ° W. 8.75 chains.
S. 44 ° W. 6.50 chains. Coal here.
S. 53½° W. 7.50 chains.
S. 76 ° W. 6.50 chains.
S. 84 ° W. 5.50 chains.
N. 74 ° W. 5.00 chains.
N. 66 ° W. 12.00 chains.
S. 88 ° W. 3.44 chains, to meander corner on west boundary between sections 7 and 12.
Banks about 8 feet, except at coal bank—there 25 or 30 feet.

DIAGRAM B.

Township Nº 89 N. Range Nº 29 W. 5th Mer.

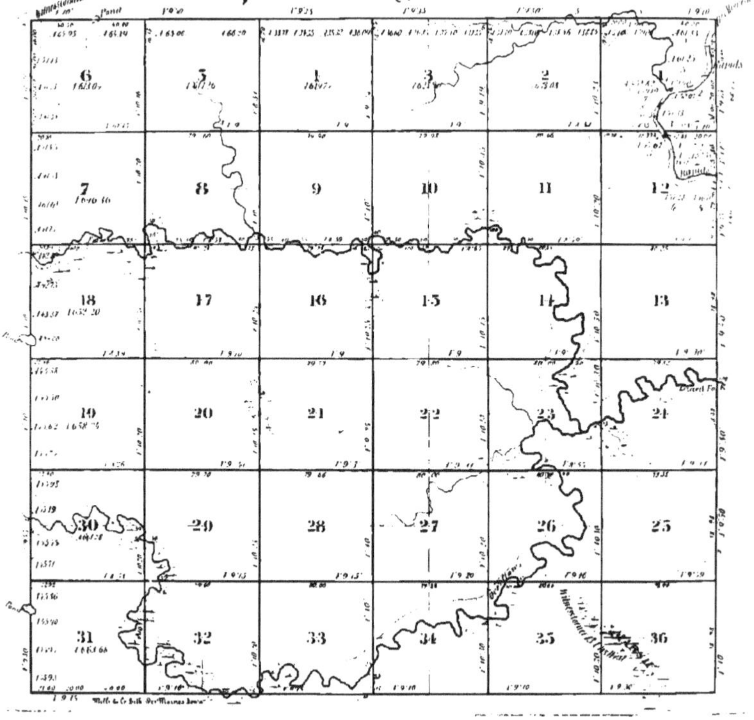

6	5	4	3	2	1
7	8	9	10	11	12
18	17	16	15	14	13
19	20	21	22	23	24
30	29	28	27	26	25
31	32	33	34	35	36

Township 89, *R.* 28 *W.*, *5th Meridian.*

Meander of island in section 19, in Des Moines river. Set post on right bank of island, course from meander post on right bank of river, between sections 18 and 19 --N. 43° E. 3.46 chains.

Bearing to said post, cluster white maple—one marked 20 inches—N. 67½ E. 18 links.

Courses.	Chains.	
N. 46½° W.	7.25.	
N. 25½° W.	2.50.	
N. 14 ° E.	15.00.	To head of island.
S. 34 ° E.	10.00.	
S. 11 ° E.	4.00.	
S. 7½° W.	4.50.	
S. 9 ° E.	1.25.	
S. 40½° W.	1.68.	
S. 29 ° W.	3.50.	
N. 60 ° W.	.70,	to place of beginning.

Timber: maple, hackberry, and elm; soil, sandy, subject to overflow.

The sub-divisions of fractional sections into forty acre lots, (as near as may be), are to be so laid down on the official township plat in *red* lines, as to admit of giving to each a specific designation, if possible, according to its relative position in the fractional section, as per examples afforded by Diagram B, as well as by a number, in all cases where the lot cannot properly be designated as a quarter-quarter. Those fractional sub-division lots which are not susceptible of being described according to relative local position, are to be numbered in regular series: No. 1 being (wherever practicable, and as a general rule) either the northeastern or the most easterly fractional lot, and proceeding from east to west, and from west to east, alternately, to the end of the series; but such general rule is departed from under circumstances given.

* * * * * * * * *

Sub-division of sections.—The following are the rules and instructions relating to the sub-divisions of sections:

DEPARTMENT OF THE INTERIOR,
GENERAL LAND OFFICE, May 12, 1870.

C. C. CARPENTER, ESQ., *Register S. L. O., Des Moines, Iowa.*

SIR:—In reference to the subject of your letter of the 22d ultimo, I have to state that the following directions for the sub-division of sections of the public land are in strict accordance with the acts of Congress relating to the public surveys, now in force:

1st. The original corners, when they can be identified, must stand as the true corners.

2d. Under the provisions of the act of February 11, 1805, the course to be pursued in the sub-division of sections is to run straight lines from the established quarter-section corners—United States surveys—to the opposite corresponding corners, and the point of intersection of these lines will be the corner common to the several quarter-sections.

3d. In the sub-division of fractional sections where no opposite corresponding corners have been or can be fixed, the sub-division lines should be ascertained by running from the established corners, due north, south, east or west lines, as the case may be, to the water-course, Indian boundary line or other external boundary of such fractional section.

4th. Upon the lines closing on the north and west boundaries of a township, the quarter-posts are established by the United States Deputy Surveyors at precisely *forty chains* to the north or west, as the case may be, of the last interior section corner and the excess or deficiency in the measurement is thrown on the outer tier of lots, as per act of May 10, 1800.

5th. In the sub-division of quarter-sections, the quarter-quarter corners are to be established at points *equi-distant* between the section and quarter-section corners *except* on the last half mile of the lines closing on the north and west boundaries of a township, where they are to be placed at a distance of twenty chains—original measurement—to the north or west of the quarter-section corners.

6. The sub-division lines of fractional quarter-sections should be run from points on the section lines intermediate between the section and quarter-section corners due north, south, east or west to the lake, water-course or reservation which renders such tracts fractional.

In regard to the restoration of lines of the public surveys, where the same may be obliterated by time or accident, the same can only be legally effected when done in strict accordance with the laws of the United States relating to the subject.

Very respectfully, your obedient servant,

JOS. S. WILSON, *Commissioner.*

Restoration of lost corners.—The following are the rules for the restoration of lost corners:

GENERAL LAND OFFICE,
June 29th, 1863.

D. W. MAXON, ESQ., *Cedar Creek, Washington Co., Wis.*

SIR:—Your letter of the 12th inst., asking for information as to the proper mode of establishing lost corners of the public surveys, etc., is received. As stated in my communication of the 2d inst., this office does not assume to exercise any control over the surveying operations of county surveyors.

For information of surveyors who may be called upon to re-establish lost corners of the public surveys, or sub-divide sections, the following general principles, based upon the laws of Congress, and the regulations of the land department in accordance therewith, may be stated:

1st. Section and quarter-section corners as established by the government survey, must, by law of Congress, stand as the true corners.

2d. Missing corners must be re-established at the indentical point where the original posts were planted by the United States deputy surveyors.

3d. The legal presumption is, in the absence of any evidence to the contrary, that lost section and quarter-section posts were originally established at the distance indicated in the field-notes.

4th. Half-quarter-section corners must be established *equi-distant* from the section and quarter-section posts.

The first proposition above is in accordance with a law of Congress, approved, Feb. 11th, 1805. To divide a section into quarters a right line should be run from the quarter-section post in one section line to the corresponding quarter-section post in the opposite section line, even though one or more of these posts may have been established nearer to one section corner than the other, thereby giving to one quarter-section more than 160 acres, and to another less.

The second proposition grows out of the first, and is in accordance with the laws of Congress. It is the duty of the surveyor to re-establish missing posts in the exact locality where they were originally placed in the government survey, The proof or locality first sought to be obtained should be the "witness trees," or any other means of identification contained *in the field-notes*, and next, clear and unquestionable testimony of any other kind.

If no bearing trees, or other evidences in the field-notes or elsewhere exist by which the locality of the missing posts can be identified or determined in the field, then, as stated under the third head, the legal presumption is, that the missing section or quarter section corners were originally established in conformity with the distances expressed in the field-notes, and the surveyor should so re-establish them.

Extinct quarter-section corners, except on fractional section lines, when they cannot be identified as above, should be re-established *equi-distant* between the section corners, in a right line between the the nearest noted "line trees" each side of it, if there are any, but if none are found, then in a right line between the section corners. Extinct quarter-section posts on section lines which close on the north and west boundaries of townships should be re-established, according to the original measurement thereof at forty chains from the last interior section corner.

Extinct section corners may be re-established by running a right line between the nearest noted "line trees" north and south and east and west of the lost corner, if there be any such trees within the distance of the nearest quarter-section, or section corners; but if no line trees be found, then between the nearest quarter-section corners, and at the point of intersection of the two lines thus run, establish the section corner, with new bearings, to the nearest and most desirable objects.

The quarter-mile posts are not established in government surveys, but are, by law, understood to be equi-distant from the section and quarter-section corners, as stated under the fourth head, and should be so established by the county surveyor. It may be remarked, that where the measurement of any section line by the county surveyor does not correspond with the original measurement recorded in the field-notes, lost corners should be re-established at proportional distances from each other, between the known corners.

A proper application of the principles embraced herein will enable the practical surveyor to sub-divide the public lands and re-establish the lost corners of the public surveys, in conformity with law and the regulations and usages of the land department.

There are some anomalous cases, such, for instance, as double corners on the north and west boundary lines of townships, an explanation of which must be omitted, owing to the length of this communication. The general principles which should govern the county surveyor are, however, indicated with sufficient clearness to guide him in the rightful performance of his duties.

Very respectfully, etc.,

JAS. M. EDMUNDS, *Commissioner.*

Sub-division: lost corners, etc.—The following observations of Hon. C. C. Carpenter are taken from his valuable compilation of "Laws, Rules and Instructions relating to the duties of

County Surveyors," to which the surveyor is referred for more full instructions relating to this matter:

The sub-division of, or restoration of lost corners to fractional sections, also the manner of proceeding to establish quarter-corners on township and range lines, on which are double sets of section corners.

Prior to 1846 the instructions of the Commissioner of the General Land-Office differed from those subsequent to that date, in reference to closing upon the north and west boundaries of a township. The instructions then provided that, in closing upon the north line of a township, the line should be run from the last interior section corner south of that line; at forty chains a quarter post should be set, and on intersecting the north boundary line, a section corner was established at the point of intersection, the surveyor noting in the field-notes the distance it fell either east or west, or north or south of the section corner for the two adjacent sections, north or west of the corner established when the township line was run. This course is still pursued when closing upon a correction line. But in the case of ordinary township and range lines, the instructions and practice are now, and have been since 1846, to close upon the north and west boundaries by running randoms and correcting back, the same as in making closings east upon interior section corners. This difference, however, will be observed: upon interior section lines running east and west the quarter-section posts were set equi-distant between the two section corners, while in closing out upon the north and west boundaries, the quarter-section corner was established just forty chains from the last interior corner south or east, thus throwing the fraction entirely upon the most northerly and westerly half-sections.

It will be seen, therefore, that upon many township and range lines, as upon all correction lines, there are double sets of corners. It will also be seen by the instructions published herein, that deputy surveyors were instructed not to run the boundary lines upon which these closings were made, as they would not be paid therefor.

It, therefore, devolves upon the county surveyor, engaged to sub-divide a section next south or east of a township or range line, upon which are two sets of corners, to establish the quarter-section corner on the north or west boundary of the section. And, in doing so, he will find the following letter of instruction and the accompanying Diagram B will be of value to him:

DEPARTMENT OF THE INTERIOR,
GENERAL LAND OFFICE,
May 26th, 1870.

C. C. CARPENTER, ESQ., *Register of the State Land Office, Des Moines, Iowa:*

SIR:—I am in receipt of your letter of the 18th instant, desiring information in regard to the proper method of establishing the quarter-corners on the northern boundaries of the northern tier of sections in a township where there is a double set of section corners on the township line.

In reply, I have to say that the quarter-corners should be established at points equi-distant between the northeast and northwest corners of the sections, *except* in section *six*, where the quarter-corner should be placed at precisely forty chains (original measurement) west of the northeast corner of the section.

Very respectfully,

Your obedient servant,

JOS. S. WILSON, *Commissioner.*

(B.)

PART OF TOWNSHIP 90, NORTH RANGE 3 WEST. 5TH MER.

as Originally surveyed in 1837, and as patented.

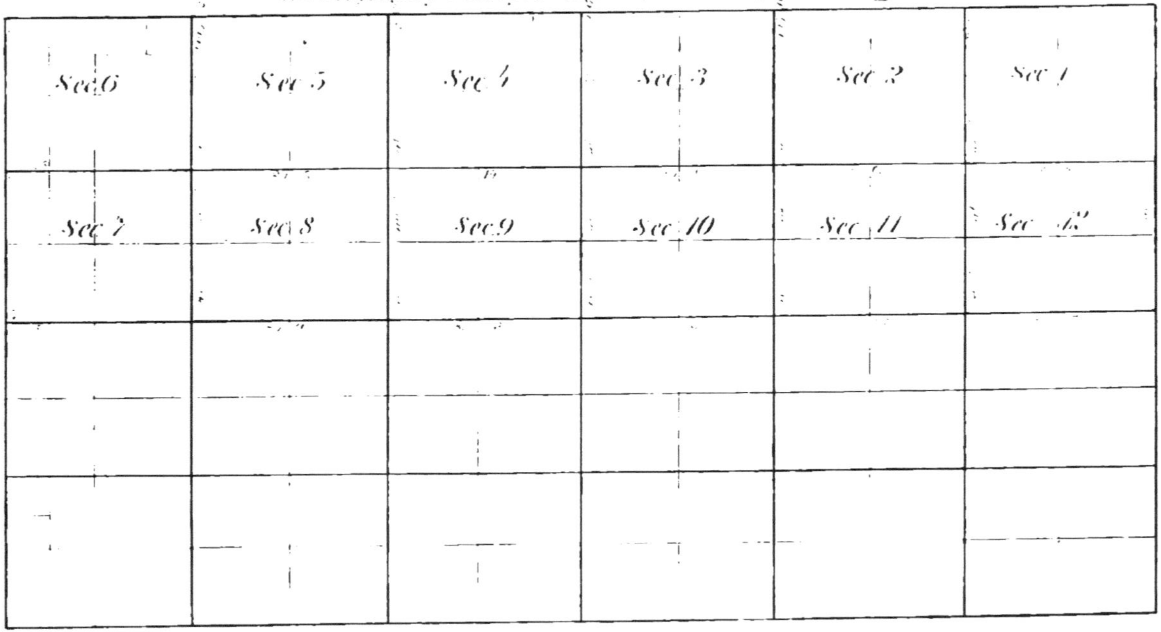

Sec 6	Sec 5	Sec 4	Sec 3	Sec 2	Sec 1
Sec 7	Sec 8	Sec 9	Sec 10	Sec 11	Sec 12

As found upon a Resurvey by the U. S. in 1852.

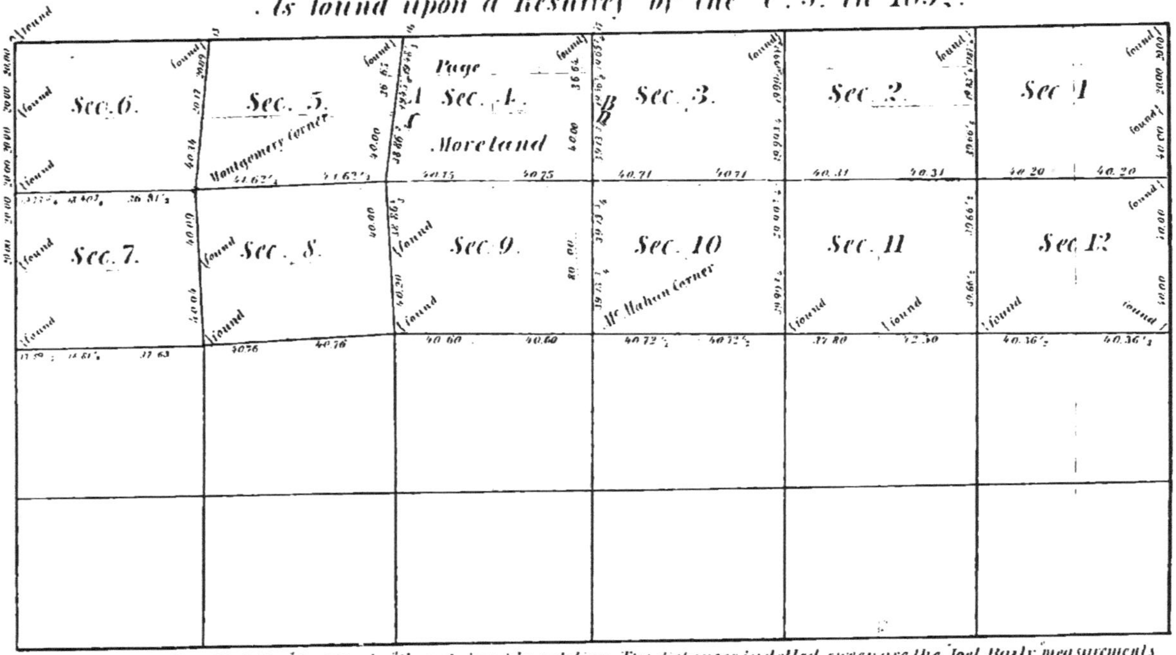

Sec. 6. Sec. 5. Sec. 4. Sec. 3. Sec. 2. Sec. 1

Montgomery Corner

Page

Moreland

A B

Sec. 7. Sec. 8. Sec. 9. Sec. 10 Sec. 11 Sec. 12

McMahon Corner

NOTE The dotted line A B. is the "Joel Baily" line claimed in petition. The distances in dotted sweep are the "Joel Baily" measurements

V. DECISIONS ILLUSTRATING THE FOREGOING RULES.

In establishing a lost survey, courses and distances must yield to fixed monuments. All ascertained surrounding monuments must be allowed their due weight in determining the locality of the unascertained, under the system by which the survey was originally made.

Where on a line of the same survey between remote corners, the whole length of which line is found to be variant from the length called for, in re-establishing lost intermediate monuments as marking sub-divisional tracts, we are not permitted to presume merely that the variance arose from the defective survey of any part, but must conclude, in the absence of circumstances showing the contrary, that it arose from the imperfect measurement of the whole line, and distribute such variance between the several sub-divisions of such line in proportion to their respective lengths. Unknown corners must be found by corroborative testimony of all known corners, with as little departure as may be from the system adopted on the original survey without giving preponderance to the testimony of any one monument above another. Moreland v. Page, 2 Iowa, 139.

In the case above cited, Moreland, the plaintiff, claimed he was the owner of the east half of the south-west quarter, and the west half of the south-east quarter of section four, in township ninety, north of range three west, and of right entitled to the possession of the same; that the northern boundary of said lands, is a line surveyed by Joel Bailey, as per diagram marked "C," that the defendant, Page, is in possession of so much of said lands as lie between lines marked "A. B.," and "C. D." as shown by said diagram; and that the defendant claims to be the owner of the land so by him possessed, and claims that the said line marked "C. D." on said diagram "C.," is the proper line between plaintiff and defendant. The defendant denied that the line claimed by the plaintiff is the true boundary, and insists that the line marked "C. D." on said diagram "C," is the true line of boundary. The Supreme Court held that the instructions of the Surveyor-General of Wisconsin was to be the rule, and that in accordance therewith the line "between plaintiff and defendant, as ascertained by this mode of survey, falls south of that claimed by plaintiff, about two and one-half chains. It will be observed by a careful examination of the description of the found corners, as hereinbefore given, that the *quarter* section corner on the west line of section nine, and the section corner at the south-east of said section, are corners found and identified on the examination, and the same were recognized on the re-survey."

Field-notes of government surveyors.—In construing a patent from the United States which describes the land granted by the number of the section, township and range, courts will look to the plat and field-notes made and returned to the Surveyor General's office by the government surveyors, in order to locate the land. 11 Ill. R., (McClintock v. Rogers.)

The lines actually run upon the ground, by the original surveyor, become the true external boundaries of all the lands sold by the government, if they can be ascertained by reference to the monuments erected upon the land by the surveyor.

The monuments erected upon the land are facts.—The field-notes and plat returned by the surveyor indicating course, distance, and quantity, are but descriptions which serve to assist in ascertaining those facts. 11 Ill. R., (McClintock v. Rogers.)

What established monuments show.—Established monuments not only serve to show with certainty the boundary of the tract upon which they are erected, but may be resorted to, in connection with field-notes and other evidence, to fix the original location of a monument or line which has become lost or obliterated by time, accident, or design.

The law cannot satisfactorily determine, in all cases, whether course or distance shall control, when they do not correspond; this must be determined by concurring testimony, and the circumstances of each particular case. The one that convinces the judgment most must be selected. The monuments erected at the two extremities of a township line, are not entitled to a more controlling influence, in determining the actual location of the intermediate line, than the section corners established along the line, if they can be found.

Where a township line is lost, the monuments of the adjacent sections may be resorted to for the purpose of ascertaining where the lost line was actually run by the original surveyor. A township line is not necessarily straight in all cases; a deflected line, if established by satisfactory evidence, will be adopted by the court as the true line originally run by the government surveyor. Quantity, although the least reliable, and the last to be resorted to, of all descriptions in a grant or deed, in determining the boundaries of the premises conveyed, may sometimes be considered in corroboration of other evidence. 11 Ill. R., (McClintock v. Rogers.)

Field-notes and plat.—The directions of the statute relating to mile-posts, and other monuments, and the making of field-notes and plats, are directory; and a failure to comply therewith by the surveyor, will not render the proceedings void. 24 Iowa, 362; 9 Iowa, 583.

VI. RE-SURVEY OF CITY AND TOWN PLATS.

The re-survey of city and town plats is provided for in Chapter 54, of the acts of the 15th General Assembly, as follows:

Where any town plat is lost, same may be re-surveyed.—SECTION 1. *Be it enacted by the General Assembly of the State of Iowa*, That in all cases where the original town-plat of any city, town, or village of this state, or any of the additions to any such city, town, or village, shall have been heretofore or may hereafter be lost, mislaid, or destroyed after the sale and conveyance of any sub-division, block, or lot thereof, by the original owner or proprietor, to any person or persons, before the same shall have been recorded, it shall be lawful for any three persons interested in such city, town, village, or addition thereto, to have such original city, town, village, or addition to any such city, town, or village re-surveyed and re-platted, and such plat made a matter of record as hereinafter set forth: *Provided*, That in no case shall such re-plat be made a matter of record without the consent in writing, indorsed thereon, of the original owner or proprietor of such city, town, village, or addition thereto, if he be alive and his residence known to those who desire such re-plat recorded.

Duty of county surveyor.—SEC. 2. The county surveyor of any county of this state in which is situate any such city, town, village, or addition thereto as contemplated in section one of this act, is hereby authorized, empowered, and upon payment to him of his legal fees by the persons interested, required to re-survey any such city, town, village, or addition thereto, and shall make out a plat of such city, town, village, or addition so re-surveyed, which plat shall in all respects, as near as possible, conform to the original lines of said city, town, village, or any addition thereto, that may be re-surveyed, and it shall in all respects be made out as required by section 559 of the code. And in order to the perfect completion of such re-survey and plat, the surveyor is empowered and authorized to subpœna witnesses, administer oaths, and *to* take evidence touching said original plat, lines, sub-divisions of said city, town, village, or addition thereto sought to be surveyed and re-platted; also as to whether the original proprietor be dead or living, and touching all things necessary to enable him to accurately establish the lines and boundaries of the said city, town, village or addition thereto, and the various sub-divisions thereof: *Provided*, That in all cases, before any such re-survey shall be made, the county surveyor of the proper county shall give four weeks' notice in some newspaper published in the county, if there be any, of such contemplated re-survey and, in case there is no such paper published in the county, then by posting up four written notices in four of the most public places in the county, one of which shall be in said district proposed to be re-surveyed.

Surveyor to certify to plat.—SEC. 3. When the surveyor shall have completed said plat, as hereinbefore contemplated, he shall attach his certificate thereto, to the effect that said plat is a just, true, and accurate plat of said city, town, village, or addition so surveyed by him; and the said plat and certificate thereto shall be filed for record in the office of the recorder of deeds of the proper county, and from the date of such filing it shall be regarded and treated, in all courts of law and equity in this state, as though the same had been made by the original owners or proprietors of said lands so re-surveyed and re-platted: *Provided*, That any person or persons deeming themselves aggrieved by said re-platting may at any time, within six months from the date of filing said plat for record, commence action by bill in chancery in the circuit or district court against the persons employing the surveyor as aforesaid and setting up their causes of complaint, and asking that said record be canceled.

VII. FEES OF THE COUNTY SURVEYOR.

The Code provides as follows:

SECTION 3800. The county surveyor is entitled to charge and receive the following fees:

For each day's service actually performed in traveling to and from the place where any survey is to be made, and for making the same and return thereof, three dollars;

For certified copy of the plat or field-notes, twenty-five cents.

In addition to which, as we have already seen, he is entitled to four dollars a day, when engaged in laying out and changing highways.

CHAPTER XXXVI.

THE CORONER.

I. ANTIQUITY OF THE OFFICE, AND HIS DUTY.

The office of coroner is of equal antiquity as that of sheriff, and, like the sheriff, his powers were both judicial and ministerial.

His principal duty.—His principal duty now consists in inquiring, when any person is killed or dies suddenly, concerning the manner and cause of his death. His ministerial acts are only as the sheriff's substitute.

Provisions of the Code.—The Code provides:

May act as Sheriff.—SECTION 349. It is the duty of the coroner to perform all the duties of the sheriff when there is no sheriff, and in cases where exception is taken to the sheriff, as provided in the next section.

Serve process.—SEC. 350. In all proceedings in the courts of record, where it appears from the papers that the sheriff is a party to the action; or where, in any action commenced or about to be commenced, an affidavit is filed with the clerk of the court, stating that the sheriff and his deputy are absent from the county, and are not expected to return in time to perform the service needed; or stating a partiality, prejudice, consanguinity, or interest, on the part of the sheriff, the clerk or court shall direct process to the coroner, whose duty it shall be to execute it in the same manner as if he were sheriff.

SEC. 351. When there is no sheriff, deputy sheriff, or coroner, qualified to serve legal process, the clerk of the court may, by writing under his hand and the seal of the court certifying the above fact, appoint any suitable person specially in each case to execute such process, who shall be sworn, but he need not give bond, and his return shall be entitled to the same credit as the sheriff's when the appointment is attached thereto.

Inquest.—SEC. 352. The coroner shall hold an inquest upon the dead bodies of such persons only as are supposed to have died by unlawful means. When he has notice of the dead body of a person supposed to have died by unlawful means, found or being in his county, he is required to issue a warrant to a constable of his county, requiring him to summon forthwith three electors of the county to appear before the coroner at a time and place named in the warrant.

Warrant.—SEC. 353. The warrant may be in substance as follows:

STATE OF IOWA, }
. . . . County. }

To any constable of the said county:—In the name of the state of Iowa you are hereby required to summon forthwith three electors of your county, to appear before me at [name the place,] at [name the day and hour, or say forthwith], then and there to hold an inquest on the dead body of . . . . , there lying, and find by what means he died.

Witness my hand this . . . day of . . . , A. D. 18 . .

A B, Coroner of . . . county.

Service.—SEC. 354. The constable shall execute the warrant, and make return thereof at the time and place named.

Jurors.—SEC. 355. If any juror fails to appear, the coroner shall cause the proper number to be summoned or returned from the bystanders, immediately, and proceed to empanel them and administer the following oath in substance:

"You do solemnly swear (or affirm) that you will diligently inquire, and true presentment make, when, how, and by what means the person whose body lies here dead came to his death, according to your knowledge and the evidence given."

Subpœnas: contempt.—SEC. 356. The coroner may issue subpœnas within his county for witnesses, returnable forthwith, or at such time and place as he shall therein direct, and witnesses shall be allowed the same fees as in cases before a justice of the peace, and the coroner has the same authority to enforce the attendance of witnesses, and to punish them and jurors for contempt in disobeying his process as a justice of the peace has when his process issues in behalf of the state.

Oath.—SEC. 357. An oath shall be administered to the witnesses in substance as follows:

"You do solemnly swear that the testimony which you shall give to this inquest, concerning the death of the person here lying dead, shall be the truth, the whole truth, and nothing but the truth."

Testimony.—SEC. 358. The testimony shall be reduced to writing under the coroner's order, and subscribed by the witnesses.

Verdict.—SEC. 359. The jurors having inspected the body, heard the testimony, and made all needful inquiries, shall return to the coroner their inquisition in writing, under their hands in substance as follows, and stating the matters in the following form suggested, as far as found:

STATE OF IOWA, }
. . . County. }

An inquisition holden at . . . , in . . . county, on the . . . day of . . . , A. D. 18 . , before . . . . , coroner of the said county, upon the body of . . . . , (or a person unknown) there lying dead, by the jurors whose names are hereto subscribed. The said jurors upon their oaths do say [here state when, how, by what person, means, weapon, or accident, he came to his death, and whether feloniously.]

In testimony whereof the said jurors have hereunto set their hands, the day and year aforesaid:

[which shall be attested by the coroner.]

Kept secret.—SEC. 360. If the inquisition find that a crime has been committed on the deceased, and name the person whom the jury believe has committed it, the inquest shall not be made public until after the arrest directed in the next section.

Arrest.—SEC. 361. If the person charged be present, the coroner may order his arrest by an officer or any other person present, and shall then make a warrant requiring the officer or other person to take him before a justice of the peace.

Warrant.—SEC. 362. If the person charged be not present, and the coroner believes he can be taken, the coroner may issue a warrant to the sheriff and constables of the county, requiring them to arrest the person and take him before a justice of the peace.

Same.—SEC. 363. The warrant of a coroner in the above case shall be of equal authority with that of a justice of the peace, and when the person charged is brought before the justice, such justice shall cause an information to be filed against him, and the same proceedings shall be had as in other cases under information, and he shall be dealt with as a person held under an information in the usual form.

Form of.—SEC. 364. The warrant of the coroner shall recite substantially the transactions before him, and the verdict of the jury of inquest leading to the arrest, and such warrant shall be a sufficient foundation for the proceeding of the justice instead of an information.

Inquest: return.—SEC. 365. The coroner shall then return to the district court, the inquisition, the written evidence, and a list of the witnesses who testified material matter.

Disposition of body.—SEC. 366. The coroner shall cause the body of a deceased person which he is called to view, to be delivered to his friends if any there be, but if not, he shall cause him to be decently buried, and the expense to be paid from any property found with the body, or, if there be none, from the county treasury, certifying an account of the expenses, which, being presented to the board of supervisors, shall be allowed by them, if deemed reasonable, and paid as other claims on the county.

When no coroner.—SEC. 367. When there is no coroner, and in case of his absence or inability to act, any justice of the peace of the same county is authorized to perform the duties of coroner in relation to dead bodies, and in such case he may cause the person charged to be brought before himself by his warrant, and may proceed with him as a justice of the peace.

Surgeons.—SEC. 368. In the above inquisition by a coroner, when he or the jury deem it requisite, he may summon one or more physicians or surgeons to make a scientific examination, and shall allow in such case a reasonable compensation instead of witness fees.

Prohibited from acting as attorneys.—The provisions of the Code prohibit coroners, as well as sheriffs and constables, from appearing in court as attorney for any party, or making any writing, or process, to commence, or be in any manner used in any court, or from becoming a purchaser, either directly or indirectly, of any property by them exposed for sale. Code, sections 342, 343.

Election and qualification.—The election of the coroner takes place at the same time of the sheriff, in each odd-numbered year, and he continues in office for the same term. His mode of qualification is the same as the sheriff's, and reference may be had to the directions and forms given in considering the subject of sheriffs, for a guide to the coroner in such cases.

Liability when acting as sheriff.—When the coroner acts in the place of a sheriff, as a ministerial officer, in all cases, his duties and liabilities are the same as the sheriff's in similar cases, and reference may be had thereto by the coroner, as given in this volume.

Special coroners, when appointed.—Where the sheriff is interested, his deputy, by reason of his relation to the sheriff, is equally disqualified to act; but where the sheriff is sick, absent from the county, or prevented from acting temporarily, the deputy should serve process, and it is improper to direct it to the coroner; and when both sheriff and coroner are disqualified, absent, sick, or otherwise prevented from acting, the clerk should appoint a special coroner, and the writ may be directed to said special appointee, or if the writ has been issued before the disqualification is known, the appointment and the reason for it may be indorsed on the back of the writ, or annexed to it; but the certificate or appointment need not contain the oath of the appointee. 11 Iowa, 91.

Coroner to determine when to act.—The supposition of death by unlawful means, of course, should be reasonable, and should amount to probable cause of death by unlawful means, of which the coroner, in the exercise of his judgment, after reasonable investigation and inquiry, must determine. It is not every vague rumor or supposition of such a death by other parties that would impose on the coroner the duty of an investigation, but it would be his duty to exercise reasonable diligence, and determine for himself his duty in the premises; and he cannot hold an inquest except a body be found.

Summons, oaths, etc.—The form of the summons for the jurors in such cases, is given in the statute, as well as the oath to be administered to them, and the witnesses, and the form of their inquisition and finding in the matter.

Warrant.—The warrant for the arrest of the party found by the inquisition to be the person who has committed the deed, may be in the following form:

WARRANT OF CORONER.

No. 125.

STATE OF IOWA, }
...... County. } ss.

The State of Iowa, To any sheriff or constable of said county:

WHEREAS, the undersigned, coroner of said county, on the .... day of ...., 18...., caused to be summoned three electors of said county as jurors to hold an inquest over the dead body of ...., deceased, supposed to have died by unlawful means, and WHEREAS, said jurors, after being duly sworn, inspected said body, and having heard the testimony, returned to me their inquisition in writing under their hands on the .... day of ...., 18.., wherein they find that a crime has been committed on said deceased, and that said deceased came to his (or her) death by means of a blow on the head, with an ax, inflicted by one ...., (or, state any other means of death, caused by the party charged as found by the jurors.)

You are therefore commanded to forthwith arrest the said ...., and bring him before ...., a justice of the peace of said county, to be dealt with according to law.

Witness my hand at ...., this .... day of ...., 18...

C.... D...., *coroner of said county.*

II. FORMS OF FINDINGS ON INQUISITIONS.

The following forms will serve to guide the jurors in different cases, in stating when, how, and by what means, weapon or accident, the deceased came to his death, to be inserted in their inquisition.

FINDING IN CASE OF MURDER.

No. 126.

That on the .... day of ...., 18.., one C.... D...., at ...., in said county, did then and there, with a certain ax, (or, other instrument known or unknown,) which he, the said C.... D...., then and there held in his hands, willfully and maliciously inflict a mortal wound on the head of the said E.... F...., of which said mortal wound, the said E.... F.... then and there instantly, (or, on the .... day of ...., 18..,) died; and so the jurors aforesaid say that the said C.... D.... did, as they believe, then and there feloniously kill and murder, in the manner aforesaid, the said E.... F.....

FINDING IN CASE OF SUICIDE.

No. 127.

That the said C D, (or, person unknown), did on the .... day of ...., 18.., at the ...., in said county, voluntarily inflict a mortal wound upon the body of him, the said C D, (or, person unknown,) of which said mortal wound the said C D, (or person unknown), instantly, (or on the .... day of ...., 18..,) died.

And so the jurors aforesaid, say that the said C D, (or person unknown,) did then and there, in manner aforesaid, and at the place aforesaid voluntarily kill and murder himself.

FINDING IN CASE OF DROWNING BY ACCIDENT.

No. 128.

That on the .... day of ...., 18.., the said C D, (or person unknown,) at ...., in the county aforesaid, went into the .... river to bathe, (or state the fact, as the case may be,) and then and there casually and accidentally was drowned in the water of said river, and by means of which the said C D, (or person unknown,) then and there died, and so we the said jurors say that said C D, (or person unknown,) in the manner and by the means aforesaid, casually, accidentally and by misfortune came to his (or her) death, and not otherwise.

FINDING IN CASE OF MARKS OF VIOLENCE, AND THE PERPETRATOR UNKNOWN.

No. 129.

That on the .... day of ...., 18.., the said C D, was found lying dead on the highway in ...., in said county, (or as the case may be,) and that the body of said C D when so found as aforesaid, appeared to have been stabbed twice with some sharp instrument, (or otherwise as the case may be,) in or near the left breast, (or otherwise as the case may be,) and thereby received a mortal wound inflicted, by some person to the jurors unknown, and so the jurors aforesaid say that the said C D, (or person unknown,) came to his death by the said wounds (or injuries) appearing upon his body as aforesaid.

FINDING IN CASE OF FEMALE INFANT.

No. 130.

That the body of said female infant was found lying entirely naked and dead, in a yard of E F, in the town of ...., in said county, on the .... day of ...., 18.., (or in a barn or out-house as the case may be;) that the said body of said female infant, when so found appeared to have received an injury on the head and body, (or state such marks of violence or injury as there were;) that said female infant at the time of her death was of the age of about ...., and that the parents, or guardians of said infant are to the jurors unknown, and the said jurors say that said infant came to her death, by means of violence and injuries received as aforesaid, from some person or persons to the jury unknown, (or state any other finding of the jury.)

FINDING IN CASE OF NATURAL DEATH.

No. 131.

That the said C D, (or person unknown,) on the .... day of ...., 18.., was found lying dead on the common, (or park, or highway, or street,) in the city of ...., in said county, and that he had no marks of violence appearing on his body; and so the jurors do say that the said C D, (or person unknown,) died in a natural way and not otherwise.

The beginning and conclusion of the inquisition made by the jurors can be in the form pointed out by the statute in any of the above cases.

To be attested.—The findings thus made, in writing, should be attested by the coroner, and may be as follows:

"Attested this .... day of ...., 18..

C.... D...., *Coroner*."

III. TESTIMONY AND WITNESSES.

The statute requires the testimony to be reduced to writing, by direction of the coroner, and with the inquisition, returned by the jury to him, should be by him returned to the clerk of the District Court of the county, with a list of the material witnesses. The following forms may be used for this purpose.

FOR TAKING THE TESTIMONY BEFORE CORONER.

No. 132.

State of Iowa, ... County. } ss.

At an inquisition held at ...., in said county on the .... day of ...., 18.., before C D, coroner of said county, and E F, G H, and I J, three electors of said county, duly summoned and sworn to inquire into and a true presentment make when, how and by what means K L, (or a person unknown,) whose body lay there dead before them, came to his death, the following testimony was taken in writing by O P, by direction of said coroner to wit:

M N, of lawful age being produced, sworn and examined, testified as follows:

[Here insert in a narrative form, the testimony of the witness on the inquisition which should be subscribed and sworn to in the following form.]

M.... N....

Subscribed and sworn to by the said M N, before me this .... day of ...., 18..

C.... D...., *Coroner*.

Proceed in this manner with all the witnesses, and when completed, and the jurors have returned their inquisition in writing, attach the same to the written testimony, to which a certificate in the following form may be made and attached, and the whole returned to the clerk of the District Court as required by law.

FORM OF CERTIFICATE OF CORONER.

No. 133.

STATE OF IOWA, }
......County, } ss.

I, C D, coroner of said county, hereby certify and return, that the foregoing is the testimony of the witnesses sworn and examined before me, and the jurors aforesaid, taken at the inquisition as aforesaid, and that the inquisition hereto attached, was made by said jurors, and returned to me as aforesaid, and that M N, O P, (and the other witnesses naming them,) testified to material matter on said inquisition.

Witness my hand this .... day of ...., 18..

C.... D...., *Coroner.*

IV. THE CORONER'S FEES.

In regard to his fees the Code provides:

SECTION 3799. The coroner is entitled to charge and receive the following fee:

For a view of each body and taking and returning an inquest on same, five dollars;

For a view of each body and examination without inquest, three dollars;

For issuing subpœna, or order for a jury, twenty-five cents;

For each mile traveled to and returning from an examination or inquest ten cents;

Which fee shall be paid out of the county treasury when they cannot be obtained from the estate of the deceased;

For all other services, the same fees as are allowed sheriffs in similar cases, to be paid in like manner.

Witness, surgeons and jurors fees.—It is customary for the coroner to certify to the correctness of the claims of witnesses, surgeons, and jurors summoned on an inquisition held before him, as well as to any expenses incurred in the burial of the deceased, where no property is found on the body with which to pay these expenses; and these claims, together with the fees of the coroner duly verified, should be filed with the auditor of the county for allowance by the board of supervisors at their subsequent meeting.

It may be here remarked, that the fees of the witnesses in such cases are the same as before justices of the peace, that is, fifty cents per day, and five cents a mile each way. There seems to be no express provision of the statute for jurors fees in such case, but they should be allowed a reasonable compensation by the board, as well as the surgeon who may be summoned to examine the body.

CHAPTER XXXVII.

NOTARIES PUBLIC.

I. THE OFFICE, AND EVIDENCE.

Notaries are of very ancient origin; they were well known among the Romans, and exist in every State of Europe, particularly on the Continent. Their acts have long been respected by the custom of merchants and by the courts of all nations. They are appointed by the executive, or other appointing power, under the laws of the different States, and their duties are generally prescribed by such laws.

Act of Congress in relation to notaries.—By act of Congress, Sept. 16, 1850, it is provided: "That in all cases in which under the laws of the United States, oaths or affirmations or acknowledgments may now be taken or made before any justice, or justices of the peace of any State or Territory, such oath, affirmations or acknowledgements may be hereafter also taken, or made by or before any notary public, duly appointed in any State or territory; and when certified under the hand and official seal of such notary, shall have the same force and effect as if taken or made by or before such justice, or justices of the peace. And all laws, and parts of laws, for punishing perjury or subornation of perjury, committed in any such oaths or affirmations, when taken or made before any such justice of the peace, shall apply to any such offense committed in any oaths or affirmations which may be taken under this act before a notary public, or commissioner, as hereinafter named: *Provided always*, That on any trial for either of these offenses, the seal and signature of the notary, shall not be deemed sufficient in themselves to establish the official character of such notary, but the same shall be shown by other and proper evidence." Minot's Statutes at Large, 458.

II. STATUTES OF IOWA—APPOINTMENT—DUTIES.

The following are the provisions of the Code in reference to Notaries Public:

For what time appointed.—SECTION 258. The governor may appoint and commission one or more notaries public in each county, and may at any time revoke such appointment. The commissions of all notaries public heretofore, or hereafter, issued prior to the fourth day of July, A. D., 1876, shall expire on that day, and commissions subsequently issued shall be for no longer period than three years, and all such commissions shall expire on the fourth day of July in the same year. The secretary of state shall, on or before the first day of June, A. D. 1876, and every three years thereafter, notify each notary when his commission will expire.

What done before commission issued.—SEC. 259. Before any such commission is delivered to the person appointed, he shall:

1. Procure a seal on which shall be engraved the words "notarial seal" and "Iowa," with his surname at length, and at least the initials of his christian name;

2. Execute a bond to the state of Iowa in the sum of five hundred dollars, conditioned for the true and faithful execution of the duties of his office, which bond shall be approved by the clerk of the district court of the proper county;

3. Write on said bond, or a paper attached thereto, his signature, and place thereon a distinct impression of his official seal;

4. File such bond with attached papers, if any, in the office of the secretary of state;

5. Remit to such secretary the fee required by law;

When the secretary of state is satisfied that the foregoing particulars have been fully complied with, he shall deliver the commission to the person appointed.

Secretary to forward copy.—SEC. 260. When the secretary of state delivers the commission to the person appointed, he shall make a certified copy thereof and forward the same to the clerk of the district court of the proper county, who shall file and preserve the same in his office, and it shall be deemed sufficient evidence to enable such clerk to certify that the person so commissioned is a notary public during the time such commission is in force.

Revocation.—SEC. 261. Should the commission of any person appointed notary public be revoked by the governor, the secretary of state shall immediately notify such person, and the clerk of the district court of the proper county, through the mail.

Powers.—SEC. 262. Each notary is invested with the powers and shall perform the duties which pertain to that office by the custom and law of merchants.

Keep record of notices sent.—SEC. 263. Every notary public is required to keep a true record of all notices given or sent by him, with the time and manner in which the same were given or sent, and the names of all the parties to whom the same were given or sent, with a copy of the instrument in relation to which the notice is served, and of the notice itself.

Vacancy: records to be deposited: when.—SEC. 264. On the death, resignation, or removal from office, of any notary, his records with all his official papers, shall, within three months therefrom, be deposited in the office of the clerk of the district court in the county for which such notary shall have been appointed; and if any notary, on his resignation or removal, neglects for three months so to deposit them, he shall be held guilty of a misdemeanor and be punished accordingly, and be liable in an action to any person injured by such neglect; and if an executor or administrator of a deceased notary willfully neglects for three months after his acceptance of that appointment, to deposit the records and papers of a deceased notary which came into his hands in said clerk's office, he shall be held guilty of a misdemeanor and punished accordingly.

Removal: resignation.—SEC. 265. If a notary remove his residence from the county for which he was appointed, such removal shall be taken as a resignation.

Duty of clerk.—SEC. 266. Each clerk aforesaid shall receive and safely keep all such records and papers of the notary in the cases above named, and shall give attested copies of them under the seal of his court, for which he may demand such fees as by law may be allowed to the notaries, and such copies shall have the same effect as if certified by the notary.

Regulations of the Executive Department.—The following regulations have been made by the Executive of the State in reference to the appointment of notaries:

STATE OF IOWA,
EXECUTIVE DEPARTMENT,
April, 1874.

The attention of those who desire the performance of specific acts by the Executive, is respectfully invited to the following regulations and usages of this department:

NOTARIAL COMMISSIONS.

I. Every application for appointment to the office of notary public should be accompanied by a recommendation stating that the applicant has proper qualifications, in point of ability and integrity, for such commission; and that he has resided in the State, and in the county in and for which he desires appointment, a sufficient length of time to entitle him to vote therein. Such recommendation should be made or indorsed by a member of the General Assembly, a State officer, a District or Circuit Judge, a District Attorney, or county officers.

II. The application may be made directly to the Governor, through the Secretary of State, and should be accompanied by the fee, $1.25. It is desired that the first or other given name be furnished in full for insertion in the commission.

III. The commission, when issued by the Governor, will be forwarded by the Secretary of State.

IV. No person can be a notary for more than one county. In case a notary public remove from the county in and for which he is or may be appointed, he is required to communicate the fact of such removal, with the date thereof, to the Secretary of State.

V. The seal of a notary must have engraved thereon his surname at length and at least the initials of his Christian name, with the words "notarial seal" and "Iowa." Lacking either of these requirements, a seal is worthless.

VI. No minor will be appointed a notary public.

VII. Upon the resignation of a notary public, or his removal from the county for which he is appointed, he will also be required, before being commissioned for another county, to transmit to the Secretary of State a certificate of the clerk of the District Court of the county from which he removes, that such notary public has made with said clerk the deposit of records and official papers required by sections 263 and 264 of the Code, or else a certificate from himself that he has done no official business demanding such record.

The mode of proceeding suggested by the statute to secure a commission as notary public, is to request the Governor of the State, by petition or otherwise, to appoint and commission the applicant as notary public in the county in which he resides.

PETITION FOR THAT PURPOSE.

No. 134.

To the Governor of the State of Iowa:

The undersigned respectfully recommend A B, of .... county, Iowa, as a person of the proper age, qualifications, ability, and integrity, for a notary public in and for .... county, where he has resided for the last .... years.

And they request that he may be appointed and commissioned as notary public in and for said county.

Witness our hands this .... day of ...., 18..

C.... D....,
E.... F....,
G.... H...., etc.

If the Governor complies.—If the Governor complies with the request, he will so advise the applicant through the Secretary of State, whereupon the applicant should procure a seal on which should be engraved the words, "Notarial Seal," and Iowa," with the surname of the applicant, and, at least, the initials of his Christian name.

BOND OF NOTARY PUBLIC.

No. 135.

Know all men by these Presents :

That we, ..., as principal, and ...., as sureties, of the county of ...., in the State of Iowa, are held and firmly bound unto the county of ...., in said State, in the penal sum of five hundred dollars, for the payment of which sum well and truly to be made, we bind ourselves, jointly and severally, firmly by these presents.

Dated the .... day of ...., A. D. 18..

The above bond is to be void upon condition that as notary public, of said State in and for said county, the said ...., will render a true account of his office, and of his doings therein, to the proper authority, when required thereby or by law; that he will promptly pay over to the person or officer entitled thereto, all money which may come into his hands by virtue of his office;

that he will promptly account for all balances of money remaining in his hands at the termination of his office; that he will hereafter exercise all reasonable diligence and care in the preservation and lawful disposal of all money, books, papers, securities or other property appertaining to his said office, and deliver them to his successor or to any other person authorized to receive the same, and that he will faithfully and impartially, without fear, favor, fraud or oppression, discharge all the other duties now or hereafter required of his office by law.

Witness our hands on the day and in the year above written.

....,
....,
....,
....

The above bond is approved, as to form and manner of execution, and also of the sureties thereto.

J.... C.... D....,
Clerk of the District Court of said county.

STATE OF IOWA, }
.... County. } ss.

I, ..., do solemnly swear that I will support the Constitution of the United States and the Constitution of the State of Iowa, and that to the best of my knowledge and ability, I will perform all the duties of the office of notary public of said State, in and for .... county, as provided by the condition of my bond above written. ....

Subscribed and sworn to before me this .... day of ...., A. D. 18.. ....

The seal to be impressed on the bond.—On such bond duly approved should be made a distinct impression of the seal of the notary, and the written signature of the applicant, and the same filed with the Secretary of State, and his fees paid.

Fees in such cases, are as follows:
For the commission, $1.25.

III. LAW RELATING TO HIS DUTIES—DEPOSITIONS—PROTEST, ETC.

By the statute, the notary is invested with the powers, and may perform the duties which pertain to that office by the custom and law of merchants. The most common of these duties are to administer oaths, take depositions, take the acknowledgements of deeds and other instruments in writing, and protest notes, bills of exchange, etc.

Days of grace.—Bills of exchange and promissory notes, negotiable or otherwise, payable at a certain day, are by the custom and law of merchants, not payable until the third day after the day expressed for payment. These are called "days of grace," and no action can be brought on these instruments until they have expired.

The owner of negotiable paper may hold the same so long as he pleases, and not lose his claim against the maker of a note, or the acceptor of a bill, unless he is cut off by the statute of limitations.

But in order to hold the indorser of a note, he must have notice as required by the statute, of a demand and non-payment of the note, or the protest thereof for non-payment, and the drawer and indorser of a bill must have notice of the non-acceptance or non-payment of the same, or of the protest thereof for non-acceptance or non-payment as required by law.

The Code provides in reference to notice, demand, and protest as follows:

GUARANTEE.

Definition of.—SECTION 2089. The blank indorsement of an instrument for the payment of money, property, or labor, by a person not a payee, indorsee, or assignee thereof, shall be deemed a guarantee of the performance of the contract.

Guarantor: how charged.—SEC. 2090. To charge such guarantor, notice of non-payment by the principal must be given within a reasonable time; but the guarantor is chargeable without notice, if the holder show affirmatively that the guarantor has received no detriment from the want of notice.

SEC. 2091. A guarantor, as contemplated in the two preceding sections, is also liable to the action of an indorsee, assignee, or payee, if due diligence in the institution and prosecution of a suit against the maker or his representative has been used.

GRACE—PROTEST.

Grace.—SEC. 2092. Grace shall be allowed upon negotiable bills or notes payable within this state, according to the principles of the law merchant; and notice of non-acceptance or non-payment, or both, of said instruments shall be required according to the rules and principles of the commercial law.

Demand.—SEC. 2093. A demand at any time during the days of grace, will be sufficient for the purpose of charging the indorser.

Holidays: protests made on preceding day.—SEC. 2094. The first day of the week, called Sunday; the first day of January, the fourth day of July; the twenty-fifth day of December; and any day appointed or recommended by the governor of this state, or by the president of the United States, as a day of fasting or thanksgiving, shall be regarded as holidays for all purposes relating to the presenting for payment or acceptance, and the protesting and giving notice of the dishonor of bills of exchange, bank checks, and promissory notes; and any bank or mercantile paper falling due on any of the days above named, shall be considered as falling due on the preceding day.

Notice of protest: how served.—SEC. 2095. In case of a demand of payment of any promissory note, bill of exchange, or other commercial paper, by a notary public, and a refusal by the maker, drawer, or acceptor, as the case may be, the notary making said demand may inform the indorser, or any party to be charged, if in the same town or township, by notice deposited in the nearest post-office to the parties to be charged on the day of demand, and no other notice shall be necessary to charge said party.

Damages for non-acceptance or non-payment.—SEC. 2096. The rate of damages to be allowed and paid upon the non-acceptance or non-payment of bills of exchange, drawn or indorsed in this state, when damage is recoverable, shall be as follows: If the bill be drawn upon a person at a place out of the United States, or in California, Oregon, Nevada, or any of the Territories, five per cent upon the principal specified in the bill, with interest on the same from the time of the protest; if drawn upon a person at any other place in the United States, other than in this state, three per cent with interest.

Mode of computing time.—If a bill or note is payable in a certain number of days from date, sight, or demand, in counting these days, the day of the date, sight, or demand, is excluded, and the day on which it falls due is included. A note, therefore, dated on the first day of May and payable in sixty days, would, with the days of grace, become due on the third of July.

Demand, when made.—The demand may be made at any time on the day the bill or note falls due. If a note or bill is payable on demand, the demand should be made in a reasonable time, and if no time is expressed, it is held payable on demand. But, under our statutes, it will be observed that a demand during the days of grace, at any time, is sufficient to charge an indorser.

Where the demand should be made.—The demand should be made at the place of business of the maker, or acceptor, within business hours, or at the place of payment, where it is expressed; and where he has no place of business, it should be made at his dwelling house. If a place of payment is designated, a presentment there to any person, or at the door of the house, if it be closed up, is sufficient.

If the payer has absconded, demand should be made at his last place of residence.

Where a bill or note is not presented for payment, or not presented at the time required by law, all the parties but the maker or acceptor are discharged.

The presentation may be made by any party, but in case of a foreign bill, there should be a regular protest by a notary, and usually all bills, if not accepted, and all bills and notes, if unpaid, are protested.

The bill, in case of protest, should be presented by the notary himself.

Notice of the presentment and demand of payment, and non-payment of a bill or note, should be given to all indorsers of the same, that it is desired to hold responsible therefor, but notice of protest is sufficient notice of demand and refusal.

The notice and protest should describe the bill or note sufficiently to identify it. No copy of the protest need be sent to indorsers, but information of the protest should be given them.

The statute provides that the service of notice, where the party to be charged resides in the same town, may be made by depositing the same in the nearest postoffice to the party on the day of the demand. In other cases the notice may be deposited on the day of the demand in the postoffice, and directed to the party to be charged, at the nearest postoffice to his residence, or to the place of his residence, or to the place where the notary, after due diligence and inquiry, deems his place of residence to be. Notice may be given to any or all of the indorsers, and may be given in all cases personally by the notary.

If the party it is desired to charge is dead, notice should be given to his personal representatives.

If the indorser directs notice to be sent to any place, it may be so sent, and it may be presumed, in the absence of any knowledge that can be obtained as to the residence of the party to be charged, after due diligence to obtain the same, that his residence is at the place where it was drawn or indorsed, and the notice may be so directed.

A demand at any time during the days of grace will be sufficient, under the statute, to charge an indorser.

The following forms may be used by the notary on protest:

PROTEST OF A NOTE FOR NON-PAYMENT.

No. 136.

STATE OF IOWA, }
...... County, } ss.

I, G W, a notary public of said State, within and for said county, hereby certify, that at the request of C D, [insert the name of the holder of the note,] I did on the .... day of ...., 18.., present for payment the promissory note hereto attached, to E F, the maker of said note at his place of business in the city of ...., in said county, and demanded payment thereof which was refused; and thereupon at the request of the said C D, I did protest and by these presents do solemnly and publicly protest, as well against the maker and indorsers of said note, as against all others whom it may concern for exchange, costs, damages already incurred and to be hereafter incurred for failure to pay the same.

And I do further certify, that on the day aforesaid, notice of the protest aforesaid, was given to G H and I J, indorsers thereon personally (or by depositing said notice in the post-office, postage paid, at said city of ...., and directed severally to each of said indorsers at the place of residence of each respectively, or in case the indorsers reside in the same town; by depositing the notice thereof in the post-office in said city, postage paid, and directed to the said indorsers, residents of said city; said post-office being the nearest post-office to the said parties.)

Witness my hand and notarial seal this .... day of ...., 18..

G.... W...., *Notary Public.*

FEES:—

For protest $0.75.
For register protest .50.

ANOTHER FORM OF PROTEST ON NON-PAYMENT.

No. 137.

STATE OF IOWA, }
...... County. } ss.

I, A B, a notary public of said State within and for said county, do hereby certify that at the request of C D, [insert the name of the holder of the note,] [*] I did on the .... day of ...., 18.., present for payment the promissory note hereto attached, at the banking house of ...., in the city of ...., in said county, where the same is made payable, and demanded payment thereof, which was refused; and thereupon, [conclude as in the last form.]

No. 138. ANOTHER FORM OF PROTEST ON NON-PAYMENT.

STATE OF IOWA, }
.... County. } ss.

I, A B, (same as in last form to [*]and then add,) I did on the .... day of ...., 18.., for the purpose of presenting and demanding payment of the promissory note (or bill,) hereto attached make diligent search and inquiry for E F, the maker of said note, (or drawee of said bill,) and his place of business, and dwelling house in the city of ...., in said county where said note (or bill,) is made payable; but was unable to find the said E F, (or the drawee,) or his place of business, or his dwelling house, and was therefore unable to make a demand of the payment of the same.

And I do further certify, [concluding as in form No. 136, with the requisite change to suit the facts where the maker or drawee cannot be found.]

No. 139. ANOTHER COMMON FORM OF PROTEST.

STATE OF IOWA, }
...... County. }

Be it known, that on this ... day of ...., A. D., 18.., I ...., a notary public in and for said county and State, duly appointed, commissioned and qualified, at the request of ...., the holder of the original .... presented the annexed .... at ...., in the town of ...., Iowa, to .... and demanded .... which was refused ....

Whereupon, I, the said notary, at the request aforesaid, have protested, and do solemnly protest, as well against the .... and indorser of said .... as against all others concerned therein, for exchange, re-exchange, and all costs, charges, damages and interest, suffered, by reason of the non.... of said original ......

And I do further certify, that on the same day and year above written, I gave notice to the .... and indorser of said ... of the non.... of the same, in writing and print, and put into the post-office at ...., Iowa, postage pre-paid, as follows, to-wit:

A notice for................ directed to ....
A notice for................ directed to ....
A notice for................ directed to ....
A notice for .... directed to ....
A notice for................ directed to ....
A notice for................ directed to ....

Each of the above named places being the reputed places of residence of the persons to whom the notices were respectively directed.

In witness whereof, I have hereunto subscribed my name and affixed my seal of office. ...., *Notary Public.*

NOTARY'S FEES.
For protest $0.75.
For recording .50.

NOTICE OF PROTEST FOR NON-ACCEPTANCE.

No. 140.

To A.... B....:

Notice is hereby given that your bill for $...., drawn at sight, (or .... days from sight,) on C D, has this day been protested by me, for non-acceptance (or, non-payment). Witness my hand and notarial seal.

E.... F....,
Notary Public in and for .... county, Iowa.

NOTICE OF PROTEST FOR NON-PAYMENT OF NOTE.

No. 141.

To A.... B....:

Notice is hereby given that the note executed by you to C D, for $ ...., dated ...., 18..., and payable .... days after date at the banking house of ...., in ...., Iowa, and indorsed by E F, and G H, has this day been protested by me for non-payment.

Dated at ...., this .... day of ...., 18..

Witness my hand and notarial seal.

I.... J....,
Notary Public for Iowa, in and for .... county.

ANOTHER FORM OF NOTICE.

No. 142.

$..... ...., IOWA, ..., A. D. 18..

To ....:

SIR:—Take notice, that on this .... day of .... A. D. 18.., at the request of the holder thereof, I protested for non-..... a .... of the following description, to-wit: Dated ...., 18..; amount, $....; payable ....; drawn by ....; in favor of ....; drawn on ....; made by ....; indorsed by ...., ... And that ...., the holder.. thereof, look.. to you for payment of the same, with all costs, damages, etc.

...., *Notary Public.*

IV. HIS RECORD.

The notary should keep a record of all notices given or sent by him, with the time and manner in which the same were given or sent, and the names of the parties to whom the same were given or sent, with a copy of all instruments in relation to which the notice is served, and of the notice itself.

This record should embrace the certified protest, notices, and note, bill, or other instrument protested. A book with the most common printed forms for this purpose, might be procured by the notary for greater convenience, in which forms, say Nos. 139 and 142, could be printed.

Acknowledgements and evidence.—The Code provides that notaries may administer oaths, and take and certify the acknowledgement of instruments in writing; Code, Secs. 277 and 1955; and that the usual protest of a notary public without proof of his signature or notarial seal, is *prima facie* evidence of what it recites concerning the dishonor and notice therof of a bill of exchange or promissory note, and that a copy from his record, properly certified to by him, shall receive such faith and credit as it is entitled to by the law and custom of merchants. Code, Sec. 3668.

A notary public is a public officer, and when he is acting as such *de facto*, though not *de jure*, his acts cannot be collaterally assailed. 14 Iowa, 464.

The official acts of a notary should be authenticated by a seal and signature; and when the *jurat* of an affidavit is not evidenced both by the seal and signature of the notary before whom it purports to have been made, it is fatally defective. 10 Iowa, 305, 593.

V. NOTARIES' FEES.

The Code provides for his fees as follows:

SECTION 3801. Notaries public shall be entitled to charge and receive the following fees:

For every protest of a bill or note, seventy-five cents;

For registering any protest, fifty cents;

For being present at a demand, tender, or deposit, and noting the same, fifty cents;

For administering an oath, five cents;

For certificate under seal, twenty-five cents;

For certifying to the same under his official seal, twenty-five cents;

For other services, the same fees as are allowed justices of the peace for similar services.

PART SECOND.

OF TOWNSHIP OFFICERS.

CHAPTER I.

TOWNSHIP OFFICERS.

I. ELECTION, QUALIFICATION AND DUTIES.

The provisions of the Code relating thereto are as follows:

Officers of.—SECTION 389. In each township there shall be elected three trustees, one clerk, one assessor, two constables, and two justices of the peace, but where a city or incorporated town is situate in a township, the trustees of the township may order the election of one or two additional justices and constables, and at least one justice and constable shall reside within the limits of such city or town.

When township contains a city or town.—SEC. 390. In any township in which is situate any city or incorporated town, two township assessors shall be elected, one by the voters of said township residing without the corporate limits of such city or town, at the general election, and the other by the voters thereof residing within such limits at the municipal election in such city or town, and each in the discharge of his duties as assessor shall be confined to that portion of his township in which he is elected as hereinbefore provided; and said city or town assessor shall hold his office for one year from the first of January next ensuing.

Officers elected annually.—SEC. 591. Three township trustees, a township clerk, one assessor, and one highway supervisor for each highway district in each civil township in the State, shall be chosen by the qualified voters of each township at the general election annually, and shall hold their offices for the term of one year.

Additional justices and constables.—SEC. 592. One or two additional justices of the peace and one or two additional constables may be elected in each township if the trustees so direct, by posting up notices of the same in three of the most public places in the township, at least ten days before election.

Justices and constables considered county officers.—SEC. 593. Justices of the peace and constables shall be considered as county officers under the provisions of this Title, but they shall be voted for by the voters of their respective townships.

Refusing to serve.—SEC. 394. Any person elected to a township office and refusing to qualify and serve, shall forfeit the sum of five dollars, which may be recovered by action in the name of the county for the use of the school fund in the county, but no person shall be compelled to serve as a township officer two terms in succession.

CHAPTER II.

TOWNSHIP TRUSTEES.

I. THEIR POWERS AND DUTIES GENERALLY.

The provisions of the Code relating thereto are as follows:

To designate place of holding elections.—SECTION 391. The trustees shall designate the place where elections will be held; and whenever a change is made from the usual place of holding elections in the township, notice of such change shall be given by posting up notices thereof in three public places in the townships, ten days prior to the day on which the election is to be held.

Record to be kept.—SEC. 392. They shall cause a record to be kept of all their proceedings.

The trustees: what they are.—SEC. 393. The township trustees are the overseers of the poor, fence viewers, and the township board of equalization and board of health, and shall have charge of all cemeteries within the limits of their township, dedicated to public use, when the same is not controlled by other trustees or incorporated bodies.

II. POWERS AND DUTIES, AS OVERSEERS OF THE POOR.

The provisions of the Code, relating to their duties and powers as overseers of the poor, are as follows:

Who liable to maintain.—SECTION 1330. The father, mother, and children of any poor person who is unable to maintain himself by work, shall, jointly or severally, relieve or maintain such poor person in such manner as may be approved by the trustees of the township where such poor person may be; but these officers shall have no control unless the poor person has applied for aid.

May apply to court for order.—SEC 1333. Upon the failure of such relatives so to relieve or maintain a poor person who has made application for relief, the township trustees may apply to the circuit court of the county where such poor person resides, for an order to compel the same, * * * *

The court may order execution.—SEC. 1341. If any person fails to render the support ordered, on the affidavit of one of the proper trustees showing the fact, the court may order execution for the amount due, rating any support ordered in kind as before assessed.

Abandoned property seized.—SEC. 1343. Whenever a father or mother abandons children, or husband abandons his wife, or wife her husband, leaving them chargeable, or likely to become chargeable, upon the public for their support, the trustees of the township where such abandoned person may be, upon application being made to them, may apply to the clerk of the circuit court or judge of any county in which the parties reside, or in which any estate of such absconding father, mother, husband or wife, may be, for an order to seize the same, and, upon due proof of the above facts, the clerk of the court or judge may issue an order authorizing the trustees or the sheriff of the county to take into their possession the goods, chattels, things in action, and lands of the person absconding.

SEC. 1344. By virtue of such order, the trustees or sheriff may take the property wherever the same may be found, and shall be vested with all the right and title to the personal property, and to the rents of the real property, which the person absconding had at the time of his departure.

When affecting real estate.—SEC. 1345. Such order, when affecting any real estate, may be entered in the incumbrance book, and all sales, leases, and transfers of any such property, real and personal, made by the person after the issuing and entry of the order shall be void.

Inventory of.—SEC. 1346. The trustees or sheriff shall immediately make an inventory of the property so seized by them, and return the same, together with the proceedings, to the court, there to be filed.

Warning to depart.—SEC. 1355. Persons coming from other states or counties who are, or of whom it is apprehended that they will become county charges, may be prevented from obtaining a settlement in a county by warning them to depart from the same or any township thereof, and thereafter they shall not acquire a settlement except by the requisite residence for one year uninterrupted by another warning.

How given and served.—SEC. 1356. Such warning shall be in writing, and may be served upon the order of the trustees of the township, or of the board of supervisors, by any person; and such person shall make a return of his doings thereon to the board of supervisors; and, if not made by a sworn officer, it must be verified by affidavit.

Removal when settlement is in another county.—SEC. 1357. When a poor person applying for relief in one county has a settlement in another, he may be removed to the county of his settlement, if he be able to be removed, upon the order of the trustees of the township or board of supervisors of the county where he applied for relief, and delivered to any officer charged with the oversight of the poor in the county where his settlement is, giving written notice of the fact to the county auditor; or the trustees of the township, or board of supervisors of the county where he applied for relief, may, in their discretion, cause the auditor of the county where he has a settlement to be notified of his being a county charge, and, thereupon, it will become the duty of the latter board to order the removal of the poor person, if he is able to be removed, and, if not able, then to provide for his relief and for all expenses incurred in his behalf.

When trustees shall afford relief.—SEC. 1361. The township trustees of each township shall provide for the relief of such poor persons in their respective townships as should not in their judgment be sent to the county poor-house. But where a city of the first or second class is embraced within the limits of any township, the board of supervisors may appoint an overseer of the poor, who shall have within said city all the powers and duties conferred by this chapter on the township trustees. The relief may be either in the form of food, rent, or clothing, fuel and lights, medical attendance, or in money; and shall not exceed two dollars per week for each person for whom relief is thus furnished, exclusive of medical attendance. When medical services are rendered by order of the trustees or overseers of the poor, no more shall be charged or paid therefor than is usually charged for like services in the neighborhood where such services are rendered.

Families of Iowa soldiers.—SEC. 1362. In no case shall the widows or families of Iowa soldiers, or other persons in families requiring public relief, be sent to the county poor-house, when they can and prefer to be relieved out of the poor-house, to the extent above provided.

Expenses to be paid out of county treasury: limit.—SEC. 1363. All moneys expended as contemplated in the two preceding sections, shall be paid out of the county treasury, after the proper account rendered thereof shall have been approved by the board of supervisors of the respective counties, and in all cases the necessary appropriations therefor shall be made by the respective counties. But the board of supervisors may limit the amount of relief thus to be furnished.

Where there is no poor-house.—SEC. 1364. The trustees in each township in counties where there is no poor-house, have the oversight and care of all poor persons in their township, and shall see that they receive proper care until provided for by the board of supervisors.

Application made to trustees.—SEC. 1365. The poor must make application for relief to the trustees of the township where they may be, and if the trustees are satisfied that the applicant is in such a state of want as requires relief at the public expense, they may afford such relief as the necessities of the person may require, and shall report the case forthwith to the board of supervisors, who may continue or deny relief as they find cause.

SEC. 1366. All claims and bills for the care and support of the poor shall be certified to be correct by the proper trustees and presented to the board of supervisors, and if they are satisfied that they are reasonable and proper, they are to be paid out of the county treasury. In no case shall a trustee, or either of the trustees, or overseer of the poor, draw an order upon himself or upon either of the board, for supplies for the poor, except such trustee or supervisor has a contract to furnish such supplies.

Allowance of in certain cases.—SEC. 1367. The board may in its discretion allow and pay to poor persons who may become chargeable as paupers, and who are of mature years and sound mind, and who will probably be benefitted thereby, such sums or such annual allowance as will not exceed the charge of their maintenance in the ordinary mode.

Appeal.—SEC. 1368. If any poor person, on application to the trustees, is refused the required relief, he may apply to the board of supervisors, who, on examination into the matter, may direct the trustees to afford relief, or they may direct specific relief.

May bind the county, when.—The township trustees, in counties where there are no poor-houses, may bind the county for medical services rendered at their instance during the vacation of the said board of supervisors, to poor sick persons in the township. 24 Iowa, 211.

III. DUTY AS FENCE VIEWERS.

Provisions relating to fences.—The Code provides, that if any party neglect to repair or re-build a partition fence, or a portion thereof which he ought to maintain, the aggrieved party may complain to the fence viewers, who, after due notice to each party, are required to examine the same; and, if they determine the fence is insufficient, shall signify it in writing to the delinquent occupant of the land, and direct him to repair or re build the same within such time as they shall judge reasonable. Code, Sec. 1490.

The notice.—The notice to the respective parties may be in the following form:

No. 143.

.... County, Iowa, }
..... Township. } ss.

To S.... B.... and F.... B ...:

You are hereby notified, that on the complaint of said S B, made to the undersigned trustees of said township, of the neglect of the said F B, to re-build a partition fence, which he ought to maintain between you, as the owners of adjoining lands, on the west line of the nw. qr. of the se. qr. of sec. 12, tp. 84 n., range 4, west of the 5th P. M. We have appointed the .... day of ...., 18.., at .... o'clock, A. M., of said day, when we will meet at the place where said fence is located, and determine what shall be done in the premises, if anything.

Dated the .... day of ...., 18..

A.... B.... }
C.... D.... } *Trustees.*
E.... F.... }

TRUSTEES' CERTIFICATE.

No. 144.

.... County, Iowa, }
..... Township. } ss.

Whereas, S B and F B, are the owners of certain adjoining and inclosed lands in said township, and complaint having been made to the undersigned trustees of said township by the said S B, that the said F B has neglected to repair or re-build a partition fence on the line between their said premises, to-wit: [on the west line of the nw. qr. of the se. qr. of sec. 12, tp. 84 n, range 4, west of 5th P. M.], which he ought to maintain:

Now, therefore, the undersigned do certify, that after due

notice to said parties, we this day met and examined said partition fence, and heard the allegations of said parties in reference thereto; and do determine, that said fence is insufficient, and that it should be re-built by said F B; and the said F B is directed and required to have the same re-built, so as to make a good and lawful fence, within sixty days. And we further certify that our fees for services herein are as follows:

A.... B...., fees for one day's service, $2.00.
C.... D...., fees for one day's service, $2.00.
E.... F...., fees for one day's service, $2.00.
And have been paid by the said S. B.

Dated, ..., 18..

A ... B.... }
C ... D.... } *Trustees.*
E.... F.... }

Failure to repair or re-build.—The statute provides, in case the fence is not repaired or re-built, as required by the fence viewers, as follows:

Penalty, if order of fence viewers is not complied with.—Sec. 1491. If such fence be not repaired or re-built accordingly, the complainant may repair or re-build it, and the same being adjudged sufficient by the fence viewers, and the value thereof, with their fees, being ascertained by them and certified under their hands, the complainant may demand of the owner of the land where the fence was deficient the sum so ascertained, and, in case of neglect to pay the same for one month after demand, may recover it with one per cent a month interest by action.

CERTIFICATE OF THE SUFFICIENCY AND VALUE OF FENCE.

No. 145.

.... County, Iowa, }
.... Township. } ss.

We, the undersigned, two of the trustees and fence viewers of said township, do hereby certify, that upon the application and request of S B, the owner of inclosed lands adjoining the inclosed lands of F B, in said township, made to us to determine the sufficiency, and appraise the value of a certain partition fence, alleged to have been built by the said S B, [here describe the line, as to-wit: on the west line of the nw. qr. of se. qr. of sec. 12, tp. 84 n, range 4, west of 5th P M,] in said township, on the neglect of the said F B, who was required and directed by us, (or the fence viewers of said township,) on the .... day of ...., 18.., to repair or re-build the same within sixty days from that date, we this day proceeded to examine said fence, and do determine that said fence is a good, lawful, and sufficient fence, and that the same is of the value of .... dollars.

And we further certify that our fees for services herein, are as follows:

A.... B...., services one day........................ $2.00
C.... D...., services one day........................ 2.00

Which have been paid by the said S B.
Dated .... day of ...., 18..

A.... B ...,
C.... D .... } *Trustees.*

In case of controversy.—The Code provides in case of controversy, and other cases, as follows:

Disputes: fence viewers to settle.—SEC. 1492. When a controversy arises between the respective owners about the obligation to erect or maintain partition fences, either party may apply to the fence viewers, who, after due notice to each party, may inquire into the matter and assign to each his share thereof, and direct the time within which each shall erect or repair his share in the manner provided above.

Failure to comply.—SEC. 1493. If a party neglect to erect or maintain the part of fence assigned to him by the fence viewers, it may be erected and maintained by the aggrieved party in the manner before provided, and he shall be entitled to double the value thereof, to be recovered as directed above.

Repair.—SEC. 1494. All partition fences shall be kept in good repair throughout the year, unless the owners on both sides otherwise agree.

Who required to maintain.—SEC. 1495. No person not wishing his land inclosed and not occupying nor using it otherwise than in common, shall be compelled to contribute to erect or maintain any fence between him and an adjacent owner; but when he incloses or uses his land otherwise than in common, he shall contribute to the partition fences as in this chapter provided.

Inclosed in common: proceedings where division is sought.—SEC. 1496. When lands owned in severalty have been inclosed in common without a partition fence, and one of the owners is desirous to occupy his in severalty, and the other refuses or neglects to divide the line where the fence should be built or build a sufficient fence on his part of the line when divided, the party desiring it may have the same divided and assigned by the fence viewers, who may, in writing, assign a reasonable time, having regard for the season of the year for making the fence, and if either party neglect to comply with the decisions of the viewers, the other, after making his own part, may make the other part, and recover as directed above.

When it is desired not to inclose.—SEC. 1497. In the case mentioned in the preceding section, when one of the owners desires to throw open any portion of his field not less than twenty feet in width, and leave it uninclosed to be used in common by the public, he shall first give the other party six months' notice thereof.

When owner incloses he must pay for partition fence.—SEC. 1498. When land which has lain uninclosed is inclosed, the owner thereof shall pay for one-half of each partition fence between his lands and the adjoining lands, the value to be ascertained by the fence viewers, and if he neglect for thirty days after notice and demand to pay the same, the other party may recover as before provided; or he may, at his election, re-build and make half of the fence, and if he neglect so to do for two months after making such election he shall be liable as above provided.

Division of fence recorded.—SEC. 1499. When a division of fence between the owners of improved lands may have been made, either by fence viewers, or by agreement in writing, recorded in the office of the clerk of the township where the lands are, the owners and their heirs and assigns shall be bound thereby, and shall support them accordingly, but if any desire to lay his lands in common and not improve them adjoining the fence divide as above, the proceedings shall be as directed in the case where lands owned in severalty have been inclosed in common without a partition fence.

Definition of "owner" and "fence viewers."—SEC. 1500. In the provisions of this chapter, the term "owner" shall apply to the occupant or tenant when the owner does not reside in the county, but these proceedings will not bind the owner unless notified. The term "fence viewers" means the fence viewers of the township in which the division line in controversy is, and if that line is between two townships, and both parties live in the same, then it means the viewers of that township, but if the parties live in different townships, one viewer at least shall be taken from that of the party complained against.

Fence on another's land may be removed.—SEC. 1501. When a person has made a fence or other improvement on an inclosure, which, on afterward making division lines is found to be on land of another, and the same has occurred through mistake, such first person may enter upon the land of the other and remove his fence or other improvement and material within six months after such line has been run, upon his first paying, or offering to pay, the other party for any damage to the soil which may be occasioned thereby, and when the parties cannot agree as to the damages the fence viewers may determine them as in other cases.

SEC. 1502. But such fence or other improvement, except substantial buildings, shall not be removed if they were made or taken from the land on which they lie, until the party pays the owner the value of the timber to be ascertained by the fence viewers, nor shall a fence be removed at a time when the removal will throw open or expose the crop of the other party, but it shall be removed in a reasonable time after the crop is secured, although the above six months have passed.

Disputes: fence viewers to determine.—SEC. 1503. When any question arises between parties, other than those above stated, concerning their rights in fences, or their duties in relation to building or supporting or removing them, such question may be determined by the fence viewers upon the principles of this chapter.

Lines: fence on.—SEC. 1504. A person building a fence, may lay the same upon the line between him and the adjacent owners, so that the fence may be partly on one side and partly on the other, and the owner shall have the same right to remove it as if it were wholly on his own land.

SEC. 1505. The foregoing provisions concerning partition fences shall apply to a fence standing wholly upon one side of the division line.

Other proceedings.—SEC. 1506. The foregoing provisions of this chapter do not bar any other legal proceedings for the determination of the title to land, or the dividing line between contending owners, nor do they preclude agreements by the parties.

Lawful fence defined.—SEC. 1507. A fence made of three rails of good substantial material or three boards not less than six inches wide, and three-quarters of an inch thick, such rails or boards to be fastened in or to good substantial posts, not more than ten feet apart, where rails are used, and not more than eight feet apart, where boards are used, wire either wholly or in part, substantially built and kept in good repair, or any other kind of fence, which in the opinion of the fence viewers shall be equivalent thereto, shall be declared a lawful fence; *provided*, that the lowest or bottom rail or board shall not be more than twenty nor less than sixteen inches from the ground, and that such fence shall be fifty-four inches in height; *provided further*, that all partition fences may be made tight at the expense of the party desiring it, and such party may take from such fence the same material by him added thereto whenever he may elect; and, *provided further*, that when the owner or occupants of adjoining land use the same for the purpose of pasturing swine or sheep, each of said owners or occupants shall keep their respective share of the partition fence sufficiently tight to restrain such swine or sheep.

Where stock is restrained.—SEC. 1508. That all the provisions of this chapter in relation to partition fences, shall be alike applicable to counties or townships having restrained, or which may restrain, stock from running at large.

CERTIFICATE IN PROCEEDINGS UNDER SEC. 1492.

No. 146.

...... COUNTY, IOWA, ⎫
...... Township. ⎭ ss.

WHEREAS, a controversy exists between S B, and F B, owners of certain adjoining lands in said township, in relation to the obligation of the said F B. to erect and maintain a portion of a partition fence between said lands, on the [here describe the line as to-wit: west line of the nw. qr. of se. qr. of sec. 12, tp. 84, n. range 4, west of 5th P. M ,] in said township; and whereas the said S B, has applied to us to determine said controversy; and due notice of the meeting of the undersigned to determine the controversy, having been given to said parties:

Now therefore, we, the undersigned, trustees of said township, do hereby certify, that we this day met to determine said controversy, and proceeded to examine said premises and hear the allegations of said parties; and we do determine that said partition fence should be maintained by said parties in equal shares, and that the said S B, shall erect and maintain his share on the north half of said line; and the said F B, shall erect and maintain his share thereof on the south half of said line, and that said partition fences shall be built (or re-built or repaired,) good and lawful fences, within sixty days from this date, by the parties respectively as aforesaid.

We further certify, that our fees herein are as follows:

A.... B...., one day's service........................$2.00
C.... D...., one day's service........................ 2.00
E.... F...., one day's service........................ 2.00

All of which have been paid by the said S B.

Dated this .... day of ...., 18..

A.... B....,
C ... D...., *Trustees.*
E.... F.....

The foregoing forms will furnish the trustees a sufficient guide as fence viewers, under the statutes relating to partition fences.

The fence viewers, a local forum.—It is the policy of the law, to have all controversies relating to fences determined by the fence viewers, as a local forum. In fact there is no other remedy in such cases but through the fence viewers. 28 Iowa, 509; and 22 Iowa, 572.

Their acts should receive indulgent consideration.—The statute does not in terms require a written notice of the meeting of the fence viewers, although such notice should properly be given in writing, and proceed from the fence viewers; but where a party appears upon notice verbally given by the other party, and without objection, it is a sufficient compliance with the statute. 28 Iowa, 509; 22 Iowa, 572; 31 Iowa, 254.

A party cannot evade the statutes.—One party cannot evade the provisions of the law, by erecting his fence a few feet from the line, after a decision of the fence viewers. 28 Iowa, 509; 22 Iowa, 572; 31 Iowa, 254.

Recent exposition of the statute.—The Supreme Court has recently held, that although the decision of the fence viewers is conclusive upon matters which are within their jurisdiction, still, in order to confer jurisdiction, the fence respecting which they decide, must in fact be a partition fence. And that "they cannot conclusively bind a party by determining that to be a partition fence which in fact is not." Bills v. Belknap, May Term, 1874, (not published.)

The proceeding in this case was under Sec. 1492. There was a controversy about the obligation of the defendant to maintain a portion of a partition fence.

It is difficult to comprehend the meaning of that section, taken in connection with the other sections relating to fences and fence viewers unless the fence viewers have jurisdiction to determine a controversy in such cases; although this may involve the question whether the adjoining lands are inclosed in such a manner as to impose on the owner the obligation to erect and maintain a portion of a partition fence. The court say in the case last referred to, that the fence viewers "cannot conclude a party, using his land in common, and not wishing it inclosed, by a determination that he shall erect a partition fence." But is not this very question whether the land is "in common," or "inclosed," a fact which may well be left to this *local forum*, to determine?

IV. POWERS AND DUTIES AS A BOARD OF EQUALIZATION.

The provisions of the statute in reference thereto are as follows:

Who composes.—SECTION 829. The township trustees shall constitute a board of equalization for their respective townships, and have power to equalize the assessments of all tax-payers within the same, except in such cities and incorporated towns as elect a township assessor, in which case the city council shall be the board of equalization, and shall perform such duties in substantially the same manner, as is required of a township board of equilization, by increasing or diminishing the valuation of any piece of property, or the entire assessment of any tax-payer, as they may deem necessary for an equitable distribution of the burden of taxation upon all the property of the township; *provided*, that such boards shall keep a record of their proceedings.

Time of meeting.—SEC. 830. Said board shall meet for that purpose at the office of the township or city clerk, on the first Monday in April of each year, and continue from day to day until completed; and at such meeting they may also add to the assessment as returned by the assessor, any taxable property in the township, city, or incorporated town, not included therein, placing the same to the name of the owner, if known, and assessing the value thereof.

May correct assessment: appeals.—SEC. 831. Any person who may feel aggrieved at anything in the assessment of his property, may appear before said board of equalization in person, or by agent, at the time and place mentioned in the preceding section, and have the same corrected in such manner as to said board may seem just and equitable, and the assessors shall meet with said board and correct the assessment books as they may direct. Appeals may be taken from all boards of equalization to the circuit court of the county where the assessment is made.

Remedy for unequal assessments.—It will be seen from these provisions of the statute that it is the privilege of parties aggrieved by assessments, to apply to this board for relief. In fact, the only remedy for parties in such cases, is through this board and by appeals from its decisions.

The county board: no power to act.—The practice has been quite common, for parties conceiving themselves aggrieved by unequal assessments, to neglect application to this board, and apply to the board of supervisors of the county for a correction thereof. This course is not authorized by law; the county board of equalization have no authority to act in such cases.

The county board should refuse to act in such cases, for beside the want of authority, it involves much trouble and confusion in the proceedings for the collection of taxes; especially after the action of the county board of equalization, required to be had at their June meeting in each year, and after the county auditor has transmitted to the Auditor of State an abstract thereof, which he is required to do before the third Monday of June in each year.

For, thereupon, the State board of equalization, at their July meeting, equalize the assessments among the several counties of the State, and the several county auditors are required to correct the assessments of their counties in accordance with the action of the State board, and transcribe the corrected assessments into a suitable book; after which the county board should levy thereon the requisite taxes, which they are required to do at their September meeting, and thereupon the county auditor is required to deliver these books to the county treasurer for collection of the taxes, on or before the first day of November in each year, and at the same time he is required to send the Auditor of State a certified statement showing the aggregate valuation of the several kinds of property, and the aggregate amount of each separate tax, as shown by the tax book, when each county is then charged with the amount of tax levied for State purposes.

After all, or any, of these various proceedings for the collection of taxes, it will cause trouble and extra labor to change the assessments of individuals who may be aggrieved, and which must be apparent to any one who comprehends the revenue system of the State, in all its relations and complications.

V. POWERS AND DUTIES AS A BOARD OF HEALTH.

The provisions of the Code in relation thereto are as follows:

Board of health.—SECTION 415. The township trustees shall have power to make whatever regulations they deem necessary for the protection of the public health, and respecting nuisances, sources of filth and causes of sickness within their respective townships; *provided*, that their jurisdiction as such board shall not extend to any city or incorporated town situated therein.

Regulations published.—SEC. 416. Notice shall be given of all regulations made, by publishing the same in a newspaper published in the township, or, where there is no newspaper, by posting in five public places therein.

Power: how executed.—SEC. 417. The trustees may order the owner or occupant, at his own expense, to remove any nuisance, source of filth, or cause of sickness found on private property within such time as they deem reasonable, and if such person neglects to do so he shall forfeit a sum of not exceeding twenty-five dollars for every day during which he knowingly permits such nuisance or cause of sickness to remain after the time prescribed for the removal thereof. The order shall be in writing, and served by any constable of the town in the usual way of serving notices in civil suits. If the owner or occupant fails to comply with such order, the trustees may cause the nuisance, source of filth, or cause of sickness to be removed, and all expenses incurred thereby shall be paid by such owner or occupant.

Use means necessary.—SEC. 418. The trustees shall have power to employ all such persons as shall be necessary to carry into effect the regulations adopted and published according to the powers vested in the trustees and to fix their compensation; to employ physicians in case of poverty, and to take such general precautions and actions as they may deem necessary for the public health.

Violation: punishment.—SEC. 419. Any person who shall willfully violate any of the regulations so made and published by the trustees, shall be guilty of a misdemeanor, and upon conviction thereof shall be subject to a fine or imprisonment, such fine not to exceed one hundred dollars, and such imprisonment, not to exceed thirty days.

Expenses: how paid.—SEC. 420. All expenses, now or hereafter incurred by the trustees of a township in the exercise of the powers heretofore or herein conferred, shall be borne by the township. The trustees shall certify the amount required to pay such expenses to the board of supervisors of the county, and that board shall, at the time it levies the general taxes, and in addition thereto, levy on the property of such township a sufficient tax to pay the amount so certified by the trustees. The tax so levied shall be collected by the county treasurer with the other taxes, and be by him paid over to the township clerk.

The regulations.—The regulations provided for, should be prepared in the form of rules or ordinances, and cover all the ground deemed requisite and necessary, for carrying out the object of the board; and on their adoption by the board, should be entered with all other actions of the board, on the records to be kept by the township clerk, and also published or posted as required by law.

Certificate of expenses.—The certificate of the amount required to pay the expenses of the board, may be in the following form:

No. 147.

CERTIFICATE OF TRUSTEES.

...... COUNTY,
.... Township. } ss.

To the Board of Supervisors, of .... county, Iowa:

We, the undersigned, trustees of said township, hereby certify to the board of supervisors of said county, that we, as a board of health of said township, have made regulations for the protection of the public health of said township, and that the expenses now and hereafter to be incurred in the exercise of our powers as such board of health, is $....; and we request you at the time of the levy of the general taxes, and in addition thereto, to levy on the property of said township, a sufficient amount to pay said sum.

Dated .... day of ...., 18..

A.... B ...,
C.... D...., } *Trustees.*
E.... F.....

VI. POWER AND DUTY TO FILL VACANCIES.

The statutes in relation thereto provide:

In office of justice.—SECTION 794. Whenever a vacancy occurs in the office of a justice of the peace or a constable more than thirty days prior to any general election, the county auditor shall immediately notify the clerk of the township in which the vacancy exists, and the township clerk, within five days after receiving such notice, shall notify each of the trustees of his township in writing, fixing the time and place that they shall meet for the purpose of filling such vacancy by appointment. Such notice may be served by any constable of the township, and shall be served at least five days prior to such meeting.

Trustees to appoint: qualification.—SEC. 795. The trustees shall meet in accordance with such notice, and fill such vacancy, and in five days after such appointment has been made, the township clerk shall record it in the township record book, and shall cause a notice to be served upon the person so appointed, informing him of his appointment, by any constable in the township in the manner prescribed by law for the service of notices, and any person so appointed and notified, shall qualify within ten days after such notice has been served upon him. The auditor may approve of the bond of a justice of the peace and constable so appointed, by the recommendation of the sufficiency of the sureties upon such bond, signed by any member of the board of supervisors.

VII. POWERS AND DUTIES RELATING TO HIGHWAYS.

The Code provides, relating thereto, as follows:

Time of meeting.—SECTION 969. The township trustees of each township shall meet on the first Monday in April, or as soon thereafter as the assessment book is received by the township clerk, and on the first Monday in October in each year. At the April meeting said trustees shall determine:

Power and duty of trustees.—1. Upon the amount of property tax to be levied for highways, bridges, guide-boards, plows, scrapers, tools, and machinery adapted to the construction and repair of highways; and for the payment of any indebtedness previously incurred for highway purposes, and levy the same, which shall not be less than one nor more than five mills on the dollar on the amount of the township assessment for that year;

2. Whether any portion of said tax shall be paid in labor, and, if so, what portion may be so paid;

3. Upon the amount that will be allowed for a day's labor done by a man, and by a man and team, on the highway;

4. At the October meeting, said trustees shall divide their respective townships into such number of highway districts as they may deem necessary for the public good, and, at said meeting, they shall settle with the township clerk and supervisors of highways.

General township fund: clerk to give bond: custody of implements.—SEC. 970. The trustees shall set apart such portion of the tax specified in the preceding section of this chapter, as they may deem necessary for the purpose of purchasing the tools and machinery and paying for the guide-boards mentioned in said section, and the same shall constitute a general township fund; and such trustees shall require the township clerk to give bond in such sum as they deem proper, conditioned as the bonds of county officers, which bond, and the sureties thereon, shall be approved by said trustees. Said clerk shall take charge of and properly preserve and keep in repair such tools, implements, and machinery as may be purchased with said general township fund, and shall have authority to determine at what time the supervisors of the several districts may have the use and custody of the same or any part thereof, and shall be responsible for the safe keeping of the same, when not in the custody of some one of the supervisors for use in working the highways in his district, and shall receive such compensation as the trustees shall provide to be paid out of such fund.

Control of fund.—SEC. 971. The trustees shall order and direct the expenditure of the general township fund.

VIII. POWERS AND DUTIES RELATING TO DRAINAGE.

The Code, in relation thereto, provides:

Application for, by petition.—SECTION 1217. Any person owning any swamp, marsh, or wet land, desiring to drain the same by cutting a ditch through the land of others, and who is unable to agree upon the terms thereof with such other persons, may make application in writing to the township trustees of the township where such swamp or marsh land is situated, with a description of such land, the commencement and termini of the proposed ditch, and a description of the land belonging to others, with their names, through which it will pass. Such petition shall be filed by the township clerk.

Meeting: notice given.—SEC. 1218. When the application is filed the clerk shall notify the trustees, who shall immediately determine upon the time and place they will meet to consider the application, and shall cause the applicant and all persons owning land through which said ditch is to pass, who are residents of the county, to be notified of the time and place of said meeting, which notice shall be served ten days previous to such day in the same manner as original notices, and if any of such owners of land are non-residents of the county, said notice shall be served on them by posting up copies thereof in three public places in the township. Satisfactory proof by affidavit of such posting, and places where posted, shall be furnished said trustees and filed with the clerk.

Hearing: adjournment of.—SEC. 1219. Upon the day fixed for the hearing, the trustees, if satisfied that the requirements of the preceding section have been complied with, may proceed to hear and determine the matter of the application, or they may adjourn the same to a future day, and, if necessary, may cause another notice to be served in the manner above required. But such adjournment shall not be for a longer period than twenty days.

Trustees determine course, width, and depth of ditch: record of made.—SEC. 1220. If the trustees are satisfied from a personal examination of the premises, or from evidence of witnesses, that such swamp or marsh lands are a source of disease, that the public health will be promoted by draining the same, that such ditch is necessary for the proper cultivation of such lands, that the permanent value thereof will be increased thereby, and that it is necessary, in order to drain said lands, that such ditch should pass through the lands of others, they shall determine the direction, depth, and width of such ditch, as near as may be, and, if necessary, may employ the county surveyor to assist them, and after such examination, or hearing such evidence, said trustees may order or refuse the construction of said ditch. All the findings and doings of the trustees shall be reduced to writing, and entered of record by the clerk.

Costs: by whom paid: bond required.—SEC. 1221. The applicant shall pay all costs of the proceedings before the trustees, and they may require, before fixing the day of meeting as above provided, such applicant to give bond with sureties to be approved by the township clerk, conditioned to pay all such costs and expenses.

Trustees to assess damages to land owners.—SEC. 1222. If the trustees are satisfied the ditch will damage the land of any person, other than the applicant for the ditch, through which it has been located, they shall assess the amount to be paid the owner, and after payment, or tender of the same, to the person entitled thereto within thirty days after the same is assessed or ascertained on appeal in the circuit court, or, in case no damages are assessed, the applicant may enter upon the land through which the ditch passes, with the necessary implements to accomplish the work.

Appeal: how taken.—SEC. 1223. The applicant, or any person through whose land the ditch is located, may appeal from so much only of the order or action of the trustees as relates to the assessment of damages to the circuit court, in the same manner as to bond, the conditions thereof, notice of appeal, and the time within which it is to be taken, as is provided by law in cases of appeals from the assessment of damages on the location of highways. The township clerk shall approve the bond and make out a transcript of the proceedings before the trustees within ten days after the bond is filed and approved, and file the same with the clerk.

Trial of: in Circuit Court.—SEC. 1224. On the trial of such appeal, the person claiming damages shall be plaintiff and the applicant defendant, and if the appeal is taken by any person other than the applicant, judgment shall be rendered by the court for the amount found due such person as damages, which may be enforced as are other judgments; and if the appeal is taken by the applicant, no judgment shall be rendered for the amount found due any person as damages, but the amount thereof shall be certified to the township clerk, and the same shall thereafter be regarded as if the same had been assessed by the trustees at the time so certified. The court shall make such disposition of the costs, as is required in similar cases in appeals from the assessment of damages on the location of highways. But the payment or acceptance of the damages assessed by the trustees shall bar the right to appeal.

Drain bridged.—SEC. 1225. If said drain shall cross a highway, it shall be bridged or covered at the expense of the applicant.

Ditch repaired.—SEC. 1226. If the ditch becomes out of repair, the applicant or any one interested therein, may make application in writing to the township trustees for leave to repair the same, whereupon such trustees shall make such orders in relation thereto as they deem proper, and may empower such applicant or other interested person to enter upon the land of another for the purpose of repairing such ditch.

Notice to be served.—The notice required to be served on the applicant and the owners of land through which the ditch is to pass, may be in the following form:

No. 148.

FORM OF NOTICE OF DRAIN.

...... COUNTY, IOWA, }
...... Township. } ss.

To C D, E F, and G H.

WHEREAS, said C D, has made application in writing to the trustees of said township and filed the same with the clerk of said township, stating that he desires to drain the following described lands situate in said township to-wit: [here describe the lands,] by cutting a ditch through the lands of you the said E F and G H, and that he is unable to agree with you upon the terms thereof.

Now, therefore, you are hereby notified that the said trustees will meet at the office of the said township clerk in ...., on the .... day of ...., 18.., at .. o'clock, .. M., of said day to consider said application, and the terms on which said ditch may be made.

By order of the Trustees.

Dated this .... day of ...., 18..

A.... B...., *Clerk.*

No. 149.

FINDING AND DECISION—DRAIN.

.... COUNTY, IOWA, }
.... Township. } ss.

WHEREAS, C D made application to the undersigned, trustees of said township, in writing, and filed the same with the township clerk of said township on the .... day of ...., 18.., in which he states he is the owner of the following described lands situate in said township, to-wit: [here describe the lands,] and that he desires to drain the same by cutting a ditch through the center line north and south of the lands owned by E F, described as follows: [here describe the lands,] and also through the center line north and south of the lands owned by G H, described as follows: [here describe the lands,] and afterward the undersigned caused due notice to be given to said applicant and the said owners of said lands of the time and place of meeting of the undersigned, to consider said application, and determine the conditions upon which said ditch might be dug; and having met for this purpose at the time and place designated in said notice, to-wit: the .... day of ...., 18.., at the office of said clerk in ....; and having satisfied ourselves from a personal examination of said premises, and the testimony of witnesses, that said lands of the applicant are marsh lands, and a source of disease; that the public health will be promoted by draining the same; that such ditch is necessary for the proper cultivation of said lands; that the permanent value thereof will be increased thereby, and that it is necessary in order to drain said lands that said ditch should pass through the said lands of the said C D and E F, as aforesaid, and that the location and direction thereof should be as aforesaid, and that said ditch should be of the depth of four feet, and of the width of three feet at the top, and eighteen inches at the bottom; and having inquired into the damages said C D and E F will sustain by reason of the location of said ditch across their said lands as aforesaid, do find and determine that the said C D will sustain damages thereby in the sum of .... dollars, and the said E F will sustain damages by reason thereof in the sum of .... dollars.

Wherefore, we, the undersigned do determine and decide that said ditch may be dug across the said lands of the said C D and E F, as aforesaid, on the payment of the damages aforesaid to them as provided by law.

We further certify that the costs and expenses herein are as follows:

FEES.

A B, 2 day's services....	$4.00
J K, 2 day's services................	4.00
L M, 2 day's services..............	4.00
A B, Clerk, filing application.......	.50
A B, Clerk, 1 day's service recording	2.00
O P, Const., serving notices.........	2.50
Total.......	$17.00

Dated this .... day of ...., 18...

A.... B...., }
J.... K...., } *Trustees.*
L.... M...., }

IX. POWERS AND DUTIES RELATING TO TRESPASSING ANIMALS.

The provisions of the Code are as follows:

Lien for damage.—SECTION 1451. The owners, or person in actual possession, of any cultivated lands in this state, shall have a lien from the time of distraint on all and any stock that shall trespass on such lands.

Payment of.—SEC. 1452. The owner of any stock trespassing on the improved lands of another, shall pay to the owner or person in actual possession of the lands so damaged, the actual amount of damages so sustained.

Person in possession may restrain.—SEC. 1453. The person who is in possession of the lands so trespassed upon, may distrain any trespassing stock and retain the same in some safe place at the expense of the owner thereof until said damages are paid, as provided in the three following sections.

Township trustees notified to assess damages: sale of stock.—SEC. 1454. Within twenty-four hours after the stock has been distrained, Sunday not being included, the party so injured, or his agent, shall notify the owner of said stock, when known, and if said owner shall fail to satisfy the owner of, or occupant cultivating said land, he shall, within twenty-four hours thereafter, notify the township trustees to be and appear upon the premises to view and assess the damages; such notices to be either verbal or in writing. When two or more trustees have assembled, they shall proceed to view and assess the damages and the amount to be paid for keeping said stock; and if the person or persons owning such distrained stock refuse to pay such damages so assessed, then the trustees shall post up notices in three conspicuous places in the township where such damages were done, that the said stock, or so much thereof as is necessary to pay said damages with costs of sale, will be sold to the highest bidder; any money or stock left after satisfying such claims shall be returned to the owner of the stock so disposed of; said sale shall take place at the inclosure where such stock was distrained between the hours of one and three P. M. on the tenth day after the posting of said notice; *provided*, that if any one or more of said trustees are interested in said damages, the trustee or trustees not so interested shall appoint some one or more, as the case may require, to act in the place of the person or persons so interested; the owner of the stock, or the person entitled to the possession thereof, when known, shall also be notified of the time and place of the meeting of said trustees to assess said damages. When either trustee is absent so that notice cannot be served upon him, then any justice of the peace shall appoint a suitable person, having the qualifications of a juror, to supply the place of the absent trustee, and the person so appointed shall serve as such trustee for all the purposes of this and the following sections.

Assessment filed with clerk: appeal from.—SEC. 1455. The trustees shall make their assessment in writing and file the same with the township clerk, to be of record in his office. Any person aggrieved by the action of the trustees under this chapter, may appeal to the circuit court of the proper county. The bond shall be filed with the clerk of the township in a penalty double the value of the property distrained, or if the value of the property exceed the amount of the damage claimed, then double the amount of the damage. Notice of such appeal shall be given in the same time and manner as in appeals from a judgment of a justice of the peace, with good and sufficient securities, to be approved by the clerk; and from and after the filing of the appeal bond, the same shall operate as a supersedeas. In case the owner of such be appellant the same shall be delivered to him. The clerk, after the appeal is taken, shall certify all the original papers to the clerk of the circuit court within the time prescribed for the appeal.

Assessment of damages.—The assessment of damages by the trustees in such cases must be in writing and may be in the following form:

CERTIFICATE OF DAMAGES ASSESSED—TRESPASSING STOCK.

No. 150.

...... County, Iowa, }
...... Township. } ss.

We, the undersigned trustees of said township, do hereby certify that having been duly notified by J K, to be and appear upon the premises of the said J K, in said township, (or premises in his actual possession), to view and assess the damages done by trespassing stock, to-wit: [here designate the animals] distrained by him, as alleged, doing damage upon his said premises, and having met for that purpose at said premises where said stock was distrained on the .... day of ...., 18.., we proceeded to view and assess the said damages done by said stock, and the amount to be paid for the keeping of said stock as follows:

1. The damages done by said stock on said premises we appraise at.....................................$40 00
2. The amount to be paid for the keeping of said stock to date..................................... 4 00
3. The amount to be paid for the keeping of said stock after this date, per day........................ 2 00

And we further certify that our fees for services herein are as follows:

A.... B...., one day's services.......................$1 00
C.... D...., one day's services....................... 1 00
E.... F...., one day's services....................... 1 00

Dated this .... day of ...., 18..

A.... B...., }
C.... D...., } *Trustees.*
E.... F...., }

When the owner refuses to pay.—The notice required when the owner refuses to pay the damages so assessed, should be posted in three conspicuous places in the township, and may be in the following form:

NOTICE—SALE OF TRESPASSING STOCK.

No. 151.

.... County, Iowa, }
.... Township, } ss.

To all whom it may concern:

Whereas, the undersigned, trustees of said township, on the .... day of ...., 18.., did appraise the damage done by trespassing stock, to wit: [designate the animals], distrained doing damage on the premises of J K, in said township, at the sum of .... dollars, and the amount to be paid for the keeping thereof at the sum of .... dollars, and for the keeping of the stock thereafter at the sum of .... dollars per day, and the owner of said stock having failed to pay the damages so assessed or any part thereof:

Now, therefore, the undersigned will offer said stock for sale to satisfy said damages and costs at public auction to the highest bidder for cash at the premises of the said J K, in said township, on the .... day of ...., 18..,at .. o'clock, .. M. of said day.

Dated this .... day of ...., 18...

A.... B....,
C.... D...., *Trustees.*
E.... F....,

X. DUTIES RELATING TO SCHOOL FUND.

The duties of trustees relative to the school fund are very important, and are often neglected. It is important to the proper security of this valuable trust that they should faithfully perform their duties. The Code provides as follows therein:

Duty as to waste of school fund.—SECTION 1858. The township trustees in each township shall see that no waste be committed upon any school lands lying in their township, and in case any such waste be attempted, they shall apply by petition to the district or circuit court, or to any judge thereof, for an injunction to stay waste, and the same, if granted, shall be without bond. The court may make such order in the premises as shall be equitable and calculated to secure the school lands from waste or destruction, and may adjudge damages against the party for injuries done in such cases; the costs shall abide the event of the suit, and the damages shall be paid to the county treasurer, and constitute a part of the permanent school fund.

XI. FEES AND COMPENSATION.

The provisions of the Code relating thereto are as follows:

Township trustees.—SECTION 3808. The township trustees shall receive:

For each day's service of eight hours necessarily engaged in official business, to be paid out of the county treasury, to each trustee, two dollars;

For each day engaged in assessing damages done by trespassing animals, one dollar per day each, to be paid as are other costs in such cases;

But when acting as fence viewers, or viewing or locating any ditch or drain, or in any other case where provision is made for their payment otherwise, they shall not be pa paid out of such treasury.

CHAPTER III.

THE TOWNSHIP CLERK.

I. HIS ELECTION AND QUALIFICATION.

Elected every year.—Each township should elect a township clerk annually. Code, Sec. 591.

How to qualify.—He is required to qualify before the board of supervisors of the county. Code, Sec. 680. But it seems the township trustees may require him to give a further bond in such penalty as they may deem proper, conditioned as the bonds of county officers, which bond and the surety thereon shall be approved by the trustees. Code, Sec. 970. It is presumed that this bond is not strictly an official one, but to secure the general township fund and the proper discharge of his duty as keeper of the tools, implements, and machinery purchased for the repair of highways.

May resign.—The resignation of the township clerk may be made to the township trustees, and the vacancy in such case may be filled by appointment of the trustees, in which case the person appointed should qualify the same as persons regularly elected. Code, 793, 786.

II. HIS DUTIES.

Records.—SEC. 395. The township clerk shall keep accurate records of the proceedings and orders of the trustees, and perform such other acts as may be required of him by law.

Oaths.—SEC. 396. He is authorized to administer the oath of office to all the township officers, and he shall make a record thereof, and also of all who file certificates of their having taken the oath before any other officer authorized to administer the same.

Notify auditor.—SEC. 397. The clerk, immediately after the election of officers in his township, shall send a written notice thereof to the county auditor, stating the names of the persons elected; and the time of the election, and shall enter the time of the election of each officer in the township record.

To administer the oath of office.—He is required to administer the oath of office to all township officers, and approve their official bonds, except those of justices of the peace, constables, collectors, and his own, who are required to qualify before the board of supervisors.

He should make a record thereof.—He is required to make a record of qualifications of officers before the trustees, and of their oaths, and of the approval of their bonds by him, and also of those cases where the officers file certificates of their having taken an oath of office before some other officer authorized to administer the same.

To send a written notice thereof to the county auditor.—Immediately after the election of officers, or of their appointment, he is required to send a written notice thereof to the county auditor, stating the names of the persons elected, and the time of the election, and shall enter the name and the time of the election of each officer in the record.

To act as clerk of election.—He is required to act as one of the clerks at the general election held in the township, and if the township is divided into precincts, then in the precinct in which he resides. Code, Sec. 606.

To preserve the poll books.—He is required to file and preserve in his office one of the poll-books containing the returns of the judges of the general elections in each township, or precinct thereof, with the register of election attached thereto. Code, Sec. 629.

To keep the ballots, etc.—It is his duty to keep the ballots and tally list of the general election in each township and precinct, deposited with him by the judges of election, until the time for contesting the election of any officer has expired, and if there are two or more precincts in the township, he is required to meet with the trustees on the day after the election, and canvass the votes given for township officers, as shown by the returns from the precincts. Code, Secs. 630, 631.

When there is a tie.—When there is a tie between two persons for a township office, the clerk should notify them to appear at his office at a given time to determine the same by lot, before one of the trustees, and the clerk; and the certificate of election is to be given accordingly, and if either party fails to appear or take part in the lot, the clerk should draw for him. Code, Sec. 632.

To post notices of the elected officers.—Within five days after the ballots for township officers have been canvassed, the clerk is required to post up in three public places in the township written notices containing the names of the persons elected to township offices, at each election, and requiring each of them to appear before a proper officer and qualify according to law. Code, Sec. 633.

To make a list of voters in certain cases.—The Code provides in reference thereto as follows:

Assessor to make lists of voters.—SECTION 594. At every annual assessment the township assessor shall record in a separate book, the full name and residence of every resident of the township who is, or will become, a qualified elector previous to the next general election; and shall deliver said list, properly certified, to the township clerk, on or before the first day of July in each year.

Trustees and clerk board of registry.—SEC. 595. The township trustees and clerk shall constitute the board of registry, and shall meet, annually, on the first Monday in September, at nine o'clock A. M., and make a list of all qualified electors in their township, which shall be known as the register of elections.

Register of elections: what to contain.—SEC. 596. The register of elections shall contain the names at full length, alphabetically arranged, with the residence set opposite. It shall be made from the assessor's list and the poll books of the previous election, and shall be kept by the township clerk, and shall at all times be open to inspection at his office without charge. He shall, also, within two days after the adjournment of the board, post up a certified copy thereof in a conspicuous place in his office, or in such other place as the board may direct.

Board: where to meet.—SEC. 597. The board of registry shall hold a meeting at the place where the last general election was held, or if from any cause it cannot be held at such place, then at some place to be designated by notice published in at least one paper printed in the township, or posted in at least three public places therein, on the Tuesday preceding the general election of each year, at which they shall revise, correct, and complete the register of elections, and shall hear any evidence that may be brought before them in reference to such correction. Their session shall be from nine o'clock A. M., till five P. M., and from day to day thereafter until they shall deem the register properly completed. The names of all persons not qualified as electors shall be stricken from the register, and any person appearing to register his name may be challenged by any elector or member of the board, and, in case of such challenge, shall be examined on oath touching his qualifications as an elector, which examination may, in the discretion of the board, be reduced to writing: and if it shall appear upon such examination that the person is entitled to be registered, in the opinion of the board, or if, after such examination, the said person will take an oath that he is, or will be at the election for which the registry is made, a legal voter, stating the ward, district, or township in which he resides, and complying in other respects with the oath now administered to an elector in case of his being challenged, then the board shall cause the name of said person to be registered. But no name shall be added to the register within five days next before the election.

Board appoint clerk.—SEC. 598. The board of registry may appoint a clerk in the absence of the township clerk, and may administer oaths in all cases coming before them for action.

Clerks of cities and incorporated towns to prepare register.—SEC. 599. In corporation elections, the clerk of the city or town shall prepare from the poll-books of the last preceding annual election of said corporation, an alphabetical register of the electors as provided in section five hundred and ninety-six of this chapter, showing the residence of each person by number of dwelling if there be a number, and the name of the street or other location of the dwelling-place of each person. And he shall post up one copy thereof in each ward at the place where the last preceding election was held one month preceding each election, and furnish the original to the board of registry at their next meeting. The board of registry for said cities and towns shall consist of the mayor, assessor, clerk, and marshal, who shall meet for the purpose of correcting the registry one week before each election, at the usual place of meeting of the city council or trustees, and, after having corrected the registry of voters in each ward as contemplated in the general provisions of this chapter, said board shall cause a certified copy of said registry for each ward to be delivered to the election board of such ward at or before the time of opening the polls. After the canvassing of the votes, the registries shall be attached to the poll-books, and filed in the office of the clerk of the city or town for the use of the succeeding board of registry. The general provisions of this chapter shall extend to incorporated towns and cities as far as the same may be applicable. But no residence in such cities or towns shall be deemed sufficiently stated, unless the street or other location, and number, if any, are specified in the list.

Special elections.—SEC. 600. In cases of special elections, the township clerk shall furnish a certified copy of the corrected registry for the last preceding general election, and the same shall be corrected and completed at a meeting of the board o registry of each township, held on the Tuesday preceding the special election at the usual place, in the manner hereinbefore provided.

Board in new townships.—SEC. 601. When a new township has been formed, by division or otherwise, the persons appointed to act as judges and clerks of the first election in such new township shall also constitute the board of registry therein; and the clerks of the township or townships from which the territory of the new township has been taken, shall furnish to such board a list of the registered legal voters residing in such territory.

When not applicable.—SEC. 602. This chapter shall not apply to townships, incorporated towns, or cities, having a population of less than six thousand inhabitants, as shown by the last preceding census.

To notify trustees of vacancies in township offices.—When notified by the county auditor of a vacancy in the office of justice of the peace or constable of the township, the clerk should within five days thereafter, notify each trustee of the township, and of the time and place when they are required to meet for the purpose of filling such vacancy by appointment.

After the appointment.—After the appointment he is required to record the same in the township record book, and cause a notice to be served upon the person so appointed, informing him of his appointment, by any constable of the township in the manner prescribed by law for the service of notices, and the person so appointed and notified should qualify within ten days thereafter. Code, Secs. 794, 795.

III. DUTY AND POWERS RELATING TO HIGHWAYS.

The Code provides as follows:

Furnish supervisor with plat.—SEC. 972. The township clerk shall furnish each supervisor, to be by him transferred to his successor in office, with a copy of so much of the map or plat furnished such clerk by the auditor as relates to the highways in the district of such supervisor, and, from time to time, to mark thereon the changes in or additions to such highways as the same are certified to him by the auditor.

Furnish tax list: duty of county auditor.—SEC. 973. The township clerk shall, within four weeks after the trustees have levied the property tax, make out a tax list for each highway district in his township, which list shall be in tabular form and in alphabetical order, having distinct columns for lands, town lots, and personal property, and carry out in a column the amount of the tax on each piece of land, and town lot, and on the amount of personal property belonging to each individual; and he shall carry out the amount of tax to be paid in money, due from each individual in a colum by itself; which list shall contain the names of all persons required to perform two days' labor upon the highway as a poll-tax; and to enable the township clerk to make out such tax list, the assessor shall furnish the township clerk of each township, on or before the first day of April of each year, a correct copy of the assessment lists of said township for that year, which list shall be the basis of such tax list. The county auditor shall furnish the several township clerks of his county with printed blanks necessary to carry into effect the provisions of this chapter.

List: what to contain.—SEC. 974. The township clerk shall make an entry upon such tax list showing what it is, for what highway district, and for what year, and shall attach to the list his warrant under his hand, in general terms, requiring the supervisor of such district to collect the taxes therein charged as herein provided; and no informality in the above requirements shall render any proceedings for the collection of such taxes illegal. The clerk is hereby required to cause such lists to be delivered to the proper supervisors of his township within thirty days after the levy, and take receipts therefor; and such list shall be full and sufficient authority for the supervisor to collect all taxes therein charged against resident property-holders in his district.

When taxes have not been paid.—SEC. 975. The township clerk shall, on or before the second Monday in October in each year, make out a certified list of all land, town lots, and personal property on which the highway tax has not been paid, and the amount of tax charged on each parcel of land, town lot, or personal property, designating the district in which the same is situated, and transmit the same to the auditor, who shall enter the amount of tax to each piece of land or town lot and person taxed for personal property in the column ruled for that purpose, the same as other taxes, and deliver the same to the county treasurer, charging him with the same, which shall be collected by such treasurer in the same manner that county taxes are collected; and in case the township clerk shall fail or neglect to make such return, he shall forfeit and pay to the use of the township, for highway purposes, a sum equal to the amount of tax on said land, which may be collected by suit on his official bond before any court having competent jurisdiction.

County treasurer to pay clerk.—SEC. 976. The county treasurer shall, on the last Monday in March and September in each year, pay to the township clerk all the highway taxes belonging to his township which are at such times in his hands, taking the duplicate receipts of such clerk therefor, one of which shall be delivered by such treasurer, on or before the first Monday in April and October in each year, to the trustees.

To approve bonds of the road supervisors.—Road supervisors are required to give bonds for the faithful discharge of their duties, and township clerks have the approval of the same.

To notify supervisors of roads.—It is his duty to notify each supervisor of roads of his township, within five days after his election or appointment of the same, and if he fail to appear before said clerk, unless prevented by sickness, within ten days thereafter, and give bond and take the oath of office, he forfeits and is required to pay the sum of five dollars, to be recovered by his successor in office. Code, Secs. 978, 979.

After a highway has been established and certified to him by the county auditor, he is required to direct the road supervisor to have the same opened and worked. Session Laws, 1874, Chap. 19.

IV. DUTY IN PROCEEDINGS RELATING TO DRAINAGE.

We have already observed in the treatment of township trustees, that the township clerk is required to file the written applications of claimants in such cases, and to give notice thereof to the trustees; to approve the bonds that the trustees may require of applicants for the payment of the costs and expenses of the proceeding, and on appeal being taken from the decision of the trustees in such cases, he has the approval of the appeal bond, and within ten days thereafter must make out and certify a transcript of the proceedings, and file the same with the clerk of the Circuit Court. Code, Secs. 1218, 1221, 1223.

V. IN CASES OF TRESPASSING ANIMALS.

He is required to file and record the assessment of damages done by trespassing animals made by the township trustees. Code, Sec. 1455.

VI. HIS ACCOUNT WITH THE ROAD FUND.

The township clerk must necessarily keep an account with the road fund of his township, which may be in the following form:

ACCOUNT WITH THE ROAD FUND.

No. 152.

JOHN ROE, Township Clerk ... Township, ... County, Iowa, in account with said township:

1870.	Dr.	
Jan. 10.	To cash received of County Treasurer......	$450.00
Jan. 25.	To cash received of Sam Hitch.............	100.00
May 1.	To cash received of R. Doe..............	4.50
June 10.	To cash received of Sam Patch	1 75
Oct. 1.	To cash received of Dick Hixon...........	10.00
	Total....................................	$566.25

	Cr.	
Aug. 1.	By cash paid for scraper, receipt No. 1.....$	10.00
Aug. 10.	By cash paid to Dick Hixon, receipt No. 2..	25.00
Aug. 11.	By cash paid A. Knapp for lumber, receipt No. 3..............................	100.00
Aug. 15.	By cash paid S. Toby for work by order of Trustees, receipt No. 4................	200.00
Sept. 1.	By balance cash on hand.................	231.25
	Total....................................	$566.25

ACCOUNT WITH SUPERVISORS.

No. 153.

DICK HIXON, Road Supervisor of Road Dist. No. 1, ...

Township, ... County, in account with said township:

1870.	Dr.	
April 1.	To tax list of said township	$ 500.00
Aug. 10.	To cash	25.00
	Total	$ 525.00
	Cr.	
Oct. 1.	By tax collected in labor, as shown by book	$ 300.00
Oct. 3.	By tax collected in cash, as shown by book	100.00
Oct. 5.	By cash paid for work, as per voucher	15.00
Oct. 21.	By delinquent tax list returned	100.00
Sept. 1.	By cash returned to clerk	10.00
	Total	$ 525.00

VII. THE TOWNSHIP RECORD BOOK.

His duty herein.—The most important duty, as well as one requiring the most care and ability, is that of keeping proper records of the proceedings of the board and of official acts of the trustees.

The following form may be of service to them in the performance of this duty:

TOWNSHIP RECORD BOOK.

No. 154.

Township Record Book.

.... Township, ... County, Iowa,
April .., 18.., it being the first Monday in April.

At a meeting of the trustees of .... township, ... county, Iowa, held at the office of the township clerk of said township, this .... day of April, 18.., there were present E M H, L C N, and A A M, trustees, and V C W, clerk.

E M H was duly elected chairman of the board.

Whereupon the following proceedings were had:

On motion of L C N, the board proceeded to equalize the assessments of the township.

The petition of J J for the reduction of his assessment on the s ½ of the nw. qr. sec. 10, 84, 4, was granted, and the assessment thereon was reduced from $.... to $ ....

The petition of H M to reduce his assessment on moneys and credits was refused.

The petition of W S to increase the assessment of J W on shares in the First National Bank of ...., was granted, and said assessment was ordered to be increased from $.... to $.....

It appearing to the board that Lot No. .., in Sec. .., in .... Tp., is omitted from the assessment list, and not assessed, it was ordered that said property be listed by the assessor, and assessed at $.....

It appearing to the board that the ne. qr. of the ne. qr. of Sec. one in .... Tp., is not assessed sufficient to make it equal with other real estate, it was ordered that the assessment thereof be increased from $.... to $....

It appearing to the board that the assessment on merchandise in the township is not made equal with other property, it was ordered that the assessment in all cases be increased .... per cent.

On motion the board adjourned till to-morrow morning at 9 o'clock.

APRIL ...., 18..

The board met pursuant to adjournment. The members being all present.

Whereupon the following proceedings were had:

The following resolution was adopted:

Resolved, That there be levied for highways in the township a tax of three mills on the dollar, on amount of the assessment.

On motion, it was ordered that one-half of the amount of said tax be payable in highway labor.

It was further ordered, that the amount allowed for a day's labor done by a man on the highway shall be $1.50, and for a man and team $3.00.

The board then on motion adjourned *sine die*.

V.... C.... W...., *Clerk*.

OCTOBER ...., 18..

This being the first Monday in October, the trustees of the township met at the office of the clerk of said township. Present E M H, L C N and A A M, trustees, and V C W, clerk.

The board was then duly organized by the election of L C N, chairman; whereupon the following proceedings were had:

It was thereupon ordered and directed by the board that the township be divided into four highway districts, and numbered and described as follows:

Highway District No. 1, shall embrace all of sections No. ....

Highway District No. 2, shall embrace all of sections No. etc., etc.

Highway District No. 3, shall embrace, etc., etc.

Highway District No. 4, shall embrace, etc., etc.

The board on motion adopted the following rules and regulations for the protection of the public health, to-wit: [here insert the rules and regulations adopted by them as a township board of health.]

And thereupon it was resolved by the board, that the board of supervisors of the county be directed to levy a tax on the property of the township, sufficient to raise $200, for the purpose of carrying out the rules and regulations of the board of health in addition to the general taxes.

The board then proceeded to examine the accounts, and settle with the township clerk and supervisors of roads:

The account of the clerk is as follows: [here state the account which should be carefully examined by the board, and the vouchers which the clerk may hold for moneys paid out to ascertain its correctness, and if the accounts are found correct add:]

And said account and the vouchers of said clerk being fully examined by the board, were found correct, and were approved by the board.

[And so continue the record of the settlement with the supervisors of roads].

The board then adjourned *sine die*.

V.... C.... W ..., *Clerk.*

The above forms will probably furnish a sufficient guide to the clerk.

Other matters to be recorded.—If the trustees make any order on an application to drain lands, or make any appointment to fill a vacancy in office, certify a division of a partition fence, or the amount of damage done by trespassing animals distrained, as provided by law, these and various other acts and proceedings should be recorded by the clerk.

VIII. CERTIFIED COPIES OF HIS RECORD AS EVIDENCE.

A copy of any record in his office duly certified by him, is evidence in all cases of equal credibility, with the original record.

TOWNSHIP CLERK'S CERTIFICATE OF RECORD.

No. 155.

.... COUNTY, IOWA, }
.... Township. } ss.

I, V C W, township clerk of said township, hereby certify that the foregoing transcript is a copy from the records of said township in my office; that I have compared it with the original record, and the same is a correct transcript therefrom, and of the whole of such original.

Witness my hand this ... day of ...., 18...

V.... C.... W...., *Clerk.*

IX. FEES AND COMPENSATION.

The provisions of the Code, in reference to his compensation are as follows:

Township clerk.—SECTION 3809. The township clerk shall receive:

For each day of eight hours necessarily engaged in official business, where no other compensation or mode of payment is provided, to be paid from the county treasury, two dollars;

For all money coming in his hands by virtue of his office, five per cent;

For filing each application for a drain or ditch, fifty cents;

For recording each person's mark or brand for animals, twenty-five cents;

For making out and certifying the papers in any appeal taken from an assessment by the trustees of damages done by trespassing animals, such additional compensation in such cases as the board of supervisors may deem reasonable and allow.

In addition to the above provisions for fees, it would appear that he is entitled to ten cents for every one hundred words in making out a transcript on appeal from the decision of the trustees in proceedings for drainage of marsh and swamp lands, and for all other records certified by him the same amount. Code, Sec. 3819.

CHAPTER IV.

CONSTABLES.

I. ELECTION AND QUALIFICATION, ETC.

The provisions of the Code, relating to the election and qualification of constables may be found on pages 4 and 335. From these provisions it will be seen that they should be elected at the general election in each even numbered year, and that they hold their offices for the term of two years.

Removal—suspension—additional security, etc.—The general provisions of the Code in reference to removal, suspension from office, additional security, and vacancies in office, apply to constables; and the general directions and forms given in treating of these matters in connection with the office of the clerk, may be consulted by the constable in such cases.

Vacancies, how filled.—When a vacancy occurs in the office of constable more than thirty days prior to any general election, it may be filled by appointment made by the township trustees, and the person so appointed must qualify within ten days after notice thereof, from the township clerk, has been duly served upon him, and the auditor may approve of the bond of the constable so appointed, on the recommendation of the sureties upon such bond, signed by any member of the board of supervisors. Code, Sec. 794.

II. HIS DUTIES.

To serve process.—Provisions of the Code.

Constables: duty.—SECTION 398. The constables shall serve all warrants, notices, and other process, lawfully directed to them by the trustees or clerk of the township, or any court, and perform such other duties as are or may be required by law.

SEC. 399. Constables are ministerial officers of justices of the peace.

To execute warrants of the coroner.—He is required to execute the warrants of the coroner for the summoning of jurors to hold an inquest, and also for the arrest of any party found by the coroner's jury to have committed a crime on the body of the deceased. Code, Sec. 362.

To attend elections.—The Code provides for his attendance at the place of elections and his authority and duty there as follows:

Order: preservation of.—SEC. 612. Any constable of the township who may be designated by the judges of election is directed to attend at the place of election, and he is authorized and required to preserve order and peace at and about the same; and if no constable be in attendance, the judges of the election may appoint one or more specially, by writing, who shall have all the powers of a regular constable.

SEC. 613. If any person conducts in a noisy, riotous, or tumultuous manner at or about the polls so as to disturb the election, or insults or abuses the judges or clerks of election, the constable may forthwith arrest him and bring him before the judges, and they, by a warrant under their hands, may commit him to the jail of the county for a term not exceeding twenty-four hours; but they shall permit him to vote.

To administer oaths and take answers of garnishees.—The constable has the same power to administer oaths to the garnishee, and take his answers, as is given to the sheriff in cases of attachment. Code, Sec. 3607.

His duty, powers, etc., same as the sheriff.—In the execution of process properly directed to him, he has the same power, and his duty in all respects is similar to that of the sheriff in similar cases, and his duty as a peace officer is also the same; and he is referred to the treatment of the subject of in Chapter VIII, *et seq.*, for full directions and a complete guide in all these official duties and acts. Code, Sec. 3632.

The full consideration of these matters there given, renders a repetition of the same here unnecessary.

III. OFFENSES IN OFFICE.

Acts prohibited.—The constable is prohibited from appearing in any court as the attorney of any party, or from making any process to commence, or to be in any manner used in the same; and also from becoming the purchaser, either directly or indirectly, of any property by him exposed for sale under any process of law. Code, Secs. 342, 343.

General provisions.—The general provisions of the Code relating to offenses in office and their punishment may be found in Chapter One, page 14.

IV. FEES AND COMPENSATION.

The provisions of the Code providing for the fees and compensation of the constable, are as follows:

SECTION 3805. Constables shall be entitled to charge and receive the following fees:

For serving any notice or civil process on each person named therein, fifty cents;
For copy thereof when required, ten cents;
For serving attachment or order for the delivery of property, fifty cents;
For travelling fees, going and returning, per mile, five cents;
For summoning a jury, including mileage, one dollar;
For attending the same on trial, for each calendar day, one dollar;
For serving execution, besides mileage, fifty cents,
For advertising and selling property, seventy-five cents;
For advertising without selling, twenty-five cents;
For return of execution when no levy is made, ten cents;
For serving each subpœna, besides mileage, fifteen cents;
For posting up each notice required by law, fifteen cents;
For serving each warrant of any kind, seventy-five cents;
For attending each trial in a criminal case, for each calendar day, one dollar;
For serving each mittimus or order of release, besides mileage, thirty cents;
For all money collected on execution and paid over, except costs, five per cent., which shall constitute part of the costs.

In criminal cases.—SEC. 3806. The fees contemplated in the two preceding sections in criminal cases shall be audited and paid out of the county treasury in any case where the prosecution fails, or where such fees cannot be made from the person liable to pay the same, the facts being certified by the justice and verified by affidavit.

Officers seizing intoxicating liquors.—SEC. 3807. A constable or other officer who serves any warrant for the seizure of intoxicating liquors shall be allowed:

For such service, one dollar;
For the removal and custody of such liquor, his reasonable expenses;
For the destruction of such liquor under the order of the court, his reasonable expenses and one dollar;
For posting and leaving notices in such cases, one dollar.

Other fees.—Besides the above fees he is entitled to twenty-five cents for each warrant served on appraisers on proceedings in respect to estrays. Code, Sec. 3822.

24

V. SUMMARY PROCEEDINGS AGAINST.

Judgments on motion.—Judgments may be obtained by plaintiffs in executions on motion against constables for the recovery of money or property collected by them. Code, Sec. 2906.

CHAPTER V.

TOWNSHIP ASSESSOR.

I. ELECTION AND QUALIFICATION.

Election.—One assessor is required to be elected annually in each township, and he holds his office for one year.

Qualification.—The penalty of his official bond should be fixed by the board of supervisors of the county. Code, Sec. 678.

But the bond must be approved by the township clerk, and assessors should take the usual oath of office. Code, Sec. 675.

II. DUTIES AND POWERS.

To make a list of voters.—At every annual assessment he is required, in townships having a population of six thousand inhabitants and over, to record in a separate book the full name and residence of every resident of the township who is or will become a qualified elector previous to the next general election, and deliver said list properly certified to the township clerk on or before the first day of July in each year. Code, Sec. 594.

To assess the township.—The provisions of the Code relating to his duty as assessor, are as follows:

When to begin: how to list property.—SECTION 822. Each assessor shall enter upon the discharge of the duties of his office on the third Monday in January of each year, and shall, with the assistance of each person assessed, or who may be required by law to list property belonging to another, enter in the books furnished him for that purpose, the several items specified in the preceding section; entering the names of the persons assessed in alphabetical order, so far as practicable, by alloting to each letter its requisite number of pages in each of the said books. He shall note opposite each piece or parcel of property by him assessed, in a column of his book prepared for that purpose, the number of the highway, independent school districts, district township, or sub-district in which said property is situated.

Assess values: penalty for refusal to take oath.—SEC. 823. The assessor shall list every person in his township, and assess all the property, personal and real, therein, except such as is heretofore specifically exempted; and any person who shall refuse to assist in making out a list of his property, or of any property which he is by law required to assist in listing, or who shall refuse to make the oath required by the next section, shall forfeit the sum of one hundred dollars, to be recovered in the name of the county for the use of common schools therein; and the assessor shall assess such person according to the best information he can get.

SEC. 824. The assessor shall administer an oath, or affirmation, to each person assessed, to the effect that he has given in a full, true, and correct inventory of all the taxable property owned by him, and all property which he is required by law to list, to the best of his knowledge and belief; and in case any one refuse to make such oath, or affirmation, the assessor shall note the fact in the column of remarks opposite such person's name, and should it afterwards appear that such person so refusing has not given a full list of his property, or that which he was required by law to list, any property so omitted shall be entered on the book at double its ordinary assessable value and taxed accordingly.

Deliver books to township clerk and county auditor.—SEC. 825. Each assessor shall, on or before the first Monday in April of each year, deliver to the clerk of his township, one of the assessment books, to be used by the trustees for the equalization of assessments, and for the levy of taxes for township and highway purposes. Said book shall have the several columns of numbers and values correctly footed up, and amount of personal property assessed to each person carried forward into a column under the head of "total personal property;" the other book he shall return to the office of the county auditor, on or before the third Monday in May of each year, which book shall be a correct copy of the first, after the same has been corrected by the township board of equalization.

Owner unknown.—SEC. 826. When the name of the owner of any real estate is unknown, it shall be lawful to assess such real estate without connecting therewith any name, but inscribing at the head of the page the words, "owners unknown;" and such property, whether lands or town lots, shall be listed, as near as practicable, in the order of the numbers thereof; and no one description shall comprise more than one town lot, or more than the sixteenth part of a section or other smallest subdivision of the land according to the government surveys, except in cases where the boundaries are so irregular that it cannot be described in the usual manner in accordance with such surveys.

Penalty for neglect.—SEC. 827. If any assessor shall fail or neglect to perform any of the duties required of him by this chapter, at the time and in the manner specified, he shall be liable to a fine of not less than twenty nor more than five hundred dollars, to be recovered in an action brought in the district court in the name of the county, and judgment shall be against him and his bondsmen.

To meet the board of equalization.—It is the duty of the assessor to meet with the township board of equalization on the first Monday in April in each year, and correct his assessment book as they may direct. Code, Sec. 831.

To make lists of persons subject to military duty.—It is his duty at the time of making the annual assessment to make and return to the auditor of the county a correct list of persons subject to military duty, and to post up in at least two public places in the township written or printed lists containing the names of all persons subject to military duty.

The provisions of the Code relating thereto, are as follows:

Who compose.—SECTION 1039. All the able-bodied male citizens of the state, between the ages of eighteen and forty-five years, who are not exempt from military duty agreeably to the laws of the United States, constitute the military force of this state.

Who exempt.—SEC. 1040. All officers, non-commissioned officers, and privates who have served in the United States service for the period of two years, and have been honorably discharged, are exempt from duty under the military laws of this state. But nothing in this section shall be so construed as to prohibit the executive from calling upon such persons in times of public danger to the state or national government.

Assessors to make list.—SEC. 1041. Assessors in each township are required to make and return to the county auditor of their respective counties, at the time of making the annual assessment, a correct list of persons subject to military duty, and to post up in at least two public places in their respective townships, written or printed lists containing the names of all persons subject to military duty.

To enumerate the children of deceased soldiers.—The provisions of the Code in relation thereto are as follows:

Assessor to enumerate children of deceased soldiers.—SECTION 1635. The assessor of each ward and township, when he is making assessment for each term of two years, shall take an enumeration of all the children of deceased soldiers who were in the military service of the government of the United States from his ward or township, naming the company, regiment, battery, battallion, or organization to which the deceased soldiers belonged, and make accurate returns to the board of supervisors of his county, designating the name, age, and sex of the children belonging to the family of the deceased, for which the assessor shall receive the same compensation as for other services.

Supervisors to revise.—SEC. 1636. The board of supervisors shall revise said enumeration list of orphans from time to time, by adding thereto or striking therefrom as they may deem proper.

Auditor to furnish blanks.—SEC. 1637. The county auditor shall furnish to the assessors of the several townships in his county, such blanks as may be necessary for taking the aforesaid enumeration.

III. COMPENSATION.

The Code provides for compensation of the township assessor as follows:

SECTION 3810. Each township assessor shall receive for each day of eight hours necessarily engaged in the discharge of his official duties, to be paid out of the county treasury, two dollars.

CHAPTER VI.

TOWNSHIP COLLECTOR.

I. ELECTION AND QUALIFICATION.

The Code provides in reference thereto as follows:

When elected.—SECTION 400. There shall be elected at the general election in every year, a township collector in and for each organized township in every county, except the township in which the county seat is located, who shall hold office for one year; *provided*, the board of supervisors of the county shall order the election of township collectors as in this chapter hereinafter provided.

Qualification of.—SEC. 401. He shall qualify as other elective officers, and give a bond to the county in a penal sum equal to double the whole amount of tax to be by him collected, which shall be presented to and approved by the board of supervisors of the county and recorded the same as the bond of county officers.

II. POWER AND DUTY.

The provisions of the Code are as follows:

Powers of.--SECTION 402. The auditor, in counties where township collectors are elected, shall make out a duplicate tax-list of each township, and deliver the same, with the original, to the county treasurer.

SEC. 403. The county treasurer shall deliver to each township collector in the county, as soon as he has qualified, such duplicate tax-list of his township, and take his receipt therefor, specifying the total amount of the tax charged in such list, and charge the same over to each township collector, in a book to be kept for that purpose; and such duplicate tax-list, when so made out and delivered to the township collectors, may be used as an execution, and shall be sufficient authority for them to collect the taxes therein charged in any township in the county, by distress and sale or otherwise, as now provided by law for the collection of taxes by the county treasurer; and the county treasurer shall not receive or collect any of the taxes charged in any duplicate tax-list so delivered, except the tax of non-residents of the township until the same has been returned to him, as hereinafter provided. The said county treasurer shall procure for and deliver to each township collector, with said tax-list, a tax receipt-book, with a blank margin or stub, upon which the said township collector shall enter the number and date of the tax receipt given to the tax-payer, the amount of tax and by whom paid, which said tax receipt-book shall be returned to the county treasurer, with the said duplicate tax-list as hereinafter provided.

To give notice.—SEC. 404. Upon the receipt of said tax-list, each township collector, immediately, shall cause the notice of the reception thereof to be posted up in some conspicuous place in every school-district in the township, and in every ward of any city therein, so located as will be most likely to give notice to the inhabitants thereof, and also publish such notice for four weeks in one or more weekly papers, if any published in the township, designating in such notice a convenient place in such township where he will attend from nine o'clock A. M. to four o'clock P. M., at least once in each week, on a day to be specified in said notice until March first following, for the purpose of receiving payment of taxes, and each collector shall attend accordingly, and he shall proceed to collect and receipt for all taxes therein charged, in the same manner as now provided by law for the collection of taxes by the county treasurer, and all the laws which apply to and govern the collection of taxes by county treasurers, shall apply to and govern the collection of taxes by said township collector, when not inconsistent with the provisions of this chapter.

Demand taxes.—SEC. 405. Every collector, after the first of March in each year, shall call at least once on each person whose tax remains unpaid, or at the place of his usual residence, if in the township for which such collector has been chosen, and demand the payment of the taxes charged to him on his property; in case any person shall attempt to remove from the township property on which tax is due without leaving sufficient to pay such tax, at any time after the duplicate comes into his hands, the collector shall attach such property, and hold the same until the tax is paid, or make the tax out of such property. In case any person shall refuse or neglect to pay the tax, or shall have removed from said township, the collector shall levy the same by distress and sale of the goods and chattels of the person who ought to pay the same, or of any goods and chattels on which said tax was assessed wheresoever the same may be found within the county. The collector shall give public notice of the time and place of sale, and of the property to be sold at least six days previous to the sale, by advertisements to be posted up in at least three public places in the township where such sale shall be made. The sale shall be made by public auction, and if the property shall be sold for more than the amount of the tax, penalty, and costs, the surplus shall be returned to the person in whose possession such property was when the distress was made.

Make monthly statements.—SEC. 406. The township collectors shall make monthly statements to the county treasurer of the amount of tax collected by them on each fund, and pay the same over to the county treasurer, and take his receipt therefor; and they shall complete the collection of the tax charged in the said duplicate tax lists, by distress and sale or otherwise, on or before the first Monday in May next after the receipt of said duplicate tax list, and pay over the amount so collected to the county treasurer, and return to him the said tax lists and receipt-books, and make a full and complete settlement for the taxes so collected with the county treasurer, which settlement shall be subject to examination and correction by the board of supervisors of the county at its next session.

Unpaid taxes.—SEC. 408. After the return of said duplicate tax-lists and settlement as provided above, the county treasurer shall receive, receipt for, and collect any unpaid taxes in the county, and shall proceed to advertise and sell the real estate in the county upon which the taxes have not been paid, for the unpaid taxes thereon as provided by law.

Failure to collect.—SEC. 408. If any of the taxes mentioned in the tax list shall remain unpaid, and the collector shall not be able to collect the same, he shall deliver to the county treasurer an account of the taxes so remaining due; and upon making oath before the county auditor, or in case of his absence before any justice of the peace, that the sums mentioned in such account remain unpaid, and that he has not, upon diligent inquiry, been able to discover any goods or chattels belonging to or in the possession of the person charged with or liable to pay such sums, whereon he could levy the same, he shall be credited by the county treasurer with the amount thereof, but such oath and credit shall only be presumptive evidence of the correctness thereof.

Liability.—SEC. 410. Such collector and his sureties shall be liable for the loss by theft or otherwise, of any money collected by him and in his possession.

Election of.—SEC. 411. The board of supervisors of each county in the state, having a population exceeding seven thousand inhabitants, as shown by the last preceding census, are hereby authorized and empowered to order an election of a township collector in each organized township in their county, by a resolution to that effect, passed at their regular meeting in June in any year by a two-thirds vote of the board, which shall be spread upon the records of the board, and the first election of township collectors in such county shall be held at the next general election after the passage of such resolution, and every year thereafter until the said resolution is repealed by the board, by a like vote, at their regular meeting in June in any year. They shall be voted for and elected in the manner of the other township officers, and in all counties in the state where such resolution is not in force, as provided in this section, then sections four hundred and one to four hundred and eleven, inclusive, of this chapter, shall be inoperative and of no effect.

Notice required.—The notice of the reception of the list required to be given by the collector may be in the following form:

NOTICE OF TOWNSHIP COLLECTOR.

No. 156.

.... COUNTY, IOWA, }
.... Township. } ss.

To all whom it may concern:

Notice is hereby given that I, as collector, of said township have received the tax list of said township for the year 18.., and am ready to receive the taxes thereon, and that I shall be in attendance at ...., in said township on each Tuesday from 9 o'clock, A. M., until 4 o'clock, P. M. of said day, until the first day of March next, for the purpose of receiving payment of the taxes due on said tax list.

Dated this .... day of ...., 18..

A.... B...., *Township Collector.*

NOTICE OF THE SALE OF PROPERTY, DISTRAINED FOR THE PAYMENT OF TAXES.

No. 157.

.... COUNTY, IOWA, }
.... Township. } ss.

Notice is hereby given that by virtue of a tax list of said township for the year 18.., delivered to me, the undersigned township collector of said township, I have seized and distrained the following described property of C D, for the payment of taxes due on said list from the said C D, amounting to $...., said taxes having been duly demanded of the said C D, and the said C D, having refused (or neglected,) to pay the same.

Now therefore, by reason of the premises I shall offer said property, to-wit: (as for example, one white four year old cow and one red two year old steer,) for sale at public auction to the highest bidder for cash, at ...., in said township on the .... day of ...., 18.., at 10 o'clock, A. M. of said day, to satisfy the amount of said taxes, penalty and costs.

Dated this .... day of ...., 18..

A.... B...., *Township Collector.*

MONTHLY STATEMENT OF COLLECTOR.

No. 158.

Monthly statement of taxes collected in the month of ...., 18.., by A.... B...., collector of .... township, ... county, Iowa.

	Dollars.	Cents.		Dollars.	Cents.
School House, Dist. No. 1, .	....	...	Polls.......	....	...
School House, Dist No. 2, .	....	...	Consolidated . .	....	...
School House, Dist. No. 3, .	....	...	School House. .	....	...
School House, Dist. No. 4, .	....	...	Teachers'. . . .	....	...
School House, Dist. No. 5, .	....	...	Railroad	....	...
School House, Dist. No. 6, .	....	...	Road.	....	...
School House, Dist. No. 7, .	....	...	. . . . . .	....	...
School House, Dist. No. 8, .	....	...	Interest.	....	...
School House, Dist. No. 9, .	....	...		....	...
School House, Dist. No. 10, .	....	...	Total	....	...
		...			
Total	....	...			

A.... B...., *Collector of*
.... *Township.*

FINAL STATEMENT OF COLLECTOR'S ACCOUNT.

No. 159.

A.... B...., Collector, etc., in account with .... county, Iowa.

1874.		DR.	CR.
Jan.	To tax list Fairview township	$9121 00	....
Feb.	By amount of taxes collected and paid county treasurer .	....	$895 00
March	By amount of taxes collected and paid county treasurer .	....	1500 00
April	By amount of taxes collected and paid county treasurer .	....	2070 75
May	By amount of taxes collected and paid county treasurer .	....	4540 95
May	By amount of taxes remaining uncollected	....	114 30
		$9121 00	$9121 00

Affidavit required.—If any of the taxes on the tax-list remain unpaid, and the collector shall not be able to collect the same, he shall deliver to the treasurer an account of the taxes so remaining due, and he is required to make oath that the sums mentioned in such account remain unpaid, and that he has not upon diligent inquiry been able to discover any goods or chattels belonging to or in the possession of the person charged with, or liable to pay such sums, whereon he could levy the same, he shall be credited with the amount thereof. Code, Sec. 409.

The affidavit may be in the following form:

AFFIDAVIT OF UNPAID TAXES.

No. 160.

STATE OF IOWA, } ss.
...... County. }

I, A B, collector of .... township, in said county, being duly sworn, depose and say that the foregoing account with .... county, is just and true, that the amount of taxes of said township unpaid is as therein stated, that the annexed tax-list of said township shows the amount of said unpaid taxes, and the persons from whom due, (except non-residents,) amounting to $ ...; that I have not been able to discover any goods or chattels belonging to or in the possession of the persons charged with, or liable to pay said upaid taxes and sums whereon I could levy the same.

A.... B....

Subscribed and sworn to this .... day of ...., 18.., by the said A B, before me.

...., *Auditor of said county.*

(Or, in the absence of the Auditor, before some Justice of the Peace.)

The tax-list his justification.—The tax list is a complete justification to the collector to seize property when required for the payment of the taxes, the same as property is taken by virtue of an execution.

Cannot distrain property exempt.—The collector is not authorized to distrain property exempt from execution, and his liability in such a case would be the same as the sheriff's who should seize exempt property by virtue of an execution.

III. FEES AND COMPENSATION.

The Code provides as follows:

SEC. 407. Each township collector shall receive for his services the following compensation:

1. Two per cent. of all sums collected by him on the first thousand dollars, and one per cent. on all sums in excess thereof collected by him otherwise than by distress and sale, to be paid out of the county treasury;

2. Five per cent. upon all taxes collected by him by distress and sale, which percentage and costs shall be collected of the delinquent tax-payer, and the same fees in addition to the said five per cent. as constables are entitled to receive for the sale of property on execution.

CHAPTER VII.

OFFICERS DE JURE AND DE FACTO.

An officer de jure.—An officer *de jure* is one who not only acts as an officer in fact, but who has an absolute and indefeasable right to the office.

An officer de facto.—An officer *de facto* is one who is acting under color of an election or appointment not strictly legal, or without having qualified by the requisite tests, or by holding over after the period prescribed for a new appointment. 2 Kent, (8 ed.), 345.

He is one who exercises the duties of an office under a claim and color of right; being distinguished on the one hand from a mere usurper, and on the other, from an officer *de jure*. Black. T. T. (3 ed.), 92; Burrell's Law Dic. Tit. *De facto*.

The mere claim to be a public officer, or the performance of a single or any number of acts in that character, will not constitute any officer *de facto;* there must be some color to the claim under an election or appointment, or an exercise of official functions, or an acquiescence on the part of the public for a length of time which would afford a strong presumption of a colorable right. *Id.*

He must have the form of election or appointment.—He must be one who comes in by the form of an election or appointment, and who thus acts under claim and color of right, but who in consequence of some informality, omission or want of qualification could not hold his office, if his right was tried in a direct proceeding in the nature of a *quo warranto*. 16 Iowa, 377.

The color of right need not be perfect.—It is not necessary that there be color of an election or appointment by the only power which has the right to elect or appoint. 38 Conn., 449, S. C.; 9 Am. Rep., 409.

His acts cannot be assailed collaterally.—The acts of an officer *de facto* cannot be assailed collaterally; and where a notary public was duly appointed by the executive, but failed to file a bond in the manner prescribed by law, it was held that he was an officer *de facto*, but not *de jure*, and that his acts in taking depositions in a cause were lawful so far as third parties were concerned and could not be attacked collaterally. 14 Iowa, 464.

There must be an office.—Before one can be a *de facto* officer, there must be a law creating the office. The office must be one *de jure;* the officer may then be one *de facto.* 25 Iowa, 12.

A recent decision illustrating fine distinctions.—A recent decision of the Supreme Court of Iowa illustrates the law on the subject of officers *de facto*, and the nice distinctions sometimes made in exposition of the law relating thereto. As this decision is not yet published, we give place to it here, with the dissenting opion of Judge COLE, taken from the WESTERN JURIST of June, 1874, decided at the April Term, 1874:

BAILEY *v.* FISHER.

Appeal from Jones District Court.

1. ASSESSMENT: ELECTION OF ASSESSOR.—The town of A. is in F. township. At a general election the people of F. Tp. elected two assessors, one for A. and the other for F. The town assessor was not chosen at a municipal election. The assessor chosen for the town assessed land outside the borders of the town. For several years it had been the custom of assessors of that town to assess such land. *Held*, that the assessment was void.

2. OFFICER DE FACTO.—In order to support the acts of one, on the ground that he is a *de facto* officer, they must have been done under color of the office, the duties of which must have been assumed and discharged by the person claiming to fill the office.

Action in equity to set aside a tax deed to defendant for land of plaintiff, on the ground that the lands were sold for taxes without having been legally assessed. A preliminary injunction was allowed restraining defendant from the sale of the land and from disposing of the timber thereon. A motion to dissolve the injunction was overruled and from this judgment of the court, defendant appeals. The facts of the case involved in the questions of law decided, are found in the opinion.

BECK, C. J. The facts of the case are as follows: The land in controversy is situated in Fairview Township, Jones county, and was sold for taxes of 1867 to defendant and a deed was made therefor. As the law then stood, in addition to township assessors, there was chosen by each incorporated town at its municipal election, an assessor who listed all property within its limits. The township assessors were elected at the general election for State and county officers. Acts 9th Gen. Assembly, Chap. 173, § 2, Acts 10th Gen. Assembly, Chap. 26, § 2. The incorporated town of Anamosa is in Fairview township—at the general election of 1866 one Arnold was elected Assessor of Fairview township, and one Dott, at the same election, and not at a municipal election, was chosen Assessor of Anamosa, and gave bond and took the oath of office as required by law. It appears that both of these assessors were voted for by all the electors of the township, including those who lived within the limits of the town of Anamosa. The Wapsipinecon river divides the township. Anamosa is in that part of the territory lying north of the river. The land in controversy is a considerable distance from the town. From 1863 until after the assessment of the taxes in question, it was the custom of the assessor of Anamosa to list the lands north of the river and lying without the town. The other part of the township was assessed by the township assessor. No question seems to have been raised during this time as to the regularity of such assessments, which were made under a misapprehension of the law. The plaintiff is a non-resident of the State.

The only question we are called upon to decide is this: Was the assessment of the land in 1867 by Dott, the assessor of Anamosa, valid?

While the election of Dott was irregular he may be regarded as the assessor *de facto* of the town of Anamosa, and all his acts as such within the limits of his official powers are valid, so far as they involve the interests of third persons and the public.

Dott, as the assessor of Anamosa, listed lands of the township including the tract in controversy; he did not assess them as the township assessor and it is not claimed that he acted as such. We then have the simple case of one officer performing an act which the law requires of another, without claiming or assuming his functions. The question does not arise whether Dott was *de facto* assessor of Fairview township. He did not act as such nor assume the duties of that office. He simply performed acts in his official capacity as assessor of Anamosa, which the law required another officer to do. The discussion upon the point made by defendant's counsel, that Dott was the assessor *de facto* and his acts are therefore valid, does not apply to the facts of the case. Had Dott made the assessment as the assessor of Fairview township, the arguments of counsel on this point would be applicable to the case. But the distinction between such a case and the one before us is obvious.

It is not claimed that where an officer *de jure* or *de facto* assumes duties not imposed upon him by law, and which pertain, under the law, to another officer, that in such a case, his acts are valid on the ground that he is an officer *de facto*. We have seen no authority supporting such a rule. Yet this is the precise case before us.

In order to support the acts of one on the ground that he is a *de facto* officer, they must have been done under color of the office, the duties of which must have been assumed and discharged by the person claiming to fill the office. This we think is essential to give one the character of an officer *de facto* and render his acts valid. These views we think are not contested by appellant's counsel and are certainly in accord with all the authorities to which we have been referred.

The fact that Dott made the assessment under a custom extending his powers and duties in a manner and to subjects unauthorized by law, which was acquiesced in by the officer, charged with such duties cannot make his acts valid. Customs of this kind cannot abrogate the law. Neither can it be pretended that a mistaken idea as to the extent of the powers and duties of an officer, though honestly entertained by himself and the people, will validate acts done in excess of his authority.

We are of the opinion that the assessment by Dott was a nullity, and that the tax sale for this reason is void.

The judgment of the District Court in overruling the motion to dissolve the injunction is therefore AFFIRMED.

COLE, J., dissenting.

COLE, J., *dissenting*. It seems to me that Dott was the assessor *de facto* of the territory actually assessed by him; and that the distinction sought to be made by the foregoing opinion, respecting the name under which he assumed to act, has no foundation in principle, and it certainly has no support in precedent. True, he was denominated the Assessor for Anamosa, and was elected by the voters of the entire township of Fairview; while another, elected by the same voters, was styled the assessor of Fairview township. Each was an assessor *de jure* within and for the territory indicated by his title, notwithstanding illegal votes may have been cast at their election. Any mere irregularity or collateral illegality in an election, does not change the character of an officer *de jure*, into one *de facto*, merely. If the election or appointment was wholly without authority, then such would be its effect. The People v. White, 24 Wend. 520; Cooke v. Halsey, 16 Peters, 71; The State v. Bloom, 17 Wis. 521; The State v. Westmore, 14 Wis. 163; Laver v. McGlachlin, 28 Wis. 364; The Commonwealth v. McCombs, 50 Penn. St. 436; Brown v. O'Connell, 36 Conn. 432.

Although Dott was elected by the voters living within the territory north of the river, and outside the limits of Anamosa, yet as to that territory he was assessor *de facto*, because they had no authority to elect him. He did, however, exercise the duties of the office of assessor over that people and territory, and there has been such a continued acquiescence on the part of the public as does afford presumption at least of a colorable election or appointment. This constitutes him an officer *de facto*. Wilcox v. Smith, 5 Wend. 231; ex parte Strong, 21 Ohio St. 610; Carleton v. The People, 10 Mich. 250; Kimball v. Alcorn, 45 Miss. 151; Brown v. Lunt, 37 Me. 423; Gilliam v. Reddick, 4 Ind. 368. The fact that another person was an assessor *de jure* for that people and territory, would not, of itself, and without any claim by him to exercise the office, defeat the character or colorable title of the assessor *de facto*. Very many *de facto* officers would cease to be such, and the public be deprived of the protection afforded by their acts, if this was the rule. For instance, at an election to fill a vacancy in the office of justice of the peace, sheriff, or judge, the contest is close, and the certificate of election is given to one, and he enters at once upon the exercise of the duties of his office; while the opposing candidate contests the election, and is successful. According to the above opinion, the occupant of the office under the certificate of election, could not be held to be an officer *de facto* while he was acting, because there was another person who was at the same time such officer *de jure*. This, it seems to me, demonstrates the error of the opinion. The very idea of an officer *de facto*, carries with it much of an implication that another has the *legal* right to the office. And it also appears to me that the fact that Dott was styled the assessor for Anamosa, cannot defeat the public right to the protection usually afforded by the acts of an officer *de facto*. To so hold would be to give to the *name* of an office, the power to limit and control its duties. He was the assessor in fact of the territory outside of Anamosa, and was so recognized and accepted by the public, and no other person claimed to exercise the duties of that office. It is this *fact* character, and not the name he bore, nor the technical legal right in another, which affords the protection to the public.

In the recent case of The State v. Carroll, 38 Conn. 449 S. C. 9 Am. Rep. 409, the question respecting an officer *de facto*, underwent a thorough examination, and it was *held*, that an officer *de facto* is one whose acts, though not those of a lawful officer, the law, upon principles of policy and justice, will hold valid so far as they involve the interests of the public and third persons, where the duties of the office were exercised:

First. Without a known appointment or election, but under such circumstances of reputation or acquiescence as were calculated to induce people, without inquiry, to submit to or invoke his action, supposing him to be the officer he assumed to be.

Second. Under color of a known and valid appointment or

election, but when the officer had failed to conform to some precedent, requirement or condition, as to take an oath, give a bond, or the like.

Third. Under color of a known election or appointment, void because the officer was not eligible, or because there was a want of power in the electing or appointing body, or by reason of some defect or irregularity in its exercise, such ineligibility, want of power or defect being unknown to the public.

Fourth. Under color of an election or appointment by or pursuant to a public unconstitutional law, before the same is adjuded to be such.

According to this, or any other case we have seen, the above opinion does not appear to be well grounded. For these reasons I dissent; but a majority say the opinion shall stand, and the judgment be AFFIRMED.

APPENDIX.

General Business Forms.

APPENDIX.

GENERAL BUSINESS FORMS.

PROMISSORY NOTE.

No. 161.

$....

.... days after date, for value received, I promise to pay John Doe or order (or bearer,) .... dollars, with .... per cent interest from date.

Richard Roe.

Iowa City, Iowa, April 1, 1866.

PROMISSORY NOTE.

No. 162.

$ ... ., Iowa, ..., 18..

.... after date .. promise to pay .... or order, ... dollars at ...., Iowa, with .... per cent interest from ....payable annually—value received.

....

PROMISSORY NOTE WITH ATTORNEY'S FEES.

No. 163.

$.... ...., Iowa, ..., 18..

.... after date, for value received, .. promise to pay to the order of ...., ... dollars. Payable at .... bank, with interest at ten per cent from .... Interest payable ...annually.

It is also stipulated that should the collection of this note be inforced by law .. per cent shall be allowed as attorney's fees, and taxed with the costs in the cause.

....

CONTRACT NOTE.

No. 164.

$.... ...., Iowa, ..., 18..

For value received, on or before the .... day of .... next, .. promise to pay ... or order, ... dollars, payable at ..., with ten per cent interest per annum, until paid, and a reasonable sum additional as attorney's fees, if collected by suit. Consent is hereby given that any Justice of the Peace may have jurisdiction on this note to an amount not exceeding three hundred dollars. And it is further agreed that the title to the ..., for which this note is given, shall remain in said ...., until this note is fully paid. For the purpose of obtaining credit, .. certify that .. own in ... own name .... acres of land, with .... acres improved, worth $.... over all incumbrances; .. own $.... worth of personal property over and above all indebtedness.

Witness, ...
P. O. ....
Residence, ...

No. 165.

FORM OF DRAFT.

$.... ...., Iowa, ..., 18..

...., pay to the order of ...., ... dollars. Value received. And charge the same to the account of ....

To ....

No. 166.

WARRANTY DEED.

Know all men by these presents: That ...., of .... county, State of ...., in consideration of the sum of .... dollars, in hand paid by ...., of .... county, and State of ...., do hereby sell and convey unto the said ...., the following described premises, situate in .... county, Iowa: [here describe the premises.]

And .... do hereby covenant with the said .... that .... lawfully seized in fee simple of said premises, and that they are free from incumbrance, that .... ha.. good right and lawful authority to sell and convey the same, and .... do hereby covenant to warrant and defend the said premises and appurtenances thereto belonging, against the lawful claims of all persons whomsoever, and the said .... hereby relinquishes all her right of dower in and to the above described premises. ....

Signed the .... day of ...., A. D. 18.. ....

In presence of ....

No. 167.

ACKNOWLEDGEMENT TO DEED.

STATE OF IOWA, }
...... County, } ss.

On this .... day of ...., A. D. 18.., before me ...., in and for said county, personally came ...., to me personally known to be the identical person. whose name. .. affixed to the foregoing deed as grantor., and acknowledged the execution of the same to be .... voluntary act and deed.

Witness my hand ...., the day and year above written.

....

QUIT CLAIM DEED.

No. 168.

Know all men by these Presents :

That ...., of the county of ...., and State of ...., for the consideration of the sum of .... dollars in hand paid, do hereby quit claim unto ...., of .... county, State of ...., all .... right, title and interest in and to the following described real estate, situate and lying in .... county, and State of ...., viz: [here describe the premises], and the said .... releases all .... right of dower in and to the above described premises.

Witness .... hand., this the ... day of ...., A. D. 18..

Attest: ....

[Acknowledge same as in last form.]

MORTGAGE—SHORT FORM.

No. 169.

This indenture, made on the .. day of .... A. D. 18.., between ...., of the first part, and ...., of the second part, Witnesseth, that the said part.. of the first part, for the consideration of .... dollars, the receipt whereof is hereby acknowledged, do.. by these presents, grant, bargain, sell and convey unto the said part... of the second part, ... heirs and assigns forever, the following described tract of real estate, lying and being situated in the county of ...., and State of Iowa, to-wit: [here describe the land].

The intention being to convey hereby an absolute title in fee simple, including all the rights of homestead, to have and to hold the premises above described, with all the appurtenances thereto belonging, unto the said second party, and to .... heirs and assigns forever.

Provided always, and these presents are upon the express condition, that if the said ...., .. heirs, executors, or administrators, shall pay or cause to be paid to the said ...., .. executors, administrators or assigns, the sum of

.... dollars, on the .... day of ...., 18..;
.... dollars, on the .... day of ...., 18..;
.... dollars, on the .... day of ...., 18..;

with interest thereon .... according to the tenor and effect of the promissory note of the said ...., bearing even date with these presents, then these presents to be void, otherwise to be and remain in full force

And the said .... hereby relinquishes her right of dower to the premises hereby conveyed.

In witness whereof, the said part.. of the first part ha.. hereunto set his hand and seal the date first above written.

Acknowledgment same as No. 167. ....
....

No. 170.

MORTGAGE WITH STIPULATIONS.

This indenture made on the .... day of ...., A. D. 18.., between ...., of the first part, and ...., of the second part, witnesseth, that the said part.. of the first part, for the consideration of .... dollars, the receipt whereof is hereby acknowledged, do by these presents grant, bargain, sell and convey unto the said party of the second part, .. heirs and assigns forever, the following described tract of real estate, lying and being situated in the county of ...., and State of Iowa, to-wit: [here describe the land.]

The intention being to convey hereby an absolute title in fee-simple, including all the rights of homestead, to have and to hold the premises above described, with all the appurtenances thereto belonging unto the said second party, and to .. heirs and assigns forever.

Provided always, and these presents are upon the express condition, that if the said .... heirs, executors, or administrators shall pay or cause to be paid to the said .... executors, administrators, or assigns, the sum of

.... dollars, on the .... day of ...., 18..;
.... dollars, on the .... day of ...., 18..;
.... dollars, on the ... day of ...., 18..;

with interest thereon .... according to the tenor and effect of the .. promissory note of the said ...., bearing even date with these presents, then these presents to be void, otherwise to be and remain in full force, but in case of default of the said first party to pay either of said notes when due, all of said notes shall become due immediately, and shall be considered as due from and after the date of such default, anything expressed in said notes to the contrary notwithstanding. It is expressly stipulated and agreed that the said first party shall pay all taxes levied on said premises, and shall keep the buildings on the same insured in some good and reliable insurance company for the benefit of said second party, to the extent of his mortgage interest therein; and in case of ... failure so to do, the said second party may pay such taxes and insure said buildings, and all money paid therefor shall bear ten per cent. interest from the date of such payment, and shall be considered as a part of the sum secured by this mortgage. It is further agreed that in case of foreclosure of this mortgage the said first party shall pay ten per cent. additional as attorney's fees therefor, which shall be taxed in as costs in said foreclosure suit.

And the said .... hereby relinquishes her right of dower to the premises hereby conveyed.

In witness whereof the said party of the first part ha.. hereunto set .. hand and seal the date first above written.

[Sign, and acknowledge same as in No. 167.]

CHATTEL MORTGAGE.

No. 171.

Know all men by these presents: That I, ..., of the county of ...., and State of ...., in consideration of the sum of .... dollars to me in hand paid, by ...., of ...., party of the second part, the receipt whereof is hereby acknowledged, have bargained and sold, and by these presents do grant and convey unto the said party of the second part, his heirs, assigns, etc., the following described goods and chattels, to-wit: [here describe the property]. To have and to hold the same forever; and I, the said party of the first part, will forever warrant and defend the same against all persons whomsoever; upon condition, however, that if the said .... shall pay to the said ...., his heirs, assigns, etc., his promissory notes, dated .... and described as follows, to-wit:

One for .... dollars, payable ...., 18..;
One for .... dollars, payable ...., 18..;
And one for .... dollars, payable ...., 18..;

(Or if to secure the delivery of property, or future advances, or an account, so state), with interest at the rate of .. per cent. per annum, according to the tenor thereof, then these presents to be void, otherwise in full force.

And I, the said ...., do hereby covenant and agree to and with the said ...., that in case of default made in the payment of the above mentioned promissory notes, or in case of my attempting to dispose of, or remove from the said county of .... the aforesaid goods and chattels, or any part thereof, or whenever the said mortgagee shall choose so to do, then and in that case it shall be lawful for the said mortgagee or his assigns, by himself or agent, to take immediate possession of said goods and chattels, wherever found, the possession of these presents being his sufficient authority therefor, and to sell the same at public auction, or so much thereof as shall be sufficient to pay the amount due, or to become due, as the case may be, with all reasonable costs pertaining to the taking, keeping, advertising, and selling of said property. The money remaining, after paying said sums, if any, to be paid on demand to the said party of the first part. Said sale to take place ......, in the county of ...., and State of Iowa, after giving at least ten days' notice thereof, by posting up written notices in three public places in said county.

And I hereby further authorize the person conducting said sale, to adjourn the same, if deemed in his opinion necessary, from time to time until the said property be sold, and to give a bill of sale to the purchaser thereof, which shall be conclusive as to the regularity of all the proceedings connected herewith, and convey absolutely all of my right and title therein. If from any cause said property shall fail to satisfy said debt, interest, costs and charges, I covenant and agree to pay the deficiency.

Witness my hand and seal this ... day of ...., 18...

[Sign and acknowledge same as No. 167, except in the acknowledgment say "foregoing instrument in writing," in the place of "foregoing deed as grantor."]

No. 172.

SATISFACTION OF MORTGAGE.

I, A B, of the county of ...., and State of ...., do hereby certify that a certain mortgage bearing date the .... day of ...., A. D. 18.., made and executed by C D, of the county of ...., and State of ...., of the first part, to E F, of the second part, on the following described real estate situate in the county of ...., and State of Iowa, to-wit: [here describe the property,] which mortgage was recorded in the office of the recorder of said .... county, Iowa, in book .. of mortgages, page .., on the .... day of ...., A. D. 18.., [if the mortgage has been assigned, here state the fact as follows: "and which mortgage was duly assigned to me by the said C D, on the .... day of ...., 18.., and recorded in the office of the recorder of said .... county in book .. of mortgages at page .. on the .... day of ...., 18..], is fully paid, satisfied, and discharged.

Signed the .... day of ...., A. D. 18..

(Signed and acknowledged same as last form.)

No. 173.

TITLE BOND.

Know all men by these Presents:

That ...., of .... county, and State of ...., am held and firmly bound unto ...., of .... county, and State of ...., in the penal sum of .... dollars, for the payment of which, well and truly to be made, ... bind ....sel.., heirs, executors, and administrators jointly and severally by these presents.

WHEREAS, The above bound .... ha.. this day bargained and sold unto the said ...., the following described real estate, situated in the county of ...., and State of ...., viz: [here describe the property], according to the tenor and effect of the .... promissory note.., bearing date .... Now, the conditions of this obligation are such that if the said .... shall pay, or cause to be paid, the principal and interest of said note at .... maturity, and shall in meantime pay all taxes which shall hereafter accrue upon said real estate. And the above bound .... shall make, execute, and deliver, or cause to be made, executed, and delivered, a good and sufficient ... deed, conveying a fee-simple title to the above described real estate, then this obligation shall be null and void, otherwise to remain in full force and virtue, both in law and equity.

And .... wife of said ...., hereby agrees that upon the performance of the conditions of this bond, they will sign and execute the proper conveyances to said real estate.

And it is hereby further expressly agreed by and between the .... parties hereunto that ....

[Signed, and acknowledged same as No. 167.]

No. 174.

POWER OF ATTORNEY.

Know all men by these Presents:

That I, A B, of ... county, State of ...., have made, constituted and appointed, and by these presents do make, constitute and appoint, C D, of .... county, State of ...., my true and lawful attorney for me and in my name, place, and stead, to ...., giving and granting unto my said attorney, full power and authority to do and perform all and every act and thing whatsoever, requisite and necessary to be done in and about the premises, as fully, to all intents and purposes, as I might or could do if personally present, with full power of substitution and revocation, hereby ratifying and confirming all that my said attorney or his substitute shall lawfully do or cause to be done by virtue hereof ...

In witness whereof, I have hereunto set my hand, this .... day of ...., 18.. ....

Signed and delivered in presence of ....

[Signed, and acknowledged same as No. 167.]

No. 175.

LEASE.

This article of agreement, made and entered into on this .... day of ...., A. D. 18.., by and between A B, of the county of ...., and State of ...., of the first part, and C D, of ...., of ... , of the second part, *Witnesseth:* That the said party of the first part has this day leased unto the party of the second part the following described premises, to-wit:...., for the term of ...., from and after the .... day of ...., A. D. 18.., at the .... rent of ...., to be paid as follows, to-wit:....

And it is further agreed that if any rent shall be due and unpaid, or if default be made in any of the covenants herein contained, it shall then be lawful for the party of the first part to re-enter the said premises, or to distrain for such rent; or he may recover possession thereof, by action of forcible entry or detainer, notwithstanding the provision of section 3612 of the Code, of 1873; he may use any or all said remedies.

And the said party of the second part agrees to pay to the party of the first part the .... rent of .... dollars, to be paid as follows, viz: ...., except when said premises are untenable by reason of fire from any other cause than the carelessness of the party of the second part, or of persons of .... family, or in .... employ, or by superior force and inevitable necessity. And the said party of the second part covenants that .... will use said premises as a ...., and for no other purposes whatever; and that .... especially will not use said premises nor permit the same to be used for any unlawful business or purposes whatever; that .... will not sell, assign, underlet or relinquish the said premises without the written consent of the lessor, under the penalty of a forfeiture of all .... rights under this lease, at the election of the party of the first part; and that .... will use all due care and diligence in guarding said property, with the buildings, gates, fences, trees, vines, shrubbery, etc., from damage by fire, and the depredations of animals; that .... will keep the buildings, glass, gates, fences, etc., in as good repair as the same now is, or may at any time be placed in by the lessor, as often as the same shall require it, damages by superior force, inevitable necessity, or fire from any other cause than from the carelessness of the lessee, or persons of .... family, or in .... employ excepted; and, that at the expiration of this lease, or upon a breach by said lessee of any of the covenants herein contained, ... will without further notice of any kind quit and surrender the possession and occupancy of said premises in as good condition as reasonable use, natural wear and decay thereof will permit, damages by fire as aforesaid, superior force, or inevitable necessity, only excepted.

In witness whereof, the said parties have hereunto subscribed their names on the date first above written.

A.... B....
C.... D....

In presence of ....

[The above lease may be signed and acknowledged the same as No. 167, and recorded, if desired.]

ASSIGNMENT OF AN INSTRUMENT IN WRITING.

No. 176.

In consideration of .... to me in hand paid, I hereby assign and set over to C D, all my right, title, and interest in and to the within instrument.

Witness my hand this .... day of ..., 18...

A.... B.....

(Acknowledgment same as No. 167.)

CONTRACT FOR SALE OF LANDS.

No. 177.

This agreement made and entered into this .... day of ...., 18.., between A B, of .... county, and State of Iowa, of the first part, and C D, of .... county, of the second part, *witnesseth:*

That the said party of the first part, in consideration of the agreement hereinafter contained, to be performed by the party of the second part, agrees to sell unto the party of the second part all that piece or parcel of land described as follows, to-wit: [here describe the land], for the sum of .... dollars. And the said party of the second part in consideration thereof agrees to pay the said party of the first part the said sum of .... dollars in manner following, to-wit: .... dollars on the execution hereof, and .... dollars on the .... day of ...., 18.., with interest at the rate of .. per cent. thereon from this date until the time of payment thereof; and .... dollars on the .... day of ...., 18.., with interest thereon at .. per cent. from this date until the time of the payment thereof; also to pay all taxes hereafter levied on said real estate when they become due.

And the said party of the first part agrees that on the payment of said sums at the times aforesaid, he will execute and deliver to the party of the second part, at his own cost and expense, a good and sufficient deed for the conveying and assuring to him, the party of the second part, the fee simple of said premises, free from all incumbrances, and with full covenants.

It is understood that the party of the second part is to have immediate possession of the premises.

A.... B....
C.... D....

[It may be acknowledged the same as No. 167.]

ACKNOWLEDGEMENT BY AN ATTORNEY IN FACT.

No. 178.

STATE OF IOWA, } ss.
...... County. }

On this .... day of ..., 18.., before me, a .... in and for said county, personally came A B, to me personally known to be the identical person whose name is subscribed to the foregoing (or within) deed (or other instrument), as attorney in fact for C D, the grantor therein named, and acknowledged the same and the execution thereof to be the act and deed of the said grantor, by him as his attorney, voluntarily done and executed.

Witness my hand this .... day of 18..

E.... F...., *Justice of the Peace.*

PETITION TO ESTABLISH, VACATE OR ALTER A HIGHWAY.

No. 179.

To the Board of Supervisors of ......county, Iowa:

The undersigned ask that a highway commencing at ...., running thence ...., and terminating at ...., be established (or altered or vacated as the case may be).

A.... B....
C.... D....
E.... F...., etc.

Before filing the petition the petitioner is required to file a bond in the office of the county auditor, which said bond may be in the following form:

No. 180.

HIGHWAY BOND.

STATE OF IOWA, } ss. To ....,
.... COUNTY, } ...., A. D. 18..

Know all men by these presents: That we, [insert the names of principal and surety,] of the county of ...., and State of Iowa, are held and firmly bound unto the State for the use of .... county, in the sum of .... dollars, for the payment of which, well and truly to be made, we bind ourselves, our heirs, executors, administrators, and every one of them, firmly by these presents.

The condition of the above obligation is such, that whereas [insert the names of one or more petitioners] has this day made application by petition to the [board of supervisors or county auditor as the case may be] of said county, to appoint a commissioner to view and ....locate a road, to be called ....

Now, if the said [insert the name of petitioner for road] shall pay all costs that may be adjudged against him by the board of supervisors, in accordance with the statute in such cases made and provided, then is this obligation to be void, otherwise to be and remain in full force and virtue.

Witness our hands this .... day of ...., A. D. 18...

G.... H....
I.... J....
K.... L....

Approved this .... day of ...., A. D. 18...

M.... N.....
....

OFFICIAL BOND AND OATH FOR COUNTY OR TOWNSHIP OFFICERS.

No. 181.

Know all men by these presents: That A B, as principal, and C D and E F, as sureties, are held and firmly bound unto the ...., and State of Iowa, in the penal sum of .... dollars, for the payment of which we bind ourselves firmly by these presents.

The condition of the above obligation is, That whereas, the above bound A B has been elected .... in and for ....

Now if the said A B shall render a true account of his office, and of the doings therein to the proper authority, when required thereby or by law; and shall promptly pay over to the person or officers entitled thereto, all money which may come into his hands by virtue of his office; and shall faithfully account for all balances of money remaining in his hands at the termination of his office; and shall hereafter exercise all reasonable diligence and care in the preservation and lawful disposal of all money, books, papers, and sureties, or other property appertaining to his said office, and deliver them to his successor, or to any person authorized to receive the same; and if he shall faithfully and impartially, without fear, favor, fraud, or oppression, discharge all other duties now or nereafter required of his office by law, then this bond to be void, otherwise in full force.

Signed this .... day of ...., 18... A.... B....
C.... D....
E.... F....

STATE OF IOWA, }
.... County, } ss.

I, A B, solemnly swear that I will support the Constitution of the United States and the Constitution of the State of Iowa, and that I will faithfully and impartially discharge the duties of the office of ......, according to the best of my ability.

A.... B....

Subscribed and sworn to by A B, before me this .... day of ...., A. D. 18...

M.... N....

ACCOUNT BETWEEN ROAD SUPERVISOR AND THE DISTRICT.

No. 182.

DICK HIXON, Road Supervisor of Road District No. 1, ... Township, ... County, Iowa, in account with said district.

1870.		DR.	
April	1.	To tax list this day received	$500,00
Aug.	10.	To cash this day received	25.00
		Total	$525.00
		CR.	
Oct.	1.	By road tax collected	$400.00
Oct.	7.	By cash, D. Hart, for work, voucher No. 1.	4.00
Oct.	9.	By cash, S. Stack, for lumber, voucher No. 2.	7.00
Oct.	15.	By cash, B. Smith, for teaming, voucher No. 3	4.00
Oct.	29.	By cash, delinquent tax-list returned	100.00
Sept.	1.	By cash paid township clerk	10.00
		Total	$525.00

STATE OF IOWA, }
.... COUNTY, } ..... Township,
District No. ....

To the Township Clerk of
...... Township, }
..... County. }

The undersigned Supervisor of Road District No. ..., herewith presents his semi-annual report, as follows:

NAMES of persons required to perform labor and pay tax for road purposes.	No. of days required.	Days worked.	Paid in cash.	Property tax.	Paid in labor.	Paid in cash.	No. sued for per diem.	Amount collected.	No. sued for property tax.	Amount collected.
John Doe	2	2	. .	$ .75	$ .75	. .	. .	. .	. .	. .
R. P.	2	2	$1.25	.50	.50	. .	. .	. .	. .	. .
T. T.	2	2	. .	1.00	1.00	. .	. .	. .	. .	. .
R. H.	2	2	. .	.50	. .	$ .50	. .	. .	. .	. .
A. H.	2	2	. .	. .	. .	. .	1	$2 50	. .	. .
T. F.	2	2	. .	1.00	. .	. .	. .	. .	1	$1.00
Total	. .	.	$1.25	$3.75	$2 25	$ .50	1	$2 50	1	$1 00

LIST OF NON-RESIDENT LANDS ON WHICH ROAD TAX REMAINS DUE.

No. 183.

S. E. qr. S. E. qr.	1	87	4	$ 1.50	. . . .	1
S. W. qr.	1	87	4	5.00	. . . .	1
S. W. qr.	4	87	4	4.50	. . . .	1
Total	.	.	.	$ 11.00	. . . .	.

To the above report must be added the items contemplated in Divisions 7, 8, 9 and 10, Section 987. By a strict observance of this section, township officers will save much confusion, and contribute greatly to the interest of the Road Fund.

Section 975 requires the township clerk to make a report of all non-resident lands and town lots on which road tax has not been paid, which may be the same as form No. 183.

All these blanks should be ruled and printed, and furnished to the clerks by the county, so as to insure uniformity.

The Supervisor should give each tax-payer a receipt, which may be in the following form:

ROAD SUPERVISOR'S RECEIPT.

No. 184.

Date . . . . 18 . .	. . . . . . County, Iowa,
Name	. . . . . . , 18 . . .
Amount, $	Received of . . . . the sum of
. . . . Tax, $ . . .	. . . . . . dollars, ... cents, in . . . in
Description, ...	full of his Poll and Personalty Road Tax, and Road
. . . . Tax, $ . . .	Tax on . . . . for
Paid in	the year 18 . . .
	A . . . B . . . .
	Supervisor Road District No. . . .
	$ . . . . Township.

NOTE.—The above should be furnished, bound in convenient sized books.

INDEX.

INDEX OF FORMS.

www.ingramcontent.com/pod-product-compliance
Lightning Source LLC
Chambersburg PA
CBHW031812270326
41932CB00008B/396

* 9 7 8 3 3 3 7 3 6 7 9 2 3 *